Fodor's

HEALTHY
ESCAPES

284 Resorts and Retreats
Where You Can Get Fit,
Feel Good, Find Yourself,
and Get Away from It All

COMPLETELY REVISED

NEW EDITION

www.fodors.com

Fodor's Travel Publications ∘ New York, Toronto, London, Sydney, Auckland

Fodor's Healthy Escapes

EDITOR: Mark Sullivan

Editorial Consultant: Lisa Alcalay Klug

Editorial Contributors: Michele Bardsley, Jim Baxter, Eve Becker, Karen Bressler, Jeff Boswell, Cathy Byrd, Denise DeGennaro, Robert DiGiacomo, John Doerper, Robin Dougherty, Jordan Elgrably, Betty Fullard-Leo, Melisse Gelula, Tom Griffith, Marilyn Haddrill, Kimberly Harwell, Lynn Hicks, Robin Kane, Delinda Karle, Barbara Kastelein, Mike Kelly, Sue Kernaghan, Jane McConnell, Diana Lambdin Meyer, Kay Michael, Hilary Nagle, Chip Nold, Pamella S. Picon, Tom Reale, Susan Redstone, Kristin Rodine, Bill and Kay Scheller, Marcia Schnedler, Elizabeth Thompson, Katherine Thompson, Chelle Koster Walton, Gisela Williams, Kay Winzenreid, Jane Zarem

Editorial Production: Stacey Kulig

Design: Guido Caroti

Production/Manufacturing: Robert B. Shields

Photography:

Corbis: *Roger Ressmeyer*, cover.

PhotoDisc, cover.

Corbis: 2. *Dave Bartruff*, 312. *Robert Holmes*, 250. *Anne Krause*, 7. *Tim Thompson*, 219. *Nik Wheeler*, 9.

PhotoDisc, i, 275, 327.

Stone Images, 11.

Original edition written by Bernard Burt.

Copyright

Seventh Edition

ISBN 0–679–00588–9

ISSN 1057–8048

Special Sales

Fodor's Travel Publications are available at special discounts for bulk purchases for sales promotions or premiums. Special editions, including personalized covers, excerpts of existing guides, and corporate imprints, can be created in large quantities for special needs. For more information contact your local bookseller or write to Special Markets, Fodor's Travel Publications, 280 Park Avenue, New York, NY 10017. Inquiries from Canada should be directed to your local Canadian bookseller or sent to Random House of Canada, Ltd., Marketing Department, 2775 Matheson Boulevard East, Mississauga, Ontario L4W 4P7. Inquiries from the United Kingdom should be sent to Fodor's Travel Publications, 20 Vauxhall Bridge Road, London, England SW1V 2SA.

PRINTED IN THE UNITED STATES OF AMERICA

10 9 8 7 6 5 4 3 2 1

CONTENTS

How to Use This Book v

Introduction 1

UNITED STATES 11

Alaska 13

Arizona 14

Arkansas 23

California 25

Colorado 62

Connecticut 75

Florida 78

Georgia 98

Hawai'i 101

Idaho 111

Illinois 113

Indiana 114

Iowa 116

Kentucky 118

Maine 120

Massachusetts 122

Minnesota 128

Missouri 131

Montana 133

Nevada 137

New Hampshire 143

New Jersey 145

New Mexico 148

New York 153

North Carolina 162

Ohio 165

Oregon 168

Pennsylvania 171

South Carolina 175

South Dakota 177

Tennessee 179

Texas 180

Utah 187

Vermont 191

Virginia 197

Washington 203

West Virginia 210

Wisconsin 214

Wyoming 217

CANADA 219

Alberta 221

British Columbia 224

Ontario 235

Québec 242

MEXICO   *250*

Baja California *252*   Mexico *262*

Baja California Sur *254*   Morelos *267*

Guanajuato *258*   Nayarit *271*

Jalisco *259*   Quintana Roo *273*

THE CARIBBEAN, THE BAHAMAS, BERMUDA   *275*

Aruba *277*   Jamaica *294*

The Bahamas *279*   Martinique *299*

Belize *282*   Nevis *300*

Bermuda *284*   Puerto Rico *302*

Bonaire *287*   St. John *306*

Dominican Republic *289*   St. Lucia *307*

Grenada *290*   St. Martin/St. Maarten *310*

Guadeloupe *292*

HEALTH & FITNESS CRUISES   *312*

Glossary *327*

Directory 1: Alphabetical Listing of Resorts *333*

Directory 2: Listing of Resorts by Program *339*

HOW TO USE THIS BOOK

Fodor's Healthy Escapes surveys the entire range of fitness holiday opportunities in North America. In the pages of this guide, the in-depth profiles of spas, fitness resorts, and cruise ships provide the detailed information anyone needs to begin to plan a vacation with a purpose.

In the **Introduction,** we explain why more and more people are taking wellness-oriented vacations, with a brief synopsis of recent trends in the industry. This is followed by practical information on how to plan your spa vacation, including descriptions of the various types of fitness vacations from which you can choose.

Spa reviews are organized by destination: United States, Canada, Mexico, the Caribbean, and cruises. In each **chapter introduction** we give you the lowdown on what to expect from spas in that particular destination. Within each chapter spas are organized alphabetically by state or region. For each of the spas and fitness resorts profiled in this book, we have indicated the particular focus of the program (*see* Planning Your Escape, *below,* for an explanation of the six designations we use). Following the overall description of each spa, resort, or fitness cruise is practical information covering facilities and services, accommodations, dining (including sample meals), rates and packages, and location.

If you wish to look up all the spas that share a particular designation, consult the **directories** in the back of the book: Directory 1 gives the complete list of each type of resort and indicates the page on which each review appears; Directory 2 lists all the resorts alphabetically. For those unfamiliar with spa terminology, we've defined commonly used terms such as acupressure and kur in the **Glossary** that appears after the last spa review.

Insider Tip: To help you get the most out of your spa experience, we have added a new feature to this edition. Our writers have given you the inside scoop on each spa, whether it's the best time of year to visit, a wonderful new treatment to try, or a suggestion on how to get the most for your money.

Equipment: Because most spas constantly update their equipment, we list the generic names for machines such as treadmills and stair climbers. In addition to the exercise equipment listed, almost all full-scale spas have steam baths, saunas, and whirlpools, usually with separate facilities for women and men. We only mention these facilities if they are unusual in some way.

Services: We provide a representative sampling of the types of spa treatments offered, including various kinds of massage, body treatments, and water treatments. In addition to standard spa services, most full-service spas have salons that provide hair, nail, and skin care. Reservations for spa and beauty services are always a good idea, as appointments generally get booked quickly. If the service you request is unavailable, many spas will let you leave your name on a waiting list; same-day cancellations are also worth checking into. Tipping is expected for all services at most spas. A 15%–20% tip is the norm, though you may tip as little or as much as you feel is appropriate.

Classes and Programs: We let you know what is available in addition to the usual health and beauty treatments, from aerobics to yoga. We also note more unusual offerings, such as courses on low-fat cooking or wine tasting, instructions on pottery or dancing, or lectures on local lore.

Recreation: Up for a game of tennis or a round of golf? We let you know what's available at all the spas and resorts. If it's hiking, kayaking, cross-country skiing, or dogsledding you're after, we give you the lowdown on what you might find in the vicinity.

Children: Many spas have a minimum age requirement of 16 or 18, so always call ahead if you're planning on bringing a child. Some spas have programs for younger children; these are noted when applicable.

Accommodations: Following the ▨ icon, we let you know the types of rooms available at each facility. If none is available on-site, we list nearby lodging possibilities.

Dining: Does a particular spa or resort offer low-calorie or low-sodium cooking, vegetarian options, or organic foods? Are the meals included in the room rate, or are they à la carte? Is there more than one restaurant on the premises? We let you know all this, plus we give you sample lunch and dinner options following the ✕ icon. If a spa doesn't serve food, we tell you about nearby options.

Rates and Packages: Following the ⌺ icon we list the rates for a standard room in the high season. Some states levy a hotel tax in addition to a sales tax, which can add quite a bit to your bill. In many reviews we've also listed rates for one or more spa packages. These usually include accommodations, meals, and selected spa services for one or more days. Deposits usually must be received in advance of your arrival, and a cancellation charge applies to most bookings. Each spa makes its own policy with respect to accepting payment by personal check, traveler's check, money order, or credit card. The following abbreviations are used to indicate the types of credit cards accepted: AE, American Express; D, Discover; DC, Diners Club; MC, MasterCard; V, Visa.

Directions: Following the ⊠ icon we give the address of each spa, as well as telephone and fax numbers.

Contributors

A former staff writer for the Associated Press and the *Los Angeles Times,* editorial consultant Lisa Alcalay Klug started her search for the ultimate massage following injuries to her back and neck. Combined with a program of exercise and a pursuit of wellness, her rehabilitation eventually led to what has since become an expertise in spa writing. Her assignments have taken her to the spas of France, Switzerland, Israel, Hawai'i and, thanks to ocean liners, the high seas. She contributes to *Men's Fitness, Shape,* and

other national publications. She has also covered San Francisco's parks, outdoor activities, and spas for *Fodor's City Guide San Francisco* and *Fodor's San Francisco 2001.* She is a Phi Beta Kappa graduate of the University of California at Berkeley and earned a master's degree at the University of California at Berkeley's Graduate School of Journalism.

Don't Forget to Write

You can use this book in the confidence that all prices and opening times are based on information supplied to us at press time; Fodor's cannot accept responsibility for any errors. Time inevitably brings changes, so always confirm information when it matters. In addition, when making reservations be sure to speak up if you have a disability or are traveling with children, if you prefer a private bath or a certain type of bed, or if you have specific dietary needs or other concerns.

Were the spas we recommended as described? Did they exceed your expectations? If you have complaints, we'll look into them and revise our entries when the facts warrant it. If you've discovered a special resort that we haven't included, we'll pass the information along to our correspondents and have them check it out. So send us your feedback, positive or negative: e-mail us at editors@fodors.com (specifying Healthy Escapes on the subject line) or write the *Healthy Escapes* editor at Fodor's, 280 Park Avenue, New York, NY 10017. And enjoy your journey toward wellness!

Karen Cure

Karen Cure
Editorial Director

INTRODUCTION

When you walk into a spa these days, there are more choices than ever before. You may be smeared with rich moor mud and relax to the sounds of New Age music. You might opt to plunge into a series of hot and cold baths in the ancient Greco-Roman tradition. Or you may simply enjoy the same type of facial your mother and grandmother did.

And these are just a few of your options. Although spas in North America once drew on European traditions, they now offer treatments that cross all national borders. Some pamper you with the Javanese lulur treatment, a two-hour extravaganza from Indonesia that begins with a rubdown using jasmine-scented oil and ends with an exotic flower bath. Some help you relax with rasul, which borrows from the tradition of communal steam rooms found in the classic Turkish bath. Others allow you to indulge in abhayanga, the ultimate four-handed massage that is part of a 5,000-year-old Indian philosophy.

Fueling this trend toward the new and different is the continued popularity of the type of pampering only a spa can provide. In the brief interlude since our last edition of *Fodor's Healthy Escapes,* the spa industry has burgeoned into a $60 billion industry. From 1998 to 2000 the number of spas in hotels and resorts across the country has increased by 53%, according to Spa Finder, the world's largest spa travel and reservation company. With so much competition, spas both old and new are seeking out novel treatments.

Nowhere is this trend more evident than in California, where the boom in high-tech industries is matched on a somewhat smaller scale by the boom in the spa industry. Always the trendsetter, California is now responsible for many of the cutting-edge therapies gaining popularity in the rest of the country. Treatments using antioxidant-rich grape seeds from the Napa Valley, for instance, are slowly making their way to other parts of the country. At Canyon Ranch, in Las Vegas, you can now sample a grape-seed mud wrap created by Jeanette O'Gallagher, a former wine expert who now markets spa products. If this treatment isn't yet available in your area, it likely will be soon.

Spas are also looking closer to home for indigenous ingredients for their signature treatments. Green Valley Spa, in St. George, Utah, formulates its own skin-care line out of desert botanicals such as sage and juniper and uses salt extracted from the nearby red-rock canyons in its spa treatments. The Sonoma Mission Inn, in Boyes Hot Springs, California, serves up "evening primrose wraps" and "lavender kurs" relying on local products. And milk baths at the Raj, in Fairfield, Iowa, incorporate a product delivered fresh from a dairy down the road.

Many spas focus on your health and fitness IQ. You can follow your herbal wrap or massage with classes on power yoga and stress management.

As spas continue to evolve, so do their clientele. Although a few facilities—the Golden Door, in Escondido, California; Cal-A-Vie, in Vista, California; and the Greenhouse, in Arlington, Texas—restrict their clientele to women, most welcome men as well. Many even offer special programs for men, such as a massage for golfers that targets areas of the body most affected by your game—hands, arms, shoulders, and lower back—offered by Casa del Mar Golf Resort & Spa, in Baja California. The Aspen Club, in Colorado, where half the U.S. Olympic ski team trains, and Banff Springs Hotel, in Alberta, British Columbia, which features a state-of-the-art strength-training room with views of the Canadian Rockies, also go out of their way to attract a male clientele. The push to offer amenities for men is simply an acknowledgment that more and more men are accompanying their wives to spas, or even going solo. Men, who accounted for less than 10% of all spa visitors just a few years ago, now make up more than a quarter of the clientele.

But men aren't the only ones discovering that they look better and have more energy after a trip to a spa. Forget whatever preconceived notions you have about what a visitor to a spa might look like. If you think spas have an older clientele, think again. According to Spa Finder, more than half are between 30 and 55. And spas aren't reserved for the rich. In 1992 only 8% of spa visitors made less than $50,000, but by 1998 that number had jumped to about 22%. Do you still believe most spa goers are urbanites heading to the country for a little R&R? In 1991 less than 20% of spa goers lived outside major urban areas. Today that figure has doubled.

Whether you're ready for some luxury pampering, a kick start to a healthier lifestyle, or a retreat from city life, a spa vacation can be ideal. Slowing your hectic daily routine with a combination of early morning walks, yoga, meditation, fitness classes, treatments, beauty services, and self-discovery—whatever it is that you're looking for—is available practically everywhere. And that's where our latest edition of *Fodor's Healthy Escapes* comes in. We have scoured the United States, Canada, the Caribbean, and Mexico for the best places offering a respite from everyday life.

With everything from wellness centers to yoga ashrams, rustic retreats to pure palaces of pampering, we've got it covered. You'll find it all here, with our newly expanded and revised guide to spa destinations, resorts, and cruises. And take note of another new feature with this edition: we've added an "insider tip" to each listing to give you the skinny on making the most of your spa experience.

WHAT'S NEW

The most successful contemporary spas not only offer unique treatments, they also focus on your health and fitness IQ. You can follow your herbal wrap with a class on anything from power yoga and meditation to stress management and ayurvedic nutrition. In today's work-hard/play-hard world, such healthy escapes are no longer an indulgence but almost a requirement. And an ever-growing number of spas is meeting this increased demand with programs that build up a sagging psyche as well as a depleted body.

Canyon Ranch in Tucson, Arizona, and its sister site in Lenox, Massachusetts, are two spas that take a proactive approach to your mental health by offering an on-site shrink. Ten Thousand Waves, in Santa Fe, New Mexico, not only offers watsu—an underwater treatment that blends acupressure, massage, and yoga—but it also teaches you the technique to practice on your loved ones. Spa experts laud Miraval, in Catalina, Arizona, for its Outward Bound–style exercises that strive to lift your self-confidence. And Rancho La Puerta, in Tecate, Mexico, offers dozens of fitness options including NIA, an exhilarating aerobic fusion of modern dance with yoga, tai chi, and other Eastern practices.

To help them have a lasting impact on their visitors, many spas also emphasize another growing trend: self-care. They prescribe extensive regimens for upkeep between facials and massages and usually market the same products they use in treatments. Golden Door, in Escondido, California, sends you an exercise cassette to help you get in shape before your visit. It also markets a post spa package of bath products to create your own "luxurious retreat" or "private oasis" at home.

In the same way that your local grocery store probably carries herbal formulas, healing teas, and homeopathic remedies, most spas now offer treatments, such as aromatherapy massage, once considered far from mainstream. The staff at the Aspen Club, in Colorado, for instance, performs herbal remedies, lymphatic drainage, and sound therapy. Treatments like massage and acupuncture are no longer considered mere indulgences but are also prescribed for back trouble, digestion problems, and even modern ailments such as carpal tunnel syndrome.

This more holistic approach to health is paired with an increasing emphasis on spirituality. Canyon Ranch, in Arizona, one of America's first destination spas, advises guests to take at least one class a day in "spiritual fitness." Subsequently, attendance in breathing and relaxation classes has increased ten fold within the last several years. Likewise, Miraval, in Catalina, Arizona, encourages guests to adopt a Zen-like approach, paying full attention to the present moment, whether they are cycling, hiking, or sipping tea. And guests, who keep returning year after year in greater numbers, clearly endorse the method.

As spas are embracing these innovations, they are also softening the dogma. Nowadays it's not unusual to enjoy a glass of wine with dinner or to reserve tee times at the golf course.

PLANNING YOUR ESCAPE

The first and most important decision about your spa vacation is where you'll go. And the most basic choice you'll need to make is whether you'll opt for a destination spa or a resort. The differences are critical.

Destination spas are self-contained environments. All guests are there precisely to enjoy the spa experience, and because of that, you'll usually find a sense of camaraderie. If you're looking to start a weight-management program, embark on a fitness regimen, or make other lifestyle changes, a destination spa is best. You'll be totally immersed in an atmosphere of wellness along with other like-minded people, away from the temptations found at most resorts.

On the other hand, if you want to spend time with your family on vacation, sneak in a few games of tennis, or simply indulge in a little pampering, a resort spa is a better choice. Exercise facilities and spa services are added amenities at resort spas. And yet many, such as the Marriott Desert Springs, in California's Palm Desert, can be quite extravagant. Boats there ferry you across a lagoon to the spa, where nearly every conceivable treatment beckons.

A few resorts blend both approaches. The Pritikin Longevity Center at Loews Santa Monica Beach Hotel, for instance, offers a rigorous one- to three-week medically supervised program in a beautiful setting overlooking the beach. When you're finished with your nearly three hours of exercise each day, you can stroll along the boardwalk or take a ride on the Ferris wheel on the picturesque pier.

The total number of destination and resort spas has jumped since our last edition—from 160 in 1998 to 190 in 2000, according to Spa Finder. In fact, nearly every luxury hotel these days lists a spa among its amenities, so you won't have any trouble finding one that suits your needs.

Although most resort spas included in this edition boast full-scale fitness facilities with regularly scheduled classes, nearly all also offer body- and skin-care treatments. Standard massages and facials are available as well as more unusual services. Many resorts also serve spa cuisine of some kind or at least include heart-healthy options on the menu. A few destinations in this edition do not fit these criteria, but we have included them because other exceptional features, such as mineral springs or athletic instruction, make them unique.

Certain spas also stand out because they are particularly known for other qualities. Some, such as the Grand Wailea Resort, in Hawaii, are ideal for honeymoons. Others, such as the Lodge at Skylonda, in Woodside, California; the Mountain Trek Fitness Retreat, in Ainsworth Hot Springs, British Columbia; and Two Bunch Palms, in Desert Hot Springs, California, are among the most tranquil. If you're looking for the best choice for a family vacation, consider the Marriott's Spa at Camelback Inn, in Scottsdale, Arizona, or the Sanibel Harbour Resort, in Fort Myers, Florida. If you're up for a mother-daughter retreat, Green Mountain at Fox Run, in Ludlow, Vermont, is a good option. If your priority is a beachfront spa, call Punta Serena, in Jalisco, Mexico; the Hilton Waikoloa Village, in Waikoloa, Hawaii; or the Half Moon Golf, Tennis & Beach Club, in Montego Bay, Jamaica. Be sure to make your special needs known to any of the spas listed in this edition. You may be surprised at how many will go out of their way to accommodate you.

An alternative to the destination or resort spa is a spa at sea. An increasing number of luxury liners offer full-scale spas featuring gyms, fitness classes, swimming pools, personal trainers, and aerobics on deck. Some ships also book special fitness and beauty cruises, with lectures on everything from nutrition to sports medicine, and shore excursions to local golf courses and fitness centers.

To help you decide on a destination, resort spa, or a spa at sea, consider what you're hoping to get out of your vacation. Some guests prefer to retreat to a posh resort. Others find gratification in a rigorous schedule. If you are interested in trying yoga, meditation, or a vegetarian diet, consider a New Age retreat. If your goal is smoking cessation, coping with diabetes, or weight loss, a medical wellness program will help you make lasting change. If you are more concerned with preventative medicine, look for programs that emphasize a holistic approach that emphasizes an understanding of the relationship between body and mind.

WHAT A SPA COSTS

The costs of spa vacations vary almost as much as the clients enjoying them. The most opulent spas, such as Golden Door, Cal-A-Vie, in Vista, California, and the Greenhouse, in Arlington, Texas, offer week-long programs for about $5,000. But shop around and you may find luxury for less. The Kerr House, in Grand Rapids, Ohio, is a well-kept secret for just six or eight women at a time. And although the ratio of staff to guests is three to one, the price for five days is only $2,375—about half the cost of the other spas in its category.

Budget-conscious travelers can also find options for less than $200 a day, often including meals, nutritional counseling, and other services. At Tennessee Fitness Spa, in Waynesboro, a week of no-frills costs about $595. Mexico offers even better deals, with Qualton Club & Spa Vallarta, in Jalisco, offering a seven-night package for about $950—and this is for luxury pampering, not merely the basics. Most upscale resort facilities, however, also offer inexpensive day passes. Many establishments waive such fees when you book spa treatments. And in some regions the off-season brings markedly reduced rates and bargain packages. Simply call ahead.

To ease the process of selecting a spa, we've categorized the entries in this book under six headings to reflect the types that are available: luxury pampering, nutrition and diet, sports conditioning, holistic health, medical wellness, and mineral springs. Many spas fit more than one category. Refer to the categories below to help guide you toward a spa vacation that will bring the results you're hoping for.

LUXURY PAMPERING

Imagine entering a world where a staff, which outnumbers the guests by three to one, remembers your name and is eager to take care of your every need. That is the essence of luxury pampering. You are immersed in a fantasy of care, attention, and detail to relax, inspire, and rejuvenate you. You can indulge in nearly every treatment you've ever heard of: aromatherapy, dulse scrubs, haysack wraps, and more.

If the concept still seems foreign, try a little guided imagery. Picture a day beginning with an early morning walk, invigorating fitness classes in a beautiful studio, water aerobics under the bright sun, and sumptuous spa meals that don't taste like diet food. Cap off the day with a series of indulgent treatments, a sauna, and a good night's sleep under luxurious linens. Repeat. You may feel you will have to do some sort of penance after all this indulgence, but you are likely to agree that it is well worth it.

NUTRITION AND DIET

Learning how to lose pounds and maintain a healthy body weight is the basis of many spa programs. Rather than forcing dramatic weight loss in a few days, most teach proper eating habits for long-term health. The carefully controlled diet and exercise regimen at most spas is typically tailored to each guest's fitness level and health needs. A team of specialists, ordinarily therapists and nutritionists, coaches you on beginning and maintaining an individualized program.

And then there is the food. Spa meals are typically light but nutritious. They aren't always gourmet, but they can be. Several spas, such as Nemacolin Woodlands, in Farmington, Pennsylvania, are known for their terrific cuisine. Great food is also a signature service at La Costa Resort & Spa in Carlsbad, California; Norwich Inn & Spa, in Norwich, Connecticut; the Phoenician, in Scottsdale, Arizona; and Turnberry Isle Resort & Club, in North Miami, Florida. Cal-a-Vie, in Vista, California and the nearby Golden Door, in Escondido, also offer truly wonderful spa cuisine, as well as cookbooks to help you reproduce their memorable meals at home.

Many sports-focused resorts are based in areas well suited to outdoor pursuits, where mountain biking and hiking take you through incredible terrain.

Many spas also focus on vegan or vegetarian meals. These include the Raj, in Fairfield, Iowa; Red Mountain Spa & Fitness Resort, in Irvins, Utah; the Ashram, in Calabasas, California; the Chopra Center for Well-Being, in La Jolla, California; Global Fitness Adventures, in Aspen, Colorado; Hippocrates Life Change Center, in West Palm Beach, Florida; Northern Pines Health Resort, in Raymond, Maine; Rancho La Puerta, in Tecate, Mexico; and Vatra Natural Weight Loss Spa, in New York's Catskill Mountains.

SPORTS CONDITIONING

When it comes to active vacations, a week at a spa or resort is a great option. Whether your sport of choice is golf, tennis, skiing, horseback riding, or simply intensely grueling workouts, you can find it almost anywhere across the country. Many spas offer programs to increase endurance, workouts with a trainer, or the chance to try out the latest in exercise equipment. And many sports-focused programs are based in areas well suited to outdoor pursuits, where mountain biking and hiking take you through incredible terrain in milder temperatures. Come winter, you can ski or snowshoe in the Rockies or New England. The Lodge & Spa at Cordillera in Colorado; Stoweflake Resort, in Stowe, Vermont; and the Vatra Natural Weight Loss Spa, in Hunter, New York, are just a few more possibilities.

The Casa del Mar Golf Resort & Spa, in Los Cabos, Mexico; Château Élan, outside Atlanta, Georgia; and the La Quinta Resort & Club, near Palm Springs, California, are just a few options for serious golfers. Tennis aficionados will love the Broadmoor, in Colorado Springs, Colorado; Topnotch Resort & Spa, in Stowe, Vermont; and Safety Harbor Resort & Spa, in Safety Harbor, Florida. And the Cloister, in Sea Island, Georgia; Westglow Spa, in Blowing Rock, North Carolina; and the Inn at Manitou and the Hills Health Ranch, both in Canada, are among the destinations offering excellent horseback riding.

Following the lead of professional athletes, mental conditioning is often incorporated into these programs. Trainers lead guests through guided relaxation, affirmations, and visualizations to improve their competitive edge. Rehabilitation for sports-related injuries is another feature at select resorts. Some specialize in the mind-body relationship, utilizing martial arts, yoga, and tai chi to promote physical and spiritual development. The options are so diverse, you will certainly find a match for your needs.

HOLISTIC HEALTH

The premise of holistic programs is that true fitness depends on emotional, intellectual, and spiritual wholeness, not just physical well-being. Illness, the theory goes, results from a lack of balance within the body that can be restored without the use of traditional medicine. Instead, holistic programs make use of positive thinking, visualizations, and workouts synchronizing body and mind.

Since they are focused on spiritual healing, spas specializing in holistic health are usually in secluded sites to minimize distractions and externally induced tensions. Wandering through wild pastures surrounding a destination such as the Ashram, in Calabasas, California, or glancing up at the stars while soaking in a hot tub at the Esalen Institute, in Big Sur, California, adds to the experience. Combined with an ed-

Some spas and resorts specialize in the mind-body relationship, utilizing yoga, martial arts, and tai chi to promote physical and spiritual development.

ucational program, a week at a holistic retreat can help you achieve lifestyle change.

MEDICAL WELLNESS

Prevention of illness is the focus of many spas. The Pritikin Longevity Center at Loews Santa Monica Beach Hotel, and the Preventive Medicine Research Institute at the Claremont Resort, Spa & Tennis Club, in Berkeley, California, are just two destinations that integrate the services offered by spas and medical clinics. These programs are designed for guests seeking to maintain good health, as well as for those dealing with serious medical concerns, from cardiovascular disease to obesity.

Typically, wellness programs are carefully structured and fully supervised. Sometimes they are also developed in consultation with your own physician. You will work with teams of doctors to modify self-destructive behavior. One-on-one training with fitness instructors, nutritionists, and psychologists will help act as blueprints for achieving your personal goals.

Wellness programs follow a scientific approach to health and fitness and combine traditional medical services with preventative measures. Fitness testing, counseling on nutrition and stress reduction, and exercise programs constitute the bulk of the day. But you can always cap your workouts with massage and other spa treatments.

MINERAL SPRINGS

The word spa is borrowed from the Belgian town of Spa, where those seeking a cure have bathed since the time of the Romans. Some say the town's name is an acronym for the Latin phrase salus per aqua, which means "health by water." Today taking the waters—which may involve drinking six to eight glasses of mineral water daily—is practiced for health and relaxation at fashionable spas around the world.

The popularity of water-based therapies and mud baths is far from a recent phenomenon. In fact, the Native American Wappo tribe considered the geysers at Calistoga Spa Hot Springs in northern California to be sacred. The springs later attracted 17th-century Spanish explorers who named them agua caliente, or "hot water." The same is true for the Spa Hotel & Casino in Palm Springs, which is still owned by the Agua Caliente band of the Cahuillia tribe.

The integration of European and American approaches to maintain a healthy body and glowing skin has revived interest in bathing. The repertoire has expanded to incorporate seaweed, algae, and seawater at spas that specialize in thalassotherapy or hydrotherapy.

For the purist, dunking sans clothing in a communal outdoor hot spring promises the ultimate in stress reduction. But you may prefer soaking in a bathing suit, whether privately or in a public setting. The epitome of the hot springs experience is perhaps Two Bunch Palms, in Desert Hot Springs, where artesian springs feed a giant pool. Visitors here do not chat, choosing instead to simply soak silently. But no matter how or where you draw your bath, you will soon be wishing you could stay in it forever.

That said, may our guide be the first step toward your own particular form of self-renewal. And may every healthy escape it inspires bring you continued well-being, self-awareness, and serenity.

–Lisa Alcalay Klug

UNITED STATES

I f you were to map out all the spas and resorts in the United States, you would find most are clustered on either coast. It's no accident that some of the nation's most famous spots for rest and relaxation overlook the rocky cliffs of the Pacific or the spectacular shorelines of the Atlantic. But spread throughout the rest of the country are a host of other destinations that offer a vast array of healthy escapes. All feature a variety of ways to soothe both the body and the soul. In California this translates to treatments based on local products, such as cleansing olive-oil salt scrubs at the Sonoma Mission Inn, or the smoothing grape-seed body polishes at Meadowood in St. Helena.

In certain parts of the country, treatments hearken back to indigenous cultures. At California's Ojai Valley Inn & Spa, a domed room called a kuyam, from a Native American word meaning "a place to rest together," evokes the spirit of the Chumash Indians who once lived in the area. In the kuyam you slather yourself with rich mud, inhale herbalized steam, and relax to the sounds of New Age music. The Hyatt Regency Kauai, in Poipu, lets you sample traditional Hawaiian lomi lomi in open-air treatment rooms where warm ocean breezes caress you. Drawn from exercises developed for canoe paddlers 5,000 years ago and employing ancient chants, lomi lomi is a type of massage that releases stress and realigns the body.

American spas differ from those in other parts of the world in their focus on wellness. The Hilton Head Health Institute, in South Carolina, features a series of specialty programs that let you learn about how to prevent cancer by focusing on nutrition, exercise, and behavior modification. The Pritikin Longevity Center in Florida teaches how changing your diet can help you fight diabetes. The Preventative Medicine Research Institute, in California, gives advice on how changing your lifestyle can reverse the progression of cardiovascular disease. Numerous spas focus on techniques for reducing stress. For example, the Kripalu Center for Yoga and Health, in Massachusetts, wins kudos for its prize-winning yoga instruction.

To top it all off, pampering that is nearly beyond belief can be had at some of the world's most luxurious spas. The cost can be $5,000 or more for a week's stay, but the number of people who return year after year say they wouldn't go anywhere else. At the Golden Door, in Escondido, California, the staff warms your robe, spritzes lavender scent on your pillow, and helps you relax with a short massage at bedtime. The Greenhouse, in Arlington, Texas, spoils you with chauffeured limousines, Egyptian cotton linens, fine china, and your own masseuse and aesthetician.

But you don't always need to expend quite so much money in order to receive such memorable service. The Wyndam Peaks Resort, in Telluride, Colorado, offers such signature touches as boot warming and the best in après-ski pampering. And the Fisher Island Club, in Florida, offers the exclusivity of an island reachable only by boat.

ALASKA

CHENA HOT SPRINGS RESORT

MINERAL SPRINGS

A soak at the historic Chena Hot Springs Resort, near Fairbanks, brings to mind pioneer days. Cabins and pools here were built in the early 1900s, when most visitors were gold miners who had traveled by dogsled and on horseback in search of relief from rheumatism and arthritis in the hot springs. Images of the miners still smile from Victorian-era photographs that decorate the dining room and lounge.

The old-time character of the resort has not changed despite several renovations. The hot mineral water that bubbles to the surface at 156°F is cooled to a tolerable 110°F in the soaking pools, 90°F in the swimming pool. Thermal water also heats the lodge rooms, three whirlpools, and the 10 rustic cabins.

The cluster of cabins around the main lodge has the general appearance of a mining camp. The machinery, carts, and tools the miners once used now dot the gardens between the steaming ponds where the spring waters run into a creek. Moose have been spotted wandering the grounds, and antlers adorn some of the buildings.

Recreational activities include snowmobiling and dogsledding in winter and self-guided history and nature hikes or horseback-riding excursions in the summer.

INSIDER TIP This is a great place to watch the aurora borealis, better known as the northern lights, because of its location in the northern region and its distance from city lights.

Swimming: Indoor pool, spring-fed lake. **Recreation:** Dogsledding, fishing, hiking, horseback riding, horseshoes, ice-skating, skiing, snowmobiling, volleyball.

⊞ 80 lodge rooms, some with shared bath; 10 cabins. Campsites available.

✕ Meals à la carte. American food is served in the Chena Hideaway Restaurant. **Sample Meals:** Roast beef, ham, roast turkey (lunch and dinner).

▧ Nightly rate $125–$200. Cabins $110–$200. AE, D, DC, MC, V.

✉ *57 Chena Hot Springs Rd., Fairbanks, AK 99707,* ☎ *907/452–7867 or 800/478–4681 (in Alaska),* FAX *907/456–3122. www.chenahotsprings.com*

ARIZONA

ARIZONA BILTMORE

LUXURY PAMPERING

Crowned the "Jewel of the Desert" when it first opened in 1929, the Frank Lloyd Wright–inspired Arizona Biltmore remains both an architectural landmark and a fashionable resort. Entering the grand hall is like stepping back to a time when movie stars and captains of industry gathered on the palm-fringed golf course to escape from the pressures of the world. With the addition of a spa linking the swimming pool and tennis complex, the Biltmore has even more appeal for sophisticated travelers in search of privacy, pampering, and attentive service.

The fascinating history of the Biltmore accounts for much of its allure. In order to produce the more than 250,000 bricks needed for the signature "Biltmore block" (which features a geometric design inspired by the trunk of a palm tree), a temporary factory was established on site. When the estimated $1 million construction cost doubled, chewing-gum magnate William Wrigley Jr. became the sole owner of the hotel and oversaw the installation of the legendary Catalina Pool, with its intricately tiled bottom, and the Aztec Room, with its gold-leaf domed ceiling supported by 40-ton filigreed-copper beams.

A 32,000-square-ft spa, a more recent addition to the property, includes an aerobics room, fitness center, full-service beauty salon, eight tennis courts, and both indoor and outdoor treatment rooms and lounge areas. The Cactus Flower Wrap is a feast for the taste buds as well as the skin. Organically grown products, including prickly pear juice, grapefruit zest, and avocado oil, are used to gently exfoliate and nourish your skin.

On the residential side of the resort, covered garden promenades and flower-edge walkways meander to a variety of lodging annexes, where guest rooms and suites feature mission-style furnishings, desert palettes of sand and ivory, and 1930s-style lamps. Most rooms have balconies or patios with views of the landscaped grounds. The Paradise Wing is closest to the spa, but the newer Arizona Wing has its own Olympic-size pool. A complex of villas is ideal for those in search of seclusion; each has one or two bedrooms and bathrooms, a kitchen, indoor and outdoor dining areas, and an oversize patio or balcony with views of Squaw Peak and the Camelback Mountains.

Relaxing in the open-air lounge or over tea in the lobby, guests savor Biltmore traditions. Try a thirst-quenching Biltmore Breezes (raspberry tea with lemonade). For lunch, dinner, or Sunday brunch you can dine at Wright's, the hotel's Aztec mural–decorated restaurant featuring seasonal New American cuisine. The informal Grill Room is a popular choice because of its 1930s ambience and selection of heart-healthy items.

INSIDER TIP If you want to really feel elite, rent the private outdoor cabanas near the Paradise Pool that are equipped with phone, shower, and refreshing mineral water. It's a steal at $250 per day.

Equipment: Free weights, rowing machines, stationary bikes, stair climbers, treadmills, weight-training circuit. **Services:** Aromatherapy, balneotherapy, hot stone massage, lymphatic drainage, paraffin wrap, reflexology, seaweed body mask, shiatsu. **Swimming:** 8 pools. **Classes and Programs:** Aquaerobics, cooking classes, fitness evaluation, golf and tennis clinics, qigong, wine tasting, yoga. **Recreation:** Biking, croquet, golf, hiking, tennis. **Children's Programs:** Kids Kabana for ages 4–12.

🏨 600 rooms, 50 villas.

✗ Meals à la carte. American cuisine at Wright's and the Biltmore Grill & Patio. **Sample Meals:** Charred tuna with wasabi crème fraîche, peanut-crusted lobster cakes, ginger-miso poached salmon (lunch); grilled halibut with couscous and parsnip cakes, smoked venison loin with black-truffle spaetzle and garlic spinach, grilled lamb chops with polenta and roasted-fennel sauce (dinner).

💴 Nightly rate $165–$330 per room. 1-night Spa Indulgence package $420–$620, includes lodging, breakfast, spa treatment. AE, D, DC, MC, V.

✉ *24th St. and Missouri Ave., Phoenix, AZ 85016,* ☎ *602/955–6600 or 800/950–0086,* FAX *602/955–6013. www.arizonabiltmore.com*

THE BOULDERS

LUXURY PAMPERING ○ HOLISTIC HEALTH

Before designing the Boulders, architect Bob Bacon pitched a tent near the massive rock formations that are the area's most striking feature and camped out for a few weeks. The result of his obsessive study of the site is a grouping of luxurious southwestern-style structures that blend into the surroundings and allow the magnificent landscape of the Sonoran Desert foothills to dominate. Paths lined by a variety of blooming cacti and frequented by jackrabbits lead to the main building, the spa, and other facilities.

In the first half of 2001 the resort's spa will move to a newly built 34,000-square-ft structure hugging the boulders. The newest Golden Door facility will keep much of the Japanese ascetic that the original spa in California is known for, but is designed to blend in with its surroundings. To improve the existing spa, which was rated one of the top 20 resort spas for 2000 in *Condé Nast Traveler*'s readers choice poll, Golden Door plans to add quite a few amenities. You can already choose from several options of Golden Door cuisine at all five resort restaurants.

The spa's exercise program will be expanded, although Denise Hamilton-Hatch's popular treadmill training class will still be offered. In addition, outdoor tai chi and yoga classes are planned. Along with hikes in the nearby hills, the spa will continue to offer a unique variety of sports for the more adventurous, such as mountain biking and rock climbing. Guide Brian Koepke works patiently so even the most hesitant novice can rise to the challenge of the rocky cliffs. At night he and other guides take you out for hikes with night-vision glasses. You'll never see so many stars in the sky.

INSIDER TIP Don't think meditation can help your swing? You might want to try the spa's extremely popular yoga for golfers class.

Equipment: Free weights, stair climbers, stationary bikes, treadmills, weight-training circuit. **Services:** Aromatherapy, body wrap, golfer's massage, maternity massage, mud wrap, reflexology, rock massage, salt glow, shirodhara. **Swimming:** Pool. **Classes and Programs:** Aerobics, aquaerobics, stretch, tennis. **Recreation:** Biking, golf, hiking, horseback riding, hot air ballooning, kayaking, rock climbing.

⌂ 160 casitas and 39 1-, 2-, and 3-bedroom villas.

✗ Meals à la carte. The Latilla serves American cuisine, Cantina del Pedregal serves Southwestern cuisine, the Palo Verde serves seafood, and the Boulders Club and the Bakery Café serve casual America fare. All menus offer Golden Door cuisine options. **Sample Meals:** Chicken quesadilla, fajita steak salad (lunch); rack of lamb, poached salmon, beef tenderloin (dinner).

▨ Nightly rate $265–$565 per room for a casita, $415–$1,175 for a villa. 4-night package $1,182–$2,630, includes lodging, breakfast, 1 dinner, and choice of couple's massage or balloon ride. AE, D, DC, MC, V.

✉ Box 2090, Carefree, AR 85377, ☎ 480/488–9009 or 800/553–1717, FAX 480/488–4118. www.grandbay.com/properties/boulders

CANYON RANCH

LUXURY PAMPERING ◦ NUTRITION AND DIET ◦ HOLISTIC HEALTH ◦ MEDICAL WELLNESS

If you can only go to one spa in your life, Canyon Ranch is the place. Since its opening in 1979, founders Mel and Enid Zuckerman have set the trends in the spa industry, developing programs that emphasize fitness of mind, body, and spirit. A high staff-to-guest ratio means for every guest there are nearly three staff members, including doctors and psychologists, nutritionists and movement therapists. There are more than 40 fitness classes daily, plus golf, tennis, hiking, and biking programs, and spiritual awareness classes such as meditation, tai chi, and yoga. Workshops in stress management, disease prevention, smoking cessation, and weight loss appeal to those with serious issues, while rejuvenating spa treatments and a spectacular setting make for a health-oriented but thoroughly pleasant vacation.

Low-lying adobe-style cottages accommodate up to 240 guests at the sprawling resort, which is set on 70 acres in the foothills of the Santa Catalina Mountains near Tucson. Walking trails weave through natural desert vegetation, and the grounds are landscaped with flowers, cactus gardens, and tropical trees. In the midst of all this is a 62,000-square-ft spa complex with seven gyms; aerobics studios; squash, racquetball, and basketball courts; and a yoga and meditation dome. An 11,000-square-ft aquatic center has massage pools, aquatic therapy pools, and cross-training and lap pools. The golf center has a practice area and is staffed with PGA pros who give lessons for beginner to advanced players.

A day at Canyon Ranch can be as busy or as low-key as you like. Unlike more rigidly programmed resorts, Canyon Ranch allows you to select your own activities, and program coordinators are on hand to help you plan your days. Several hikes of various lengths begin at dawn along paths through the desert landscape of cacti, mesquite, acacia, and paloverde trees. There are also early morning and late-afternoon bike rides. From 8:30 AM on, fitness classes are scheduled on the hour or half hour until 5 PM. The last class of the day is usually meditation in the yoga dome—a great way to wind down after a day of physical challenges.

Dining at the ranch is an integral part of the wellness experience. Here you'll learn that healthy eating does not require depriving yourself. You can choose from traditional dishes, regional specialties, vegetarian fare, daily chef's specials, and even dessert—all low in fat and nutritionally balanced. Information about the nutritional content of each item is provided so that you can learn about healthy eating as you enjoy it.

At the Life Enhancement Center those committed to making serious lifestyle changes are teamed with specialists on physical and emotional problems. Workshops deal with everything from diet to healthy aging, with experts on health, nutrition, stress management, and prevention of illness conducting one-on-one sessions. A medical checkup is included in the program fee. Participants share meals in a private dining room and bunk in special living quarters, but also have access to the spa's facilities and services.

INSIDER TIP Canyon Ranch periodically offers theme weeks for those with special needs. These range from Living with Arthritis to Exploring Spiritual Wellness.

Equipment: Cross-country ski machine, free weights, rowing machines, stair climbers, stationary bikes, treadmills, weight-training circuit. **Services:** Aloe-algae mask, aroma wrap, aromatherapy, craniosacral massage, herbal wrap, lymphatic massage, mud wrap, reflexology, reiki, salt scrub, shiatsu. **Swimming:** 3 outdoor pools, 7 pools in Aquatic Center. **Classes and Programs:** Aerobics, aquaerobics, kickboxing, meditation, Pilates, qigong, Spinning, stretching, tai chi, yoga. **Recreation:** Basketball, biking, golf, hiking, racquetball, squash, tennis, volleyball.

▦ 185 rooms.

✗ Meals included. Some vegetarian choices. **Sample Meals:** Chicken fajitas, Oriental noodle salad, pasta primavera, vegetarian bean chili (lunch); lobster with tarragon sauce, roast turkey with garlic-mashed potatoes, mustard-crusted rack of lamb (dinner).

▧ 4-night package $2,050 per person, double occupancy, includes lodging, meals, spa treatments. 7-night package $3,310 per person, double occupancy, includes lodging, meals, spa treatments. AE, D, MC, V.

✉ *8600 E. Rockcliff Rd., Tucson, AZ 85750,* ☎ *520/749–9000 or 800/ 726–9900,* FAX *520/749–7755. www.canyonranch.com*

FAIRMONT SCOTTSDALE PRINCESS

LUXURY PAMPERING ○ SPORTS CONDITIONING

The towers of the Scottsdale Princess rise from the Sonoran Desert like an oasis. At the heart of the resort is the newly designed Princess Plaza, a lively gathering spot reminiscent of a bustling marketplace in old Mexico, with spouting water fountains, purple jacaranda and giant red hibiscus, and shady arcades for escaping the heat. The remodeled open-air Cazadores Bar, on the plaza, is the perfect place to people-watch.

Participating in a wide range of outdoor sports is the attraction for most guests. The fitness staff sets the pace with a 45-minute morning walk in the crisp desert air. Golfers have direct access to 36 holes within the resort. There are seven tennis courts, including a stadium court that hosts a men's tournament. Other options include sand and water volleyball and fishing. The resort can also arrange hiking in the McDowell Mountains, bike tours, or horseback riding at a nearby 400-acre equestrian park.

The spa is somewhat cramped. However, a major renovation, slated to be completed in 2001, will triple its size to 30,000 square ft. Of the treatments currently offered, the desert lavender salt glow, in which lavender oil and Dead Sea salt are briskly rubbed on your body to slough off dead skin, is surprisingly invigorating. The fitness center has complete workout facilities, including racquetball, squash, and basketball courts. Classes are offered on everything from aquaerobics to step.

Guest rooms are done in Mexican-colonial style, with terraces, wet bars, and separate living and work areas. The sun-bleached color scheme is relaxing. For extra space and privacy, the casitas are choice accommodations, each with a fireplace.

INSIDER TIP If you want to swim laps, head for the quiet East Pool. The South Pool, a 12-sided extravaganza, gets lots of use from families and conventioneers.

Equipment: Cross-country ski machines, free weights, rowing machines, stair climbers, stationary bikes, weight-training circuit. **Services:** Aloe or algae body mask, aromatherapy, four-hand massage, hot rock massage, loofah body scrub, mud wrap, reflexology, salt glow, shiatsu. **Swimming:** 3 pools. **Classes and Programs:** Aquaerobics, Pilates, tai chi, tennis clinics, yoga. **Recreation:** Basketball, biking, croquet, fishing, golf, racquetball, squash, tennis, volleyball. **Children's Programs:** Kids Klub for ages 5–12.

▥ 429 rooms, 21 suites, 125 casitas, 75 villas.

✕ Meals à la carte. The Grill offers steaks and seafood, Las Ventanas features southwestern-style fare, La Hacienda serves Mexican specialties, and the Marquesa features Catalan cuisine. **Sample Meals:** Grilled salmon with spicy couscous and lemonade vinaigrette, gazpacho, wood-roast pizza of braised vegetables and dry Jack cheese, mango quesadilla with prickly-pear vinaigrette (lunch); paella, scallops with cilantro-pesto vinaigrette, jalapeño-glazed mahimahi (dinner).

▨ Nightly rate $149–$539 per room. 2-night Royal Indulgence spa package $357–$1,335 per person, includes breakfast-spa services. AE, DC, MC, V.

✉ 7575 E. Princess Dr., Scottsdale, AZ 85255, ☎ 480/585-4848 or 800/344-4758, FAX 480/585-0086. www.fairmont.com

LOEWS VENTANA CANYON RESORT

SPORTS CONDITIONING

Nestled against the Santa Catalina Mountains on a plateau high above Tucson, the Loews Ventana Canyon is ideally situated for those looking for an active desert getaway. Many guests choose to start the day by hiking on nearby Ventana Canyon trail, or biking to Saguaro National Park to see the giant cacti found only in the area.

The stark concrete exterior of the hotel, which echoes Arizona's early cliff dwellings, allows the desert landscape to be the main attraction. An 80-ft waterfall cascades from the Catalina Mountains to feed an artificial lake at the resort's entrance. Paths meander through groves of hackberry, squaw bush, and blue paloverde.

The resort's two championship golf courses, both designed by Tom Fazio, ramble through the canyon and up steep mountain ridges; plenty of cacti and boulders make natural hazards. There are also eight tennis courts lighted for play in the evenings.

The spa is small but complete, with eight wet and dry treatment rooms, an aerobics studio with mountain views, a glass-enclosed workout room overlooking the tennis courts, and a lap pool. Try a sports massage after hiking or biking, or choose from more unusual offerings such as reiki, craniosacral massage, or the region's specialty: hot stone massage.

After a day of working out, the reward is dinner in the Ventana Room, consistently voted one of the top restaurants in the Southwest. Chef Jeffrey Russell designs two tasting menus weekly—one featuring spa cuisine—that he pairs with wines. The restaurant, on the top floor of the hotel, features panoramic views of Tucson.

Rooms in the hotel are done in restful neutrals and pine furnishings; each has a private balcony and a marble tub for two.

You will find plenty here to keep kids busy. Take them to see a miniature replica of an old western town or to the nearby Arizona Sonora Desert Museum where they can get close to a javelina, or wild desert pig.

INSIDER TIP Summer is a is a good time to go. Rates are considerably lower, and you can get your exercise in the morning and retreat from the afternoon heat to the pool or spa.

Equipment: Free weights, stationary bikes, stair climbers, treadmills, weight-training circuit. **Services:** Aromatherapy, body mask, body polish, herbal wrap, hot stone massage, mud body treatment, reflexology, reiki, shiatsu. **Swimming:** 2 pools. **Classes and Programs:** Aerobics, aquaerobics, body sculpting, fitness evaluation, golf and tennis clinics, meditation, nutritional consultation, personal training, tai chi, yoga. **Recreation:** Biking, croquet, golf, hiking, horseback riding, tennis. **Children's Programs:** Coyote Club for ages 5–12.

▣ 371 rooms, 27 suites.

✕ Meals à la carte. New American cuisine in Ventana Room, southwestern food in Flying V Bar & Grill, casual American cuisine in Canyon Cafe. Spa cuisine available in all restaurants. **Sample Meals:** Warm lobster salad with chanterelle mushrooms, Arizona tomatoes, and arugula with balsamic vinaigrette; seared ahi tuna with peppercorns, rice noodles, and stir-fried vegetables in a carrot-lemongrass broth (dinner).

▨ Nightly rate $109–$385 per room. 1-night spa packages $405–$610 per couple, includes meals and spa treatments. AE, D, DC, MC, V.

✉ *7000 North Resort Dr., Tucson, AZ 85750,* ☎ *520/299–2020 or 800/234–5117,* ℻ *520/299–6832. www.loewshotels.com*

MARRIOTT'S SPA AT CAMELBACK INN

LUXURY PAMPERING ○ MEDICAL WELLNESS

Housed within a spectacular hacienda in the foothills of Mummy Mountain, the Spa at Camelback Inn is a destination in itself. This retreat, surrounded by a striking desert landscape, combines the latest treatments with heart-healthy cuisine for a top-notch spa experience.

Discerning spa goers will not be disappointed here. Many of the therapists have degrees in physiology from the University of Arizona, while others trained in esoteric massage techniques at workshops in nearby Sedona. This is one of the few spas to offer classes in Pilates, a highly specialized program designed to correct postural alignment and strengthen the back and abdomen. Other unusual programs include healing rituals inspired by the Native American culture that use indigenous desert plants and herbs. For the adobe purification treatment, your body is coated with warm mineral-rich clay. After the mixture is removed with a cactus-fiber cloth, you are massaged with juniper and sage oils. For the desert nectar wrap, your skin is drenched with honey, buttermilk, and oats while your scalp is massaged with essential oils. You are then rubbed down with aloe vera and chamomile.

Camelback has linked up with the Institute of Aerobic Research in Texas, where testing procedures are based on those of aerobics pioneer Dr. Kenneth R. Cooper. After a one-hour assessment of body composition, flexibility, cardiovascular endurance, and body strength, a computerized evaluation of your data provides individualized recommendations for improving your level of fitness.

Most guests begin the day with a 4-mi power walk in the mountains for grand views of the surrounding desert. You can also challenge yourself with a hike up Camelback Mountain, and you'll be rewarded with a view of all Phoenix and a congratulatory T-shirt.

Guests stay in southwestern-style casitas, some with private sundecks. The most luxurious guest quarters have private pools.

INSIDER TIP This down-home western-style resort is a good place to bring the family. Kids will love the gecko pool with spurting fountains and sandbox.

Equipment: Cross-country ski tracks, free weights, rowing machines, stair climbers, stationary bikes, treadmills, weight-training circuit. **Services:** Aloe-vera rehydrating treatment, aromatherapy, hot stone massage, hydrotherapy, loofah body scrub, shiatsu, thalassotherapy. **Swimming:** 3 pools. **Classes and Programs:** Aerobics, aquaerobics, ballet stretch, body sculpting, meditation, tai chi, yoga; fitness and wellness evaluations, body-composition analysis, nutritional counseling, personal training. **Recreation:** Basketball, golf, Ping-Pong, shuffleboard, tennis. **Children's Programs:** Hopalong College for ages 5–12.

⊞ 420 casitas, 27 suites.

✕ Meals à la carte. Continental cuisine at the Chapparal, southwestern at the Navajo, spa cuisine at Sprouts Restaurant. **Sample Meals:** Grilled pompano stuffed with crabmeat, cold skinless breast of chicken (lunch); poached lamb loin, grilled ahi tuna with papaya relish, or roast breast of capon stuffed with ricotta cheese (dinner).

▦ Nightly rate $389–$409 per room. 1-night spa getaway $559 per couple, includes lodging, 1 meal, spa treatment. 3-night revitalizer package $2,339 per couple, includes lodging, meals, and spa treatments. AE, DC, MC, V.

✉ *5402 E. Lincoln Dr., Scottsdale, AZ 85253,* ☏ *480/948–1700 or 800/242–2635,* 🖷 *480/596–7018. www.camelbackinn.com*

MIRAVAL

LUXURY PAMPERING ○ SPORTS CONDITIONING ○ HOLISTIC HEALTH

One experienced spa goer called the Miraval a cross between Outward Bound and a New Age destination. Indeed, this desert resort near Tucson is more than just a spa. Part ranch, part self-discovery center, it's an upscale destination for those seeking new challenges. Accordingly, you may find yourself trying things you've never done before: jumping off a 25-ft pole (you'll be safe in a harness, of course), climbing a rock wall, or even taking a workshop on grooming horses. The goal of most programs is to teach guests how to balance their lives by challenging themselves physically and spiritually.

Besides its innovative programs, the real joy of Miraval is its spectacular setting. Sprawling over 135 acres in the foothills of the Santa Catalina Mountains of southern Arizona, this resort enjoys the same climate as neighboring Canyon Ranch. Hikes and trail rides through the Sonoran Desert are a favorite pastime, as a cool, dry energy prevails, even in the heat of summer. If you combine these with the challenging classes, no doubt you will feel invigorated.

When the desert sun is too much, you can take shelter in the fitness center and yoga studios. In addition to strength and cardiovascular training (personal trainers are on hand), there are two aerobics studios (one has a suspended hardwood floor) and a 25-meter lap pool. The spa's specialty is hot stone therapy, a form of massage using smooth, heated basalt rocks placed alongside your spine, on your stomach, and between your toes.

Accommodations in spacious stucco-walled casitas are another part of the desert experience. More than 100 adobe buildings accommodating up to 180 guests are set amid palm trees, meditation gardens, and meandering streams. Fruit and bottles of mineral water are supplied in your room. The cuisine here is inventive and healthful, relying mainly on organically grown vegetables and grains and using vegetable stock reductions in place of fattening sauces.

INSIDER TIP During lunch you can watch cooking demonstrations and take home the recipes from the spa's own cookbook.

Equipment: Free weights, stationary bikes, stair climbers, treadmills, weight-training circuits. **Services:** Body wrap, hot stone massage, hydrotherapy. **Swimming:** 4 pools. **Classes and Programs:** Cooking classes, fitness evaluation, tennis instruction, personal training. **Recreation:** Biking, croquet, horseback riding, tennis.

🛏 92 rooms, 14 suites.

✕ Meals included. Low-fat meals available in several restaurants. **Sample Meals:** Vegetarian corn crepe, braised artichokes, grilled swordfish salad (lunch); braised cactus and baby vegetables with loin of venison, vegetable lasagna, grape leaves stuffed with grilled salmon and sea scallops (dinner).

💵 Nightly rate $395–$1,070 per person, single or double occupancy. AE, DC, MC, V.

✉ 5000 E. Via Estancia Miraval, Catalina, AZ 85739, ☎ 520/825–4000 or 800/825–4000, FAX 520/792–5870. www.miravalresort.com

THE PHOENICIAN

LUXURY PAMPERING ○ NUTRITION AND DIET ○ HOLISTIC HEALTH

Luxury—cascading waters, polished marble, crystal chandeliers, and candlelit terraces—engulfs you from the moment you arrive at the Phoenician. The effect is certainly over the top but not vulgar. The crowd here ranges from conventioneers and corporate moguls to ladies taking tea, but somehow it all works.

The Phoenician Centre for Well-Being has been an integral part of the resort from its opening. The philosophy is based on the mythical phoenix that rose from its own ashes to be reborn. There are many ways to achieve that personal renewal here, whether it is taking one of the daily meditation classes, getting an astrology reading, or trying a kickboxing class.

The two-level spa complex rises from a verdant lawn surrounded by casitas, separated from the resort's main building by a series of pools. Past the reception area and boutique are a skylighted meditation atrium and 24 treatment rooms. The aromatherapy massage is a wonderfully calming experience. Exceptional service abounds. An attendant is waiting around every corner to spread towels on your chaise lounge or bring you a pitcher of ice water.

The fitness center is state of the art, with strength-training and cardiovascular equipment and a glass-walled aerobics and yoga studio. Next door are the beauty salon and barber shop; all have beautiful desert views.

Oversize guest rooms are quiet retreats with all the amenities you'd expect from a world-class resort. Although accommodations are spread throughout the resort, some of the nicest are closest to the spa. Most have oversize bathrooms with Italian marble. Suites have hand-carved travertine fireplaces.

....

INSIDER TIP Art lovers should check out the resort's $6 million collection of artwork.

....

Equipment: Free weights, rowing machines, stationary bikes, stair climbers, treadmills, weight-training circuit. **Services:** Aloe-vera wrap, aromatherapy, body scrub, desert clay wrap, herbal wrap, lymphatic drainage, moor mud wrap, reflexology, shiatsu, shirodhara. **Swimming:** 9 pools. **Classes and Programs:** Aerobics, body-composition analysis, cholesterol testing, fitness consultation, kickboxing, Spinning, tai chi, yoga. **Recreation:** Archery, badminton, biking, croquet, golf, hiking, lawn bowling, tennis, volleyball. **Children's Programs:** Funicians, for ages 5–12.

⌖ 654 rooms.

✕ Meals à la carte. Mary Elaine's serves French, Windows on the Green serves southwestern, and the Terrace serves casual American. Spa cuisine available at restaurants.

Sample Meals: Grilled-vegetable sandwich, grilled Portobello taco with roasted peppers, avocado, and cheese (lunch); grilled salmon with gazpacho relish, penne with grilled chicken, roasted peppers, and eggplant (dinner).

▱ Nightly rate $525–$655 per room. Day-spa package $95–$355. AE, DC, MC, V.

✉ *6000 E. Camelback Rd., Scottsdale, AZ 85251,* ☎ *480/423–2452 or 800/843–2392,* 🅵🅰🆇 *480/423–2582. www.the_phoenician.com*

ARKANSAS

NEW MOON SPA

HOLISTIC HEALTH

Eureka Springs became a spa town during the prosperous Victorian era, when it welcomed visitors with lavish hotels, summer homes, and picturesque cottages along the narrow streets zigzagging up wooded hills. Crowning the village was the Crescent Hotel, built in 1886.

A complete restoration of the Crescent and its sister hotel, the 1905 Basin Park, was completed in early 2000. A highlight of the Crescent is the New Moon Spa, a full-service spa. Its aerobics and exercise equipment rooms offer inspiring views of the hotel's manicured gardens and the forested mountains in the distance. You'll find ultimate relaxation in its hydrotherapy tub (with 89 jets massaging tired muscles) or its Vichy shower (with multiple showerheads raining down from above). Visitors can choose from traditional and specialized massages and custom body wraps, as well specialty energy work such as reiki.

Healthy meals and treats at the spa's award-winning café can be enjoyed at tables set among artwork and antiques. The spa's director, a former gallery owner, has commissioned members of the hill tribes in northern Thailand to make the nature-inspired jewelry and hand-loomed clothing that she designed, and you can buy them here.

INSIDER TIP The spa's Duet Room has a cedar sauna and massage area that are ideal for couples.

Equipment: Rowing machines, stationary bikes, weight-training circuit. **Services:** Body wraps, massage, reiki, Vichy shower. **Swimming:** Pool. **Classes and Programs:** Aerobics, circuit training, yoga. **Recreation:** Fishing, hiking, horseback riding, water sports.

⊞ 68 rooms at Crescent; 61 rooms at Basin Park.

✗ The New Moon Café is open 8:30–5. The Crescent and Basin Park hotels have restaurants serving American fare. **Sample Meals:** Shiitake mushroom sandwich, avocado sandwich, vegetarian lasagna (lunch).

▧ 1-night spa package $179 per couple, includes room, breakfast, and spa treatments. 2-night spa package $359 per couple, includes room, breakfast, and spa treatments. Spa treatments range from $15–$90. AE, MC, V.

⊠ *75 Prospect, Eureka Springs, AR 72632,* ☎ *501/253–2879. www.crescent-hotel.com*

HOT SPRINGS NATIONAL PARK

MINERAL SPRINGS

During a harrowing journey in 1541, Spanish explorer Hernando de Soto and his men relaxed in the 47 springs that bubble up 142°F mineral waters from the Ouachita Mountains. The area, once known as Valley of the Vapors by Native Americans because of the awe-inspiring clouds of steam, became the nation's first national park in 1832. More than 150 years later people still flock here to take the waters.

The park's 5,800 acres include the historic Bath House Row, the eight remaining spas built in the area around the turn of the last century. The most elegant is the opulent 1915 Fordyce Bathhouse, which now attracts visitors with free tours of its lavish fixtures. Exhibits at the Fordyce show the history of the hot springs, believed to alleviate numerous medical ailments. The Buckstaff Bathhouse, operated by the National Parks Service, still offers mineral baths, as it did in its heyday.

Half a dozen privately owned spas offer thermal baths and other spa treatments. The Arlington Hotel (⊠ Central Ave. and Fountain St., 71902, ☎ 501/623–7771 or 800/643–1502), a slightly faded grand dame built in 1924, has a two-level cascading swimming pool, two golf courses, an exercise room, and a beauty salon. It has been frequented by gangster Al Capone, baseball legend Babe Ruth, comic Phyllis Diller, and other notables. The Hot Springs Health Spa (⊠ 501 Spring St., 71901, ☎ 501/321–9664) offers thermal baths in large pools and hot tubs.

INSIDER TIP Not far from Bath House Row you'll find art galleries, restaurants, shops, and the boyhood haunts of President Bill Clinton.

Services: Massage, thermal water baths. **Swimming:** Nearby lakes and rivers. **Recreation:** Biking, hiking, horseback riding, water sports in area.

🏨 Numerous hotels in the area. For information call Hot Springs Convention and Visitors Bureau (☎ 800/772–2489).

⊠ *Hot Springs Visitor Center, 629 Central Ave., Hot Springs, AR 71902,* ☎ *800/772–2489. www.hotsprings.org*

CALIFORNIA

NORTHERN CALIFORNIA

BERNARDUS LODGE

LUXURY PAMPERING

Tucked away in the Carmel Valley's award-winning vineyards is this idyllic retreat combining the delights of fine country living with the service and amenities of top European hotels. In addition to sweeping mountain views, the romantic guest rooms at the Bernardus Lodge feature stone fireplaces, two-person tubs, and (since there's a vineyard on the premises) built-in wine grottoes.

In the spirit of its wine-making tradition, the spa offers a variety of therapies that incorporate products from the region, such as a scrub of crushed grape seed and red wine and a warm grape-seed oil massage. Prior to your treatment, arrive with enough time for a cup of herbal tea in the warming room, a eucalyptus steam, or a soak in the sundeck's reflecting pool. A beauty salon offers facials, manicures, pedicures, and other services. Kohls bath amenities and Essential Elements bath salts are provided to create your own private spa in the oversize tub in your guest room. Reach into the cupboards for candles to create even more ambience.

For those who appreciate viticulture, there are educational forums presented in a special exhibition kitchen just off the croquet lawn. There are also casual pool-side dining, fine dining, and creative spa cuisine to pair with Bernardus wines. And to set the tone when you arrive, you are greeted with a glass of vino as soon as you enter the classic country lodge, where overstuffed chairs and a roaring fire beckon. Each evening with turndown service, you'll enjoy a different wine, along with fruit and cheese.

In addition to a 24-hour fitness center (where you can request that your stationary bike be moved outside so you can enjoy the view), you'll also enjoy swimming, tennis, lawn croquet, and boccie. You can also visit seven local wineries, ride horses on some 4,400 acres of mountain trails, and golf at the 10 nearby championship courses.

INSIDER TIP Request a private session of meditation or yoga in a lovely studio.

Equipment: Elliptical trainers, free weights, stationary bikes, treadmills. **Services:** Aromatherapy, massage Vichy shower. **Swimming:** Pool.

Classes and Programs: Meditation, private Pilates, stretch, tai chi, tennis, yoga.

▥ 57 suites.

✕ Meals à la carte. Dine at two restaurants or outdoors alongside a stone fireplace or under the trellis by the croquet lawn. Spa menu available. **Sample Meals:** Fontina, tomato-and-basil pizza, grilled flat-iron steak (lunch); Portobello mushroom soup with goat cheese and white truffle oil, smoked salmon-fennel *brandade* (puree) with sweet English pea sauce (dinner).

▧ Nightly rate $245–$1900 per room. AE, D, DC, MC, V.

✉ *415 Carmel Valley Rd., Carmel Valley, CA 93924,* ☎ *831/659–3131 or 888/648–9463,* ℻ *831/659–3529. www.bernardus.com*

CALISTOGA SPA HOT SPRINGS

MINERAL SPRINGS

In 1859 San Franciscan developer Sam Brannan purchased a plot of land in what is now known as Calistoga in order to build a resort. There are many theories about how the town got its name, but one of the most entertaining holds that an intoxicated Brannan said he planned to create the "Calistoga of Sarafornia," a jumble of California and Saratoga Springs, then a fashionable New York hot springs.

The water here is only half the story. Calistoga's equally famous mud baths are a mixture of volcanic ash and peat. The high mineral content gives it a slightly sulfuric odor. After you lie in a vat of mud heated to just over 100°F, an attendant covers your body with another layer. As you relax, you let the heat penetrate your muscles and joints for up to 10 minutes. Next, you shower off the mud, soak for 10 or 15 minutes in a mineral-water whirlpool (filled from the hot wells), sweat it out in the steam room, and, finally, rest with a cotton blanket wrapped around you for 15 minutes. This gentle cooldown may even relax you enough to put you to sleep.

Europeans and Americans frequent Calistoga Spa Hot Springs, the best of the town's more utilitarian establishments. The spa's no-nonsense approach puts less emphasis on pampering and luxury touches than other spas, but the mud still works its magic. The resort's pluses include a gym and four outdoor pools with naturally heated mineral water of varying temperatures, including a 104°F whirlpool tub (the pools are available on a first-come, first-served basis, so be sure you get in early).

The no-frills motel-style guest rooms, which are arranged around the pools, are modern and well maintained, with kitchenettes stocked with basic pots, pans, dishes, and utensils. A grocery store about a block away provides anything for your meals.

INSIDER TIP Even if you're just passing through town, you can still stop by for mud baths and massages.

Equipment: Free weights, rowing machines, stair climbers, stationary bikes, treadmills, weight-training circuits. **Services:** Blanket wrap, massage, mud bath, mineral bath. **Swimming:** Two soaking pools, one whirlpool, one lap pool.

▥ 57 rooms.

✕ No meals served, but many restaurants are within walking distance.

✉ Nightly rate $105–$110 per room. Mud bath $48, including mineral bath, steam room, blanket wrap. Mud bath and massage $74–$98. Massage $40–$70. MC, V.

✉ *1006 Washington St., Calistoga, CA 94515,* ☎ *707/942–6269.*

CASA PALMERO

LUXURY PAMPERING

On the first tee of the Pebble Beach Golf Links, the newly opened Casa Palmero is as intimate as the nearby Inn at Spanish Bay and the Lodge at Pebble Beach are sprawling (all three have the same owner). With just 24 rooms, this Mediterranean-style hideaway near the soothing surf of Carmel Bay is an ideal getaway.

At the nearby Spa at Pebble Beach, designed to complement the three accommodations, is a private 22,000-square-ft facility surrounded by fragrant gardens, trellised walkways, and soothing fountains. A wide array of treatments and services provides a wonderful escape. You can enjoy a massage in front of a roaring fireplace or relax under a Vichy shower featuring a variety of water pressures and temperatures. Sea-salt scrubs, reflexology, craniosacral treatment, sea kelp and mud wraps, and other treatments are available. Here you'll find that classes in yoga, tai chi, meditation, and guided visualization are given right on the beach.

The spa, as well as the four golf courses and the beach and tennis club, is open to guests at all Pebble Beach Resorts. The properties overlook two of their four sister golf courses.

INSIDER TIP Park the car and forget about it. A complimentary shuttle runs between the three resorts, the spa, and the Monterey Peninsula Airport and downtown Carmel.

Services: Craniosacral treatment, hydrotherapy, massage, reflexology, sea-salt scrubs, sea kelp or mud wraps. **Classes and Programs:** Guided visualization, meditation, nature hikes, tai chi, yoga. **Swimming:** Outdoor pool. **Recreation:** Golf, hiking, horseback riding, kayaking.

🖭 21 rooms, 3 suites.

✗ Breakfast included. Variety of restaurants serve international cuisine. Spa cuisine available. **Sample Meals:** Fruit plate with yogurt, mixed greens with lemon-herb dressing and crispy croutons (lunch); thyme- and pepper-crusted ahi tuna with crispy matchstick potatoes, watercress, and red-wine peppercorn sauce (dinner).

✉ Nightly rate $550–$1,750 per room. Day spa package $50. AE, D, DC, MC, V.

✉ *1518 Cypress, Pebble Beach, CA 93953,* ☎ *831/624–3811 or 800/ 654–9300,* ᖴᴬˣ *831/644–7960. www.pebblebeach.com*

CLAREMONT RESORT & SPA

LUXURY PAMPERING

This grand, white-turreted resort hotel presiding over 22 manicured acres in the Berkeley hills beckons to frazzled city dwellers with excellent spa facilities. Although many come to be pampered, others turn out for the Life Shift programs designed to promote wellness.

The Claremont's spa wins kudos for its extensive menu of services. Trainers will help you restyle your workout routine and lead you through a wide variety classes, from stretching to tai chi. Also on the property are 10 tennis courts (six lighted for night play), four saunas, two outdoor heated pools (one Olympic size), and a whirlpool.

In true grand-resort tradition, the Claremont stands out for its cuisine and accommodations. The main restaurant, Jordan's at the Claremont, emphasizes California cuisine with a Pacific Rim influence, as well as health-oriented gourmet options called Lifestyle Cuisine. Beyond the tall windows of the elegant dining room lies San Francisco Bay. There's also a café offering beautiful views and low-calorie meals.

INSIDER TIP You won't get cabin fever here. You can easily stroll to shops and eateries in nearby Berkeley, or zip over to San Francisco by car or train.

Equipment: Free weights, rowing machines, stair climbers, stationary bikes, treadmills, weight-training circuit. **Services:** Aromatherapy, chamomile body scrub, deep-tissue massage, flotation tank, grapeseed body polish, loofah scrub, pressure-point massage, reflexology, salt glow. **Swimming:** 2 pools. **Classes and Programs:** Aerobics, nutritional counseling, personal training, tennis and swimming lessons, yoga. **Recreation:** Tennis, hiking, jogging. **Children's Programs:** Day camp for ages 4–10, swimming and tennis clinics for ages 7–16.

🛏 247 rooms, 32 suites.

✕ Meals à la carte. **Sample Meals:** Lettuce-wrapped halibut with ginger-soy marinade and Asian greens (lunch); mesquite-grilled swordfish with papaya chutney, rack of lamb with preserved lemon, sautéed spinach, and roasted tomatoes (dinner).

💳 Nightly rate $235–$850 per room. Day spa package $100–$350. AE, D, DC, MC, V.

✉ *41 Tunnel Rd., Berkeley, CA 94705,* ☎ *510/843–3000 or 800/551–7266,* 🖷 *510/843–6239. www.claremontresort.com*

DOUBLE EAGLE RESORT & SPA

LUXURY PAMPERING

Nestled in 13 acres of wooded pines on the eastern side of Yosemite National Park lies the Double Eagle Resort and Spa. This tranquil resort rests at the base of Dream Mountain, and you may find the name particularly apt. A creek runs through the property, and three waterfalls are visible from the restaurant and spa. Resident ducks live at the picturesque pond, and blue jays fly above.

The resort features 13 cabins, all in the woods or on the trout pond, where you'll enjoy fly-fishing in the summer and ice-skating in the winter. Each has its own fully equipped kitchen (don't leave food in your car, as the occasional brown bear won't leave it undisturbed). When you're ready to dine outside your cabin, meals are available à la carte at the restaurant.

Whenever you arrive, there is an array of activities available, including horseback riding and snowshoeing. The state-of-the-art fitness center is filled with cardio- and weight-training machines and offers a variety of classes including aerobics, tai chi, and yoga. There are also a whirlpool and indoor lap pool with an area designed for water aerobics. Post-workout, skiers and hikers will delight in the resort's signature deep-tissue massage, as well as a host of treatments, including hydrotherapy, mud baths, oxygenated facials, and a Vichy shower.

INSIDER TIP The tap water in June Lake is so clean, it comes straight from underground springs with no added chlorine. You won't be able to taste the difference from the pricey bottled stuff.

Equipment: Cross-country ski machines, free weights, rowing machines, stair climbers, stationary bicycles, treadmills, weight-training circuit. **Services:** Hot stone therapy, hydrotherapy, massage, mud baths, oxygenated facials. **Swimming:** Indoor lap pool. **Classes and Programs:** Aerobics, aquaerobics, tai chi, yoga. **Recreation:** Fishing, ice-skating.

⊞ 13 cabins, 1 guest house.

✗ Meals à la carte. Eagle's Landing Restaurant open for three meals daily. Meals low in fat, cholesterol, and sodium are available. **Sample Meals:** Oriental grilled chicken salad with ginger dressing (lunch); charbroiled orange roughy with an apricot, ginger, and almond glaze.

▤ Nightly rate $153–$224 per room. Day spa passes $10. AE, D, MC, V.

✉ *5587 Hwy. 158, June Lake, CA 93529,* ☎ *760/648–7134 or 877/648–7004,* FAX *760/648–8225. www.double-eagle-resort.com*

DR. WILKINSON'S HOT SPRINGS RESORT

MINERAL SPRINGS

When Doc Wilkinson arrived in Calistoga as a young chiropractor in 1946, he began combining volcanic ash, peat, and steaming mineral water straight from its source. The result was a remedy for aches and pains that is still popular today. At 82 he serves as a walking advertisement for his treatments.

His namesake resort, the oldest family-run spa in the Napa Valley, is synonymous with northern California relaxation. And treatments haven't changed much over the years. Guests still indulge in a series of spa treatments based on the mud baths, mineral baths, and therapeutic massage. Packages combine full-body mud baths with whirlpool baths, steam, wraps, and massage. Complete relaxation will be yours during these two hours of pampering. If you're ready for more, you have access to one large indoor warm mineral water whirlpool and two outdoor warm mineral pools.

You stay in individual bungalows in quiet garden surroundings or in a handsomely restored Victorian house. The spacious rooms are near sundecks, lounges, and garden patios. Cottages with full kitchens are also available.

INSIDER TIP The weekday Stress Stopper package is a bargain in the off-season.

Services: Acupressure, mud baths, mud wraps, salt glow. **Swimming:** 2 outdoor mineral-water pools.

⊞ 42 rooms.

✗ No restaurant, but many are within walking distance.

▤ Nightly rate $99–$159 per room. AE, MC, V.

✉ *1507 Lincoln, Calistoga, CA 94515,* ☎ *707/942–4102,* FAX *707/942–4412. www.drwilkinson.com*

ESALEN INSTITUTE

HOLISTIC HEALTH ○ MINERAL SPRINGS

Atop 27 acres on the spectacular Big Sur coastline is the Esalen Institute, an alternative education center where letting it all hang out is the order of the day. Clothing is optional and nudity common in the hilltop hot springs, massage area, and swimming pool. And an almost overwhelming number of seminars on everything from spiritual healing to Gestalt therapy offer an equally freeing experience.

Many who come here simply want to unwind in what easily ranks as one of California's most beautiful settings. You can book a massage, soak in mineral springs, or hike in the nearby wilderness without participating in workshops. Exercise classes are available daily, including yoga, meditation, and dance. You can also learn Esalen massage, a sensuous type of bodywork developed by the retreat's founders.

Guests share accommodations in either doubles, triples, or dormitories with four or more per room. The rooms are simple, with no televisions, phones, or air-conditioning. The buffet-style meals are just as casual as the accommodations, but the food is wonderfully wholesome, including organically grown produce.

Children are welcome here, and those between one and six can participate in the Gazebo School Park education program.

Days are spent gardening, riding ponies, learning about animal care, and exploring nature. Evenings are spent reading, learning computer, baking, or arts and crafts.

INSIDER TIP If you're ready to experience a nude hot springs, you can dive right in here. Countless others have since the 1960s.

Services: Craniosacral massage, deep-tissue massage, Hellerwork, Feldenkrais Method, Rolfing. **Swimming:** Pool. **Classes and Programs:** Dance classes, lectures, meditation, yoga. **Recreation:** Hiking. **Children's Programs:** Activities for ages 1–6.

🛏 94 beds in double and triple rooms, 16 bunk beds, 12 sleeping-bag spaces.

✗ Meals included. Most are vegan and vegetarian with some fish and chicken. **Sample Meals:** Pasta salad, potato-leek soup (lunch); spinach lasagna (dinner).

💰 Nightly rate $130–$150 per person. Weekend rate $485 per person. 5-day rate $885 per person. AE, MC, V.

✉ *Hwy. 1, Big Sur, CA 93920–9616,* ☎ *831/667–3000 or 831/667–3005 for reservations,* FAX *408/667–2724. www.esalen.org*

FESS PARKER'S WINE COUNTRY INN & SPA

LUXURY PAMPERING

Fess Parker, renowned for his portrayal of Davy Crockett and Daniel Boone in film and television, is now making a name as a wine maker and hotelier. In the heart of Santa Barbara wine county, Parker operates both a winery and an inn and spa, complete with the latest grape seed–based treatments.

This isn't exactly the best place for dieting. The wine-tasting room at the Fess Parker Winery also markets Parker's signature vinegars, dressings, and fudge sauce (you may even find the former screen star autographing bottles). To top off a day of fine vintages, executive chef Bernard Barchie serves up delicious gourmet cuisine back at inn's Vintage Room restaurant.

Due to space restrictions, the inn's low-key boutique spa is down the street from the inn. The spa is tiny but offers a nice array of treatments based on natural resources, many of them from the area. Choose from an aloe-vera wrap, hot stone therapy, crushed rose exfoliation and rose body oil massage, marine pumice scrub and algae mud wrap, salt glow, and a variety of massages, including reflexology and aromatherapy.

A number of activities are available within a short drive. Art galleries, antiques shops, horse ranches, and the replica Dutch town of Solvang are all nearby. Golf lovers will delight in the Rancho San Marcos Golf Course, River Course at Alisal, and La Purisima Course, all within 15 mi of the inn.

At the end of a long day you'll be glad to retreat to your room. Each features a fireplace and minibar, and some include a whirlpool tub.

INSIDER TIP Need something to bring home for the kids? Visit the gift shop at nearby Fess Parker Winery to pick up coonskin caps and other souvenirs from Parker's roles as Davy Crockett and Daniel Boone.

Services: Algae mud wrap, aloe-vera wrap, hot stone therapy, massage, salt glow. **Swimming:** 2 outdoor pools. **Recreation:** Golf, horseback riding nearby.

⊞ 21 rooms, 1 suite.

✕ Meals à la carte. The Vintage Room serves California cuisine. **Sample Meals:** Rosemary-garlic chicken Caesar salad (lunch); roasted Chilean sea bass with a lemon-chive crust, garlic freshwater prawns, creamy root-vegetable and white-bean cassoulet with a watercress emulsion (dinner).

✍ Nightly rate $175–$400 per room. AE, MC, V.

✉ *2860 Grand Ave., Box 908, Los Olivos, CA 93441,* ☎ *805/688-7788 or 800/446-2455,* ℻ *805/688-1942. www.fessparker.com*

FOUR SEASONS RESORT AVIARA

LUXURY PAMPERING

The rolling hills surrounding the Four Seasons Resort Aviara hold something to captivate almost everyone, from a championship golf course to the Batiquitos Lagoon, a famed wildlife preserve that is home to more than 130 species of birds.

The resort's state-of-the-art fitness center is well equipped with stair climbers (each with its own television screen), stationary bikes, treadmills, weight-training equipment, and free weights. Serious swimmers will delight in the beautiful outdoor pool, especially because another is designated for kids. There are also two heated whirlpools, a steam room, and sauna. The center provides terry robes and slippers, as well as shorts, T-shirts, socks, and athletic shoes at no charge.

Outdoors, there are six tennis courts lighted for night play. Golfers will delight in the 7,007-yard, par-72 course designed by Arnold Palmer and the Aviara Golf Academy, run by Kip Puterbaugh. Runners will appreciate the three scenic jogging loops ranging from 2.5 to 10.5 km.

Spa services include more than 20 treatments, including a variety of massages, from aromatherapy to reflexology. You can also choose from facials, body scrubs, and signature southern California treatments, such as the spirulina body wrap, using all natural, live spirulina algae harvested from pure salt lakes in the southern part of the state. Hair styling is also available in the Jose Eber Salon. Guests enjoy complimentary herbal teas, cucumber-infused water, and fresh fruit.

The resort boasts a total of five restaurants including Vivace, where Chef Alessandro Serni, a native of Milan, serves up innovative Tuscan cuisine. The four other restaurants are the family-friendly casual California Bistro; the Argyle at the golf clubhouse, which opens for breakfast and lunch; the Ocean Pool Bar & Grill, which serves lunch poolside in warm weather; and the lounge, which serves evening appetizers. The Four Seasons' own Alternative Cuisine features delectable meals that are low in sodium, fat, and cholesterol. An extensive kids' menu is available throughout the resort.

Nightly live entertainment is in the lounge. If you're not much of a night owl, another draw is afternoon tea served in the hotel's lovely lobby. An assortment of finger sandwiches, scones with rose-petal jelly, lemon curd, and Devonshire cream, delicate pastries, and petit fours are served.

INSIDER TIP Nature lovers will flock to the docent-led tours of the Batiquitos Lagoon, one of the few remaining tidal wetlands in southern California.

Equipment: Free weights, stair climbers, stationary bikes, treadmills, weight-training circuit. **Services:** Massage, spirulina body wrap, Turkish body salt scrub. **Swimming:** 2 pools. **Classes and Programs:** Personal training, yoga. **Recreation:** Golf, jogging, tennis. **Children's Programs:** Complimentary Kids For All Seasons program for ages 4–12.

⊡ 285 rooms, 44 suites.

✕ Meals à la carte. 5 restaurants feature international fare. Meals lower in fat, salt, and sodium available. **Sample Meals:** Blackened chicken salad with chipotle-honey vinaigrette and cantaloupe-melon salsa (lunch); angel-hair pasta with tomato and purple basil (dinner).

▣ Nightly rate $365–$475 per room. 1-day spa package $425–$665, includes lodging, spa treatments. 1-day Gold and Spa package $490–$530, includes lodging, golf, and spa treatments. AE, D, DC, MC, V.

✉ *7100 Four Seasons Point, Carlsbad, CA 92009,* ☎ *760/603–6800 or 800/332–3442,* FAX *760/603–6801. www.fourseasons.com/aviara*

HEALTH SPA NAPA VALLEY

LUXURY PAMPERING

Many of Napa Valley's spas are older establishments, and some lean toward the utilitarian. The proprietors of Health Spa Napa Valley knew this when they opened a facility combining a Wine Country aesthetic with the latest spa treatments and services. Luxury pampering is the order of the day. Two attendants perform the panchakarma massage, an ayurvedic treatment that involves having your skin nourished with an ample supply of warm sesame oil.

Grape-seed oil, whether used in mud wraps or for massages, is the spa's trademark product. The attendant slathers you with a mixture of French clay, lavender, and crushed grape seeds (it smells great, almost like a glass of zinfandel) and wraps you up. The clay helps draw out impurities, and the grape seeds are said to contain antioxidants that rejuvenate the skin. After 20 minutes or so, you rinse off the mud and proceed to the massage table. You can also opt to finish with a grape-seed body polish.

Before or after your massage you can work out at a compact but well-equipped fitness center where glass doors open onto the pool area. Swim laps or sunbathe by the 25-meter pool, or take a yoga class. The changing areas, which have spacious steam rooms and great-smelling hair and skin products, receive constant attention from the spa's staff.

Within the complex is a lively restaurant, Tomatina's, that serves pizza and Mediterranean fare.

INSIDER TIP To really indulge yourself, try the world famous Napa Valley eateries. The award-winning Tra Vigne and other stellar restaurants are nearby.

Equipment: Free weights, stair climbers, stationary bikes, treadmills, weight-training circuit. **Services:** Ayurvedic massage, grape-seed oil treatments, reflexology, salt glow, seaweed wrap, shiatsu. **Swimming:** Pool. **Classes and Programs:** Body-composition, fitness, Spinning, stress evaluations, yoga.

⊞ No accommodations. 20 rooms and 1 suite at nearby Inn at Southbridge (☎ 800/520–6800 or 707/967–9400).

✗ No meals at spa.

▨ Massages $40–$195. Skin-care treatments $45–$120. Spa treatment packages $110–$270.

✉ *1030 Main St., St. Helena, CA 94574,* ☎ *707/967–8800,* ℻ *707/ 967–8801. www.napavalleyspa.com*

HEARTWOOD INSTITUTE

HOLISTIC HEALTH ∘ MEDICAL WELLNESS

This budget-price country retreat north of San Francisco operates on 240 acres on California's north coast. The wilderness setting is ideal for hiking in the woods, mountain biking on nearby trails, or participating in group meditation in a straw-bale meditation temple.

Housed in a picturesque log lodge, a renovated barn, and a yurt (canvas dome), the facilities are rustic but pleasant. In addition to the massage lessons, yoga classes, and lectures on nutrition, there are occasional weekend wellness workshops that enroll between 5 and 20 participants.

A limited number of spa services is available, but you must reserve in advance. In the meantime, you can choose from a variety of rubdowns from the staff or faculty of the massage school. Also available are an outdoor hot tub, a wood-fired sauna, and an unheated swimming pool.

Accommodations are simple. You either camp outside (bring your own gear) or sleep in small, simple dormitory rooms. Three daily vegetarian meals, included in the tuition, are served buffet style in the cozy dining room or on a spacious deck in nice weather.

INSIDER TIP Bring your own mountain bike or well-worn hiking boots to explore this beautiful mountain wilderness.

Services: Body wraps, craniosacral therapy, deep-tissue massage, hypnotherapy, polarity therapy, shiatsu. **Swimming:** Pool. **Classes and Programs:** Dance classes, lectures on nutrition, massage classes, nutritional counseling, yoga. **Recreation:** Biking, hiking, swimming.

▣ 15 dormitory rooms with shared bath, 36 campsites.

✕ Meals included. 3 buffet-style meals, primarily vegetarian, served in dining room. **Sample Meals:** Indian dal (lentils), coconut rice, apple-raisin chutney (lunch); breaded baked fish fillet with spicy lemon glaze (dinner).

▥ Nightly rate $90–$150 per room, $65 per campsite. MC, V.

✉ *220 Harmony Lane, Garberville, CA 95542,* ☎ *707/923–5004 or 877/408–9663,* FAX *707/923–5010. www.heartwoodinstitute.com*

INDIAN SPRINGS RESORT

MINERAL SPRINGS

Mud baths at most resorts are a mixture of volcanic ash and peat, but Indian Springs Resort, which has a cache of ash right on its property, uses 100% volcanic ash. It truly makes a difference—you feel like an insect suspended in amber.

The mud-bath regimen here includes a 10-minute session in the mud followed by a 15-minute soak in a mineral tub (during which you rehydrate by sipping the house cooler, spring water flavored with orange and cucumber slices). Next comes a respite in the steam room and a blanket wrap. The entire process lasts about 55 minutes.

Indian Springs has a single attendant for four mud baths. She provides water, cold compresses, and assistance getting in and out of the baths. The resort encourages silence, although some chatter does occur, breaking the meditative calm a mud-bath session can provide. But the pure volcanic ash will make your skin silky smooth, and the skill of the massage technicians is generally quite high.

After your mud bath, you can have a massage (from 25 to 90 minutes), get a facial, or have a manicure. If sitting in mud doesn't appeal to you, you can opt for a mineral bath followed by a visit to the steam room and a blanket wrap.

The spa, which has operated since the late 1800s, was renamed Indian Springs in the mid-1980s. Major renovations to the 1913 bathhouse and the 1940s-era cottages (which hold studio and one-bedroom units) have preserved their character. A big plus if you're a swimmer is the naturally heated outdoor Olympic-size mineral-water pool. The pool area is surrounded with lavender, ivy, and cacti.

INSIDER TIP For the best rates try a winter special that features a one-night stay and two mud baths.

Services: Body polish, craniosacral therapy, deep-tissue massage, mud bath, polarity therapy, reflexology. **Swimming:** Pool. **Recreation:** Hiking, tennis.

▣ 2 studio duplexes, 12 1-bedroom duplexes, 2 1-bedroom cottages, 1 2-bedroom house, 1 3-bedroom house.

✕ No meals served, but there are many restaurants within walking distance.

⌦ Nightly rates $95–$500 per night. Spa treatments $65–$130. D, MC, V.

⊠ *1712 Lincoln Ave., Calistoga, 94515,* ☎ *707/942–4913,* FAX *707/942–4919.*

THE LODGE AT SKYLONDA

LUXURY PAMPERING

You're bound to feel rejuvenated after a couple of nights in the quiet calm of the Lodge at Skylonda. This elegant log-and-stone structure, set among the redwoods, combines top-notch massage therapists, excellent exercise instructors, and gourmet meals so good it's hard to believe they contain less than 15% fat. Anyone who's intimidated by the idea of working out and dieting at a spa will feel at home here, where hard-core exercise is optional. You can join any of the three early morning hikes, wander by yourself among the nearby trails, or just take it easy.

The daily schedule at Skylonda is exceedingly civilized. After an optional stretch class at 6:45 AM, there's a hearty but healthy breakfast buffet of fresh-baked muffins, homemade granola, and a hot entrée. Then you'll be given a water bottle and ushered outside for a guided hike along trails through forested canyons and grassy meadows. Although the spa occupies 16 acres of coastal hills near Silicon Valley, hikes often venture farther afield to various parks within the Santa Cruz Mountains. Along the way you'll learn about the area's ecosystem as well as bits of folklore. At the end of the trail a van will bring you back to the lodge, where hot chocolate and muffins will greet you on your return.

After lunch you're on your own to indulge in top-notch spa treatments or enjoy the gorgeous glassed-in pool or the adjoining outdoor hot tub—it's the ultimate California perch. For those with more energy to burn, classes in tai chi, stretch, yoga, and aquaerobics are available.

At 6, hors d'oeuvres are served in the Great Room, where you can relax in an overstuffed sofa near a roaring fire or challenge a friend to a game of backgammon or chess. Dinner, served from 7 to 8:30, is worth waiting for. Candles dress up the rustic dining room. Menus on every table announce the two entrée dinner choices, always featuring fresh produce (supplied by local farmers) and the day's catch from the Pacific. Calories and fat grams are noted for each. Meals are so tasty that chef Sue Chapman gives evening cooking demonstrations twice a week. Her cookbook, *The Lodge at Skylonda Recipe Collection,* sells for $12 in the gift shop.

Because every day begins early, nighttime activities are scarce—all the better to enjoy the huge rooms, complete with white-cotton reading pillows and full bathrooms with deep soaking tubs (rubber ducky and hand-cut lavender soap included). There are no televisions or radios; instead you have a private deck or patio. Choice top-floor rooms have 12-ft vaulted ceilings.

Because hiking is the focus here, cardiovascular equipment is limited. The gym doubles as the exercise studio, so you'll be ousted from the machines when classes are in session. With so many other exercise options, however, this is hardly a concern.

INSIDER TIP Don't miss a hike on the Ridge Trail, where views reveal the ocean, coastal hillsides, and masses of wildflowers.

Equipment: Free weights, stair climbers, stationary bikes, weight-training circuit. **Services:** Aromatherapy, body wraps, hot stone therapy, reflexology, salt scrubs. **Swimming:** Indoor pool. **Classes and Programs:** Aquaerobics, personal training, tai chi, yoga.

▣ 16 rooms.

✗ Meals included. Gourmet meals served in the dining room average about 1,400 calories. **Sample Meals:** Sweet potato and apple bisque with fresh thyme, quinoa salad with chicken and pumpkin (lunch); baby-arugula salad with marmalade-mustard dressing, seared swordfish with sugar-snap peas and tangerine-dill beurre blanc, New Mexican stuffed potato with black beans, goat cheese, and chipotle pepper on wilted kale (dinner).

▤ Nightly rate $265–$320 per person, double occupancy. 2-night spa package $305–$375 per person, double occupancy, includes massage. AE, MC, V.

✉ *16350 Skyline Blvd., Woodside, CA 94062,* ☎ *650/851–6625 or 800/851–2222,* FAX *415/851–4500. www.skylondalodge.com*

MEADOWOOD NAPA VALLEY

LUXURY PAMPERING

The chic town of St. Helena has a reputation for fine wineries, sophisticated restaurants, and high-style boutiques and galleries. It's no surprise, then, that the town is also home to one of the region's most elegant spas. Nestled among the oaks and pines, Meadowood Napa Valley recalls the grand old resorts of the early 1900s with its gabled lodges overlooking the manicured croquet lawn and golf course. The health spa, added in 1993, epitomizes the Napa Valley lifestyle: easy informality and superb taste.

Epicurean pleasures are a major part of the Meadowood experience. Many of the area's best wineries are nearby. Vineyard tours begin right at the resort, where resident wine tutor John Thoreen sets up guided tours and tastings. Sunday brunch and dinners in the main restaurant are superb, with chef Pilar Sanchez's seasonal menu drawing on local produce, free-range poultry, and fresh fish from the Pacific. Though vegetarian and heart-healthy meals are available, this is not the place to diet, especially if you are intent on sampling some of the area's finest vintages, served by the glass or the bottle.

The airy spa building is rarely crowded, and guests are treated like VIPs. Scheduled classes include an early morning stretch session followed by a 60-minute total-body workout. Other daily exercise sessions include aquaerobics, yoga, and step classes. Personal training is available. There's an extensive selection of spa services, massage therapies, facials, and signature Napa Valley treatments employing a variety of grape-seed products.

Creature comforts count for a lot in this sybaritic corner of the world, and accommodations are predictably up to par. Terraced up the hillside along a nine-hole golf course, most guest units are done in a French country style, with fieldstone fireplaces and high ceilings. You can opt for seclusion higher on the hill (a call to the bellman shuttles you to the spa), or select a terrace unit facing the croquet green. Wherever you choose, you're likely hear frogs croaking in the evenings.

INSIDER TIP A wine tasting at one of the many famous vineyards a short distance from Meadowood will bring added good cheer to your visit.

Equipment: Free weights, stair climbers, stationary bikes, treadmills, weight-training circuit. **Services:** Aromatherapy, deep-tissue massage, grape-seed body polish, reflexology, salt glow. **Swimming:** Lap pool, family pool. **Classes and Programs:** Aerobics, aquaerobics, body-composition, exercise consultation, nutrition analysis, personal training, step, yoga. **Recreation:** Biking, croquet, golf, hiking, tennis. **Children's Programs:** Welcoming kit with toys and animal crackers, milk turndown service, kid-size robes.

🛏 38 rooms, 47 suites.

✕ Meals à la carte. California cuisine, as well as vegetarian and heart-healthy options, are available in two restaurants. **Sample Meals:** Grilled salmon with arugula, fennel, and orange reduction, fettuccine with mushrooms, tomatoes, basil, and garlic (lunch); sea scallops steamed in corn husks with vanilla-bean butter and corn-shiitake ragout (dinner).

💳 Nightly rate $350–$710 per room. Seasonal packages available. AE, D, DC, MC, V.

✉ *900 Meadowood La., St. Helena, CA 94574,* ☎ *707/963–3646 or 800/458–8080,* ᴵᴬˣ *707/963–3532. www.meadowood.com*

MOUNT VIEW SPA

LUXURY PAMPERING

One of Calistoga's classiest spas is inside the Mount View Hotel, a restored 1930s art deco treasure that's been designated a National Historic Landmark. The hotel's casual but elegant ambience continues in the spa, where private treatment rooms with double-size whirlpools are ideal for couples. A quiet outdoor courtyard shelters a heated pool and whirlpool.

The hotel is romantic, open, and airy. Enter the lobby illuminated by skylights, and you'll find overstuffed couches, potted palms, and bouquets of unusual flowers. Cottages have private patios with hot tubs and wet bars stocked with sparkling beverages from local springs. Many rooms overlook the hotel's shaded courtyard.

Come mealtime, the acclaimed Catahoula Restaurant will tempt you with its California-Cajun cuisine prepared in a wood-burning oven. You can dine in the funky restaurant, gazing at a giant avant-garde mural and photos of the Catahoula hound for which the restaurant is named, or take your meal by the pool.

INSIDER TIP Eight theme rooms include the art deco Jean Harlow Suite and the Victorian-style Robert Louis Stevenson Suite.

Services: Aromatherapy, Dead Sea mud wrap, herbal linen wrap, reflexology. **Swimming:** Pool.

🛏 22 rooms, 8 suites, 3 cottages.

✕ Meals à la carte. California-Cajun cuisine at Catahoula Restaurant. **Sample Meals:** Caesar salad with spicy rock shrimp, pizza with andouille sausage, onion confit, and oven-roasted tomatoes (lunch); oven-roasted bone marrow with tomato-mushroom jam, spicy paella with mussels, clams, rock shrimp, and homemade chorizo, southern-fried rabbit with dirty rice and collard greens (dinner).

🎫 Nightly rate $130–$250 per room. 1-night spa package $290 per room, double occupancy, includes two treatments per person. AE, D, MC, V.

✉ *1457 Lincoln Ave., Calistoga, CA 94515,* ☎ *707/942–5789 (spa) or 800/772–8838,* FAX *707/942–9165. www.mountviewspa.com*

OSMOSIS ENZYME BATH & MASSAGE

LUXURY PAMPERING

Although enzyme baths are ubiquitous in Japan, Osmosis Enzyme Bath & Massage is the only spa in the United States offering this treatment. The ritual begins in a tea room overlooking a traditional Japanese garden, where you drink a pot of herbal tea mixed with digestive enzymes imported from Japan. After about 20 minutes you climb into a large redwood tub filled with a fragrant mixture of organic plant enzymes and finely milled cedar, fir, and rice bran. When the enzymes are combined in the tub, a chemical reaction occurs, naturally heating the water to 135°F. The attendant covers you up to your chin and for the next 20 minutes gently wipes your brow and brings you sips of water.

When you emerge, you can opt for a 75-minute massage either indoors or in one of the freestanding pagodas near the creek that runs through the property. Or you may conclude instead with a half-hour blanket wrap in a darkened room. You'll listen to specially selected music that helps you relax.

Part of the retreat's appeal is its serene setting. The spa is in a two-story clapboard house. The meditative Japanese tea garden, with a soothing fountain and intricately planted bonsai trees, is a perfect place to begin your treatment. To reach the pagodas where massages take place, you'll meander along a secluded bamboo path where you'll hear the wind in the trees and the chirping of birds.

INSIDER TIP For an added treat, visit the organic brick-oven bakery Wild Flour, just down the street.

Services: Enzyme bath, massage.

🏨 No lodging at spa.

✗ No meals provided at spa. Restaurants are within easy driving distance.

🎫 Enzyme bath and blanket wrap $65. Enzyme bath and massage $140. Massage $75 indoors, $90 outdoors. AE, MC, V.

✉ *209 Bohemian Hwy., Freestone, CA 95472,* ☎ *707/823–8231,* FAX *707/874–3788. www.osmosis.com*

POST RANCH INN

LUXURY PAMPERING

Blending in with the redwoods that line the jagged coastline called Big Sur are the wooden structures that make up the Post Ranch Inn. The most popular include a tree house (yes, built in a tree) and an ocean house with a roof covered with wildflowers and a spectacular view of the sea. Made of wood, glass, slate, and other natural materials, the rooms feature wood-burning fireplaces, hot tubs, and massage tables in case you should want to book a massage while enjoying your private view of the cliffs below.

Spa treatments are administered in three separate studios filled with fresh ocean air. Don't worry about rushing through your day to fit in your spa treatments, as appointments are scheduled until 9 PM. Depending on the weather, tai chi and yoga classes are held under the yurt (canvas-roofed structure) or outdoors. A fitness room includes cross trainers, treadmills, stationary bikes, and free weights.

Dining at the Inn's Sierra Mar Restaurant, you'll have a vantage point 1,200 ft above the Pacific Ocean. The daily-changing menu features fresh seafood and local produce. Gourmet picnics are packed on request. For more epicurean pleasures, stick around on Saturday for a mixer with other guests that includes wine and cheese.

....

INSIDER TIP Take a nature walk with Billy Post, a descendant of the original owners of the land. It's offered at 10 AM Monday, Thursday, and Saturday and leads you through the majestic Big Sur landscape.

....

Equipment: Free weights, stair climbers, stationary bikes, weight-training circuit. **Services:** Aromatherapy, body polish, deep-tissue massage, herbal wrap, hot stone therapy, reflexology. **Swimming:** Lap pool. **Classes and Programs:** Nature walks, personal training, tai chi, yoga.

▥ 30 rooms.

✕ Breakfast included. Sierra Mar restaurant features California cuisine. **Sample Meals:** Grilled Portobello mushroom with tomato and basil on homemade wheat bread, cold rosemary-lemon roast chicken with potato salad and vinaigrette (lunch); sautéed halibut with champagne caviar butter, rack of lamb with grilled eggplant and chickpea tower (dinner).

▧ Nightly rate $455–$835 per room. AE, MC, V.

✉ *Hwy. 1, Box 219, Big Sur, CA 93920,* ☎ *408/667–2200 or 800/ 527–2200,* FAX *408/667–2824. www.postranchinn.com*

PREVENTIVE MEDICINE RESEARCH INSTITUTE

NUTRITION AND DIET ○ MEDICAL WELLNESS

Changing your lifestyle to prevent or reverse the progression of cardiovascular disease is the focus of the four weeklong retreats sponsored by the Preventive Medicine Research Institute. Directed by respected nutritionist Dean Ornish and led by health-care professionals, this highly structured program includes everything from lectures on stress management to cooking instruction by celebrity chefs.

Participation in the retreat is limited to 100 at a time. Part of the fee contributes to ongoing programs at the Preventive Medicine Research Institute, a nonprofit program associated with the University of California at San Francisco.

Lodging at the Claremont Resort is arranged separately, allowing you to choose the type of room or suite that fits your budget. Specially prepared meals for program participants are served in a private dining room in the hotel. Services in the Claremont's spa and salon (not included in the price of programs) add a welcome bit of pampering to this educational, perhaps life-changing experience.

INSIDER TIP To keep your costs down, call the Preventive Medicine Research Institute to inquire about the need for volunteers.

⊞ Accommodations at the Claremont Resort arranged through the institute at a discounted rate.

✗ Meals included. All are low-fat, low-cholesterol, and mainly vegetarian. **Sample Meals:** Lentil soup and garden salad, pasta salad (lunch); vegetarian lasagna, stir-fry vegetables, and brown rice (dinner).

✉ Weekly program $2,900 per person, including meals, classes, lectures. Lodging not included.

✉ *900 Bridgeway, Suite 1, Sausalito, CA 94965,* ☎ *415/332–2525 or 800/775–7674,* FAX *415/332–5730. www.pmri.org*

ST. HELENA CENTER FOR HEALTH

NUTRITION AND DIET ∘ MEDICAL WELLNESS

Taking charge of your health often requires big lifestyle changes, and the program offered by the St. Helena Center for Health provides practically every tool you might need. A little more than an hour north of San Francisco in the beautiful town of St. Helena, the center feels more like a hotel than a medical facility, with vineyards stretching for miles below its hillside perch. Although it is part of a hospital complex run by Seventh-Day Adventists, programs are nondenominational and are structured to provide complete medical and lifestyle evaluations. Every guest leaves with a personalized plan for diet, exercise, and stress management.

Self-management and disease prevention are the goals here. Following a physical examination and diet analysis that take into account your physical condition, nutritional requirements, and weight-loss goals, health professionals prescribe a course of action intended to help you achieve a healthier lifestyle. The center's association with St. Helena Hospital enables it to draw on that facility's state-of-the-art medical facilities, if necessary. You can choose to focus on smoking cessation, recovery from chemical dependency, making your heart healthier, or dealing with pain. There's also a four-day, women-only renewal retreat.

The 10- to 12-day McDougall Program, dealing with diet and nutrition, includes discussion groups, vegetarian cooking classes, and consultations with Dr. John McDougall, the author of many books on improving personal health and well-being.

INSIDER TIP Can't find time to get out of the office? There's a one- to five-day executive health program available.

Equipment: Rowing machines, stair climbers, stationary bikes, treadmill. **Services:** Massage. **Swimming:** Pool. **Classes and Programs:** Cooking classes, exercise instruction, lectures on health-related topics, medical counseling, yoga. **Recreation:** Biking, hiking.

⊞ 22 rooms.

✗ Meals included. 3 vegetarian meals daily served buffet style. **Sample Meals:** Bean enchiladas with salsa verde, Chinese noodles (lunch); split-pea soup and polenta with marinara sauce, green pepper and tomato teriyaki with brown rice (dinner).

✉ 7-day smoking cessation program $3,100 per person. 12-day McDougall program $5,015 single per person. Medical insurance may cover part of cost. AE, MC, V.

✉ *Box 250, Deer Park, CA 94576,* ☎ *707/963–6207 or 800/358–9195,* FAX *707/967–5618.*

SIVANANDA ASHRAM YOGA FARM

HOLISTIC HEALTH

At a simple farmhouse in the Sierra foothills, you can delve into a serious study of yoga, both in practice and philosophy. Two daily sessions teaching traditional postures, breathing techniques, and meditation are intended to enhance your understanding of the mind-body connection and foster spiritual growth.

Four forms of yoga are practiced here: raja (yoga of meditation, including hatha yoga), karma (yoga of action or selfless service), phakti (yoga of devotion), and jnana (yoga of knowledge). The program is based on the yogic principles of Swami Vishnu-devananda, whose followers and new students join in practicing the 12 asanas (positions), from a headstand to a spinal twist, each believed to have specific benefits. Participants learn that the proper pranayama (breathing) in each position is essential for energy control.

A 90-minute yoga and meditation session begins the day, followed by a buffet-style brunch. A second yoga session is held in the afternoon. A half hour of silent meditation is followed by chanting and reading on a spiritual topic. From time to time the ashram also offers special programs, including workshops such as acupuncture and Chinese medicine, and hosts visits from Indian clerics.

The 80-acre farm attracts a diverse crowd, ranging from families with children to seniors. Guests typically share cabins (or pay a modest single supplement) and contribute one hour a day to the upkeep of the ashram, helping with kitchen work, painting, or gardening. Simply said, this is considered a form of karma yoga, or selfless service.

INSIDER TIP This New Age retreat prohibits smoking and alcohol. If you're trying to quit or reduce your intake of these substances, this may be the right choice for you.

Swimming: Pond. **Classes and Programs:** Lectures, meditation, yoga. **Recreation:** Hiking.

🛏 10 room. Campsites available.

✕ Meals included. 2 vegetarian meals are served buffet style. **Sample Meals:** Oatmeal, fresh fruit, dal soup, brown rice, steamed vegetables (brunch); potato-carrot curry, fresh steamed greens, ginger-soy broth, dal, scrambled tofu (dinner).

💲 Nightly rate $45–$50 per person, double occupancy, includes lodging, meals, programs. Tent space $25–$30. Dormitory beds $35–$40. MC, V.

✉ *14651 Ballantree La., Grass Valley, CA 95949,* ☎ *530/272–9322 or 800/469–9642,* FAX *530/477–6054. www.shivananda.org*

SONOMA MISSION INN & SPA

LUXURY PAMPERING ∘ MINERAL SPRINGS

Since 1840 San Franciscans have been "taking the cure" at the Sonoma Mission Inn, perhaps the best-known spa in Sonoma County. Despite its unlikely location off the main street of tiny Boyes Hot Springs, guests continue to come from afar to enjoy the extensive spa facilities and the classic spa cuisine. A few days spent on these 10 eucalyptus-shaded acres can do wonders for your spirits, which might explain why it's a frequent stopover on Wine Country tours.

Soaking in the mineral water remains one of the most popular activities at the spa. A spring funnels 135°F mineral-rich water into the exercise and swimming pools. Thanks to a recent $20 million expansion, the spa has grown to 40,000 square ft. The new facility features an elaborate Roman bathing ritual, which includes an exfoliating gel scrub, a warm mineral bath, a cooling shower, sitting in an herbal steam room and dry sauna, then another cool shower. Afterward, you can rest with complimentary juice or herbal tea in comfortable leather and wooden lounge chairs by a fireplace.

In addition, the spa now serves up more than 50 treatments, including herbal, seaweed, and mud wraps, facials, body scrubs, and Swiss and Vichy showers. Among the standout treatments is the nearly two-hour Revitalizer, which combines an invigorating herbal body scrub, detoxifying lymphatic massage, and hot linen wrap. Four others types of body wraps take place on a flotation table, which lets you float on pillows filled with warm water.

The fitness center, within the new spa, features gardens scented by roses, camellias, and jasmine. Classes are scheduled in the aerobics studio throughout the day, beginning at 7 AM with tai chi and yoga. Hikers can sign up for 90-minute morning excursions, which depart from the inn by van, as well as guided bike tours through the Wine Country.

A big part of the inn's allure is its mission-style architecture. The baronial reception hall, with its huge stone fireplace and cool tile floors, sets the mood of casual elegance. In the main building 100 of the inn's original rooms maintain a historic flavor. There are also 70 Wine Country–theme rooms and 30 luxury suites, many with fireplaces and terraces.

As expected in this part of the world, the dining is sublime: Even non-spa guests often make reservations to dine here. The fashionable Restaurant and more casual Big 3 Diner feel far removed from the rigors of calorie counting. Complementing the healthy but sophisticated cuisine is a wine list with more than 300 selections.

INSIDER TIP The large outdoor lap pool may be your healthiest swim yet. It's filled with mineral water pumped from the inn's own wells.

Equipment: Elliptical trainers, free weights, stair climbers, stationary bikes, treadmills. **Services:** Aromatherapy, body scrubs, body wraps, deep-tissue massage, reflexology, shiatsu. **Swimming:** 2 mineral water pools. **Classes and Programs:** Aerobics, aquaerobics, body sculpting, nutritional counseling, personal training, step, yoga. **Recreation:** Biking, golf, hiking.

170 rooms, 60 suites.

✕ Meals à la carte. Spa cuisine available at 2 restaurants as well as the spa snack bar. **Sample Meals:** Grilled vegetable quiche, rice lentil and sweet potato burger, ahi tuna salad (lunch); black pepper and coriander-crusted rack of lamb, horseradish-crusted grouper with French lentils, pancetta, and roasted red-pepper coulis (dinner).

Nightly rate $249–$449 per room. 2- to 4-day Spa or Golf Immersion packages $449–$1,149 per person. AE, DC, MC, V.

⊠ *Box 1447, Sonoma, CA 95476,* ☎ *707/938–9000 or 800/862–4945,* FAX *707/938–4250. www.sonomamissioninn.com*

TASSAJARA ZEN MOUNTAIN CENTER

NUTRITION AND DIET ∘ HOLISTIC HEALTH ∘ MINERAL SPRINGS

The craggy cliffs of Big Sur are a perfect setting for the Tassajara Zen Mountain Center, where resident monks lead daily sessions of meditation and teach basic Zen philosophy. The site has been a place of healing and purification for centuries. Native Americans bathed in the same hot springs that still attract people today.

Guests are invited to join student monks in their meditation schedule, which begins at 5:30 AM, when a bell awakens them for sitting in the Zendo, or Japanese-style hall that forms the center of the monastery. Watching the students, many with black robes and shaved heads, is an excellent way to learn meditation. Participation in all activities is optional, and the atmosphere is decidedly nonthreatening.

Among the retreat's most popular traditions is its gourmet vegetarian cuisine. Those who know Tassajara primarily through its cookbooks can experience cooking in a one-week workshop called "Zen in the Kitchen," led by Ed Brown, former head chef here and author of *The Tassajara Bread Book*, *The Tassajara Recipe Book*, and *Tomato Blessings and Radish Teachings*. In addition to preparing food, guests learn about the spiritual aspects of cooking.

The Zen ideal of simplicity is apparent in guest quarters. All cabins are equipped with kerosene lamps. The majority of rooms feature more traditional Western accommodations, but six Japanese Tatami cabins have shikibutons (foam mattresses) on tatami-mat floors with shoji screens or low-set windows. Most cabins are creek-side, while a few are along the gardens or the meditation hall.

INSIDER TIP Pick up any of Tassajara's cookbooks at your local bookstore for a taste of life at this Zen monastery.

Services: Mineral baths, sauna, plunge pools. **Swimming:** Pool, creek. **Classes and Programs:** Cooking classes, meditation instruction, spirituality classes, Zen workshops, yoga. **Recreation:** Hiking.

⌂ 36 cabins, 1 suite.

✕ Meals included. Vegetarian meals served family style. **Sample Meals:** Lentil loaf, steamed vegetables with tofu and brown rice (lunch); Japanese udon noodles, pasta primavera (dinner).

▦ Nightly rate $85–$150 per person, double occupancy. Dormitory $70–$84 per night. No credit cards.

⊠ *39171 Tassajara Rd., Carmel Valley, CA 93924,* ☎ *415/865–1899,* FAX *415/865–1892. www.sfzc.com*

SOUTHERN CALIFORNIA

THE ASHRAM

NUTRITION AND DIET ∘ HOLISTIC HEALTH

Barbra Streisand called the Ashram "a boot camp without food." Shirley MacLaine described it as "a spiritually involved health camp."

Most of the fairly affluent achievers who come here have high-pressure jobs, and by challenging themselves to a week of enormous physical exertion and minimal meals, they can experience what some speak of as a transcendent, positive change in attitude.

Guests are limited to 12 per week. Everyone follows the same routine of mountain hikes and yoga. A daily massage and meals are the only respite. Togetherness is emphasized in this intimate setting, and each person is required to participate in every activity.

Turning the concept of a retreat (the original meaning of the word ashram) into the ultimate challenge was the brainchild of Dr. Anne-Marie Bennstrom, now the Ashram's owner. A cross-country skiing champion in her native Sweden, Bennstrom tested her personal limits by spending five months alone in a Guatemalan jungle—an experience that inspired her to help others discover their own inner power. The Ashram has operated at this site since 1974, accepting men and women between the ages of 20 and 70.

Each day begins at 6:30 AM with yoga, stretching, and breathing exercises that help take the kinks out of sore muscles and build energy for a strenuous hike into the hills. Breakfast is a small dish of fresh fruit. The afternoon schedule usually includes an hour of lifting free weights, followed by an hour of exercise in the pool, and winds down with a game of water volleyball. Another yoga class ends the day. Instructors set the pace for the hike, so the distance varies daily, but some groups have walked more than 90 mi in a week. Each guest receives a one-hour massage each day, and you'll need it after all that hard work.

Spartan accommodations fit right in with the boot-camp theme. Guests double up in six bedrooms in a plain two-story stucco ranch house. Outside is a garden surrounded by towering eucalyptus trees, with a small swimming pool and whirlpool, a solarium for sunbathing, and a geodesic dome where guests participate in yoga and meditation sessions.

INSIDER TIP Meals here are minuscule, so bring a few energy bars if you're not ready for severe calorie cutting.

Equipment: Free weights. **Services:** Massage. **Swimming:** Pool. **Classes and Programs:** Meditation, health and spirituality lectures, nutritional counseling, yoga. **Recreation:** Hiking, water volleyball.

⊞ 6 rooms with shared baths.

✕ Meals included. 3 vegetarian meals daily. **Sample Meals:** Yogurt and cottage cheese with fruit slices (lunch); black-bean soup, baked potato, green salad (dinner).

▣ 1-week package $3,500 per person. MC, V.

✉ Box 8009, Calabasas, CA 91372, ☎ 818/222–6900, FAX 818/222–7393. www.theashram.com

CAL-A-VIE SPA & HEALTH RESORT

LUXURY PAMPERING ○ NUTRITION AND DIET

On a hillside with tea roses and flowers blooming almost everywhere, Cal-a-Vie Spa & Health Resort is simply lovely. And its serenity, spa treatments, exercise programs, and delicious spa cuisine rank it among the country's best destination spas.

Not surprisingly, Cal-a-Vie attracts a sophisticated clientele. And because the guest capacity is limited to 48, you'll get to know your fellow guests during your week's stay. You'll work out with your fellow guests, sharing a sense of achievement afterward as you munch on fresh fruit, grilled vegetables, spiced tomato juice, and other snacks. Meals feel more like family gatherings as the week progresses, creating a relaxed atmosphere that resembles the fun you had as a kid. But with simple yet elegant rooms furnished with country furniture and carved wood armoires, you'll know this is a far cry from summer camp.

A daily regimen of hikes, aerobics, and stretch and yoga classes forms the core of the program. But afternoon pampering counterbalances the effort expended during morning workouts. You'll have two plans to choose from for your stay, which determine the number of spa treatments you'll receive. The European plan includes multiple treatments daily, while the California plan includes only six treatments spread over a week. Don't worry about missing out, as additional treatments, including massages, body scrubs, wraps and facials, are offered à la carte.

Upon arrival you'll be given a computerized fitness evaluation to determine flexibility, cardiovascular capability, upper body strength, blood pressure, heart rate, and body fat percentage. Your personal diet and exercise regimens are designed to meet your personal needs.

Another important aspect of Cal-a-Vie's program is its emphasis on educating guests about healthier lifestyles. An evening lecture series addresses fitness, nutrition, stress management, and weight loss. But don't think rabbit food. These spa menus are so delicious that guests demanded the recipes. *Cal-a-Vie's Gourmet Spa Cookery* is on sale in the boutique or by mail order.

....

INSIDER TIP If you don't mind warm weather, you can save hundreds by planning a summer visit. Expect lots of sun, so bring a hat.

....

Equipment: Elliptical trainers, free weights, stationary bikes, treadmills, stair climbers, weight-training circuit. **Services:** Aromatherapy, hydrotherapy, reflexology, shiatsu, thalassotherapy. **Swimming:** Pool. **Classes and Programs:** Aerobics, aquaerobics, cooking demonstrations, Fitness lectures, personal training, stress management, weight training, nutrition lectures. **Recreation:** Tennis, volleyball.

🛏 24 rooms.

✗ Meals included. 1,200–1,400-calorie diet program optional. **Sample Meals:** Whole wheat pizza with roasted and grilled vegetables, sautéed tofu and lentils (lunch); sautéed free-range chicken with rosemary and roasted garlic, rice paper–wrapped salmon with ginger sauce (dinner).

💶 1-week all-inclusive European plan $5,150 per person. California plan $4,850. AE, MC, V.

✉ *2249 Somerset Rd., Vista, CA 92084,* ☎ *760/945–2055,* FAX *760/630–0074. www.cal-a-vie.com*

THE CHOPRA CENTER FOR WELL BEING

HOLISTIC HEALTH

Learning the precepts in Deepak Chopra's best-selling book *The Seven Laws of Spiritual Success* may be the best reason to enroll in a workshop at the Chopra Center. Inspired by the 5,000-year-old Hindu system of natural medicine known as ayurveda, Chopra founded the center in 1996. This India-born, Harvard-educated endocrinologist may not appear during your visit, but you will certainly feel his influence.

Beautifully situated in the seaside town of La Jolla, the center welcomes guests for one- to five-day programs oriented toward natural health, spirituality, and inner growth. Meals are included with each workshop, but lodging is arranged separately—either at a nearby hotel or in modestly priced rooms in private homes.

For the noninitiated, the program may feel almost too cosmic, despite a sincere openness to strangers on the part of the leaders. Beyond meditation, the focus is on education in ancient philosophies. After an introductory briefing, a staff of doctors examines you to determine which of three doshas, or mind-body types, you belong to: kapha (solid, stable, earthy), vatta (quick, changeable, airy), or pitta (intense, sharp, fiery). Based on a detailed questionnaire about your lifestyle, the staff also recommends certain foods and activities and sends you home with a prescription. Serious medical issues are treated with a combination of Western medicine and Eastern healing principles.

Bodywork is based on panchakarma, a physician-supervised cleansing program. Pizichilli is a purifying experience in which a continuous stream of warm herbalized oil is poured over the body as two therapists perform a gentle massage. Equally soothing is an herbal body wrap in which specially blended oils are applied to stress points. In shirodhara (a treatment for madness in India), warm herbalized oil drips over your forehead for a half hour, inducing a state of mental calm. Abhyanga massage entails five successive kneadings on every muscle from head to toe. Exercise consists mainly of group yoga, practiced in guided sessions.

Chopra and his full-time educators lead some workshops and seminars. The most basic of these is a three-day overview program that includes private counseling. The most advanced is a five-day ayurvedic purification program that includes medical consultations with health-care professionals, five panchakarma treatments, nutritional counseling, three gourmet organic vegetarian meals, daily group meditation, instruction in primordial sound meditation (mantras matched to your individual birth date, time, and place), and daily yoga sessions.

The center's two-story building includes treatment rooms, a yoga studio, and Quantum Soup, a sun-dappled vegetarian café open to the public. Upstairs is the hushed Meditation Room, padded with gold-brocade velvet pillows and richly colored drapes and cushions. Also upstairs is the Food Court, where diners are seated around a long mosaic table evocative of the court of King Arthur—a theme inspired by Chopra's novel, *The Return of Merlin*. The food is abundant, healthful, and truly delicious. The kitchen staff introduces each dish as it is served, explaining how each dish is meant to promote balance and harmony. Kept in easy reach are churnas (blends of spices used as condiments) and three types of mixed teas, designed to complement the three doshas: kapha (invigorating peppermint), vatta (spicy cinnamon), and pitta (mellow chamomile).

INSIDER TIP Pick up herbal tea, condiments, and even music to match your dosha at the center's lovely little shop.

Services: Ayurvedic body scrub or wrap, deep-tissue massage, pizichilli, reflexology, shirodhara, swedana, vishesh. **Classes and Programs:** Corporate-training courses, creating-health classes, mind-body medical consultation, natural-cooking class, natural skin care, prenatal course, primordial sound meditation, yoga.

⊡ No lodging at center, but hotels are available nearby.

✕ Meals included. Vegetarian food served at Quantum Soup café. **Sample Meals:** Ginger elixir, red-lentil dal, herbed couscous, ratatouille, steamed China peas, cucumber raita (yogurt salad), whole wheat bread twist, whole-grain pound cake (lunch); Italian white-bean soup, spinach polenta with roasted vegetable sauce, sautéed kale and Swiss chard with leeks, baked spaghetti squash, cocoa tofu mousse with almond praline (dinner).

▨ 1-day program $335–$565. 3-day program $1,700–$2,250. 5-day program $2,700–$3,300. À la carte treatments $55–$210. AE, MC, V.

⊠ *7630 Fay Ave., La Jolla, CA 92037,* ☎ *858/551–7788 or 888/424–6772,* FAX *858/551–7811. www.chopra.com*

GLEN IVY HOT SPRINGS SPA

MINERAL SPRINGS

Nestled in the foothills of the Santa Ana Mountains, Glen Ivy Hot Springs Spa has 15 mineral pools, mud baths, and spa services. Bathers spend the day relaxing poolside—dozing, reading, or meditating under the warm desert sun. There is no lodging available, but at less than $30 per day for admission, Glen Ivy is an affordable escape.

The waters here have been renowned for their healing powers ever since the Luiseno tribe first built mud saunas around the springs during the 14th century. The Native peoples used the Aztec word temescal, meaning "sweat house," to name the valley. Glen Ivy originally opened in 1890, but a flood in 1969 damaged the facilities. With renewed interest in natural therapies, the spa reopened, adding pools, sundecks, and landscaping.

Water temperatures vary between 90°F and 110°F at the two wells that supply a constant flow of mineral water to the pools. Don't stay in the hot water too long, particularly if you're in poor health or if the weather is very hot. A series of pools contains pure mineral water; the others are combinations of mineral water and fresh water that's refilled every day. The only organized activity is an aquaerobics class held in the large swimming pool, but it's not always offered in the winter and fall.

At "Club Mud," you moisten your skin with mineral water, then slather on soft red clay. After you coat your body and hair, relax on lounge chairs poolside and let the clay bake until it dries. It detoxifies and exfoliates the skin, and leaves it feeling smooth and refreshed.

Although there are shaded areas, you will definitely need sunscreen, and an old swimsuit and towel are recommended for the mud bath. Food and drink are available at the Spa Café.

INSIDER TIP Although the spa sells its own food, you might want to pack a picnic.

Services: Aromatherapy, body polish, moor mud wrap. **Swimming:** Pool. **Recreation:** Mineral baths.

⊡ Guests at Glen Ivy Springs stay at area hotels. Rates at the Historic Mission Inn (⊠ 3649 Mission Inn Ave., Riverside, CA 92501, ☎ 909/784–0300 or 800/843–7755) are $119–$600 per night. The Country Inn (⊠ 2260 Griffin Way, Corona, CA 92879, ☎ 909/734–2140) has rooms for $89 per night.

✕ Meals à la carte. Outdoor café serves soup, salad, sandwiches, and snacks for lunch only. **Sample Meals:** Chicken-breast sandwich, veggie burger, Caesar salad (lunch).

▢ Admission $24 weekdays, $29 weekends. AE, MC, V.

✉ *25000 Glen Ivy Rd., Corona, CA 92883,* ☎ *909/277–3529 or 800/ 454–8772,* FAX *909/277–1202. www.glenivy.com*

THE GOLDEN DOOR

LUXURY PAMPERING ◦ NUTRITION AND DIET

Imagine spending a week in the care of a full-time staff whose job is to customize a daily schedule of fitness and learning activities for you and then to ensure that you follow the schedule religiously. Welcome to the Golden Door, trendsetter and longtime favorite of serious spa goers since 1958. Secluded on 377 acres of hilly avocado country, "the Door" welcomes no more than 40 guests for a minimum four-day stay. A daily schedule arrives on your breakfast tray, so you can easily follow it, make your own changes, or take time out as you like.

Open year-round, the spa is open to men five weeks each year and to couples four weeks each year. The rest of the year this is the private domain of women.

Each day begins at 5:45 with stretches and a rigorous hike led by staff members who supply cups of cool water and a bit of fruit to sustain you until breakfast. A variety of activities—everything from fencing to Latin dance—easily fills up the rest of the day. The program can begin to feel like boot camp unless you remember that you don't need to go to every hike, lecture, or workout.

Would you prefer an easy, moderate, or challenging fitness schedule? You'll be queried about your preferences when you arrive. You will also receive a daily massage (which can be given in the hillside solarium or in your room) and a series of other treatments, including a manicure, pedicure, herbal wrap, and several facials. You can also order additional treatments and services, such as hot stone therapy.

The Door stresses the mind-body connection, so some activities have a spiritual bent. A concrete labyrinth is used as a metaphor for your journey through life. Meditation classes and lectures on stress reduction are also usually offered. Guests are encouraged to nightly record what they learn about themselves in journals they receive at the beginning of the week.

In terms of the facilities, the Door's lovely decor blends elements of a first-class resort with those of a Japanese country inn. Four exercise studios feature sliding glass walls that open to lush foliage. Guest rooms, linked by elevated wooden walkways, open onto shared garden courts, a koi pond, or a traditional sand sculpture. All rooms are single occupancy, and their subdued Asian design—sliding shoji screens, jalousie windows, and wood-block prints—promotes contemplation and serenity. Welcome creature comforts include sweats and T-shirts, yukata robes, hats, gloves, and raingear for use during your stay. There is also daily laundry service for your workout clothes and undergarments. But keep track of what you sent to the laundry, or you may not receive your undies back before the end of your stay.

The cuisine relies on fresh produce, much of it grown in the spa's organic gardens. On a designated evening each week you can join the chefs for a cooking demonstration in the kitchen. At the beginning of your stay a nutritionist will help you determine your daily caloric needs, and the dining room will serve portions according to those guidelines. Each day's menu presents lunch and dinner options, and you can request additional food. You may very well need to, because if you're working out for four to six hours a day, a drastically low calorie intake won't be enough.

Food allergies and dislikes are common, so do convey them during your stay. But keep in mind your meals won't likely be as enjoyable with substitutions. And with 40 meals being prepared simultaneously, you may encounter mistakes with special orders. Speak to the management if your needs aren't being met.

For a taste of the meals without a weeklong stay, you can always sample the *Golden Door Cookbook*. You can also bring home some of the spa's signature skin care products. These items are processed without artificial scents and dyes and with minimal preservatives.

INSIDER TIP To make the most of your stay, practice with the exercise tape Golden Door sends out in advance. And try getting up two hours earlier each day the week before arriving. You'll be ready for that 5 AM wake-up call.

Equipment: Free weights, rowing machines, stationary bikes, treadmills, weight-training circuit. **Services:** Aromatherapy, body scrub, deep-tissue massage, herbal wrap, hot stone therapy, shiatsu, Trager massage. **Swimming:** 2 pools. **Classes and Programs:** Circuit training, dance, fitness and stress evaluations, tai chi, yoga. **Recreation:** Hiking, tennis.

▦ 39 rooms, 1 villa.

✕ Meals included. Food is low in cholesterol, salt, sugar, and fat. **Sample Meals:** California rolls, grilled salmon with spinach and yogurt-dill sauce (lunch); garden greens, sprouts, and crudités with herbed balsamic vinaigrette, red bell pepper linguini with eggplant, marinara sauce, steamed baby vegetables, and Asiago cheese (dinner).

▱ $5,375 per person, per week. AE, MC, V.

✉ *777 Deer Springs Rd., San Marcos, California, CA 92069,* ☎ *760/ 744–5777 or 800/424–0777,* ℻ *760/471–2393. www.goldendoor.com*

LA COSTA RESORT & SPA

LUXURY PAMPERING ○ NUTRITION AND DIET

A huge resort designed for the fun-and-fitness crowd, La Costa Resort & Spa focuses both on recreation and pampering as well as structured wellness programs. The Racquet Club has 21 tennis courts and two championship golf courses spread over 450 acres in a valley that retains the sun's warmth all day while drawing a constant breeze off the ocean.

Unfortunately, the spa building hasn't been updated for about 30 years. You may surprised by the production-line look of rows of massage tables separated only by curtains. Fantastic service helps compensate for any flaws. Attendants are eager to help you with whatever you need.

Spanish Colonial influences prevail at La Costa. Lodgings are spread out in stucco buildings with pink-tile roofs. Some of the largest guest rooms are within the spa building itself. Other rooms overlook the golf course. There are four restaurants on the property that serve spa cuisine as well as gourmet fare. Especially enjoyable is lunch at the Poolside Terrace, where waterfalls and a pond filled with colorful koi fish provide a quintessentially Californian ambience.

Equipment: Cross-country ski machines, free weights, rowing machines, stair climbers, stationary bikes, treadmills. **Services:** Aromatherapy, exfoliating scrub, herbal wrap, loofah body scrub, reflexology, shiatsu. **Swimming:** 5 pools. **Classes and Programs:** Aerobics, aquaerobics, body-composition analysis, computerized diet analysis, fitness evaluation, nutrition counseling, personal training, step, stretch, workshops on topics ranging from restaurant dining strategies to meditation. **Recreation:** Biking, golf, tennis. **Children's Programs:** Camp La Costa for ages 5–12.

🛏 421 rooms, 77 suites.

✕ Meals à la carte. Seafood at Pisces, Mediterranean and Italian cuisine at Ristorante Figaro, California cuisine at Brasserie La Costa, casual fare at Center Court Restaurant. Spa cuisine available. **Sample Meals:** Hummus with whole wheat pita chips, grilled Santa Fe chicken with tangy lime sauce with herb fettuccine (lunch); beefsteak tomatoes and Bermuda onions with pineapple vinaigrette, grilled sea bass salad with melon salsa and orange-basil vinaigrette (dinner).

💳 Nightly rate $325–$500 per room. 4-night Total Wellness package $540 per couple per night, includes lodging, spa treatments, nutritional counseling. AE, D, DC, MC, V.

✉ *Costa del Mar Rd., Carlsbad, CA 92009,* ☎ *760/438–9111 or 800/854–5000,* FAX *760/931–7569. www.lacosta.com*

LA QUINTA RESORT & SPA

LUXURY PAMPERING

La Quinta Resort & Spa, in the rugged Santa Rosa Mountains, has long been a favorite hideaway for Hollywood icons. Legendary filmmaker Frank Capra, who was inspired to write the Oscar-winning romantic comedy *It Happened One Night* after a stay here in 1934, called it a wonderful green oasis in the middle of the desert. The same year, Greta Garbo had a rendezvous here with John Gilbert. In 1953 Ginger Rogers chose the oasis for her marriage to Jacques Bergerac.

Opened in 1926, La Quinta Resort & Club is the elder statesman of the resorts in the Palm Springs area. Set amid 45 acres of orange, lemon, and grapefruit trees, the resort is known for its stunning array of colorful gardens.

The resort's spa focuses on treatments based on the indigenous Mexican and Native American cultures. The Cahuilla sage wrap, for instance, begins with an application of a desert sage concentrate and ends with a warm herbal wrap. Many treatment rooms here have one or more fireplaces, private patios, and whirlpools. The fitness center, with an abundance of cardio machines, also offers a wide variety of classes, from body sculpting to low-impact aerobics.

La Quinta Resort offers golf at or near the resort. You can also enjoy 25 pools, 38 whirlpools, and 23 tennis courts, 10 lighted for night play.

Five restaurants offer nearly every dining experience. The Adobe Grill serves Mexican favorites in a setting that overlooks the resort's central plaza. Mediterranean cuisine is available at Montañas, and American fare is served at Morgan's and at the Tennis Clubhouse, which serves meals either poolside or courtside.

INSIDER TIP Spanish-style afternoon tea is served at the resort's elegant lounge, which features fireplaces and wide-beam ceilings.

Equipment: Free weights, stationary bikes, stair climbers, weight-training circuit. **Services:** Champagne facial, grape-seed scrub, hot stone massage, hydrotherapy, paraffin wrap, Swiss shower, thermal mud bath. **Swimming:** 25 pools and whirlpools. **Recreation:** Golf, tennis. **Classes and Programs:** Personal training, Pilates, yoga. **Children's Programs:** Camp La Quinta for ages 5–12.

▦ 613 rooms, 27 suites.

✕ Meals à la carte. Spa cuisine available at Morgan's. **Sample Meals:** Whole wheat pita wrap with spinach, Calamata olives, sun-dried tomatoes, and feta cheese with artichokes and hummus (lunch); capellini with tomatoes, spinach, carrots, mushrooms, and grilled asparagus, mango sorbet (dinner).

▨ Nightly rate $325 per room. 3-night Desert Renewal package $826 per person, includes lodging, spa treatments. AE, D, DC, MC, V.

✉ *49–499 Eisenhower Dr., Box 69, La Quinta, CA 92253,* ☎ *760/564–4111 or 800/598–3828,* ℻ *760/564–7656. www.laquintaresort.com*

MARRIOTT'S DESERT SPRINGS RESORT

LUXURY PAMPERING

Marriott's Desert Springs Resort, one of the company's grandest properties, is so large that a water taxi shuttles you to your room or to the restaurants. The lagoon actually comes into the lobby, with a small boat dock within the beautiful nine-story atrium. A series of landscaped waterfalls fills your ears with the sound of rushing water. It's no intimate getaway, but extravagance has its own rewards.

As you settle in, you'll discover five restaurants (several of which serve spa cuisine), five swimming pools, and 20 tennis courts. There are 884 rooms and suites, many with balconies boasting views of the Santa Rosa Mountains. Golfers can book their own private villas near the course.

At the spa, the biggest in the Palm Springs area, you can join any of five to seven daily scheduled classes—among them yoga, step aerobics, and body sculpting—in expansive studios flooded with light. Water is involved in many treatments and services, from hot and cold plunge pools and a Turkish bath to a vigorous aquaerobics class. Consider the European Kur Programme, a three-hour package of baths and massages, or the Ayurvedic Ritual, which includes an herbal wrap and an abhyanga massage performed by one or two therapists.

INSIDER TIP Learn your way around this massive resort by taking a tour in the charming water taxi soon after you arrive. Even then, consider carrying a map with you.

Equipment: Free weights, stair climbers, stationary bikes, treadmills, weight-training circuit. **Services:** Aromatherapy, body scrub, body wraps, reflexology, shiatsu. **Swimming:** Pool. **Classes and Programs:** Aerobic walk, aquaerobics, computerized fitness and body-composition analysis, nutritional counseling, step, strength and flexibility training, yoga. **Recreation:** Croquet, golf, miniature golf, hot-air ballooning, tennis, volleyball. **Children's Programs:** Kids Klub for ages 5–12; sitters available.

🛏 833 rooms, 51 suites.

✗ Meals à la carte. 5 restaurants; several serve spa cuisine. **Sample Meals:** Spinach salad, fruit smoothies (lunch); grilled Pacific tuna salad with artichoke hearts, Roma tomatoes, herbed feta, and vinaigrette, horseradish-crusted salmon with tarragon vinaigrette, potato croquette and sautéed vegetables (dinner).

🕿 Nightly rate $175–$495 per room. 1-night Spa Experience package $349–$609 per couple, includes lodging, lunch, spa treatments. Day spa package $150–$340. AE, D, DC, MC, V.

✉ *74855 Country Club Dr., Palm Desert, CA 92260,* ☏ *760/341–2211 or 800/331–3112,* FAX *760/341–1872. www.marriott.com*

MERV GRIFFIN'S RESORT HOTEL

LUXURY PAMPERING

Luxury seekers come to Merv Griffin's Resort Hotel to enjoy an atmosphere of exclusivity. The mood is formal and traditional, with more emphasis on luxury pampering than on fitness. Money is no object to most guests, who pay up to $160 per treatment.

One of the most striking features of this Givenchy-designed Versailles of the West is its manicured gardens resplendent with roses (although it does seem out of place among the palm trees). The gardens separate the spa complex from the dazzlingly white, contemporary French Renaissance–style buildings, appropriately named the Pavilion and the Trianon. Strolling the 14 lushly landscaped acres, you're bound to feel like Marie Antoinette or Louis XIV.

In keeping with the French philosophy that youth and wellness have more to do with beauty than fitness, the Givenchy Spa caters mainly to those who want to be primped and pampered. The beauty salon is under the direction of Gerald Alexandre, who loves to mingle with the stars. While you wait for a haircut or pedicure, check out one of his scrapbooks documenting his career with hundreds of celebrities, from singer Paul Anka to advice guru Dr. Ruth Westheimer. If you are interested in working out, there's a good chance you'll have the pristine gym all to yourself.

When it comes to dining, chef Gerard Vie obviously subscribes to the idea that food is meant to be enjoyed. Want caviar? Champagne? A chocolate soufflé? Chances are you'll find all three at Gigi's, the main restaurant, where men are required to wear collared shirts but jackets aren't necessary. You can also take your meal at the less formal Garden Terrace. During your day at the spa, however, you may prefer to dine, between treatments, at the charming Spa Café, which looks like something out of a French impressionist painting and serves guilt-free cuisine légère.

As in many elite European spas, the Givenchy Spa has separate facilities for men and women, including separate treatment rooms and even swimming pools. This traditional approach extends to the guest rooms, some of which have separate his-and-her bathrooms. Most rooms are in the Trianon, although there are also 12 private single-floor villas in the middle of the central gardens ideal for entertaining, with a butler pantry and a separate living room. High-rolling celebrities, politicians, and the occasional sheik opt to stay in the Grand Suite, which has four bedrooms, a living room with a grand piano, and a reception salon.

INSIDER TIP Be sure to ask about your accommodations when your book as some suites don't provide double beds.

Equipment: Cross-country ski machines, rowing machines, stair climbers, stationary bicycles, treadmills. **Services:** Aromatherapy, deep-tissue massage, herbal wrap, hydrotherapy, lymphatic massage, mud wrap, reflexology, seaweed wrap, shiatsu. **Swimming:** 2 pools. **Classes and Programs:** Aquaerobics, personal training, Pilates, tai chi, yoga. **Recreation:** Biking, golf, tennis.

⚏ 52 rooms, 40 suites, 12 villas.

✕ Meals à la carte. Meals served in Le Restaurant and in Garden Terrace, spa cuisine in the Spa Café. **Sample Meals:** Romaine salad in a tulip of Parmesan cheese, fresh berries and crème brûlée (lunch); crispy sea bass wrapped in threads of potato with saffron sauce (dinner).

⊠ Nightly rates $185–$350 per person, double occupancy. 2-night spa package $530 per couple, includes lodging, breakfast, spa treatments. AE, D, DC, MC, V.

⊠ *4200 E. Palm Canyon Dr., Palm Springs, CA 92264–5291,* ☎ *619/770–5000 or 800/276–5000,* FAX *619/324–6104. www.merv.com*

THE OAKS AT OJAI

NUTRITION AND DIET

Fitness and weight-control programs are the raison d'être at this no-frills spa. The clientele—working women, grandmothers, and a sprinkling of men—come to burn calories, condition the heart and lungs, and tone the body. With its daily program of 16 exercise classes and diet of fresh, natural foods totaling only 1,000 calories, this is the perfect place for shaping up and slimming down.

Sheila Cluff, a physical fitness instructor and former professional ice skater, along with her husband, Don, developed the fitness facilities in the 1970s. Since then they have expanded their focus with programs on such topics as spa cooking, stress management, and yoga.

Occupying an entire block in downtown Ojai, in a valley near Los Padres National Forest, the dignified wood-and-stone structure was built in the 1920s. The complex now includes coed saunas, an aerobics studio, a large swimming pool, and a cluster of guest bungalows, plus a main lodge with additional guest quarters. All rooms are simple but comfortable.

INSIDER TIP Don't be shy if you feel you're not getting enough calories. You can always ask for seconds.

Equipment: Free weights, stair climbers, stationary bikes, treadmills, weight-training circuit. **Services:** Aromatherapy, body wraps, hot stone therapy, reflexology, scalp massage. **Swimming:** Pool. **Classes and Programs:** Aerobics, aquaerobics, body-composition analysis, fitness counseling, step, strength training, stretching, tai chi, yoga. **Recreation:** Hiking, tennis.

⚏ 27 rooms, 19 cottages.

✕ Meals included. Food includes no salt, sugar, or white flour. **Sample Meals:** Tostada with Mexican bean salad, gazpacho (lunch); lemon-broiled salmon salad of baby greens (dinner).

🖃 Nightly rate $145–$189 per person, double occupancy. 5-day program $725–$945 per person, double occupancy. Day spa package $99. AE, D, MC, V.

✉ *122 E. Ojai Ave., Ojai, CA 93023,* ☎ *805/646–5573 or 800/753–6257,* FAX *805/640–2004. www.oaksspa.com*

OJAI VALLEY INN & SPA

LUXURY PAMPERING

The terra-cotta roofs, decorative ironwork, and flagstone terraces of the Ojai Valley Inn & Spa hint that this resort is different from most. You enter the complex through the traditional River of Life doors and cross the courtyard to the Fountain of the Sun, whose waters are meant to symbolically wash away the cares of life.

A bell tower rises 50 ft over the spa's mission-style courtyard, where guests mingle as the chefs prepare meals on the outdoor grill in warmer weather. Inside, the spa carries on the Spanish Colonial theme, with mosaics made of hand-painted tile. Each of the 28 treatment areas has stenciled walls painted in warm shades, and many have fireplaces. Thoughtful touches, such as citrus-infused drinking water and iced aromatherapy cloths to cool yourself in the steam room, make you feel even more pampered.

Local ingredients are used in the spa's treatments, such as the hydrating elderberry wrap. The Ojai Honey Scrub uses local orange essential oils, and an exfoliation treatment called "Petals" uses fragrant crushed rose petals and rose powder to soothe the skin. The spa's signature treatment is the kuyam, a Chumash Indian word meaning "a place to rest together." This traditional healing treatment begins with the application of clays and herbs. Herb-infused steam then fills the domed room, softening the clay and providing inhalation therapy. A walk-through shower helps cool you down. Afterward you'll be wrapped in a clean, plush robe and left to relax in the lounge, where you'll sip a refreshingly sweet mint tea.

An incredible variety of fitness classes is scheduled each week at the spa. You'll find everything from Irish dance aerobics to restorative yoga taught by experienced teachers in an airy, well-lighted studio. There are also seminars on everything from painting to journal writing.

More active guests will gravitate toward the George C. Thomas–designed 18-hole championship golf course, three heated swimming pools, and the first-rate fitness center. For those who prefer a less structured approach, the beautiful Ojai Valley is easily explored on foot, bike, or horseback. The inn's 220 acres of softly rolling hills include a ranch with stables where you can get outfitted for a trail ride. The staff offers guided hikes through Los Padres National Forest, and the concierge can arrange bird-watching tours at nearby Lake Casitas. But you can always borrow a bike—gratis—and explore on your own.

When it comes to accommodations, most of the inn's rooms are decorated in a contemporary California mission style. The original building, however, features 1920s-style rooms with four-poster beds, Morris chairs, pedestal sinks, and the original hardwood floors. The top floor of the spa also houses a 3,500-square-ft penthouse with two suites, each with two bedrooms. These private suites are decadently outfitted with carved chests, fringed ottomans, oversize sofas, and fireplaces. Four cottages, each with a fireplace and private terrace, face the golf greens.

INSIDER TIP Don't miss the organic garden that features a variety of herbs and edible flowers like calendulas and nasturtiums. Make a bouquet for your room, or ask the chef to incorporate your favorites into your dinner.

Equipment: Elliptical trainers, free weights, stair climbers, stationary bikes, treadmills, weight-training circuit. **Services:** Aromatherapy, craniosacral therapy, deep-tissue massage, ginger herbal wrap, green-tea treatment, herbal baths, hydrotherapy, reflexology, shiatsu. **Swimming:** 3 pools. **Classes and Programs:** Aerobics, aquaerobics, guided meditation, labyrinth walks, painting and drawing classes, personal training, qigong, Spinning, tai chi, yoga. **Recreation:** Biking, bird-watching, fishing, golf, hiking, horseback riding, kayaking, surfing, tennis. **Children's Programs:** Camp Ojai for ages 3–12.

🛏 191 rooms, 11 suites, 4 cottages.

✕ Meals à la carte. Two restaurants feature spa cuisine. **Sample Meals:** Tortilla soup with chicken, avocado salsa, ranchero cheese, and cilantro (lunch); pan-roasted venison loin with apple cider–forest mushroom sauce, warm caramelized bananas and toasted peanuts on citrus-caramel au jus (dinner).

💳 Nightly rate $245–$320 per room. Spa Discovery package $578–$680 per person, double occupancy. Day spa package $145–$525. AE, D, DC, MC, V.

✉ *905 Country Club Rd., Ojai, CA 93023,* ☎ *805/646–5511 or 800/ 422–6524,* 📠 *805/646–7969. www.ojairesort.com*

THE PALMS

NUTRITION AND DIET

This relatively small spa, sister property to the Oaks in Ojai, attracts mostly women, who come in search of a serious weight-loss and fitness-oriented program. Devoted fans of Sheila Cluff come for her workouts and one-on-one fitness training, as well as her trademark 1,000-calorie diets.

This "come as you are" spa offers plenty of options and has no attendance requirements. Goal-oriented guests can have programs tailored to suit their abilities, interests, and needs. Activity centers on a large swimming pool, set amid bungalows and well-landscaped grounds where organic herbs are grown for meals. Classes are held either there, indoors in a small aerobics studio, or outside under the palms. Massage rooms and a sauna and whirlpool are tucked into the complex.

INSIDER TIP Take some time to enjoy the attractions of the Palm Springs area, especially since many can be found within walking distance of the spa.

Equipment: Free weights, stair climbers, stationary bikes, treadmills, weight-training circuit. **Services:** Body scrubs, biofeedback, hypnotherapy, massage, reflexology. **Swimming:** Pool. **Classes and Programs:** Body-composition analysis, fitness consultations, health evaluations, makeup classes. **Recreation:** Biking, hiking, golf, horseback riding nearby.

🛏 29 rooms, 8 bungalows.

✕ Meals included. 3 meals daily, totaling 1,000 calories. No salt, sugar, or chemical additives. **Sample Meals:** Vegetable burgers, stir-fry vegetables, vegetable crepes (lunch); broiled red snapper in tomato sauce, vegetarian lasagna (dinner).

✉ Nightly rate $225–$238 per person, double occupancy. 5-night package $1,127 per person, double occupancy, includes lodging, meals, spa treatment. Day spa package $89, includes meals. AE, D, MC, V.

✉ 572 N. Indian Canyon Dr., Palm Springs, CA 92262, ☏ 760/325-1111 or 800/753-7256, FAX 760/327-0867. www.palmsspa.com

PRITIKIN LONGEVITY CENTER

LUXURY PAMPERING ○ MEDICAL WELLNESS ○ NUTRITION AND DIET ○ SPORTS CONDITIONING

The Pritikin Longevity Center has inspired wellness programs around the country since 1976. Based on the diet and exercise regimen created by the late Nathan Pritikin, the center is designed to help participants take charge of their health, prevent disease, and improve their quality of life. Programs, which vary from one to three weeks, are held at the newly renovated Loews Santa Monica Beach Hotel. With its picturesque view of the Pacific and the Santa Monica Pier, this beachfront hotel provides an idyllic setting for the medically supervised program.

Learning to love Pritikin's low-fat, low-calorie diet is not too difficult. Since these tasty meals are served buffet style, you won't feel like you're starving.

For all participants the daily schedule includes three supervised workouts, such as cardiovascular training on treadmills, as well as elective exercise classes such as aquaerobics and yoga. A typical day also features several educational workshops that focus on applying Pritikin principles to real life, whether eating at home, dining out, or shopping for groceries. Classes on low-fat cooking and other topics provide sound, practical strategies for healthy living. You also have access to the spa and salon on the premises.

The environment is supportive, positive, and encouraging. And graduates of the program receive a complimentary alumni newsletter to help reinforce what is learned. So if you're serious about making a long-lasting lifestyle change, this is one great place to get started.

INSIDER TIP To help you incorporate better eating habits into your daily routine, pick up a handy packet of Let's Dine Out cards, which give you tips on eating smart at your favorite restaurants.

Equipment: Cross trainers, free weights, stair climbers, stationary bikes, treadmills. **Services:** Aromatherapy, body polish, mud bath, salt glow, seaweed body masque. **Swimming:** Pool, beach. **Classes and Programs:** Aquaerobics, personal training, Pilates, yoga.

🛏 327 rooms, 13 suites.

✗ Meals included. Buffet-style meals are low fat, low calorie. **Sample Meals:** Vegetarian lasagna, steamed vegetables, vegetable soup (lunch); salmon and shiitake mushroom risotto, chicken primavera stir-fry (dinner).

✉ 6-night program $1,995 per person. MC, V.

✉ 1700 Ocean Ave., Santa Monica, CA 90401, ☏ 310/829-6229 or 800/421-9911, FAX 310/829-0259. www.pritikinca.com

SPA HOTEL & CASINO

MINERAL SPRINGS

The Spa Hotel & Casino rests on the site of hot mineral springs used by Native Americans for centuries. The Agua Caliente band of the Cahuilla tribe still owns the land, as well as the hotel and the adjoining casino.

More than 40 services are available at the spa, which opened in 1964 and is a now a Palm Springs landmark. On view are Native American–influenced murals, clay-tile flooring, and a display of artifacts and photographs emphasizing its unique cultural heritage.

The best way to get a sense of the Spa Hotel is to indulge in the Spa Experience, a five-step treatment similar to a Roman bathing ritual. First, you'll spend 10 minutes each in steam and a sauna, followed by a stint breathing in the eucalyptus-scented steam of the Inhalation Room. Next, you'll soak for about 20 minutes in a ceramic-tile whirlpool. Finally, you can nap in the Tranquillity Room or head for a massage or other pampering treatment.

INSIDER TIP Although the menu is not extensive, you can order a spa lunch any place on the property, even late in the afternoon.

Equipment: Free weights, stationary bikes, treadmill. **Services:** Aromatherapy, body scrub, herbal wrap, mud wrap, shiatsu. **Swimming:** Pool. **Recreation:** Cross-country skiing, golf, hiking, horseback riding, tennis.

🛏 230 rooms, 20 suites.

✕ Meals à la carte. **Sample Meals:** Salmon Niçoise salad (lunch); blackened ahi tuna with a trio of sauces, Caesar salad (dinner).

💷 Nightly rate $129–$249 per room. AE, DC, MC, V.

✉ *100 N. Indian Canyon Dr., Palm Springs, CA 92262,* ☎ *760/325-1461 or 800/854-1279,* 🖷 *760/325-3344. spahotelandcasino.com*

SPIRIT ROCK MEDITATION CENTER

HOLISTIC HEALTH

On more than 400 acres in rural western Marin County, Spirit Rock Meditation Center is a place where you can explore a variety of spiritual practices in a setting far removed from your everyday life.

Spirit Rock offers a series of classes, daylong workshops, and one- to three-week retreats funded almost entirely by donations. The purpose of the center is to help individuals find within themselves peace, compassion, and wisdom and to support the individual in taking those qualities into the world. It is nonsectarian, although the ethics and traditions of Buddhist psychology are included for guidance.

The typical day for those staying here for a week or longer begins at 5 AM and ends at 10 PM. The entire day is spent in silent meditation with alternating periods of sitting and walking meditation. One-day retreats are shorter, running from 9 AM to 5 PM. They are designed to provide an introduction to the practice of meditation. Other classes are offered on a donation basis to both the teacher and the center. No preregistration is necessary.

Eating meditation, an awareness of food and the process of nourishment, is part of the retreats. The food is vegetarian, and lunch is the main meal of the day. The lightest meal of the day is called tea and is served around 5:30 PM. Participants work in the kitchen in what is called "work meditation," which helps support the community and keep it running smoothly.

INSIDER TIP A play about the life of Buddha is the highlight of a Vesak Day celebration, held during the full moon in May.

Classes and Programs: Meditation. **Recreation:** Walks and hikes. **Children's Programs:** Weekday evening class for children 5 and up, teen program for ages 12–18. Child care provided for some adult retreats.

🛏 80 rooms.

✗ Meals included. Vegetarian meals served buffet style. **Sample Meals:** Basmati rice, vegetable curry, yellow split-pea dal, mango chutney, banana raita (lunch); carrot–yellow beet cream soup, green salad with basil vinaigrette, poached pears stuffed with hazelnuts and raisins (dinner).

💲 4- to 14-night residential retreats $200–$700. Classes $5. Day programs $30–$85. MC, V.

✉ *5000 Sir Francis Drake Blvd., Woodacre, CA 94973,* ☎ *415/488-0164,* FAX *415/488-0170. www.spiritrock.org*

SYCAMORE MINERAL SPRINGS

LUXURY PAMPERING ∘ MINERAL SPRINGS

Sycamore Mineral Springs, halfway between Los Angeles and San Francisco, has been operating this tranquil hillside resort since 1886, when two prospectors discovered mineral water instead of oil.

Accommodations are surrounded by huge oaks and sycamores, as well as an herb garden and a rose garden. Suites, including 16 new ones added in 2000, feature elegant mahogany fireplaces. But the real perk is that every room has its own private spa filled with mineral water.

The resort's Gardens of Avila restaurant is known as the most romantic restaurant on California's central coast, thanks to its lush garden. Chef Christian Raia serves California cuisine for three meals daily.

INSIDER TIP Even if you are staying elsewhere, you can still test out Sycamore Springs by renting a private outdoor redwood hot tub on an hourly basis.

Services: Facials, massage. **Swimming:** Pool.

🛏 26 rooms, 44 suites.

✗ Meals à la carte. The Gardens of Avila restaurant serves international fare. **Sample Meals:** Arugula and spinach salad with goat cheese, Portobello mushrooms, capers, smoked bacon, and caramelized apples (lunch); chicken or vegetable pot stickers sautéed in plum wine, coconut cream, and red curry, grilled Hawaiian swordfish with cilantro, grape seed, and pepper oil, served with shrimp (dinner).

💲 Nightly rate $135–$169 per room. Suites $239–$350 double occupancy. 1-night Rub, Tub, and Grub package $299–$349, includes lodging, breaks and dinner, and 2 spa treatments. AE, D, MC, V.

✉ *1215 Avila Beach Dr., San Luis Obispo, CA 93405,* ☎ *805/595–7302 or 800/234–5831,* ℻ *805/781–2598. www.sycamoresprings.com*

TWO BUNCH PALMS

LUXURY PAMPERING ○ MINERAL SPRINGS

The gates of Two Bunch Palms lead you to another world. This desert hideaway earned its moniker in 1907 when a U.S. Camel Corps survey team discovered two groves of palm trees towering over a hot springs. Almost a century later it's popular among Hollywood executives, writers, and stars who savor the area's stunning beauty.

Two Bunch Palms is best suited for those who prefer not to have a dawn-to-dusk schedule. You can take a tai chi class or play a game of tennis, but the main focus here is relaxation. You can meditate on green meadows surrounding two ponds of colorful koi, stroll along a creek, or soak in a warm, therapeutic pool fed by geothermal springs. The water—cooled a bit because it comes out at 148°F—splashes over a rock waterfall into a turquoise grotto framed by tropical shrubbery and a canopy of fan palms and tamarisk trees. (Moviegoers might recognize the beautiful pool from Robert Altman's satirical film *The Player.*) For a special treat you can try soaking in the water under the stars.

The dry heat of the desert induces a certain lethargy. To avoid the sun, guests indulge in Two Bunch's spa treatments. One innovation is the Esoteric Massage, "designed to balance and harmonize the physical, emotional, and spiritual bodies." Another specialty is watsu, in which you float in a hot mineral pool while enjoying a hand and foot massage. Another option is a mud bath in the shaded Clay Cabana, filled with warm clay from the property's own wells. Follow your mud treatment with sunbathing, a steam, and a soak in the mineral pool. A final massage with one of the experienced therapists may bring you closer to nirvana than you ever thought possible.

Throughout the grounds are spacious villas and motel-like rooms. Many guests request No. 14, a two-bedroom suite that goes for a whopping $495 a night. The big draws here are the bullet hole in the mirror and a desktop inscribed with the initials A.C., for none other than Al Capone, who was rumored to frequently hide out here. Each suite has a private patio, whirlpool, and kitchenette.

All guests dine on a healthy breakfast buffet in the Casino Restaurant, a former gaming room whose walls are dedicated to movie memorabilia. You may also have lunch and dinner here or order meals to go and dine privately. This is, after all, a bastion of privacy. If you're longing to socialize, look elsewhere. But if you crave solitude, this may be your slice of heaven.

....

INSIDER TIP Visit the lovely grapefruit orchard and pick one of the golden beauties. You'll be amazed by its intense sweetness.

....

Services: Aromatherapy, deep-tissue massage, herbal wrap, mud wrap, reflexology, salt glow, shiatsu, Trager massage. **Swimming:** Pool. **Recreation:** Biking, tennis.

▣ 19 villas, 9 rooms, 6 spa suites, 6 2-bedroom apartments.

✗ Breakfast included. No spa cuisine, but salads, grilled fish and chicken, and seasonal fresh fruit available. **Sample Meals:** Whole wheat enchilada with cheese and grilled vegetables, albacore tuna and sprouts on seven-grain bread (lunch); rosemary rack of lamb, grilled sword-fish (dinner).

✉ Nightly rate $175–$625 per room. AE, MC, V.

✉ *67425 Two Bunch Palms Trail, Desert Hot Springs, CA 92240,* ☎ *760/329–8791 or 800/472–4334,* FAX *760/329–1317. www.twobunch-palms.com*

VENTANA INN & SPA

LUXURY PAMPERING

Hidden within the redwoods on the Big Sur coast is a 243-acre retreat called Ventana. Named for the Spanish word for window, Ventana is a gateway to a world where remarkable natural beauty meets warm hospitality, delicious food, and Japanese-style baths.

A sumptuous wine-and-cheese spread greets you on check-in. An equally delicious breakfast is served every morning (and can be delivered to your room should you wish). In addition, you can enjoy fine dining at Cielo, where chef Jeffrey Regester serves fabulous meals in a hilltop restaurant just a 10-minute walk (or a short shuttle-bus ride) away. Innovative gourmet dishes rely on regional ingredients prepared with robust flavors.

When it comes to recreation, the staff will provide you with a list of day trips as well as guided hikes (order a picnic lunch the night before). Local draws include the Julia Pfeiffer Burns State Park, where a spectacular waterfall flows directly into the ocean. Another option is to explore the area's many interesting historical sites. Henry Miller came to live here in 1944 and his writings made Big Sur famous. His nearby namesake memorial library is full of books and other memorabilia.

From November to January you may even witness the annual southward migration of California gray whales. The playful whales swim very close to shore and can be seen spouting and breaching out of the water. The northward trip in March and April is harder to see since the whales travel farther from shore. If you miss them in person, you can always watch a documentary on whales in your room. All accommodations are equipped with VCRs. Most have fireplaces, and some include hot tubs.

When you're ready for pampering, the Allegria Spa offers a wide variety of services, including massages, wraps, and scrubs. Certain massage rooms also offer an ocean view, as does the small fitness center. Signature treatments include the Pine Forest Scrub, which features an application to the body and face of an essential pine-oil mixture combined with cornmeal, oatmeal, and clay. This 90-minute treatment includes a wrap, gentle scrub, shower, and full-body application of Essence of Big Sur massage oil. In the evening you can lounge by the lovely outdoor pool and Japanese baths, which are open until 2 AM. The plethora of stars makes this an ideal escape for two.

All this attracts a long list of celebrity guests. Over the years Robert Redford, Pierce Brosnan, Oprah Winfrey, and Goldie Hawn have spent the night here. And with the unique combination of rustic elegance, solitude, and incredible pampering, it's not hard to understand why.

INSIDER TIP The delicious homemade granola served at breakfast is for sale at the spa's gift shop.

Equipment: Free weights, rowing machines, stationary bicycles, treadmills. **Services:** Massage, salt scrubs. **Swimming:** 2 pools. **Classes and Programs:** Meditation, qigong, tai chi, yoga. **Recreation:** Horseback riding.

🛏 62 rooms.

✗ Breakfast included. Cielo restaurant serves California cuisine. **Sample Meals:** Steamed Castroville artichoke with buttermilk-herb sauce, thyme-roasted Portobello sandwich, grilled onions and potato steak on Francesca bread (lunch); black radish and anchovy salad with lemon vinaigrette, roasted swordfish medallions, oak-grilled beef tenderloin, almond-milk flan (dinner).

💳 Nightly rate $340–$975. AE, D, DC, MC, V.

✉ *Hwy. 1, Big Sur, CA 93920,* ☎ *831/667–2331 or 800/628–6500,* FAX *831/667–2419. www.ventanainn.com*

COLORADO

ASPEN CLUB

LUXURY PAMPERING ○ NUTRITION AND DIET ○
SPORTS CONDITIONING ○ MEDICAL WELLNESS

A holistic approach to health care is the philosophy of the Aspen Club. The club now consists of four facilities—a state-of-the-art fitness club, a full-service spa, a sports medicine center, and a center for well-being—all under one roof. The latter, counting chiropractors, acupuncturists, and sports psychologists among its staff, provides the cornerstone to owner Michael D. Fox's approach toward medicine. Here you can try sessions in biofeedback or sound therapy, get a metabolic test, or even take home a Chinese herbal medicine prescription or a personalized blend of aromatherapy oils.

A two-story workout facility, capped by a 50-ft skylight, forms the core of the club. The architecture communicates vitality and energy through a vibrant red, green, and gold color scheme and an abundance of natural light. You can challenge yourself with classes in Spinning, Pilates, or four kinds of yoga. The club can also arrange snowshoeing and hiking excursions right from the property. There's even an indoor simulated ski- and snowboard-training studio where an instructor helps first-timers learn the skills by using a harness on a treadmill ramp. Afterward, you can head outdoors to try the real thing. The club counts tennis legend Martina Navratilova among its members, and about half the U.S. Olympic ski team trains here. You can drop in to use the fitness facilities or get spa treatments, or you can meet with a staff member to design a workout plan.

At Spa Aspen traditional European treatments range from a detoxifying thermal mineral kur to therapeutic bath and massage. You can relax between treatments in a lounge overlooking a meditation garden, lulled by the sound of a waterfall. The Sports Medicine Institute treats injuries and provides preventive treatments like sports-specific training and orthotics design.

The Aspen Club does not have its own lodging; instead it works with hotels throughout the area to arrange accommodations. Breakfast and lunch are included in the rates at the Aspen Club. For dinner Aspen's many restaurants are within easy driving distance.

INSIDER TIP A day spa package here makes a good addition to an Aspen ski vacation.

Equipment: Free weights, rowing machines, stationary bikes, stair climbers, treadmills, weight-training circuit. **Services:** Alpine body wrap, aromatherapy, Feldenkrais, hydrotherapy, thermal mineral kur, thermal scrub. **Swimming:** Indoor pool. **Classes and Programs:** Blood-profile analysis, body-composition analysis, fitness and nutrition seminars, kickboxing, maximal stress test, nutritional and food-allergy evaluation, personal training, Pilates, postinjury therapy, Spinning, strength and flexibility testing, yoga. **Recreation:** Basketball, cycling, fencing, hiking, racquetball, skiing, squash, tennis, volleyball. **Children's Programs:** Camp Aspen Club for ages 6–12.

🖿 No accommodations. Lodging can be arranged at nearby hotels.

✗ Meals à la carte. Low-fat breakfast and lunch included in spa packages and served in dining room. **Sample Meals:** Tofu scramble, organic maple granola (breakfast); Thai soba-noodle salad, chicken pesto wrap (lunch).

▥ 1-day Spa Aspen Trio package $155, includes 2 two meals, massage, manicure, facial. 1-day Absolute Rapture package $355, includes 2 meals, massage, body scrub, manicure and pedicure, hairstyling, facial. AE, D, MC, V.

✉ *1450 Crystal Lake Rd., Aspen, CO 81611,* ☎ *970/925–8900 or 800/554–2773,* ℻ *970/925–9543. www.aspenclub.com*

THE BROADMOOR

LUXURY PAMPERING

Visiting the Broadmoor, a mountain retreat on 3,000 well-groomed acres, is like taking a step back to the golden era when Colorado Springs attracted health seekers from around the world. With the addition of a two-level lakefront spa and fitness complex, the Broadmoor is now considered one of the top health resorts in the Rocky Mountains.

A major draw is the dramatic mountain setting. Within a few miles are the red-rock canyons of the Garden of the Gods and the mineral waters of Manitou Springs. You can ride the original cog railway on Pikes Peak, float above the clouds in a hot-air balloon, or ride horseback into the foothills.

You might never leave the resort, choosing instead to spend all your time enjoying the spa, which overlooks 12 tennis courts and three championship golf courses. There is an aerobics studio for scheduled classes in yoga and tai chi, a complete weight room, and cardiovascular equipment. Families can splash in the huge indoor swimming pool under a soaring skylighted ceiling, while adults have a two-lane outdoor lap pool to themselves. Alongside the pool is a juice bar, with tables on a sunny terrace overlooking the golf course's first tee.

A visit to the spa is a pure Colorado experience, infused with scents of spruce and cedar, decorated with columbine (the state flower), and invigorated by mountain air. The spa offers an exclusive line of body treatments using native Colorado ingredients. The Broadmoor Falls Water Massage is a surprisingly invigorating experience: In a shower with heated granite walls, your scalp and body are massaged by 17 hot and cold jets of pure mountain water. Seven kinds of therapeutic baths are used to soothe sore muscles, smooth the skin, and encourage circulation. The spa lounge is an ideal place for relaxation—it's warmed by a log fire so you can sip tea or lemonade while contemplating the changing sunlight on the mountains.

Equipment: Free weights, rowing machines, stationary bikes, stair climbers, weight-training circuit. **Services:** Aromatherapy, herbal wrap, hydrotherapy milk-whey bath, mud bath, salt glow, shiatsu. **Swimming:** 3 outdoor pools, 1 indoor pool. **Recreation:** Biking, golf, horseback riding, hot-air ballooning, ice-skating, paddleboats, shuffleboard, skeet and trapshooting. **Children's Programs:** Bee Bunch for ages 3–12.

☷ 591 rooms, 109 suites.

✗ Meals à la carte. Ten restaurants serve varied cuisine. Cuisine Vivant items on all menus are lower in fat. **Sample Meals:** Grilled swordfish steak with Mediterranean sauce, sautéed Colorado red trout fillet (lunch); broiled red snapper and halibut, vegetable ravioli with shiitake mushrooms (dinner).

☕ Nightly rate $294–$455 per room. 1-night Spa Splurge package $222 per person, double occupancy, includes lodging, spa treatments. 3-night Spa Spectacular package $1,002 per person, double occupancy, includes lodging, spa treatments. AE, D, MC, V.

✉ *Box 1439, Colorado Springs, CO 80901,* ☏ *719/634–7711 or 800/634–7711, ext. 5770,* FAX *719/577–5700. www.broadmoor.com*

GLENWOOD HOT SPRINGS LODGE & POOL

MINERAL SPRINGS

Join the crowd soaking in the steaming waters of the Rockies' largest natural thermal-springs pool. Open year-round, even in subfreezing temperatures, the mineral water flows constantly at 122°F. Dashing into the pool past trees covered with icicles is a bracing experience.

In summer, though, the hot springs really come alive. A 405-ft swimming pool that's usually filled with families is cooled for comfortable swimming, while a smaller therapy pool is equipped with underwater jets for massage. Both are ozone-filtered, cutting down considerably on the chlorine level. Together, the pools contain 1.1 million gallons of mineral water (it's changed four times daily).

If you opt to stay at the geothermally heated lodge, you'll have direct access to the outdoor pools and the fitness facility, including saunas and whirlpools. There are fitness classes in aerobics, aquaerobics, and Jazzercise. You'll also get to use the racquetball, handball, and walleyball courts.

Equipment: Stationary bikes, stair climbers, weight-training circuit. **Services:** Massage, reflexology. **Swimming:** 2 pools. **Recreation:** Fishing, handball, hiking, miniature golf, racquetball, water slides.

☷ 107 rooms.

✗ Meals à la carte. Meals served at deli.

☕ Nightly rate $68–$115 per room. Daily pool admission for nonguests $9. AE, DC, MC, V.

✉ *Box 308, 415 E. 6th St., Glenwood Springs, CO 81602,* ☎ *970/945–6571,* FAX *970/947–2950. www.hotspringspool.com*

GLOBAL FITNESS ADVENTURES

NUTRITION AND DIET ∘ SPORTS CONDITIONING ∘ HOLISTIC HEALTH

Holistic health authority Rob Krakovitz and former fashion model Kristina Hurrell designed a program that promotes health and fitness by arranging hiking trips in some of the world's most beautiful settings. Though based in Aspen, the husband-and-wife team has put together a traveling spa, with weeklong programs in eight locations around the world, from domestic destinations such as Arizona and California to tropical islands like Kaua'i and Dominica to international destinations such as Kenya. You can hike with Africa's Masai tribes, attend Balinese temple ceremonies, or paddle across Lake Como.

The program is limited to 12 participants. Hikes of 5–16 mi geared to individual fitness levels fill most mornings. Afterward, guests can challenge themselves with sports such as horseback riding, scuba diving, and kayaking. Days begin with yoga and meditation—in Sedona, Arizona, these activities take place on a rock outcropping with incredible views—and end with dinners by candlelight. Cultural outings, cooking classes, and other experiences are often available.

Each retreat is structured around the same basic program but draws its inspiration from the beauty of its locale. Accommodations, always upscale, range from country inns to villas to jungle lodges. A Colorado trip houses guests in a lodge at the base of a mountain, one block from the town of Aspen. In Sedona the lodgings, in southwestern-style houses in Oak Creek Canyon, have fireplaces and wooden decks.

The combination of healthy eating and extensive daily exercise forms a basis for weight loss. Spa-cuisine meals are mostly vegetarian, with some organic chicken or freshly caught fish as part of the fare. By adhering to a course of exercise and attending classes on topics ranging from improving communication skills to enhancing mental, emotional, and physical energies, you'll soon be on the road to peak vitality.

....

INSIDER TIP The trips offered by Global Fitness Adventures are great for those who are traveling alone.

....

Services: Massage, natural-healing bodywork. **Classes and Programs:** Medical consultations, meditation training, health and nutrition workshops. **Recreation:** Canoeing, horseback riding, fishing, rafting.

🛏 Accommodations vary by locale, from mountain cabins to country inns to jungle lodges.

✗ Meals included. 3 mostly organic meals served daily family style. **Sample Meals:** Salad with tofu, lemon-garlic tempeh, sprout sandwich (lunch); steamed squash, steamed brown rice with vegetables, grilled trout (dinner).

💲 Rates and packages vary for each program. For Aspen, 1-week trips $2,696 per person, double occupancy, includes lodging, meals, spa treatments, cultural activities. No credit cards.

✉ *Headquarters: Box 330, Snowmass, CO 81654,* ☎ *970/927–9593 or 800/488–8747,* FAX *970/927–4793. www.globalfitnessadventure.com*

GOLD LAKE MOUNTAIN RESORT & SPA

LUXURY PAMPERING ∘ SPORTS CONDITIONING

In the mountains west of Boulder, this turn-of-the-last-century fishing resort is now an unusual small spa. Inspired by the environmentally conscious Post Ranch Inn in Big Sur, California, owners Alice and Karel Starek set out to create a high-end resort high in the mountains where art and natural beauty would blend harmoniously. What they created is an eclectic blend of rusticity and luxury.

Gold Lake itself is the focal point for most of the resort's activities: hiking its perimeter, paddling around it in a canoe or kayak, ice-skating in winter, or simply luxuriating in one of four hot pools built into the rocks above the lake. There are purposely no indoor fitness facilities or classes here—the intent is for guests to be outdoors, soaking in the splendor of the Rockies. You may want to do nothing more than sit in a hot pool and listen to the wind whistle through the evergreens.

The indoor environment is, however, carefully crafted. Guests stay in log cabins with exquisite slate-and-copper bathrooms and log beds with raw silk and hemp duvets. Alice's Restaurant is a rough-hewn beauty, with unpeeled birch-log furniture and a copper fireplace. And it's all the more enjoyable thanks to the Mountain Spa Cuisine menu developed by chef Eric Skokan. He uses organically grown vegetables and grains to create richness and texture but also incorporates wild game and fresh fish. About half the menu is vegetarian.

Spa treatments such as radiance technique and polarity therapy are designed to work on a spiritual as well as a physical level. The dual massage, however, is just plain decadent: Two masseurs or masseuses work in tandem, synchronizing their strokes. Imagine having your scalp and feet massaged at the same time.

INSIDER TIP If you're bringing the family, one of the cabins has two suites that can be combined into a single four-bedroom unit.

Services: Aromatherapy, clay body treatments, massage, salt glow, thalassotherapy. **Recreation:** Biking, canoeing, fly-fishing, horseback riding, ice-skating, kayaking.

▦ 17 1- or 2-bedroom log cabins; 1 3-bedroom house.

✕ Breakfast included. Lunch at Karel's Bad Tavern, dinner at Alice's Restaurant. **Sample Meals:** Grilled trout salad with blackberries and sweet potatoes, chickpea and vegetable biryani with cayenne raita (lunch); duck confit and amaranth pudding, pan-roasted pheasant with roasted friar plums, persimmon cake with black-walnut ice cream and maple juice (dinner).

✉ Nightly rate $195–$345 per room. Day spa package $113–$253, includes lunch, spa treatments. AE, DC, MC, V.

✉ 3371 Gold Lake Rd., Ward, CO 80481, ☎ 303/459–3544 or 800/450–3544, ℻ 303/459–9080. www.goldlake.com

HYATT REGENCY BEAVER CREEK RESORT & SPA

LUXURY PAMPERING ∘ SPORTS CONDITIONING

The Allegria Spa at the Hyatt Regency Beaver Creek was designed using the Chinese concept of feng shui, and you feel the influence of the Eastern philosophy of environmental harmony as soon as you walk past the reception desk. Passing between cascading waterfalls—aged copper fountains set in sandstone troughs—you enter the inviting lounge and tea bar. A Colorado buff-sandstone floor, richly textured fabrics in a natural palette of lavender, spruce, and wheat, and indirect lighting all create an environment that is soothing and sophisticated.

The feng shui influence extends to the spa's signature treatments, dubbed Balance, Peace, and Energy. In the Balance treatment two therapists—one male and one female, to balance the body's yin and yang energies—perform a synchronized massage with an oil of spikenard, ylang ylang, and cypress, said to bring harmony and balance to the body. Other innovative treatments include the wild-mountain-berry scrub, which uses fresh raspberries, sea salt, and honey, and the Japanese-mint hot-oil wrap.

For relaxing before or after a treatment, the sanctuary room features chaise lounges, a fireplace, and a trompe l'oeil dome ceiling. To renew the spirit, classes are taught in watercolor and pottery painting. For more athletic pursuits, Spinning and Pilates are taught in a studio overlooking the mountain. The state-of-the-art health club also has an indoor/outdoor lap pool.

The ski-in, ski-out resort sits at the base of Beaver Creek Mountain. The ultimate in ski convenience is having your boots warmed and skis waiting when you step out the door. The hotel's grand main lobby has a magnificent chandelier made of antlers, wall-size fireplaces, and floor-to-ceiling windows overlooking the ski slopes. The Hyatt has its own on-staff storyteller/historian, who weaves tales about the area around the outdoor fire pit.

Beaver Creek became a year-round destination in 1998, with the addition of an outdoor ice-skating rink and, directly beneath it, the Vilar Center for the Arts, a 530-seat theater showcasing top musical, dance, and comedy performances. Patina, the hotel's fine-dining restaurant, features Pacific Rim/southwestern fare, along with a spa menu. Rooms are done in French provincial style, with knotty pine furniture and heated towel racks.

INSIDER TIP Guided snowshoe tours in the winter are a great way to enjoy the spectacular scenery.

Equipment: Free weights, stationary bikes, stair climbers, treadmills, weight-training circuit. **Services:** Aromatherapy, body scrub, hydrotherapy, Japanese-mint body wrap, reflexology, salt glow, shiatsu, spirulina body wrap. **Swimming:** Pool. **Classes and Programs:** Aerobics, kickboxing, personal training, Pilates, Spinning, tai chi, yoga. **Recreation:** Golf, hiking, ice-skating, tennis, skiing, snowshoeing. **Children's Programs:** Camp Hyatt for ages 3–12.

🛏 271 rooms, 5 suites.

✕ Meals à la carte. Patina features Pacific Rim/southwestern fusion. Spa menu available. **Sample Meals:** Grilled vegetable wrap, seared ahi tuna over hothouse greens (lunch); grilled fish bouillabaisse over jasmine rice in a light saffron shellfish broth (dinner).

💳 Nightly rate $85–$850 per room. 4-night spa package $2,366 per couple, includes lodging, some meals, 3 spa treatments, fitness classes. AE, D, DC, MC, V.

✉ *Box 1595, Avon, CO 81620,* ☎ *970/949–1234 or 800/554–9288,* FAX *970/949–4164. www.allegriaspa.com*

INDIAN SPRINGS RESORT

MINERAL SPRINGS

The hot springs at Indian Springs Resort were first developed for prospectors during the local gold rush, and devotees of taking the waters have traveled from around the world to bathe in them ever since. Three springs with temperatures ranging from 104°F to 125°F provide the therapeutic waters. Although no scientific claims have been made for the healing powers of the waters, experts cite the benefits of bathing for those who suffer from arthritis and rheumatism.

The main pool, filled with 90°F mineral water, is surrounded by tropical foliage beneath an arched glass roof. Below are separate men's and women's caves, with soaking pools cut out of the rocks. Bathing suits are taboo in the caves. For those who are sheepish about public nudity, private tubs can be booked by the hour—a popular alternative for couples and families.

Though the historic resort is definitely beginning to show its age, it's still a bargain getaway. Both day visitors and overnight guests are welcome. The latter stay in an atmospheric, if slightly worn, Victorian hotel, built in 1905. Rooms in the original building have half baths and a few modern conveniences; those in the newer adjoining inn have more amenities.

INSIDER TIP Unlike most hot springs, the waters here do not smell of sulfur.

Services: Massage, salt glow. **Swimming:** Pool. **Recreation:** Fishing, hiking, horseback riding.

⌘ 68 rooms.

✕ Meals à la carte.

🖃 Nightly rate $50–$85 per night. Campsite $18. Admission to pool $18. MC, V.

⊠ *Box 1990, Idaho Springs, CO 80452,* ☎ *303/989–6666,* ꜰᴀx *303/567–9304. www.indianspringsresort.com*

THE LODGE & SPA AT CORDILLERA

LUXURY PAMPERING ∘ SPORTS CONDITIONING

Imagine spending the morning fly-fishing on a private 3-mi stretch of the Eagle River, then indulging in the afternoon with a facial. Finish by dining on sophisticated cuisine prepared by a renowned chef and then retiring to your own private estate, where a butler has turned down your bed and fluffed your pillow.

Set on 2,500 acres of its own mountaintop between the resort towns of Vail and Beaver Creek, the Lodge & Spa at Cordillera is secluded and intimate. With stone-and-stucco walls and deeply sloping roofs of Chinese slate, it was built to resemble a manor house in the Pyrenees. Most of its 56 spacious rooms have fireplaces and glass doors opening onto terraces with sweeping views of the mountains. Private luxury estates in the Cordillera residential community can also be rented, complete with a personal butler who will serve cocktails, schedule tee times, and perform just about any task to make your vacation more enjoyable.

With Hale Irwin's 18-hole Mountain Course and Tom Fazio's Valley Course—and a Jack Nicklaus course scheduled for completion in 2001—Cordillera is one of the country's top golf destinations. You can take advantage of 12 mi of privately maintained trails for hiking, biking, or cross-country skiing, as well as tennis courts. The glass-wall fitness center, adjacent to an indoor lap pool and an aerobics studio, has the latest equipment.

After a day on the slopes or in the spa, you'll be ready for an epicurean performance in the Picasso restaurant, named for its original Picasso lithographs. Chef Fabrice Beaudoin uses vegetable and fruit reductions and herbs from the Cordillera kitchen garden in place of butter and cream to create a lighter style of French cuisine. Afterward, retire to the lobby to sink into a plush sofa in front of a carved limestone fireplace. This is getting away in style.

INSIDER TIP You can rent a luxurious private home to really indulge in the lifestyle of the rich and famous.

Equipment: Rowing machine, stationary bikes, stair climbers, treadmills, weight-training circuit. **Services:** Algae body wrap, aromatherapy, body polish, hydrotherapy. **Swimming:** 1 indoor pool, 1 outdoor pool. **Classes and Programs:** Aerobics, endurance testing, fitness assessment, personal training, Pilates. **Recreation:** Badminton, biking, croquet, dogsled rides, fishing, golf, hiking, ice-skating, skiing, snowmobiling, tennis.

⊞ 48 rooms, 3 suites, 5 lofts. Home rentals available.

✕ Breakfast included. Four restaurants serve varied cuisines. Low-fat menu available. **Sample Meals:** Chicken breast marinated in sherry vinaigrette, salmon fillet wrapped in grape leaves (lunch); veal loin Provençale, fish of the day steamed with vegetables julienne (dinner).

▨ Nightly rate $150–$595 per room. Spa packages vary seasonally. AE, D, DC, MC, V.

✉ *Box 1110, Edwards, CO 81632*, ☎ *970/926–2200 or 800/877–3529*, FAX *970/926–2486. www.cordillera-vail.com*

THE PEAKS RESORT & SPA

LUXURY PAMPERING ∘ NUTRITION AND DIET ∘ SPORTS CONDITIONING

Set amid the ski slopes in southwestern Colorado, the Peaks Resort & Spa is surrounded by majestic views of the 14,000-ft peaks of the San Juan Mountains. Outdoor enthusiasts can go hiking, horseback riding, mountain biking, and rock climbing. A gondola lift links the resort to the historic silver-mining town of Telluride, so guests can take advantage of the many activities in town.

The program at the Golden Door Spa offers the region's widest range of massages and skin-care regimens. Many of the treatments are based on southwestern traditions and Native American lore. Try a soak in a kiva whirlpool—a treatment inspired by a cleansing ritual that's part Native American sweat lodge, part Scandinavian sauna and steam— or an alpine aromatherapy massage with custom-blended oils of geranium, sage, tangerine, sandalwood, cardamom, and frankincense.

The resort's fitness program incorporates advanced concepts. One of the most unusual is "Cardio Coaching," where sensors on your body help a physiologist give you guidance on how to maximize your exercise. Another program prepares you for activity at high altitudes, since the resort is at about 10,000 ft.

Family-friendly activities are a specialty at the Peaks. Entertaining and educational programs combine with exercise and healthy meals at the resort's KidSpa, a day camp that allows parents to pursue activities without worrying about childcare. Depending on the weather, kids go on guided hikes, take swimming lessons, practice yoga, or pan for gold in nearby streams. The two-story water slide is a big hit with kids and adults alike. For budding athletes, junior ski and snowboarding lessons are available.

Next Level Spa, available in summer, is designed for vacationers looking for a "peak" experience. Guests can choose from one of five themed programs: Change, Rejuvenation, Tranquillity, Adventure, or Vigor. All include spa treatments, seminars on a variety of topics, cooking demonstrations, and outdoor options such as mountain biking, white-water rafting, fly-fishing, horseback riding, rock climbing, golf, and tennis. Next Level Spa guests have separate accommodations in 13 deluxe guest rooms with extra amenities such as a foot massagers.

Skiers and golfers will be in business here. The Peaks' location provides ski-in, ski-out access to the Telluride ski area for enthusiasts of every experience level. In summer you can take advantage of North America's highest 18-hole championship golf course.

INSIDER TIP Golfers should try "Yoga for Golf," said to help control the mind while stretching the muscles used in your swing.

Equipment: Cross-country ski machine, free weights, rowing machines, stationary bikes, stair climbers, treadmills, vertical ladder climbers, weight-training circuit. **Services:** Aromatherapy, fango wrap, hydrotherapy bath, shiatsu, shirodhara. **Swimming:** 2 pools. **Classes and Programs:** Fitness evaluation, nutrition consultation, personal training, Pilates, stress management, yoga. **Recreation:** Badminton, biking, fishing, golf, Ping-Pong, racquetball, skiing, squash, tennis. **Children's Programs:** KidSpa for kids up to 11.

⌕ 138 rooms, 36 suites.

✕ Meals à la carte. Spa cuisine available. **Sample Meals:** Bow-tie pasta with scallops in tomato-saffron broth; pizza with tomatoes, fresh mozzarella, and basil (lunch); lobster stew, grilled sea bass with chickpea-mashed potatoes (dinner).

▱ Nightly rate $150–$645 per room. 4-night Next Level spa package $2,200–$2,720, includes lodging, meals, and spa services. AE, DC, MC, V.

✉ *136 A Top Country Club Dr., Box 2702, Telluride, CO 81435,* ☎ *970/728–6800 or 800/789–2220,* ℻ *970/728–6567. www. thepeaksresort.com*

SONNENALP RESORT

LUXURY PAMPERING

In the faux-alpine village of Vail, the Sonnenalp stands out as the real thing, run with gemütlichkeit (warmth) by the Bavarian Fassler family, fourth-generation hoteliers. The sprawling resort is as luxurious and service-oriented as any four-star resort in the Alps. The staff, who dress in dirndls and lederhosen, will even ship your skis to and from your home for you or lend you a cellular phone to take with you to the mountains.

An open fireplace is the centerpiece of the sunny spa, where picture windows frame views of nearby Gore Creek. The glassed-in fitness room has a few carefully chosen pieces of equipment, and the indoor-outdoor pool is fed by a waterfall. Treatments use body-firming seaweed, salt scrubs, and moor mud. The smaller Swiss Hotel & Spa, available to Sonnenalp guests, offers facials, manicures, and pedicures as well as body treatments.

Do not plan on dieting here: Each day begins with a full European breakfast of muesli, pastries, cold cuts, fruit, and a hot entrée of eggs or pancakes, topped off by an oversize china cup of the richest hot chocolate in the Vail Valley. Ludwig's, the most elegant of the resort's three restaurants, serves sophisticated Bavarian fare. The Swiss Chalet serves calorie-laden fondue and raclette, and at Bully Ranch you can partake of ribs.

Rooms in the all-suite resort feature gas fireplaces and dark wood beams. The mammoth bathrooms have heated marble floors.

INSIDER TIP In April you can enjoy the singular experience of skiing and golfing in the same day.

Equipment: Free weights, rowing machines, stair climbers, stationary bikes, treadmills. **Services:** Hydrotherapy, massage. **Swimming:** Pool. **Recreation:** Golf, tennis, skiing.

🛏 90 rooms.

✕ Breakfast included. Three restaurants serve Bavarian and international fare. **Sample Meals:** Cheese fondue (lunch); grilled antelope chop with braised red cabbage, glazed chestnuts, gnocchi (dinner).

💳 Nightly rate $340–$950 per room. AE, DC, MC, V.

✉ *Sonnenalp Resort, 20 Vail Rd., Vail, CO 81657,* ☎ *970/476–5656 or 800/654–8312,* FAX *970/476–1639. www.sonnenalp.com*

VAIL ATHLETIC CLUB

LUXURY PAMPERING ○ SPORTS CONDITIONING

Vail is Valhalla for skiers in winter, and for golfers, hikers, and mountain bikers in summer. In the midst of the bustling village, the Vail Athletic Club Hotel and Spa is an ideal home base for a sports-centered getaway.

The fitness center and spa have a sleek, modern look, with gray-slate tiles and polished chrome fixtures. A 20-meter indoor lap pool and outdoor hot tub overlook Gore Creek and Vail Mountain. The most dramatic feature of the club is the two-story rock-climbing wall, where lessons are offered for the uninitiated. Equally impressive is the list of classes, including Pilates, Spinning, and several forms of yoga. Ballroom dancing and fencing round out the options.

Spa treatments with Dr. Hauschka's botanical oils and lotions from Germany use aromatherapy to balance and harmonize the senses. The signature Nature, Body, and Spirit treatment incorporates sage, rosemary, lavender, rose, and lemon oil on different parts of the body to alternately stimulate, calm, and refresh.

Terra Bistro, which relies on organic produce whenever possible, caters to meat-and-potatoes eaters as well as vegetarians. Hotel rooms are basic but include such amenities as ski-boot warmers, refrigerators, coffeemakers, and private balconies.

INSIDER TIP Terra Bistro claims to offer the most affordably priced bubblies of any restaurant in the United States.

Equipment: Cross-country ski track, free weights, rowing machines, stair climbers, stationary bikes, treadmills, vertical ladder climbers, weight-training circuit. **Services:** Hydrotherapy, reflexology, shirodhara, Swiss shower. **Swimming:** Indoor pool. **Classes and Programs:** Boxing aerobics, fencing, personal training, Pilates, Spinning, yoga. **Recreation:** Hiking, skiing.

▦ 38 rooms.

✗ Breakfast included. Terra Bistro serves international cuisine. No spa menu. **Sample Meals:** Coriander-rubbed tuna with tamari vinaigrette, sesame-crusted salmon (lunch); rum-soaked drunken pork chop, grilled Portobello mushroom with wild-rice pilaf and miso gravy (dinner).

▧ Nightly rate $450–$1,200 per room. Day spa $30. AE, D, MC, V.

✉ *352 E. Meadow Dr., Vail, CO 81657,* ☎ *970/476–0700 or 800/822–4754,* FAX *970/476–6451. www.vailathleticclub.com*

VAIL CASCADE RESORT

LUXURY PAMPERING ○ SPORTS CONDITIONING

A ski vacation at the Vail Cascade Resort is nearly hassle-free. The concierge has your equipment warmed and waiting for you in the morning, and the resort's own chairlift whisks you up the mountain right from the hotel.

Nonskiers, too, will find plenty to keep them busy at this 17-acre resort. The 78,000-square-ft Cascade Club has an aerobics studio with mountain views, tennis, squash, racquetball courts, and a running track—all indoors for year-round use. When summer rolls around, you can practice your swings on the golf course or go swimming in three outdoor pools. You might prefer biking or in-line skating into the village, hiking to Vail Mountain, or experiencing white-water rafting on the Colorado River.

Spa treatments are as broad in scope as the range of sports activities: The rejuvenating foot treatment is a great pick-me-up after hitting the trails. The Gore Creek hot stone massage, alpine body glow, and milk-and-honey body treatment all use ingredients from the area. A treatment room for two allows couples to share simultaneous massages.

The hotel's four-story wings are designed to look like a European chateau. Rooms are decorated in jewel tones and have courtyard or mountain views. Some rooms have doors opening right onto Gore Creek, while some suites have fireplaces and whirlpools or saunas.

INSIDER TIP Afraid of overdoing it on the slopes? A dynamic sports massage, along with assisted stretches, prepares you for a day of double-diamond descents.

Equipment: Free weights, rowing machines, stair climbers, stationary bikes, treadmills, weight-training circuit. **Services:** Body glow, herbal wrap, massage. **Classes and Programs:** Aerobics, body composition, personal training, Pilates, Spinning, yoga. **Swimming:** 3 outdoor pools. **Recreation:** Biking, racquetball, skiing, squash, tennis. **Children's Programs:** Camp Cascade for ages 4–12.

▦ 201 rooms, 28 suites.

✗ Meals à la carte. Chap's Grill & Chophouse serves game and regional specialties. **Sample Meals:** Chateaubriand for 2, Colorado trio of elk, lamb, and venison, pan-fried Colorado trout (dinner).

☎ Nightly rate $129–$409 per room. 3-night spa package $339–$399, includes spa treatments. AE, DC, MC, V.

✉ *1300 Westhaven Dr., Cascade Village, Vail, CO 81657,* ☎ *970/476–7111 or 800/420–2424* FAX *970/479–7025. www.vailcascade.com*

WIESBADEN HOT SPRINGS SPA & LODGINGS

MINERAL SPRINGS

On a starlit night, soaking in the outdoor thermal-water pool at Wiesbaden Hot Springs Spa & Lodgings can be an uplifting experience. You can indulge in this relaxing ritual at this family-owned and -operated mountainside resort that began as a motel and gradually became a full-fledged health resort.

The resort's facilities include a lodge, an exercise room, and a weight room. A massage therapist is on staff, and you can also sign up for facials, aromatherapy wraps, and acupressure treatments designed to help you achieve deep relaxation. A glass-walled lounge overlooks the swimming pool and sundeck. As in the past, however, the main attraction is the series of naturally heated outdoor pools and rock-walled vapor caves. One private soaking pool has a clothing-optional policy.

The spiritual quality of the cave was recognized by the Ute tribe and other Native Americans who traveled for days to reach the curative waters. The geothermal water that heats the motel and its pools flows from two springs at 111°F and 134°F. The original bathhouse, built in 1879, was replaced by a medical clinic in the 1920s, then by a guest lodge. Recently renovated rooms are decorated with antiques, and some have wood stoves.

At an altitude of 7,700 ft, the picturesque old mountain town of Ouray is sheltered from winds by the surrounding forest. Scenic canyons in the national forest are a major attraction for hikers. Few roads traverse these mountains, which are the source of the Rio Grande, so make sure to pick up a picnic lunch before you set out.

INSIDER TIP Dinner at the Bon Ton Restaurant, in the nearby St. Elmo Hotel, gives a taste of the town's Victorian past.

Equipment: Free weights, stair climbers, stationary bikes. **Services:** Acupressure, body wraps, reflexology, Swedish massage. **Swimming:** Pool. **Recreation:** Biking, hiking.

🛏 17 rooms, 1 cottage, 1 house.

✗ No restaurant.

☎ Nightly rate 120–$145 per room. D, MC, V.

✉ *625 5th St., Box 349, Ouray, CO 81427,* ☎ *970/325–4347,* FAX *970/325–4358. www.geocities.com/wiesbadenspa*

WOMEN'S QUEST FITNESS RETREATS

SPORTS CONDITIONING ○ HOLISTIC HEALTH

Founded in 1992 by Colleen Cannon, a former world-champion triathlete, and staffed by nationally ranked athletes including world-champion cyclist Eve Stephenson and U.S. Masters swimming champion Anna Pettis Scott, this women-only program is built on the philosophy that physical activity is one of the most powerful and perhaps most underused tools for personal discovery, balance, and transformation.

Programs take place either at rustic Woodspur Lodge Winter Park from June through August, Snow Mountain Ranch in Winter Park in February, or in Boulder in May for a new triathlon clinic. The focus of the summer programs is on instruction in trail running, mountain biking, and swimming. Winter programs teach cross-country skiing, snowshoeing, and swimming. You learn to combine these activities with yoga, meditation, and journal writing to create inner balance. The staff takes a playful, unintimidating approach, encouraging you to stretch your limits. Cooperation rather than competition is encouraged.

A typical day at a Women's Quest retreat begins with prebreakfast yoga and meditation in the Great Room of the Woodspur Lodge, where glass doors look out on the snowcapped Rockies. After breakfast there's a group mountain-bike ride. Swimming instruction, yoga, and free time for journal writing and relaxing follow lunchtime. After dinner there are lectures on subjects such as heart-rate-monitor training or nutrition and body image. On the final day, when the group has become fit, there's an all-day hike to the top of the Continental Divide.

The 35 women who attend these retreats may be as young as 17 or as old as 65, as fit as a competitive runner or as new to sports as someone who has never ridden a bicycle, and yet by the end of each session lasting friendships have inevitably formed. Camaraderie and mutual support are emphasized. All activities are done as a group. Meals are served at big common tables, giving you a chance to make new friends every evening.

INSIDER TIP On the first day of camp you are paired with a roommate, although you can opt to pay extra for a single room.

Services: Massage. **Classes and Programs:** Guided visualization and imagery, meditation, yoga. **Recreation:** Biking, hiking, swimming, skiing, snowshoeing.

▦ Accommodations vary by program.

✕ Meals included. 3 meals. **Sample Meals:** Tofu eggless salad, tuna salad, garden burgers (lunch); stir-fried vegetables with chicken, fajitas, pasta with marinara and steamed vegetables (dinner).

▨ 5-day Winter Park program $1,250. 3-day triathlon clinic $600. No credit cards.

✉ *2525 Arapahoe Ave., Suite E4-181, Boulder, CO 80302,* ☎ *303/545–9295,* ℻ *303/443–3620. www.womensquest.com*

CONNECTICUT

NORWICH INN AND SPA

LUXURY PAMPERING ○ HOLISTIC HEALTH

Combine an old-fashioned country inn with an up-to-the-minute spa, and you have a perfect escape for harried city dwellers. About three hours northeast of New York City, the imposing Georgian-style Norwich Inn and Spa blends New England traditions with sophisticated cuisine and state-of-the-art spa treatments.

Join the daily guided walk at 7 AM to learn your way around the 43-acre resort near the Thames River. Then you can work out at your own pace or with a personal trainer in a glass-walled room of cardio- and strength-training equipment, swim a few laps in a 35-ft pool, or enjoy an underwater massage in a hydrotherapy tub. You can also have any of the more than a dozen types of facials available. For an additional fee you can attend workshops on nutrition and cooking.

Country-chic comfort characterizes the living quarters. Public areas include a taproom with a large stone fireplace, a quiet sunroom full of palms and wicker furniture, and a lobby with a pair of pet finches. Standard guest rooms are small but homey, with antiques, four-poster beds, handwoven rugs, and lace curtains. For a splurge stay in one of the charming villas that border a nearby pond. Each has a fully equipped kitchen, living room with fireplace, and balcony overlooking the gardens. Villa guests have a private fitness center, swimming pool, and hot tub.

INSIDER TIP Feeling lucky? The inn is owned by the Mashantucket Pequot tribe, which also owns the nearby Foxwoods Resort Casino.

Equipment: Free weights, stair climbers, stationary bikes, treadmills, weight-training circuit. **Services:** Aromatherapy, clay wrap, herbal wrap, hot stone massage, hydrotherapy, loofah scrub, reiki, salt glow, seaweed wrap, thalassotherapy. **Swimming:** Indoor and outdoor pools. **Classes and Programs:** Aerobics, cooking demonstrations, personal training, wellness workshops. **Recreation:** Biking, golf, hiking, tennis.

🛏 49 inn rooms, 4 suites, 30 villas.

✕ Meals à la carte. Spa cuisine available. **Sample Meals:** Grilled Atlantic whitefish and seared Portobello mushrooms, oven-roasted eggplant with herbed feta in a pita pocket (lunch); blackened yellowfin tuna, salmon fillet (dinner).

💳 Nightly rate $225–$900 per room. 5-night women-only Balance Within program $3,400 per person, includes lodging, meal, treatments. AE, DC, MC, V.

✉ *607 W. Thames (Rte. 32), Norwich, CT 06360,* ☎ *860/886–2401 or 800/275–4772,* ℻ *860/886–9483.* www.norwichinnandspa.com

SAYBROOK POINT INN AND SPA

LUXURY PAMPERING

Built on the site of the Terra Mar, a hideaway for celebrities such as Frank Sinatra, Tom Jones, and Jayne Mansfield, the Saybrook Point Inn and Spa still caters to rich and famous people seeking to get away from it all. The resort, on the Connecticut River, is popular with those who cruise into the Saybrook Point Marina on their yachts and sailboats.

Many guest rooms in the sprawling main building have lovely views of the water. The best view, though, is from the room on the second floor of the lighthouse, in the marina (you can spot the building by the whimsical whale-shape weather vane on the roof). Reserve this room for a romantic experience.

A new addition here is the expanded spa facilities, which include 13 treatment rooms, a large fitness center, and a garden room where you can relax between services. Treatments at the state-of-the-art facility range from a papaya-pineapple facial to a detoxifying seaweed body wrap. You can also arrange for any number of beauty treatments—manicures, pedicures, and makeup applications. These treatments are one reason why the resort is so popular among couples getting married.

Sports activities are not as varied as beauty treatments. Many guests tend to do their own thing, although the aquaerobics class is popular with locals who use the facilities. At least a few times a week there are guided walks around the quaint colonial town of Old Saybrook.

INSIDER TIP The spa is usually filled with bridesmaids on summer weekends. Book spa appointments during the summer months a few weeks in advance.

Equipment: Free weights, stair climbers, stationary bikes, treadmills, weight-training circuit. **Services:** Body scrubs, body wraps, facials, makeup consultation, massage. **Swimming:** Indoor and outdoor pools. **Classes and Programs:** Aquaerobics, body-composition test, personal training, Pilates, tai chi, yoga. **Recreation:** Biking, fishing, golf, hiking, jogging.

🛏 81 rooms.

✗ Meals à la carte. Terra Mar Grille serves American cuisine. Many dishes are prepared without fat or sodium. **Sample Meals:** Sautéed lobster meat on toasted roll, salad of arugula, radicchio, and frisée with shaved fennel (lunch); blackened salmon medallions with red-lentil pilaf, skillet-seared Long Island duck breast, grilled maple-cured pork loin (dinner).

💲 Nightly rate $179–$485 per room. 1-night spa package $426–$505 per person, double occupancy, includes meals, spa treatments. AE, DC, MC, V.

✉ *2 Bridge St., Old Saybrook, CT 06475,* ☎ *860/395–2000 or 800/243–0212,* ℻ *860/388–1504.* www.saybrook.com

THE SPA AT GRAND LAKE

NUTRITION AND DIET ○ MEDICAL WELLNESS

At different times over the past several decades, this property has been a Jewish summer community and a weight-loss camp. In its new incarnation the Spa at Grand Lake is an affordable, homey inn that caters to mostly urban women (and a few men) looking for a healthy getaway to the country.

In the rural farming community of Lebanon, the inn attracts guests who think of it as their private hideaway. Owner Anne Rubb is extremely friendly, circulating with guests during meals and available throughout the day.

Most guests come for a full week or a weekend and follow a schedule of exercise, which may include yoga, kickboxing, and NIA, a new discipline that incorporates modern dance with martial arts. A daily massage is included in a week's package, and many opt to pay extra for manicures and other services. Although facials are given in a private room, massages are usually given in a larger room where others are getting rubbed down at the same time.

Before arrival at the spa, guests choose whether they prefer regular meals or a 900- or 1,200-calorie diet. All meals are cooked without salt or butter, although you can ask for both if you so desire. After dinner there is generally a guest lecturer on nutrition or health issues. On Friday the lecture is given up for a night of line dancing. Those who stay a week may take a trip to nearby Foxwoods Casino and hike in a nearby state park, but many choose not to leave the property at all.

Accommodations here are spare, although each room has a television and phone. Although deluxe rooms are well furnished and comfortable, the setup is similar to a dormitory.

INSIDER TIP For a kick start to a more healthy lifestyle, this spa is a good choice. The crowd is mostly over 40, and the atmosphere is friendly and not at all intimidating.

Equipment: Free weights, stationary bikes, stair climbers, treadmills, weight-training circuit. **Services:** Lymphatic drainage, massage, mud and seaweed wraps, reflexology, reiki. **Swimming:** Indoor and outdoor pools. **Classes and Programs:** Aerobics, body conditioning, yoga. **Recreation:** Hiking, tennis.

🛏 75 rooms.

✕ Meals included. Choice of regular meals or 900- or 1,200-calorie meals. **Sample Meals:** Mixed salad, carrots and celery, tuna salad over lettuce with pita pockets, stir-fried vegetables with chicken (lunch); white-bean and pepper salad, poached salmon with asparagus (dinner).

💳 2-night package $309–$369 per person, double occupancy, includes lodging, meals, 1 massage. AE, MC, V.

✉ *Rte. 207, 1667 Exeter Rd., Lebanon, CT 06249,* ☎ *800/853-7721,* 🖷 *860/642-4799. www.thespaatgrandlake.com*

FLORIDA

THE COLONY BEACH & TENNIS RESORT

LUXURY PAMPERING ○ SPORTS CONDITIONING

Long acclaimed for its excellent tennis facilities, the Colony Beach & Tennis Resort has in recent years given more attention to its intimate spa and fitness center to round out its healthful offerings.

At the small spa, which is expected to double in size in 2001, the treatments are straightforward: basic massages, facials, and a few body treatments involving herbs and algae. At the fitness center you can work out on your own or with a personal trainer on your particular needs, whether it's weight loss, posture, strengthening, or sports-specific training. You can try the latest fitness equipment or join classes in aerobics, stretch, and yoga. You may combine sports training with walks on the gorgeous 12-mi stretch of beach. Clinics, camps, and private or semiprivate lessons with the Colony's 10 tennis pros are available. Court time is free, as are weekly family tennis events.

The Colony excels at family vacationing. First of all, its 208 town-house-like suites are designed to give kids and adults their space. The Colony also earns kudos in the kitchen. The Colony Dining Room, with a popular Sunday brunch, has long been known for setting a high standard. The Colony Bistro and the Patio serve lighter, more casual fare. Vegetarian and healthy entrees are available on request. Guests can ask for a printed nutritional analysis of any dish they order.

Another fine way to exercise while staying at the Colony is by making use of its rental bicycles and cruising the paved path the length of flowery, manicured Longboat Key. On City Island, just south of the Longboat Key Bridge, visit the highly acclaimed Mote Marine Laboratory & Aquarium and the Pelican Man's Bird Sanctuary. Sarasota and its islands overflow with cultural offerings, most notably the Ringling Museum of Art. Artist colonies and boutique enclaves make this area a shopper's haven.

INSIDER TIP This resort is perfect for families with children. Beach equipment rentals, a playground, and the complimentary kids' clubs keep the kids active and interacting.

Equipment: Free weights, rowing machines, stair climbers, stationary bikes, treadmills, weight-training circuit. **Services:** Algae scrub, craniosacral therapy, herbal wrap, massage, reflexology, shiatsu. **Classes and Programs:** Aerobics, body sculpting, kickboxing, stretch, yoga. **Swimming:** Pool, beach. **Recreation:** Sailing, snorkeling, tennis. **Children's Programs:** Programs for ages 3–6, 7–12, and 13–17.

⊞ 208 1- and 2-bedroom villa suites.

✕ All meals à la carte. The Colony Dining Room serves Floridian cuisine. **Sample Meals:** Mediterranean salad, grouper panini, peppercorn-crusted salmon (lunch); shallot-glazed grouper, rack of lamb, Cajun-rubbed yellowfin tuna, fusilli with broccoli rabe (dinner).

▧ Nightly rate $195–$645 for 1- and 2-bedroom villas. 3-night Classic Spa Experience package $960–$1,260 for 2, includes lodging, spa treatments. Day spa package $305, includes lunch. AE, D, DC, MC, V.

✉ *1620 Gulf of Mexico Dr., Longboat Key, FL 34228,* ☎ *941/383–6464 or 800/426–5669,* FAX *941/383–7549. www.colonybeachresort.com*

DISNEY'S GRAND FLORIDIAN RESORT

LUXURY PAMPERING ○ SPORTS CONDITIONING

Only Disney can take an exalted aspect of real life and improve upon it. The entertainment experts have done exactly that in recalling Florida's grand era of wooden Victorian railroad hotels at the Grand Floridian Resort. The immense white clapboard structure with gingerbread trim and French doors opening out to tropical gardens is, of course, like nothing that ever existed. The resort's four-year-old spa, however, is the real thing. There are no Disney songs brainwashing you in the treatment rooms.

You might expect Disney to create, as so many modern spas do, an atmosphere of classic Rome. In keeping with the resort's theme, however, the Grand Floridian Spa seems to dwell in old Florida. Just as it doesn't pretend to be chic European, it also makes no claims to being cutting-edge, although some of its treatments, such as the blue-cornmeal scrub, are out of the ordinary. The Grand Floridian Spa is geared for first-time spa goers and strives to make the experience less intimidating. It offers a couples massage room to those who would like another person present when receiving treatments and even offers My First Facial for 10- to 14-year-olds. Steps from Disney's Wedding Pavilion, the spa is also popular with brides and wedding parties.

Twenty treatment rooms include a Vichy shower in one, a hydrobath in another, and a VIP pedicure throne room. Massages are traditional and facials most popular. The 75-minute Grand Floridian Deluxe Facial incorporates hand and foot massage and a relaxing series of steaming, massage, masking, and rehydration treatments using Australian Jurlique products. Comfort is a prime concern here. A nice touch: A small bell rests at the head of each treatment bed so that when you are unrobed and comfortable, you can summon your therapist.

Persons receiving spa treatments have run of the fitness center that same day. The staff will not allow you to use it the next day, even if your spa appointment is after a late arrival. Otherwise the fee is $12 to use the cardio and weight equipment.

The Grand Floridian, Disney's flagship resort, is very high-end and one of its most romantic, yet nonetheless it's a natural for families. Besides kid-tailored spa services, it offers daily children's activities, such as a pirate cruise, cooking classes, and fishing. In the evening the Mouseketeer Club feeds them and keeps them entertained so adults can relax with a spa treatment or dinner at the resort's haute cuisine Victoria & Albert's, the Caribbean-influenced Grand Floridian Café, or the lakeside Narcoosee, where you can order spa and vegan meals. Other restaurants, along with a deli and a tearoom, offer further options. At buffet-style 1900 Park Fare, Disney characters appear for breakfast, tea time, and dinner.

The accommodations huddle around a free-form pool and rose gardens. The rooms, larger than at most Disney properties, simulate a Victorian parlor with lacy curtains, oversize oval mirrors, daybeds, and floral wallpaper. From your balcony you can watch the nightly fireworks at the Magic Kingdom. As at all Disney resorts, guests here get early admission privileges at the parks and free transportation around Disney World and to Downtown Disney for some lively nightlife as only Disney can do it.

INSIDER TIP No Mickey Mouse operation at this spa. It specializes in the fine service Disney has come to exemplify, especially for first-time spa goers.

Equipment: Free weights, stationary bikes, treadmills, weight-training circuit. **Services:** Algae body mask, aloe wrap, aromatherapy, massage, mustard bath and wrap, reflexology, sea-salt polish, shiatsu. **Swimming:** 2 pools. **Recreation:** Boating, golf, volleyball, water sports. **Children's Program:** Mouseketeers' Club for ages 4–12.

▥ 842 rooms, 25 1- and 2-bedroom suites.

✕ Meals à la carte. Restaurants serve various cuisines, including a spa menu. **Sample Meals:** Grilled vegetable flat bread, Cuban sandwich, tomato and fresh mozzarella salad (lunch); orzo paella, pepper-seared scallops, porterhouse steak, herb-crusted spring lamb, porcini-crusted veal (dinner).

▧ Nightly rate $304–$670 per room. Ultimate Day package $430, includes lunch. AE, MC, V.

✉ *4111 N. Floridian Way, Lake Buena Vista, FL 32830,* ☎ *407/934–7639, 407/824–2332 for spa reservations. www.disney.com*

DON CESAR BEACH RESORT

LUXURY PAMPERING

Ever since its jazz-age heyday, when writer F. Scott Fitzgerald himself indulged, the Don CeSar Beach Resort has been known for its sumptuousness. Don't expect spa sparseness, even today. Modern-day guests relive the era every Sunday at a no-holds-barred buffet in the King Charles Ballroom. There you can sample more than 180 specialty dishes as well as a delicious view of the Gulf of Mexico.

This pink palace with an elegant European aura is a self-contained world of luxury. Laden with crystal chandeliers and marble floors, the 10-story hotel opened in 1928, survived the Great Depression, served as an air force convalescent center in the 1940s, and came through a succession of face-lifts to emerge as a savvy resort that attracts Europeans and American families.

At the compact but complete spa you can set your own course, selecting from a menu of nine body treatments. Four sea- and sun-oriented scrubs and polishes are recommended to prepare your skin for the full benefits of body wraps and massage therapies. The sea-salt exfoliating scrub is an invigorating loofah treatment that makes you feel you've acquired a new suit of skin. Herbal and sports body wraps, using Floraspa products imported from France, promise to revitalize and detoxify. Massages are as vigorous as you desire.

Apart from the spa, there is much to do and enjoy. Activities at the Don include water aerobics, ecology walks on the beach, poolside yoga, and ballroom dance instruction in a private studio. A supervised program for kids includes movie parties with pizza. Biking, deep-sea fishing, and sailing excursions can also be arranged.

Guest rooms range from small rooms with single beds to spacious high-ceiling suites with a small balcony facing the sea. Healthy selections appear on the menus of three restaurants. You can have dinner in the fashionable Maritana Grille, which features Caribbean-influenced fare, or the more casual Sea Porch Café, where spa cuisine is served at boardwalk tables. The Beachcomber Grill caters to the light-lunch crowd deck-side at the pool.

INSIDER TIP Visit Fort DeSoto State Park, where manatees occasionally visit the warm waters during the winter months.

Equipment: Free weights, stair climbers, stationary bikes, treadmills, weight-training circuit. **Services:** Aromatherapy, massage, reflexology, sea scrub. **Swimming:** 2 pools, ocean beach. **Classes and Programs:** Fitness assessment, nutritional consultation, personal training. **Recreation:** Tennis, water sports. **Children's Programs:** Kids Ltd. program for ages 5–12.

▣ 225 rooms, 43 suites, 2 penthouses.

✕ Meals à la carte. Spa selections included on the Sea Porch Cafe menu. **Sample Meals:** Chilled tropical fruit with fresh berry yogurt, grilled Gulf fish sandwich, shrimp and spinach frittata (lunch); Portobello panini, Caribbean grilled chicken sausage, polenta-crusted red snapper (dinner).

▦ Nightly rate $169–$389 per person, double occupancy. 3-night Pink Palace Refresher package $789–$1,214 for 2, includes lodging, breakfast, spa treatments. Day spa package $100–$275. AE, D, MC, V.

✉ *3400 Gulf Blvd., St. Petersburg Beach, FL 33706,* ☎ *727/360–1881, 800/282–1116, or 800/637–7200,* FAX *727/367–6952. www.doncesar.com*

THE DORAL GOLF RESORT & SPA

LUXURY PAMPERING ○ SPORTS CONDITIONING

With what it bills as the largest spa facility in the South, the Doral Golf doesn't just win the prize for spaciousness. It's also quite impressive for the range of services that it offers. Pampering begins when you are escorted to one of the private rooms surrounding the lofty central dining atrium dominated by dramatic dual sweeping staircases. In total there are 52 massage, facial, and wet rooms offering a wide selection of treatments, as well as an aerobics studio, a cardiovascular and weight-training room, and indoor and outdoor lap pools.

The Doral's spa blends European and American health concepts but keeps daily regimens flexible. Classes tend to be jazzy, low-impact workouts that appeal to men as well as women. Guests can work out with weight-training equipment in a fitness center that looks out onto groomed greens. Sequestered gardens allow you tranquil spots to relax after a treatment.

You can either enjoy the country club atmosphere of the main lodge or any of the other lodges, or use the spa villa as a luxurious hideaway. The spa's 48 extralarge suites are among the best accommodations at any American spa: Each has twin baths, hot tub, wet bar, and refrigerator, a VCR with access to a video library, and two dressing areas. Suites have private terraces or balconies overlooking the garden.

Golf and tennis are major attractions at Doral, and a number of tournaments and group events are scheduled. Golfers can tee off on five championship courses, including the legendary Blue Monster (a favorite stop on the PGA tour) and the Great White. Tennis instruction at the 15-court complex is furnished by well-qualified professionals.

INSIDER TIP With its new pool complex, fine kids' program, top-shelf spa, and renowned sports facilities Doral is the place for quality family time—together and apart.

Equipment: Free weights, stair climbers, stationary bikes, treadmills, weight-training circuit. **Services:** Aloe-vera wrap, aromatherapy, fango, herbal wrap, massage, reflexology, reiki. **Swimming:** 4 pools. **Classes and Programs:** Aquaerobics, body awareness, kickboxing, Spinning, tai chi, tap dancing, yoga. **Recreation:** Basketball, biking, golf, softball, tennis, volleyball. **Children's Programs:** Camp Doral for ages 5–12.

🛏 694 rooms, 48 suites.

✘ Meals à la carte. 5 restaurants serve everything from burgers to seafood. Spa serves low-fat clean cuisine. **Sample Meals:** Grilled chicken sandwich, crab-cake burger, Oriental chicken salad (lunch); grouper en papillote with mango and banana, broiled scallops with carrot-orange sauce (dinner).

📷 Nightly rate $155–$395 per room. 1-night Spa Experience package $125–$275 per person, double occupancy, includes breakfast. Day spa package $105–$295, includes lunch. AE, D, DC, MC, V.

✉ 4400 N.W. 87th Ave., Miami, FL 33178, ☎ 305/592–2000, FAX 305/591–6630. www.doralspa.com

EDEN ROC RESORT & SPA

LUXURY PAMPERING ○ SPORTS CONDITIONING ○ HOLISTIC HEALTH

Legendary as one of Miami Beach's grand 1950s hotels, the stylish art deco–style Eden Roc Resort & Spa has a prime beachfront location on a slim island between the Atlantic Ocean and the Intracoastal Waterway. Although it lies within minutes of South Beach's famed nightclubs, shops, and restaurants, it rises 14 stories above the crowds and noise.

The hotel spared no expense in creating its mezzanine-level Spa of Eden, which features air-conditioned cardiovascular and strength-training rooms complete with an ocean view. The spa solves Florida's it's-too-hot-to-exercise problem with an indoor, air-conditioned rock-climbing wall and basketball, squash, and handball courts. Spa treatments demonstrate variety and innovation, including such specialties as a Thai massage that combines acupressure and yoga as well as a hot stone massage in which therapists place heated and cooled smooth stones at strategic pressure points on the body. Daily exercise classes have guests pumping iron, dancing the mambo, and doing yoga.

Eden Roc's dramatic atrium lobby sweeps you to another era. Most rooms in the oceanfront hotel have dramatic dark ocher and black decor, deco-style furniture, and closets large enough to live in. Corner rooms feature drop-dead views of yachts on the Intracoastal Waterway.

INSIDER TIP Work off a few calories walking to South Beach, where you can take in the latest in trendy food and fashion.

Equipment: Free weights, stair climbers, stationary bikes, treadmills, weight-training circuit. **Services:** Aromatherapy, massage, reflexology, reiki, seaweed mud body wrap, shiatsu. **Swimming:** 2 pools, beach. **Classes and Programs:** Aerobics, Spinning, weight training, yoga. **Recreation:** Basketball, kayaking, racquetball, rock climbing, sailing, scuba, squash, yachting.

🛏 301 rooms, 49 suites.

✗ Meals à la carte. 2 restaurants serve contemporary American fare. Spa cuisine available. **Sample Meals:** Cuban sandwich, surf and turf salad, fruit platter (lunch); pan-seared scallops, sesame-crusted ahi tuna, roasted rack of lamb (dinner).

💵 Nightly rate $210–$439 per room. 3-night Escape to Eden package $1,220–$1,585 per person, includes breakfast and dinner, spa treatments. Day spa package $215, includes lunch. AE, D, MC, V.

✉ *4525 Collins Ave., Miami Beach, FL 33140,* ☎ *305/531–0000 or 800/327–8337, 305/674–5585 for spa reservations,* ℻ *305/531–6955. www.edenrocresort.com*

FISHER ISLAND CLUB

LUXURY PAMPERING

Privacy is the primary focus on this 216-acre island off the southern tip of Miami. Once a secluded hideaway for family and friends of William K. Vanderbilt II in the 1920s, Fisher Island Club is now a Mediterranean-style condominium community with a 9-hole golf course, 17 tennis courts, beach club, marina, and spa. It's still exclusive, partly because of its location (the only way to get there is by boat) and partly by design (you go through a security check before reaching registration).

The 22,000-square-ft spa, built in Vanderbilt's old hangar, features an indoor lap pool with retractable roof, 15 beautifully appointed treatment rooms, a salon, two aerobics studios, and a cardio- and weight-training room with views of the marina. In a secluded garden with trickling fountains you discover a whirlpool and a larger pool for aquaerobics. Among your choices of treatments are a hydromassage in a French tub fitted with 47 underwater jets and the Super Hydradermie Facial, which uses a mild electrical current to cleanse and improve the elasticity of your face.

Since there's a maximum of 20 guests at a time, the spa staff lavishes attention on you. There are between five and nine exercise classes scheduled each day, but most of your workout is tailored to your personal needs. Don't expect to interact with others, though. Club members are a mix of Europeans and locals, but there isn't much socializing with outsiders.

Accommodations, which range from villas to oceanfront condominiums, include three cottages Vanderbilt built that are fit for a millionaire's holiday. The cottages and condos have a kitchen, living room with period furnishings, and one to three bedrooms, each with a private bathroom. Villas have polished marble floors and large bathrooms with whirlpool tubs.

The lavish Vanderbilt mansion now holds an aviary and one of the island's six restaurants. Outside, guests can use the Vanderbilts' original pool. The grounds, with massive oaks and stately royal palms and peacocks strolling about, are meticulously manicured.

INSIDER TIP If a private island isn't exclusive enough for you, you can have your treatments in Fisher Island's spa within a spa, which is secluded from the rest of the facility.

Equipment: Free weights, rowing machines, stair climbers, stationary bikes, treadmills, weight-training circuit. **Services:** Aromatherapy, algae body masque, body polish, herbal wrap, hydrotherapy, reflexology. Swimming: 2 outdoor pools, 1 indoor pool, beach. **Classes and Programs:** Aerobics, aquaerobics, fitness assessment, kickboxing, personal training, yoga. **Recreation:** Biking, golf, tennis, volleyball. **Children's Programs:** Childcare available.

▣ 4 suites, 28 villas, 30 apartments, 3 cottages.

✕ Meals à la carte. 5 restaurants serve international cuisine. **Sample Meals:** Mandarin Chinese chicken salad, grilled chicken breast layered with squash, tomatoes, and mozzarella (lunch); Thai curry broth, Florida lobster tails, roasted free-range chicken, roasted rack of lamb (dinner).

▤ Nightly rate $525–$745 for villas, $655–$1,485 for cottages. 3-night spa package $2,250–$2,450 per person, includes meals, spa treatments. Day spa package $195. AE, DC, MC, V.

✉ *1 Fisher Island Dr., Fisher Island, FL 33109,* ☎ *305/535–6020 or 800/537–3708,* ℻ *305/535–6032. www.fisherisland-florida.com*

HIPPOCRATES HEALTH INSTITUTE

NUTRITION AND DIET ○ HOLISTIC HEALTH

Past guests tell miracle-cure stories about Hippocrates Health Institute, where the power of positive thinking and taking charge of your life is put into practice with strict diet and exercise.

Extreme lifestyle change is the goal at this secluded retreat near Palm Beach. A holistic health center and learning institute, Hippocrates evolved from a Boston-based program designed to revitalize the body, mind, and spirit. Under the direction of Brian and Anna Maria Clement, the program now has a permanent home in a wooded area close to the beaches.

The institute's weekly programs run from Sunday to Saturday and teach participants to be self-sufficient in matters of food and medicine. Included are physician consultation, psychological evaluation, nutritional counseling, daily exercise, and weekly massage. You learn deep-relaxation techniques to aid in prevention of illness and to enhance healing, creativity, and inspiration.

The vegetarian diet—consisting of unprocessed, organically grown fruits and vegetables—is a drastic change for most people. The institute's chefs prepare meals composed mostly of green vegetables eaten raw to preserve nutrients. Presented at a sumptuous buffet, the enzyme-rich organic food provides a sequence of new tastes and textures. Wheatgrass juice figures into the Hippocrates diet and is always available at a juice bar.

A peaceful, healing serenity pervades the grounds, where walkways wind through a semitropical natural environment to a fitness center, whirlpool, and four swimming pools, including one loaded with Dead Sea minerals. The Vapor Cave institutes an American healing tradition that uses steam to cleanse and relax the body. The therapy building offers massage and an extensive selection of spa and health services, from acupuncture to hypnotherapy.

Accommodations on the 30-acre retreat range from five luxury suites with marble-wall bath and whirlpools in the spacious main building to cottages decorated with southwestern-style furnishings to rooms in guest houses. Guest-house accommodations are singles and doubles, with private or shared bathrooms.

INSIDER TIP Want to bring home what you've learned? An on-site shop sells books, vitamins, and even wheatgrass juicers—all the materials you need to pursue a healthy lifestyle.

Equipment: Cross-country ski machines, free weights, stair climbers, stationary bikes, weight-training circuit. **Services:** Acupuncture, algae wrap, aromatherapy, body glow, craniosacral therapy, hypnotherapy, lymphatic drainage, mud wrap, paraffin back treatment, shiatsu. **Swimming:** Pool. **Classes and Programs:** Body-composition analysis, chiropractic therapy, fitness evaluation, health consultations, personal training, private yoga classes.

▥ 25 rooms, some with shared bath.

✕ Meals included. 1 day each week designated for juice fasting. **Sample Meals:** Broccoli salad with garlic and oregano, stuffed avocado, almond-basil loaf with red-pepper coulis.

▧ 1-week program $1,800–$2,300 per person, double occupancy. AE, D, DC, MC, V.

✉ *1443 Palmdale Ct., West Palm Beach, FL 33411,* ☎ *561/471 8876 or 800/842-2125,* ☒ *561/471-9464. www.hippocratesinst.com*

HYATT REGENCY PIER SIXTY-SIX RESORT

LUXURY PAMPERING

Spa LXVI is tucked away in Hyatt Regency Pier Sixty-Six Resort's 22 acres of tropical gardens. A convenient place to escape from business at the nearby convention center or to relax before boarding a cruise ship, the facility is an oasis away from the bustle of Fort Lauderdale.

Spa LXVI spoils its guests with leather couches and extravagant signature treatments such as champagne facials and pineapple loofah scrubs. In addition to a full-service salon for body, skin, and hair treatments, the recently renovated spa offers private massage rooms and a rain room for body wraps. Yoga classes are offered on the pool deck in the morning, and exercise sessions are in the sports pool. Golfers are whisked to the resort's Grande Oaks Golf Club, 15 minutes away. The roomy family pool, with waterfalls and snack bar, is popular with kids. Nearby, there's a 40-person hydrotherapy pool.

The landmark Hyatt Regency Pier Sixty-Six rises 17 stories above the Intracoastal Waterway. Rooms in the circular tower feature splendid views of the sea or city. You can also take in the vistas from the revolving lounge on the top floor. When you want to swim in the ocean, hail the water taxi at the resort's dock for a quick trip to the beach.

INSIDER TIP For a romantic meal, dine at one of the chic cafés along the Riverwalk and Las Olas Boulevard.

Exercise Equipment: Free weights, rowing machines, stair climbers, stationary bikes, weight-training equipment. **Services:** Aromatherapy, body glow, reflexology, hot stone massage, sea-salt scrub, seaweed wrap. **Swimming:** 2 pools. **Classes and Programs:** Aerobics, aquaerobics, fitness evaluation, personal training. **Recreation:** Boating, deep-sea fishing, sailing, scuba, snorkeling, tennis.

380 rooms, 8 suites.

✗ Meals à la carte. 2 of the hotel's 4 restaurants have low-calorie options. **Sample Meals:** Tuna salad wrap, grilled shrimp with angel-hair pasta, New York strip salad (lunch); crab cakes, linguine with fresh vegetables, grilled salmon (dinner).

Nightly rate $179–$330 per room. Day spa packages $163–$273. AE, DC, MC, V.

✉ 2301 S.E. 17th St. Causeway, Fort Lauderdale, FL 33316, ☎ 954/525–6666 or 800/327–3796, FAX 954/728–3541. www.hyatt.com

LIDO SPA HOTEL & HEALTH RESORT

NUTRITION AND DIET

The Lido Spa Hotel & Health Resort is the type of place where many of the older guests who make up the majority of the clientele tend to stay for weeks or the entire winter. Many return year after year. Everyone eats at long cafeteria-style tables, noshes at the juice bar, works out in the swimming pool, plays mah-jongg on the lawn, and goes shopping in the hotel van.

The Lido has a comfortable, lived-in look. The main building, opened in 1962, is flanked by one- and two-story garden wings, which house motel-style accommodations. Fifteen fully equipped apartments are nearby. The lobby is a pleasant and comfortable venue for relaxing after meals, reading, and socializing. Plans for renovations are in the works, and work has already begun on the resort's bay-front boat dock.

The daily schedule includes two exercise classes in the air-conditioned gym and pool. Otherwise you're on your own to schedule massages, swim in the two outdoor pools (one with filtered saltwater), or soak in the hot tub or whirlpools. The treatment rooms, which possess a clinical quality, are separated from hallway traffic by only a curtain. The staff nutritionist meets with each new guest to work out a weekly menu. All food prepared by the kitchen is low in salt, fat, and sugar and high in flavor.

INSIDER TIP Snowbirds looking for an inexpensive way to spend days in the sunshine will like Lido's old-fashioned approach.

Equipment: Free weights, stair climbers, stationary bikes, treadmills. **Services:** Aromatherapy, loofah body scrub, reflexology, salt glow, shiatsu. **Swimming:** 2 pools. **Classes and Programs:** Aerobics, aquaerobics, line-dance lessons. **Recreation:** Bingo, dancing, shuffleboard.

106 rooms, 15 apartments.

✗ Meals included. American cuisine served in dining room. Kosher and vegetarian food on request. **Sample Meals:** Chicken Caesar salad, broiled tilapia (lunch); stuffed lobster, veal scallopini (dinner).

Nightly rate $65–$81 per person, double occupancy, includes lodging, meals, exercise classes. AE, MC, V.

✉ *40 Island Ave., Miami Beach, FL 33139,* ☎ *305/538–4621 or 800/ 327–8363,* FAX *305/534–3680.*

PGA NATIONAL RESORT & SPA

LUXURY PAMPERING ∘ SPORTS CONDITIONING

Serious golfers, including some prominent members of the Professional Golfers Association, work on their game and work out the kinks afterward at the PGA National Resort & Spa. The 2,340-acre complex includes five 18-hole golf courses, 19 tennis courts, nine swimming pools, and a full-service European-style spa. It might sound overwhelming, but all these amenities are huddled in a conveniently compact area.

Though there is no organized spa program, you can plan your own comprehensive health and fitness regimen or create an action-oriented sport-and-spa package. As part of the latter, workouts with professional trainers are combined with spa services designed to enhance your sports performance. You can then hone your skills at golf, tennis, or even croquet.

More than 100 skin care and body services are offered in nearly 30 treatment rooms at the Mediterranean-inspired spa building, which lies secluded in a gated garden just steps from the hotel. Here you'll find outdoor therapy pools, dubbed "Waters of the World," that simulate those you'd find abroad. One pool re-creates the sensation of floating in the warm waters of the Dead Sea, while another takes you to the chilly waters of the Alps. Inside the spa aromatherapy massage is the specialty, tailored to your lifestyle. Essential oils are mixed to match whatever your need, whether you require perking up, settling down, or anything in between. The treatments, given in a dimly lighted treatment room that has the cloistered feel of a monk's cell, continue to work hours after you leave. Other signature therapies include a seaweed body mask and polish, sea-foam mud wrap, thalassotherapy gel mask, and watsu, a watery form of shiatsu.

At the Health & Racquet Club, instructors recommend workout programs to develop specific muscle groups and cardiovascular strength. Skiers might train on cross-country machines, while tennis players might work out on the treadmill. Daily yoga and aerobics classes— from step in the aerobics studio to workouts in the club's lap pool— are open to all resort guests.

Since this is national headquarters for the PGA, golf is the principal recreation. Courses designed by Jack Nicklaus, Arnold Palmer, and others challenge pros as well as amateurs. Try the daily clinics, private lessons, or sign up for the National Golf Academy. For children the PGA offers summer golf programs.

Of the resort's eight restaurants, Citrus Tree, where robed spa clients can sneak into a special private room, is dedicated to spa and sports nutrition cuisine. Arezzo offers a selection of healthy Italian items. Spa cuisine service is also available in the spa.

INSIDER TIP To see the part of Florida that isn't packed with tourists, sign up for an ecotour through mangrove-lined lakes, rivers, and scenic estuaries.

Equipment: Cross-country ski machines, free weights, rowing machines, stair climbers, stationary bikes, treadmills, weight-training circuit. **Services:** Algae wrap, aromatherapy, hydrotherapy, lymphatic massage, reflexology, salt glow, seaweed body polish, Vichy shower. **Swimming:** 9 pools. **Classes and Programs:** Aerobics, body-composition analysis, fitness evaluation, golf and tennis instruction, yoga. **Recreation:** Croquet, golf, jogging, racquetball, tennis, volleyball. **Children's Programs:** Daily baby-sitting, golf and tennis instruction.

⌨ 339 rooms, 60 suites, 65 villas.

✕ Meals à la carte. 8 restaurants serve American and Italian food. Citrus Tree serves spa cuisine. **Sample Meals:** Vegetable burrito, grilled chicken gyro, turkey burger, chicken fajita (lunch); yellowfin tuna teriyaki, spa filet mignon, spa lasagna, shrimp fra diavolo (dinner).

🖾 Nightly rate $129–$509 per room. 2-night spa plan $510–$1,030, includes lodging, some meals, spa treatments. Day spa package $275–$435, includes lunch. AE, DC, MC, V.

⌧ *400 Ave. of the Champions, Palm Beach Gardens, FL 33418,* ☎ *561/627–2000 or 800/633–9150, spa reservations 800/843–7725,* FAX *561/622–0261. www.pga-resorts.com*

PIER HOUSE

LUXURY PAMPERING

As its name implies, the nautically inspired Pier House is a Caribbean-style resort with the laid-back air of Key West. A "don't worry, be happy" mentality prevails here. The biggest event of the day may well be watching the spectacular sunset with a drink in hand.

In the heart of Key West's Old Town, the spa is the perfect place to recharge and rejuvenate after exploring the colorful houses, interesting shops, and plentiful bars of an often boisterous city that takes fun seriously. A short stroll brings you to the historic home named after nature illustrator John James Audubon, Ernest Hemingway's cat-dominated domain, Harry Truman's Little White House, and a host of other attractions.

The Caribbean Spa, in a dramatic two-story building surrounded by tropical plants, has professional trainers and aestheticians on hand to develop your personalized program. Try the Caribbean Coma, a 90-minute combination of massage, reflexology, and paraffin treatment on your hands and feet. A harbor view is the bonus to joining the daily aerobics classes, held in the resort's waterside disco. Options include step and low-impact aerobics. You can also join the aquaerobics session held in the swimming pool. Afterward you can relax on the tiny beach, where nude sunbathers bask on the rocks.

Guest rooms are in the hotel's main building and a smaller building on the beach. You'll dine mostly on seafood, with a few healthy selections. It isn't serious spa cuisine, but no one comes here to lose weight. An in-spa menu offers breakfast and lunch selections.

INSIDER TIP Reserve one of 22 spa rooms, some of which have private steam bath and sauna. Wicker furnishings, ceiling fans, and French doors that open onto private patios or balconies evoke a tropical mood.

Equipment: Free weights, rowing machine, stair climbers, stationary bikes, treadmills, weight-training circuit. **Services:** Aromatherapy, loofah scrub, mud body treatment, reflexology. **Swimming:** Pool, beach. **Classes and Programs:** Aerobics, aquaerobics, body sculpting, tai chi, yoga. **Recreation:** Jogging.

⌨ 128 rooms, 14 suites.

✕ Meals à la carte. Pier House Restaurant and Harbor View Café serve Caribbean fare, Pier House Market Bistro serves deli favorites. Spa menu available. **Sample Meals:** Purple potato salade Niçoise, cold chicken with lime dressing, grilled chili-shrimp salad (lunch); ahi tuna sushi, grilled vegetable salad, Caribbean pork tenderloin, grilled mahimahi (dinner).

🕮 Nightly rate $195–$1,600 per room. 2-night Stress Breaker Plus package $784–$1,008 per couple, includes breakfast. Day spa package $216. AE, DC, MC, V.

✉ *1 Duval St., Key West, FL 33040,* ☎ *305/296–4600 or 800/327–8340,* FAX *305/296–7568. www.pierhouse.com*

PLAZA RESORT

LUXURY PAMPERING

Small but luxurious, the Ocean Waters Spa at the Plaza Resort manages to stand up to competition from larger operations on Daytona Beach with its art nouveau touches, relaxing atmosphere, and high level of personal service.

The spa's 15 Serenity rooms include a couples massage room, a wrap room with a Vichy shower, and a computerized hydrobath room. The menu of spa treatments ranges from traditional (facials and massages) to cutting-edge (hydrotherapy and hot stone treatments). In the Utopia Room you can munch on fresh fruit and other goodies, sip mineral water, watch a big-screen television, and order a spa lunch.

Next door, the salon sports shiny new pedicure thrones and other service stations. A small fitness room down the hall has a listing of daily activities that begins with a morning stretch and beach walk. Among the activities you'll find are kickboxing, yoga, and aquaerobics.

Outside, an Olympic-size pool overlooks one of Florida's most famous beaches, where Henry Ford once speed-tested his automobiles and today's beachgoers still drive on wide, hard-packed sands. The hotel lies within walking distance of the hub of beach activity, a boardwalk amusement area and fishing pier. Go-carts, miniature golf, and a new water park along Atlantic Avenue make this a top family destination. Less than 10 minutes away, the famous Daytona International Speedway offers tours.

Plaza Resort provides a comfortable base for local explorations. Its 322 rooms and suites are stocked with coffeemakers, microwaves, and mini-refrigerators. Café del Mar promises spa cuisine and seafood prepared with an international flair. A poolside snack bar provides quick and light meals.

INSIDER TIP Plaza Resort, Daytona Beach's first destination spa, is still a bargain. Book now before the rates go up.

Equipment: Free weights, stair climbers, stationary bikes, treadmills, weight-training circuit. **Services:** Algae wrap, aromatherapy, fango wrap, floral wrap, moor mud wrap, reflexology, salt glow, shiatsu. **Swimming:** Pool, beach. **Classes and Programs:** Aquaerobics, personal training, tai chi, yoga.

🛏 322 rooms and suites.

✕ Meals à la carte. Spa cuisine served in the spa and at Café del Mar. **Sample Meals:** Gazpacho, sun-dried tomato pita, chilled poached salmon (lunch).

Nightly rate $59–$149 per room. 2-night spa package $469–$499 per person, double occupancy, includes lodging, breakfast, and lunch. 4-night spa package $749–$799 per person, double occupancy, includes lodging, breakfast, and lunch. AE, D, DC, MC, V.

✉ *600 N. Atlantic Ave., Daytona Beach, FL 32118,* ☎ *904/255–4471 or 800/767–4471,* FAX *904/253–7672. www.plazaresortandspa.com*

PONTE VEDRA INN & CLUB

LUXURY PAMPERING ∘ SPORTS CONDITIONING

Vacationers haven't always filled the 300-acre stretch of northeastern Florida coastline now occupied by the Ponte Vedra Inn & Club. Zirconium and other minerals were mined here until 1928, when some alumni of Princeton University built the hotel. The resort now includes 36 holes of golf, 15 tennis courts, four swimming pools, and miles of pristine white beaches. The full-service spa and fitness center are more recent additions.

The inn's main building, paneled in dark wood, has a clubby feel, but not to worry—guests are treated like members. Lodgings are in nine cottage-style buildings clustered around the golf courses. Most of the spacious rooms have private terraces or balconies with ocean views. Additional accommodations and a second health club are at a sister property, the Lodge, a little more than a mile from the main complex.

The 10,000-square-ft beachfront spa, which resembles a big beach house, has whitewashed walls and a terra-cotta-tile roof topped by a lighted cupola that gives it a distinctly Florida feeling. Inside there are five massage rooms, five facial rooms, a wet room with whirlpool tubs and shower beds, and a salon. More than 100 services are available. Enjoy your treatments with a beach view or in a darkened room free from distractions. The ground-floor fitness center overlooks the pounding surf through huge picture windows and has more than 50 pieces of exercise equipment. Aerobics classes open to all resort guests are held here daily, including aquaerobics sessions in the outdoor pool.

INSIDER TIP Set in an upscale neighborhood, Ponte Vedra Inn exudes an air of exclusivity but is conveniently close to the tourism scenes of St. Augustine and Jacksonville Beach.

Equipment: Cross-country ski machines, free weights, stair climbers, stationary bikes, treadmills. **Services:** Algae scrub, aromatherapy, body peel, body polish, herbal wrap, hot stone massage, sea mud pack. **Swimming:** 4 pools, beach. **Classes and Programs:** Aerobics, personal training. **Recreation:** Biking, boating, golf, sailing, tennis, water sports. **Children's Programs:** Youth camp for ages 4–12, daily baby-sitting.

🛏 162 rooms, 40 suites.

✗ Meals à la carte. 4 restaurants serve international cuisine. The Seafoam Room has a spa menu. A spa lunch is served in the spa's sunny dining room. **Sample Meals:** Broiled snapper, grilled chicken, seafood and greens salad, and pasta à la jardinière (dinner).

Nightly rate $160–$395 per room. 2-night spa package $294 per person, double occupancy, includes breakfast, spa treatments. Day spa package $155–$295. AE, D, DC, MC, V.

✉ *200 Ponte Vedra Blvd., Ponte Vedra Beach, FL 32082,* ☎ *904/285–1111 or 800/234–7842,* FAX *904/285–2111. www.pvresorts.com*

PRITIKIN LONGEVITY CENTER

NUTRITION AND DIET ○ MEDICAL WELLNESS

Like its sister center in California, the Pritikin Longevity Center in Miami Beach is both a resort and a learning center. The highly structured, medically supervised residential program provides the support many people need to take charge of their health. Pritikin is committed to helping people live healthier lives, and the program has proven beneficial to people with hypertension, diabetes, and cancer.

The low-fat diet introduced by the late Nathan Pritikin in 1974 lies at the foundation of one- to four-week programs. Exercise, stress management, and health education are all part of the core curriculum. Supervised by a team of doctors, nutritionists, and physiologists, the center's residents maintain a lively pace. A full physical examination by a physician includes a treadmill stress test and blood analysis. You'll be given a diet and exercise program tailored to your own personal history and fitness level.

Pritikin recently moved to the Turnberry Isle Resort and Club and is now housed in a handsome building adjacent to the marina. The center has also taken over and renovated the original three-tier Turnberry Isle spa, so a variety of spa treatments are available.

Guest accommodations are in two marina-side hotels encircled by lush vegetation. Rooms are designer-decorated in pale woods and earth tones.

INSIDER TIP The fitness regimen here demands discipline, so don't expect a fun-in-the-sun holiday. Along with about 100 other participants, you work out at least three times a day.

Equipment: Free weights, rowing machines, stair climbers, stationary bikes, treadmills, weight-training circuit. **Services:** Aromatherapy, herbal wrap, loofah salt glow, mud treatment, reflexology. **Swimming:** Pool, beach. **Classes and Programs:** Aerobics, aquaerobics, qigong, private counseling on nutrition and health, physical exams, stretch, yoga.

▦ 18 rooms, 56 suites.

✗ Meals included. Buffet-style breakfast and lunch, table service at dinner. **Sample Meals:** Spinach, black-bean and vegetable crepe, golden split pea soup, vegetable stir-fry, tropical fruit cup (lunch); grilled jumbo Portobello mushrooms, steamed fresh asparagus, salmon paella (dinner).

▦ 1-week program $2,730 per person. AE, MC, V.

✉ *19735 Turnberry Way, Aventura, FL 33180* ☎ *305/935–7131 or 800/327–4914,* FAX *305/935–7111. www.pritikinfl.com*

SADDLEBROOK RESORT TAMPA

LUXURY PAMPERING ○ SPORTS CONDITIONING

If you are serious about your tennis or golf game, Saddlebrook Resort's excellent programs are guaranteed to raise your score. Fitness training here is geared specifically toward your sports goals. The spa provides the finishing touches with muscle-relaxing sports massages.

The resort's Harry Hopman Tennis Program is in action daily on 45 courts featuring a variety of surfaces from traditional red clay to Wimbledon-style grass. Highly rated by Tennis magazine, the tennis camp offers sessions of varying lengths for teenagers and adults. Specialized programs are designed for players of all skill levels, and personal training for five hours is available. All programs include unlimited access to the cardiovascular and strength-building exercise equipment at the Sports Village.

Saddlebrook's golf facilities are equally impressive. The Arnold Palmer Golf Academy has its world headquarters here, employing two 18-hole courses designed by Palmer as well as a special driving range and putting green. Designed to simulate all the features of a golf course, the practice area is used for group and individual instruction. Stretching and exercises to improve your golf swing are combined with hands-on course training and video analysis. Programs are scheduled to last anywhere from a half day to five days.

The 480-acre resort encircles the free-form 50,000-gallon pool. The main building houses an elegant, clublike dining room and bar, as well as ballrooms and convention facilities. For such a vast property, navigation is incredibly easy. Paved pathways and wooden bridges provide easy access to the golf courses and swimming pool. Accommodations in two-story lodges are modern, spacious, and comfortable, with sliding glass doors to a terrace or balcony.

The spa, which was designed to complement the golf and tennis programs, provides all the necessary facilities but no structured program. Under the direction of new spa director Valarie Maloff, the spa has become wildly popular, so be sure to make reservations weeks in advance. On your first visit a therapist greets you in the lounge and leads you to one of the dozen treatment rooms. There are special therapies for sports-related problems—hydromassage (recommended for tennis tension), an herbal or seaweed body wrap, and a Vichy shower. Although the tub is, unfortunately, a bit snug for two adults, the adroit fingers of the spa's excellent therapists take care of cramped muscles and any other aches, pains, or stress. You can preorder lunch for an alfresco break in the courtyard, where you can feel comfortable dining in your spa robe.

A half-mile path through lodges and over a cypress swamp leads to the Sports Village. Facilities include 14 tennis courts, a 1⅓-acre soccer and softball field, sand and grass volleyball courts, a regulation-size basketball court, a swimming pool, a whirlpool, and a boccie court. Stretching and exercise classes are held in an open-air pavilion.

INSIDER TIP Want to see some of the top tennis stars? Pros such as Pete Sampras and Martina Hingis come here to drill for tournaments.

Equipment: Cross-country trainer, elliptical trainers, stair climbers, stationary bikes, treadmills, weight-training circuit. **Services:** Aromatherapy, balneotherapy, body polish, herbal wrap, lymphatic massage, mud wrap, reflexology, salt glow, seaweed wrap, shiatsu. **Swimming:** 3 pools. **Classes and Programs:** Aerobics, body-composition analysis, fitness evaluation, golf and tennis clinics, nutrition consultations, personal training. **Recreation:** Basketball, biking, boccie, golf, tennis, volleyball. **Children's Programs:** S'Kids Club for ages 4–12.

▥ 800 rooms and suites.

✕ Breakfast and dinner included. Spa menu contains information on calories and fat. Cypress Restaurant serves seafood, Dempsey's Steak House serves American cuisine. **Sample Meals:** Gazpacho, minted strawberry soup, fruit salad, tabbouleh pita sandwich, turkey burger, pan-seared snapper with yogurt, stir-fry tofu and vegetables (lunch); baby spinach salad, sea bass in parchment, pan-seared scallops (dinner).

⌨ Nightly rate $120–$185 per person, double occupancy, includes breakfast and dinner. Spa Escape packages $217–$377 per night per person, double occupancy, includes lodging, breakfast and dinner, and spa treatments. Day spa packages $190–$345. AE, D, MC, V.

✉ *5700 Saddlebrook Way, Wesley Chapel, FL 33543,* ☎ *813/973–1111 or 800/729–8383,* 𝖥𝖠𝖷 *813/973–4505. www.saddlebrookresort.com*

SAFETY HARBOR RESORT

LUXURY PAMPERING ○ NUTRITION AND DIET ○ MINERAL SPRINGS

Morning strolls along beautiful Bayshore Drive, swimming laps under swaying palms, and soaking in mineral-spring water count among the pleasures of a vacation at Safety Harbor Resort. Built during the 1980s fitness fad, the low-slung Mediterranean-style resort has adjusted to today's more relaxed views about fitness.

With five mineral springs on the property, hydrotherapy has become a major feature of the spa. Chemical analysis shows that each spring contains a different proportion of healthful minerals such as calcium, magnesium, sodium, and potassium. The hotel uses the thermal water in all its hot tubs, whirlpools, swimming pools, and even the water coolers.

It's not surprising that water treatments are a focus here. Private men's and women's hydrotherapy tubs are enhanced with blends of herbs and algae for stress reduction, relief of muscular tension, and toning the skin. Exercising in specially designed 3½ ft indoor and outdoor lap pools burns calories efficiently without straining the body. Even out of the water, though, exercise instructors promote low-impact routines, and the shock-absorbing floors are specially constructed to help you avoid tendonitis and shin splints. The instructors specialize in a variety of routines, from energy meditation to boxercise.

When you check in, a member of the fitness staff will check your overall physical condition, monitor your heart rate, and analyze your body-fat-to-muscle ratio. Based on a computer analysis, a specific combination of exercise and diet will be recommended. Don't expect interaction with other guests; you're pretty much on your own until meeting kindred souls on group shopping excursions or in the dining room.

For more active pursuits there's Phil Green's Tennis Academy, where one-hour classes take place daily for beginning, intermediate, and advanced players. Unlimited use of the tennis courts for daytime play, a golf driving range overlooking the water, and play at a nearby golf course are other options.

INSIDER TIP Beginners will feel comfortable here. The average guest's age is 40, with a smattering of older clients (often snowbirds on an extended vacation) and the occasional twentysomething fitness fanatic.

Equipment: Cross-country ski machines, free weights, rowing machines, stair climbers, stationary bikes, treadmills, weight-training circuit. **Services:** Aromatherapy, herbal wrap, loofah body scrub, mud wrap, reflexology, salt glow, shiatsu. **Swimming:** 2 outdoor pools, 1 indoor pool. **Classes and Programs:** Fitness evaluation, golf and tennis instruction, medical assessment, nutritional consultation. **Recreation:** Biking, tennis, volleyball.

🛏 193 rooms.

✕ Meals à la carte. Spa cuisine available in main dining room or café.
Sample Meals: Vegetable quesadillas, grouper-cake sandwich (lunch);
Oriental salad, lime-broiled shrimp and scallops, Asian vegetable stir-
fry (dinner).

▨ Nightly rate $89–$199 per room. 3-night introductory spa package
$450–$603 per person, double occupancy, includes lodging, meals, spa
treatments. 4-night spa package $880–$1,064 per person, double occupancy, includes lodging, meals, spa treatments. AE, D, DC, MC, V.

✉ *105 N. Bayshore Dr., Safety Harbor, FL 34695,* FAX *727/726–1161
or 888/237–8772 for reservations or information, 800/237–0155 for
spa appointments,* FAX *727/726–4268. www.safetyharborspa.com*

SANIBEL HARBOUR RESORT & SPA

LUXURY PAMPERING ∘ SPORTS CONDITIONING

Once known primarily as a tennis resort—it's home to a 5,500-seat
tennis stadium—Sanibel Harbour Resort & Spa's focus is changing to
overall fitness. In addition to a wide range of weight-training equipment, the gym has an impressive repertoire of free weights and a cardiovascular theater connected to a sound system. A glass-walled gym
offers more than 40 aerobics classes a week, taught at a variety of levels in a plush studio with carpeted floor. Choices range from tai chi
and interval training to fitness boxing. The spa's indoor lap pool is used
for energizing power splash classes.

The spa offers a wide range of body treatments—aromatherapy, salt-
glow body scrub, and seaweed wraps. For a sonic massage, relax on
the BETAR bed, a combination of aromatherapy and stress-releasing
musical impulses with your choice of music, from Bach to rock. One
of only 16 such systems throughout the world, it surrounds you in sound
and enhances the soothing qualities of music by sending gentle vibra-
tions through your body.

The racquet club schedules daylong tennis workouts for all skill levels with tennis star Phil Green. There are nine lighted courts, so you
can even sneak in a few games after watching a spectacular sunset. Bring
your own racket or rent equipment at the pro shop.

Rooms and suites in the resort's main building have private balconies
and Florida-style pale wood furniture. At a newer inn guests enjoy
more intimacy and European charm, but with all the same amenities.
For more space and luxury, condominium apartments in two 12-story
towers provide fully equipped kitchens and dining rooms as well as two
bedrooms and two baths. Among the resort's restaurants, Chez le Bear
is the most refined, serving Mediterranean fare. The Promenade serves
healthy selections overlooking the swimming pool and the ocean. Spa
guests may preorder from this menu for service in the spa dining room.

Recreation at Sanibel Harbor is family friendly, with sailing and boating excursions at the marina. Daily trips take you to secluded islands
for beaching and lunching, on wildlife dolphin expeditions, and on romantic dinner cruises. There's also a highly acclaimed supervised program for children.

INSIDER TIP Beautiful sunset views of island-dotted San Carlos Bay from
your balcony make this an ideal vacation hideaway.

Equipment: Free weights, stair climbers, stationary bikes, treadmills,
rowing machines, weight-training circuit. **Services:** Algae scrub, aro-

matheraphy, fango mud pack, mango salt glow, milk-and-honey body wrap, reflexology, seaweed wrap. **Swimming:** 5 outdoor pools, 1 indoor pool, beach. **Classes and Programs:** Fitness evaluation, nutritional counseling, personal training, tennis instruction. **Recreation:** Basketball, canoeing, fishing, hiking, racquetball, tennis, volleyball. **Children's Programs:** Kids Klub for ages 5–12.

▦ 281 rooms, 66 suites, 70 2-bedroom condominiums.

✕ Meals à la carte. **Sample Meals:** Seared ahi tuna salad, grilled Portobello sandwich (lunch); basil linguini, pan-seared red snapper, Colorado rack of lamb (dinner).

▦ Nightly rate $145–$549, double occupancy. 2-night spa package $400–$570 per person, double occupancy, includes lodging, meals, spa treatments. Day spa packages $99–$263. AE, D, DC, MC, V.

✉ *17260 Harbour Pointe Dr., Fort Myers, FL 33908,* ☎ *941/466–2157 (spa), 941/466–4000 (resort), or 800/767–7777,* FAX *941/466–2198. www.safetyharborspa.com*

TURNBERRY ISLE RESORT & CLUB

LUXURY PAMPERING

If you prefer a luxurious resort that feels more like a country club than a health spa, consider Turnberry Isle Resort & Spa. The verdant 300-acre grounds, tucked away within North Miami's busy Aventura, straddle the Intracoastal Waterway. Continual van service transports guests along the flower-lined roads that lead between the main hotel at the golf and tennis club, the marina, and the beach club.

The luxurious new facility, which opened in 2000, has state-of-the-art fitness, spa, and salon facilities. Turnberry's new three-level spa sweeps you away in luxury up a spiral staircase to the second floor's 26 Italian-tile treatment rooms, some with their own balconies. The range of services is extensive. For example, for the exfoliating body treatments aestheticians use Dead Sea muds, loofah salts, and citrus products. The spa recently introduced tandem massage in which two therapists use choreographed movements for twice the results. The third-floor fitness center features an aerobics studio with a skylight. The fitness center also offers private trainers and top-of-the-line equipment.

The focus of Turnberry's sport facilities is golf and tennis. Designed by Robert Trent Jones, the splashy South Course, known for the oft-photographed 18th-hole island green, has treacherous water traps on all but a handful of holes. By contrast, Jones's challenging North Course provides smooth, consistent greens. Former Wimbledon competitor Fred Stolle heads the tennis pro staff. Turnberry Isles offers a junior tennis program and special Sunday-afternoon kids' events.

Spacious executive-class accommodations are found in the Mediterranean-style complex. Rooms are in four red-tile-roofed buildings named for tropical blossoms and set amid lush gardens enclosing a patio courtyard pool. Rooms and suites are decorated with lots of wood and polish. All come with marble baths, three phones (with two lines), and a fax machine. This is Turnberry, so all rooms have fresh orchids.

INSIDER TIP Turnberry's shuttle bus can deposit you at the upscale Aventura Mall, a massive celebration of the good life. There are enough restaurants and shops for it to qualify as a small city. In the morning it's open early for power walks.

Equipment: Stair climbers, stationary bikes, weight-training circuit. **Services:** Algae wrap, aromatherapy, balneotherapy, herbal wrap, loofah salt glow, mud treatments, reflexology, shiatsu. **Classes and Programs:** Fitness profile analysis, private training. **Swimming:** 2 pools, beach. **Recreation:** Golf, tennis, yachting. **Children's Programs:** Baby-sitting and 2-hr Sun.-afternoon program.

▦ 395 rooms, suites.

✕ Meals à la carte. Four restaurants serve lower-fat items on request. **Sample Meals:** Lavosh (Armenian cracker bread) roll-up sandwich, Florida fruit salad, broiled sea bass (lunch); grilled veal chops, ginger- and soy-glazed ahi tuna, baked yellowtail snapper (dinner).

▧ Nightly rate $175–$465 per room. 2-night Rejuvenating Escape $389–$559 per person, double occupancy, includes lodging, breakfast, spa treatments. Day spa package $220–$260, includes lunch. AE, DC, MC, V.

✉ *19999 W. Country Club Dr., Aventura, North Miami, FL 33180,* ☎ *305/936–2929 or 800/223–6800,* ℻ *305/933–6560. www.turnberryisle.com*

WYNDHAM RESORT & SPA

LUXURY PAMPERING ○ SPORTS CONDITIONING

The Wyndham Resort slowly evolved into a pampering and beauty destination as it made its transition from its former life as the Bonaventure Spa. It still, however, has one of Florida's largest and best-designed spas as well as a popular spa dining room.

Guests tend to opt for either unlimited exercise classes, expert bodywork, and beauty treatments or outdoor sports at the 23-acre resort's 15 clay tennis courts, two 18-hole golf courses, and five swimming pools. A daylong schedule of activities enhances sports training with targeted workouts. Classes range from interval training to yoga to aquaerobics.

Somewhat old-fashioned, the spa is spacious, a place where one can relax in large lounges. It holds more than 50 treatment rooms. Privacy here is ensured by separate wings for men and women, each with its own lap pool and sundeck, steam room and Swiss showers, hot and cold plunge pools, and whirlpools. The aerobics studio has a suspended wooden floor, fitness equipment, and a cardiovascular theater. The salon offers makeup classes and lessons in addition to extensive hair styling, manicure, and pedicure services, as well as permanent makeup and dermatological services.

Guest rooms and suites are in nine four-story buildings amid the verdant grounds, which boast tropically landscaped free-form pools. Large rooms with balconies overlook the lake or golf course. Oversize bathrooms have a dressing area.

INSIDER TIP This is a good place to bring the kids, as Wyndham's children's program is complimentary.

Equipment: Free weights, rowing machines, stair climbers, stationary bikes, treadmills. **Services:** Algae wrap, aromatherapy massage, craniosacral therapy, herbal wrap, loofah body scrub, reflexology, shiatsu. **Swimming:** 5 pools. **Classes and Programs:** Aerobics, body-composition analysis, golf and tennis lessons, Spinning, weight training. **Recreation:** Biking, golf, tennis. **Children's Program:** Wyndham Kids Klub for ages 5–12.

🏨 400 rooms, 96 suites.

✕ Meals à la carte. Calorie-counted selections at Horizons Restaurant and on spa poolside menu. **Sample Meals:** Quesadilla with fruit salsa, grilled-shrimp and spinach salad, grilled chicken sandwich, shrimp linguini (lunch); Caribbean pan-seared salmon, braised sea bass, ricotta ravioli with lobster medallions (dinner).

💳 Nightly rate $99–$202 per room. 3-night spa package $588–$730 per person, double occupancy, includes lodging, spa treatments. 7-night Ultimate Spa Experience package $1,248–$2,267 per person, double occupancy. Day spa package $199–$249, includes lunch. AE, D, MC, V.

✉ *250 Racquet Club Rd., Fort Lauderdale, FL 33326,* ☎ *954/389–3300 or 800/996–3426, 954/349–5515 for spa reservations,* FAX *954/384–6157. www.wyndham.com*

GEORGIA

CHÂTEAU ÉLAN

LUXURY PAMPERING

Château Élan, in the beautiful northern Georgia countryside, is a picturesque romantic getaway. Days are filled with luxury treatments, gourmet meals, and activities from wine tastings to nature walks. Just a short drive from downtown Atlanta, nothing quite prepares you for the château, which resembles a 16th-century French estate. This 3,500-acre resort, which includes a winery, also boasts an equestrian center, three golf courses, seven restaurants, and a spa.

The main floor of the château includes a library, a lounge where afternoon tea is served, and a dining room with sweeping views of magnificent landscaped greenery. You can choose from 14 suites decorated according to various themes. The Laura Ashley Room features floral fabrics and white-wicker furniture, while the Lodge Loft is a two-story rustic cabin complete with a curly willow headboard, rocking chair, and skylight. Many rooms also feature elaborate tubs or showers for two. If you prefer, you may also choose from the 275 rooms at the French-style inn or 18 small villas bordering the fairways.

At the spa you have more choices to make: hydrotherapy with underwater massage jets, hot stone massage, reflexology, body scrubs, or herbal wraps. The in-house salon is staffed with hair stylists and skin and nail care specialists. You can select from a wide mix of fitness classes, from aquaerobics to yoga.

Dining options are equally numerous. The spa dining room provides low-fat choices in small portions designed to encourage weight loss. For those not counting calories, the concierge will make dinner reservations in the winery's Le Clos, which serves eight courses of classic French cuisine, or at Paddy's Irish Pub, with a menu of traditional food and drink.

More than 60 holes challenge golfers. Three golf icons—Gene Sarazen, Sam Snead, and Kathy Whitworth—designed the Legends, a course that calls to mind some of their greatest challenges. Facilities include three championship courses and a 9-hole walking course. Instruction is available in half-day clinics. The resort also features the region's largest equestrian center, featuring four all-weather arenas, riding trails, and show facility. There is also a seven-court tennis center designed by Stan Smith, as well as indoor and outdoor swimming pools. The winery offers tours and tastings daily and houses shops and a café. Summertime concerts are held in the pavilion.

INSIDER TIP Save time for a soak in the indoor hot tub with its beautiful view of the towering oaks.

Equipment: Free weights, stair climbers, stationary bikes, treadmills. **Services:** Aromatherapy, body wrap, deep-tissue massage, hot-stone massage, hydrotherapy, reflexology, salt glow, thalassotherapy. **Swimming:** 2 pools. **Classes and Programs:** Aerobics, aquaerobics, fitness evaluation, personal training, stretching, tai chi, yoga. **Recreation:** Biking, golf, hiking, horseback riding, tennis.

🛏 275 rooms, 18 villas.

✕ Meals à la carte. Le Clos serves French cuisine; Paddy's Irish Pub serves pub grub; Spa dining room serves low-fat options. **Sample Meals:** Seared red snapper, pasta with fresh vegetables and tomato sauce (lunch); shrimp salad with Japanese rolls, grilled tuna and cucumber, spaghetti (dinner).

💳 Nightly rate $170–$275 per room, includes breakfast and tea and use of spa facilities. Day spa package $228–$405, includes lunch, afternoon tea, winery tour and tasting, spa services. AE, D, DC, MC, V.

✉ *100 Rue Charlemagne, Braselton, GA 30517,* ☎ *678/425–0900 or 800/233–9463 (outside Atlanta),* 📠 *678/425–6000. www. chateauelan.com*

THE CLOISTER ON SEA ISLAND

LUXURY PAMPERING

Pack your dancing shoes for a beach escape on one of the prettiest barrier islands along the Atlantic coast. Fun and fitness meet at the Cloister on Sea Island. You can join a morning walk on the sandy beach, enjoy sophisticated pampering in the privacy of spa suites, then dance the night away to the sounds of a big band.

At the resort's white-stucco Beach Club, the Sea Island Spa is steps from swimming pools and surf. The facial treatments here become a succession of cleansing and soothing experiences as four layers of aloe, seaweed, and creams are applied. While your complexion is being detoxified and moisturized to combat the ravages of time and sun, your feet are softened with paraffin wax. The final touch may be a reflexology massage, 1 of 18 techniques offered by staff therapists. Hydrotherapy is available in a specially designed tub with underwater massage jets to enhance the soothing effect of seaweed or herbal extracts added to the bath.

Set up a personal schedule with a spa programmer prior to your arrival, as appointments for treatments tend to fill up during peak periods. The facilities are spacious, but only nine treatment rooms are available, and the aerobics studio gets full with a dozen in the class.

Sports add a special dimension to this seaside escape. The Cloister offers 54 holes of golf at two clubs, plus an acclaimed golf learning center with indoor and outdoor training by professionals. Water sports, a tennis club with 17 courts, a cycling center with nearly 500 bikes for rent, stables with 24 horses, a gun club, and docks for boat rental and fishing expeditions on the Intracoastal Waterway are also available.

Accommodations include private cottages and beach houses overlooking the Atlantic, inland waterways, or lush gardens. All oceanfront rooms have patios or balconies. Despite the modern accommodations, tradition clings to the Cloister as attractively as the Spanish moss dangling from old oak trees shading the roads. The main building, a 1928 Mediterranean palazzo designed by Addison Mizner, is the setting for gourmet meals (there's also a limited selection of spa cuisine) followed by ballroom or modern dancing. The family-oriented Beach Club bustles with breakfast and luncheon buffets, heavy on Southern specialties but also offering light fare.

INSIDER TIP Indulge in thalassotherapy, which is a major attraction here. Treatments include seaweed masks and salt scrubs to nourish and cleanse the skin.

Equipment: Elliptical trainers, free weights, stair climbers, stationary bikes, weight-training circuit. **Services:** Aromatherapy, body scrub, deep-tissue massage, herbal or seaweed wrap, mud herb bath, sea stone massage. **Swimming:** 2 pools, beach. **Classes and Programs:** Fitness evaluation, nutrition consultation, personal training. **Recreation:** Biking, boating, golf, horseback riding, sea kayaking, skeet shooting, tennis, windsurfing. **Children's Programs:** Kids' fitness classes during holidays. Teenage golf clinic. Supervised program for ages 3–12.

🛏 286 rooms.

✕ Meals included. Beach Club, Golf Club, and Island Club serve casual American fare; Dining Room serves international fare. Spa cuisine available. **Sample Meals:** Buffet salads, soups, fruit salad, club sandwiches, hamburgers (lunch); escargot, seafood bisque, hearts of romaine with tomato and goat cheese tart, lemon-pepper fettuccine, smoked pheasant, roasted veal, broiled lobster tail (dinner).

💳 Nightly rate $185–$892 per person, double occupancy. 1-day spa package $350–$660 per person, double occupancy. AE, D, DC, MC, V.

✉ *Sea Island, GA 31561,* ☎ *912/638–3611 or 800/732–4752,* FAX *912/ 638–5159. www.seaisland.com*

FOUR SEASONS RESORT HUALALAI

LUXURY PAMPERING

At the beginning of the millennium, Hualalai Sports Club and Spa was named the top resort spa in North America by *Condé Nast Traveler*. The magazine might easily have bestowed similar accolades on the entire resort. Built in 1996, this is a place that showcases the best of Hawai'i. Restaurants are so close to the ocean you wonder what happens when the tide comes in. One of the five swimming pools has a special edge that makes it appear as if the water overflows right into the deep blue sea.

Like all Four Seasons resorts, Hualalai is known for its high level of service. But unlike others in the chain, this one seems truly Hawaiian. The buildings seem to fit right into the landscape. Accommodations are in low-level complexes connected by winding, plumeria-lined pathways lighted at night with flaming torches. Well appointed and very spacious, the rooms have a serene, tropical decor. All have large lanais facing the ocean with comfortable lounge chairs and tables that make room-service breakfasts in the fresh air almost irresistible.

The spa complex is probably the best equipped in the state. Many treatments are offered indoors, particularly those involving Vichy showers, but five open-air massage tables are shaded by thatched roofs in a garden. The spa's most decadent treatment is the Decleor Deluxe. The treatment, which lasts nearly two hours, begins with a luxurious body wrap and massage, followed by a Vichy shower. Finally, aromatic oils are massaged into the back, neck, and shoulders to enhance a sense of relaxed well-being.

Exercise equipment is in a gym surrounded with glass doors that are slid open during the day. Fitness buffs can take advantage of state-of-the art exercise machines on a shaded patio.

INSIDER TIP Don't miss the two fitness hikes offered here. One takes small groups to explore a lava tube cave; the other crosses varied terrain of sand, lava, and coral to reach the peak of a cinder cone with an inspiring view.

Equipment: Free weights, punching bags, rowing machine, stair climbers, stationary bikes, treadmills, weight-training circuits. **Services:** Acupressure, acupuncture, aloe and herbal wraps, aromatherapy, craniosacral therapy, lomi ho'ola (hot rock treatment), salt glow, shiatsu. **Swimming:** 5 pools, beach. **Classes and Programs:** Aerobics, body composition, boxing aerobics, exercise and weight loss, fitness assessment, interval step aerobics, swimming lessons, tai chi, yoga. **Recreation:** Canoeing, golf, hiking, tennis. **Children's Programs:** Free children's programs.

⌶ 212 rooms, 31 suites.

✕ Meals à la carte. Beach Tree Bar and Grill, Pahu i'a Restaurant Residents' Beach House, and the Club Grille serve varied cuisine. All feature Four Seasons alternative cuisine, which is lighter and healthier fare. **Sample Meals:** Opakapaka (Hawaiian pink snapper) with shiitake mushrooms, Chinese parsley, ginger, and shoyu (dinner).

⌦ Nightly rate $450–$575 per room. 1-night Spa Enthusiast package $1,165–$1,305, includes spa treatments, breakfast. AE, DC, MC, V.

✉ *100 Ka'upulehu Dr., Ka'upulehu/Kona 96740, Box 1269, Kailua-Kona 96745,* ☎ *808/325–8000 or 800/332–3442,* ℻ *808/325–8000 or 800/332–3442,* ℻ *808/325–8100, www.fourseasons.com*

HILTON WAIKOLOA VILLAGE

LUXURY PAMPERING

Mahogany canal boats deposit guests at the Kohala Spa, secluded within the Hilton Waikoloa Village, the Big Island's largest spa resort. Overlooking Waiulua Bay, the spa offers a variety of treatments that combine Eastern and Western therapies.

The spa has spacious facilities and treatments ranging from lomi-lomi massage to thalassotherapy baths infused with limu (seaweed). A resident aromatherapist blends all the oils used in treatments. Body wraps use oils—orchid, coco-mango, rosehip-aloe, and ti leaf—produced on the island. A rain-forest massage combines a warm Vichy shower with a soothing natural bristle brush scrub that relaxes the muscles.

The spa offers Cinema Secrets professional makeup treatments, created by Hollywood-based Maurice Stein. In the full-service salon, which specializes in hair coloring and nail services, every shampoo is completed with a signature shiatsu scalp massage. Provided with a robe, you can lunch in the spa's café on a special low-fat menu.

A huge resort set on 62 acres, Waikoloa Village offers something for everyone. It has a vast swimming pool with waterfalls, hidden grottoes, and a twisting water slide. A gallery holds a collection of Asian and Pacific art. You can sign up to swim with dolphins, take horse-drawn carriage rides into the countryside, and go surfing in catamarans. You can even indulge in a spiritual walk with guided meditation to recall the ancient Kahuna people.

INSIDER TIP Most Hawaiian of the spa's treatments is the Big Island Healing Ritual, during which you sip Hawaiian kava tea while you loll in a private whirlpool bath bubbling with locally produced mineral salts.

Equipment: Cross-country ski machines, free weights, rowing machines, stair climbers, stationary bikes, treadmills, weight-training circuit. **Services:** Acupuncture, aromatherapy, balneotherapy, herbal bath, herbal wrap, lomi lomi, loofah buff, reflexology, shiatsu, thalassotherapy, vibrational therapy.

Swimming: 3 pools, seawater lagoon, beach. **Recreation:** Climbing, diving, golf, horseback riding, racquetball, sailing, skiing, snorkeling, tennis, windsurfing. **Children's Programs:** Children's day camp with lunch.

🛏 1,240 rooms.

✕ Meals à la carte. 10 restaurants serve international cuisine. **Sample Meals:** Chili chicken salad with marinated rice and vegetables in cilantro vinaigrette, poached salmon with cucumber and tomato on Bibb lettuce with dill coulis, vegetable antipasto with tuna (lunch); grilled mahimahi, vegetarian platter (dinner).

💳 Nightly rate $240–$580 per room. 4-night Pleasures in Paradise package $2,262 per person, includes spa treatments. AE, D, DC, MC, V.

✉ *425 Waikoloa Beach Dr., Waikoloa, 96738,* ☎ *808/886–1234 or 800/445–8667,* 📠 *808/886–2900. www.kohalaspa.com*

KALANI OCEANSIDE ECO-RESORT

HOLISTIC HEALTH ○ SPORTS CONDITIONING

Set beside a black-sand beach that steams with thermal springs, Kalani Oceanside Eco-Resort lets you experience the unspoiled natural beauty of the Big Island whether you're getting a massage or participating in an exercise class. Meditation sessions are held on a stunning lava point right beside the ocean.

Founded in 1982, the nonprofit resort on 113 acres of rolling hills attracts an interesting mix of people, from newcomers interested in learning yoga to professionals taking classes in holistic health and preventive medicine. Director Richard Koob says the resort takes pride in the diversity of it clients, which include families and gays.

Therapeutic services and exercise classes are the focus of a Japanese-style spa. The wooden bathhouse has a communal hot tub, sauna heated by wood-burning stove, and private massage rooms. A pool was added in 2000 for underwater massages. Four pavilions are used for yoga, aerobics, and dance performances. Nearby are a 25-ft swimming pool, a hot tub, and a fitness center.

This is perhaps the only Hawaiian spa where you can receive training in lomi lomi and other traditional healing arts. A seven-day seminar enables you to administer treatments to friends and family once you're back home.

In keeping with the spirit of old Hawai'i, most guests are housed in hales, wooden lodges made of cedar logs. Each hexagonal lodge has its own kitchen and ocean-view studio space. There is minimal furniture but many windows. The lodges are decorated with Hawaiian art and fabrics and fresh flowers. Campers can also sleep under the stars at 25 sites among the palms. Accommodations are set perhaps a half mile inland from the beach, but in the still night air the soothing sounds of the ocean are still audible.

....
INSIDER TIP A half hour away, Hawai'i Volcanoes National Park provides a close-up look at rivers of red-hot lava flowing from Mt. Kīlauea.
....

Equipment: Free weights. **Services:** Acupressure, acupuncture, shiatsu. **Swimming:** Pool, tidal ponds, thermal spring, beach. **Classes and Programs:** Culture and health workshops, hula, nutrition counseling, tai chi, sports conditioning, yoga. **Recreation:** Biking, hiking, tennis, volleyball.

🛏 40 rooms, 13 cottages.

✕ Meals à la carte. Primarily vegetarian, with fish and chicken available. Breakfast and lunch buffet, dinner at Café 'Olelo. **Sample Meals:**

Sautéed vegetables with tempeh and tahini sauce, broiled ahi tuna, spinach lasagna (lunch); grilled chicken, baked mahimahi with mushrooms in lemon-and-garlic sauce, cream of papaya-cashew soup, salad bar (dinner).

☏ Nightly rate $110–$240 per room. Tent site $30. Meal plan $27 per day. AE, DC, MC, V.

✉ R.R. 2, Box 4500, Pahoa-Beach Rd., Waikoloa, HI 96778, ☏ 808/965–7828 or 800/800–6886, FAX 808/965–0527. www.kalani.com

THE ORCHID AT MAUNA LANI RESORT

LUXURY PAMPERING

Massages are an art form at the Spa Without Walls, at the Orchid at Mauna Lani Resort, so you'll want to try more than one. Most are administered in three thatched huts beside a tinkling stream. The most romantic of the spa's treatments, a massage for couples, is given in a cabana within 10 ft of the surf.

Although Spa Without Walls has six indoor treatment rooms, Director Jean Sunderland has created healing and wellness programs that capitalize on the resort hotel's beautiful beachfront setting. Tai chi classes are conducted in the shade of palm trees, power walks progress through ancient lava flows, and yoga takes place on the beach.

Some of the oils distilled from Hawaiian plants like pikake, maile, ti, and others are used in the spa. These oils have been used for centuries in ancient Hawaiian healing techniques to relax, release toxins, and rejuvenate the body.

Three relatively new treatments are collectively called Super Body/Mind Synchronization. Each takes about 50 minutes, begins with a 15-minute massage, and then involves donning computer-controlled light-pulse glasses that coax your mind into a relaxed state. Treatments can focus on relaxing the back and neck, on deep relaxation that induces a meditative state, or on an auditory journey that sets your mind free.

INSIDER TIP The warm stone massage is one of the best anywhere in the islands. The message begins with a comforting flat rock under your abdomen and ends with a warm stone on your forehead, which seems to erase all conscious thought.

Equipment: Free weights, rowing machines, stair climbers, stationary bikes, treadmills, weight-training circuit. **Services:** Aromatherapy, lomi lomi, reflexology, shiatsu. **Swimming:** Pool, protected ocean lagoon. **Classes and Programs:** Aerobics, Pilates, tai chi, yoga. **Recreation:** Golf, hiking, tennis, water sports. **Children's Programs:** The Keiki Aloha program is a full or half day of activities for ages 5–12.

🛏 539 rooms, 54 suites.

✗ Meals à la carte. The Grill Restaurant and Lounge offers seafood and game. Brown's Beach House serves Hawai'i regional cuisine, and the Orchid Court serves American cuisine. **Sample Meals:** Smoked marinated chicken sandwich, grilled vegetable wrap, seafood fettuccine (lunch); Parmesan-crusted grilled veal chop, crispy pan-seared duck breast, steamed lobster (dinner).

☏ Nightly rate $385–$650 per room. 1-night spa package $662 per person, double occupancy, includes spa treatments. AE, DC, MC, V.

⊠ *1 N. Kaniku Dr., Kohala Coast, HI 96743,* ☎ *808/885–2000, 800/ 845–9905,* 𝖥𝖠𝖷 *808/885–1064. www.orchid-maunalani.com*

KAUA'I

HYATT REGENCY KAUA'I RESORT & SPA

LUXURY PAMPERING

What's new at the Hyatt Regency Kaua'i Resort & Spa are old Hawaiian healing treatments: the sacred red clay called alaea used as a skin softener in the sea-salt scrubs, the leaves of the ti plant used in body wraps, and the chants once performed by Kahuna high priests that begin the lomi-lomi massage.

The spa's pōhaku massage here takes the concept of a rubdown to a new level. In this treatment a therapist sets warm stones along your spine as well as at your major chakra points. In the Kaua'i Gold treatment your body is painted with clay and wrapped with cellophane and a warm bath sheet. You relax in this mummified state while your face is massaged with a light oil. After a cool shower the pampering concludes with a light 10-minute massage.

An open-air courtyard encloses the lap pool, creating a quiet place to awaken the senses. You can work out in an air-conditioned fitness facility and aerobics studio. Scheduled daily are aerobics, tai chi, and yoga classes and weight-training clinics.

Set on 50 acres of lush beachfront gardens, the long and rambling hotel is built in the style of 1930s plantations. Public areas are decorated with Asian and Pacific art. Adjacent to all this is a 5-acre saltwater lagoon for kayakers, snorkelers, and scuba divers. Surrounding the grottoes, waterfalls, and swimming pools is a Robert Trent Jones II–designed golf course.

Nature lovers and hikers who want to explore the island can schedule a tour of Limahuli Garden, in a lush, green valley dedicated to preserving Hawaiian plants. These gardens, cultivated since 1940, include remnants of a Polynesian settlement believed to have been built a millennium ago. In the rural hamlet of Waimea, where Captain Cook dropped anchor in 1778, retired sugar growers, who share stories of bygone days, will take visitors on a tour of the sugar mill or a former plantation village.

INSIDER TIP This is one of only a few island spas that serves breakfast and lunch, so you can spend a whole day indulging yourself without leaving the spa environs.

Equipment: Free weights, stair climbers, stationary bikes, treadmills, weight-training circuit. **Services:** Aromatherapy, body scrub, lomi lomi, reflexology, shiatsu. **Swimming:** Pool, beach. **Classes and Programs:** Aerobics, scuba classes, tai chi, tennis clinics, yoga. **Recreation:** Biking, golf, hiking, tennis. **Children's Programs:** Camp Hyatt day camp.

▦ 602 rooms.

✕ Meals à la carte. 5 restaurants serve international cuisine. The Kupono Café at the spa is open for breakfast and lunch. **Sample Meals:** Red-lentil chili, grilled eggplant sandwich with olives, onions, and cheese, turkey club layered with avocado, tomato, and organic leaf lettuce (lunch); hot grilled salmon salad, pasta with sautéed Roma tomatoes, sweet peppers, and carrots, grilled fresh salmon (dinner).

✉ Nightly rate $350–$520 per room. 4-night spa package $1,100–$1,450 per person, includes room, breakfast, spa treatments. AE, D, DC, MC, V.

✉ *1571 Poipu Rd., Koloa, Kaua'i, HI 96756,* ☎ *808/742–1234 or 800/55-HYATT,* ℻ *808/742–1557. www.kauai-hyatt.com*

MAUI

GRAND WAILEA RESORT & SPA

LUXURY PAMPERING

Amid the splendor of waterfalls and tranquil pools, the 50,000-square-ft Spa Grande at the Grand Wailea Resort & Spa offers the most extensive health and fitness facilities in Hawai'i. In addition to 42 individual treatment rooms, many with ocean views, there are 10 private hot tubs and Roman-style whirlpools 20 ft in diameter in the atriums of both the men's and women's pavilions.

But all the splashing on this 40-acre resort isn't in the spa. Kids will enjoy the seven water slides and a 2,000-ft artificial river encircling the beach restaurant. Among nine pools, one is specially designed for scuba lessons. For the less adventurous there's a lap pool reserved for adults.

The spa's signature treatment, the Termé Wailea hydrotherapy circuit, begins with a choice of two treatments designed to exfoliate and cleanse the skin: a loofah scrub or Japanese goshi-goshi scrub. Next you have a choice of five specialty baths in marble-and-gold mosaic tubs: aromatherapy for relaxation, Maui mud to nourish the skin, limu to open the pores, herbal to help you feel rejuvenated, and a tropical enzyme bath for toning and softening the skin. Upstairs are private treatment rooms where seven types of massage and five different facials are offered. One scalp treatment combines limu, kelp, ginger, papaya, kukui nuts, and other native Hawaiian plants.

Guests can join a morning walk for miles along a crescent of powder-soft sand or escape the sun in the spa's air-conditioned aerobics studio or fitness center. The two-level beachfront facility has ocean-view suites for couples massage as well as a relaxation room equipped with soothing mechanical massage chairs. Attendants are happy to call room service and have meals delivered so you can enjoy an al fresco meal between classes or treatments. Refreshments are also available from a self-service juice bar.

Across the street from the hotel, three 18-hole golf courses wind through manicured grounds, and a tennis club with 11 courts offers day and night play.

Set amid terraced gardens, the eight-story hotel has a wide range of accommodations, from standard lanai rooms to suites. Spectacular promenades lead to the open-air eateries and restaurants.

....
INSIDER TIP Couples might want to book a "Romantic Interlude." It includes a deliciously decadent Ali'i honey steam wrap, which involves being covered in honey, then wrapped in a sheet for a session in the steam room.
....

Equipment: Free weights, rowing machines, stair climbers, stationary bikes, treadmills, weight-training circuit. **Services:** Aromatherapy, body wraps, herbal bath, lomi lomi, loofah scrub, reflexology, seaweed body pack. **Swimming:** 9 pools, beach. **Classes and Programs:** Aerobics, boxercise, fitness, health, isometrics, nutritional consultations, stress management, stretch, tai chi, yoga. **Recreation:** Billiards, golf, racquetball, tennis. **Children's Programs:** Camp Grande for ages 5–12.

▦ 780 rooms, 52 suites.

✗ Meals à la carte. 6 restaurants serve Italian, Japanese, Mediterranean, and Polynesian fare. **Sample Meals:** Individual pizzas, pasta with grilled pesto chicken (lunch); tuna sashimi with a spicy Szechuan vinaigrette, herb-broiled mahimahi, chili-garlic marinated Hawaiian snapper (dinner).

▨ Nightly rate $390–$525 per room. 1-day spa packages $255–$389. AE, DC, MC, V.

✉ *3850 Wailea Alanui Dr., Wailea, Maui, HI 96753,* ☎ *808/875–1234 or 800/888–6100,* ℻ *808/874–2411. www.grandwailea.com*

HOTEL HANA-MAUI

LUXURY PAMPERING

The hairpin curves of the narrow road that leads to the easternmost end of Maui may have you on edge, but when you arrive at the Hotel Hana-Maui, you'll feel yourself begin to relax. After all, the hotel is near the broad curve of silver sand known as Hamoa Beach, described by author James Michener as "the most perfect crescent beach in the Pacific."

An aura of old Hawai'i pervades the hotel, which is set on an isolated coast in the middle of a 7,000-acre cattle ranch. While hiking on the beach you can see paniolos, or Hawaiian cowboys, lead white-face Hereford cattle in from pastures. In winter it is possible to spot humpback whales while you are floating in the main swimming pool. A vintage Packard transports you to the beach. During dinner in the Plantation Great House, the staff performs Hawaiian music and dance.

This is a place of soothing seclusion. Lodging is in 67 spacious cottages with wooden floors and walls, tropical furnishings, and private lanais. Many come with private hot tubs.

A nature walk begins the day at 9:30. For serious hikers there is a four-hour trek into the lush tropical forest, with a stop to swim under the cascades of a waterfall. The 66-acre complex also has a small wellness center where you can work out while enjoying panoramic views. The mirrored aerobics studio provides a varied schedule of classes, from aerobics to yoga. Spa services, however, are limited, as the emphasis here is on appreciating the island's natural beauty. You can choose from several types of facials and massages. Spa staffers will order food for you from the resort's main dining room so you can dine in your robe between treatments.

INSIDER TIP If you plan on hiking through Haleakalā Crater, you might consider booking a cottage with a private hot tub overlooking the ocean so you can ease those aching muscles.

Equipment: Cross-country ski machines, rowing machines, stair climbers, stationary bikes, weight-training circuit. **Services:** Massage. **Swimming:** Pool, beach. **Classes and Programs:** Aerobics, aquaerobics, hiking trips. **Recreation:** Baseball, hay ride, horseback riding.

▦ 67 cottages.

✗ Meals à la carte. The Plantation Great House serves Asian-Pacific cuisine. **Sample Meals:** Hawaiian sandwich with tomato, cucumber, and sprouts, island salad with roasted pine nuts, smoked turkey with brie and avocado on a baguette (lunch); seared tofu with lemon-soy sauce, linguini with red bell peppers, mushrooms, spinach, tomato, and shaved Parmesan in a garlic-cream sauce (dinner).

Nightly rate $375–$500 per room. AE, DC, MC, V.

Box 8, Hana, Maui, HI 96713, ☎ *808/248–8211 or 800/321–4262,* FAX *808/248–7202. www.hotelhanamaui.com*

THE WESTIN MAUI

LUXURY PAMPERING

Flamingos and other tropical birds roam freely around the breathtaking waterfalls and meandering streams of the Westin Maui, one of the first huge resorts to open in Hawai'i. Want some fun with the family? The pool area features five free-form swimming pools with two water slides. How about some time alone? There's a swim-up hot tub hidden away in a grotto.

The health spa and beauty salon offer weight-training equipment and an exercise room where aerobics classes are held daily. If you overdo it on the resort's golf courses and tennis courts, there's a hydrotherapy pool for relaxing your stiff, sore muscles. Massage is available by appointment.

Healthy outings can be arranged beyond the walls of the spa as well. Experienced guides weave geology, botany, and history into hikes that meander through tropical rain forests to exotic waterfalls and gorgeous views. Of course, it's easy to head off the property on your own to visit more of Maui's watery wonders. At the $20 million Maui Ocean Center you can see cruising tiger sharks and manta rays, tiny burrowing shrimp, and waving garden eels. Mā'alaea Harbor, 20 minutes from the hotel, is a takeoff point for snorkeling and whale-watching as well as sunset cruises.

Each of the hotel's two towers has 11 floors. Rooms and suites have private lanais with views of the ocean or golf courses. The Royal Beach Club rooms are especially luxurious.

INSIDER TIP If you're short of time, the spa offers some massages and facials in "half sessions" lasting 25 minutes.

Equipment: Free weights, stair climbers, stationary bikes, treadmills, weight-training circuit. **Services:** Acupressure, lomi lomi, reflexology, sea-salt therapy, seaweed wraps, shiatsu, volcanic mud masques. **Swimming:** 5 pools, beach. **Classes and Programs:** Aerobics. **Recreation:** Golf, tennis, water sports.

756 rooms.

✗ Meals à la carte. 8 restaurants serve seafood and international fare. **Sample Meals:** Grilled tuna salad with summer beans and sweet basil, whole pineapple with tropical fruit (lunch); grilled Portobello mushroom with zucchini, tofu, and eggplant in a light tomato sauce, vegetable stir-fry with crispy noodles and a coconut gravy (dinner).

Nightly rate $280–$470 per room. AE, DC, MC, V.

2365 Kaanapali Pkwy., Lahaina, HI 96761, ☎ *808/667–2525 or 800/228–3000,* FAX *808/661–5764. www.westinmaui.com*

O'AHU

HYATT REGENCY WAIKĪKĪ RESORT

LUXURY PAMPERING

The 10,000-square-ft Na Ho'ola Spa at the Hyatt Regency has the most complete spa facilities in Waikīkī. The spa is on the fifth and sixth floors of the luxurious high-rise hotel, which has a three-story open-air atrium filled with tropical flowers and cascading waterfalls. You feel tranquil as soon as you step off the elevator to face a fluttering wall of bamboo against a translucent etched-glass backdrop, then continue past a sandstone wall covered with a dozen varieties of flowering orchids.

Na Ho'ola, which means "many healers," was named to reflect the spa's commitment to rejuvenating you body, mind, and soul. Accordingly, all staff members are licensed either as massage therapists, estheticians, or cosmetologists. Na Ho'ola's high-tech machinery and treatment facilities are more impressive than anything found in older spas throughout the islands. Computerized skin analysis reveals how clogged pores are opened after treatment.

Sparkling new spa facilities encompass 19 treatment rooms, an exercise room, jet baths, and Vichy showers. Fitness equipment is limited, but there's a larger gym elsewhere in the hotel. When you have a moment between treatments, you can relax in comfortable lounges, on two levels, so you can can see out over the hotel's pool and the beautiful beach.

Because this hotel is centrally located in Waikīkī, guests are within walking distance of countless diversions. There's plenty of shopping nearby—Gucci, Armani, Chanel, and Tiffany & Co. If you're traveling with youngsters, you can try the zoo and aquarium, both only few blocks away; ambitious hikers have been known to hoof it to the top of nearby Diamond Head.

....

INSIDER TIP Clients who do not want to appear in disarray before others will be happy to know that there are private showers in every treatment room.

....

Equipment: Stair climbers, stationary bikes, treadmills. **Services:** Hawaiian salt scrubs, jet baths, lomi lomi, massage, shiatsu, ti-leaf wraps. **Swimming:** Pools, beach. **Recreation:** Golf, tennis, snorkeling, surfing.

⊞ 1,230 rooms.

✕ Meals à la carte. 5 restaurants serve seafood as well as American, Chinese, Italian, and Japanese cuisine. The Terrace Grille serves lowcal cuisine. **Sample Meals:** Red-lentil chili, spicy scallop and cucumber salad (lunch); island chowder, wild mushroom ragout, tiger prawns, fresh grilled fish, Hawaiian paniolo-style ribs (dinner).

▨ Nightly rate $250–$465 per room. 1-day spa package $240–$380, includes spa treatments. AE, DC, MC, V.

✉ *2424 Kalakaua Ave., Honolulu, HI 96707,* ☎ *808/923–1234, 800/ 233–1234,* FAX *808/923–7839. www.hyattwaikiki.com*

MARRIOTT IHILANI RESORT & SPA

LUXURY PAMPERING ○ MINERAL SPRINGS

Soak in seawater amid velvety orchid blossoms at this unique Hawaiian hydrotherapy resort. Inspired by ancient Hawaiian healing therapies, the spa at the Marriott Ihilani Resort specializes in therapies involving seawater piped directly from the ocean.

On O'ahu's western coast, the 640-acre resort is set amid thousands of coconut palm, banyan, monkeypod, and silver buttonwood trees, as well as flowering bougainvillea, firecracker plants, and fragrant plumeria. Surrounded by four tranquil lagoons and the Waianae Mountains, this property may be O'ahu's ultimate escape.

French thalassotherapy is what you'll find here. Specially designed treatment rooms have a hydrotherapy tub, a Vichy-style shower, and a needle shower with 12 heads. The treatments involve Hawaiian seaweed packs and wraps, salt scrubs, and facial masks with marine algae.

After being wrapped and steamed in herb-soaked raw linen, you can drink the same herbs in tea or taste them in spa meals made with local seafood, seaweed, and fruits. Complete your day with a lomi-lomi massage, where the traditional rhythmic strokes are accompanied by chanting and perhaps a hula dancing session.

INSIDER TIP Therapists here recommend a Hawaiian sea-salt glow followed by a green tea wrap. The salt glow removes flaking skin, and the green tea wrap soothes the skin.

Equipment: Rowing machines, stair climbers, stationary bikes, treadmills, weight-training circuit. **Services:** Aromatherapy, body scrub, herbal wrap, hydrotherapy, shiatsu, thalassotherapy, Vichy shower. **Swimming:** Pool, ocean. **Classes and Programs:** Health and fitness evaluation, personal training. **Recreation:** Golf, snorkeling, tennis, water sports. **Children's Programs:** Supervised child-care available.

▥ 387 rooms, 36 suites.

✕ Meals à la carte. Spa cuisine menus are offered at Naupaka Terrace. **Sample Meals:** Vegetarian pizza, spinach lasagna (lunch); Mediterranean-style shrimp and scallops, grilled mahimahi (dinner).

▨ Nightly rate $275–$550 per room. 1-day spa package $350–$395 per person, includes spa treatments. AE, DC, MC, V.

✉ 92–1001 O'lani St., Kapolei, O'ahu, HI 96707, ☎ 808/679–0079 or 800/626–4446, FAX 808/679–3387. www.ihilani.com

IDAHO

SUN VALLEY RESORT

SPORTS CONDITIONING

There are enough recreation, shopping, eating and entertainment options to keep you occupied for weeks at Sun Valley Resort. A ski mecca since the mid-1930s, Sun Valley is now a flourishing year-round resort. There are 2,054 acres of ski trails in winter, and great hiking and fishing in the warmer months.

Sun Valley boasted one of the world's first chairlifts, a 1930s-vintage single-chair model that now dangles above the Trail Creek Cabin, site of the resort's mountainside restaurant. It was adapted from a design to load bananas into cargo ships. It sits forlorn now, as modern high-speed quad lifts haul you to the top of the slopes.

Sun Valley is often named among the best resorts for skiing, tennis, and golf. Serious skiers revel in the challenges offered by famed Baldy Mountain, and Dollar Mountain offers a varied array of beginners and intermediate runs. With a total of 77 runs served by 18 lifts, Sun Valley ski slopes offer something for skiers of all levels.

In other seasons, 18 tennis courts and a 72-par golf course—the greens cross Trail Creek seven times in the first 9 holes—draw appreciative crowds. Other options include horseback riding, trap and skeet shooting, and fly-fishing.

The "village" surrounding the lodge and inn is jammed with specialty shops, galleries, indoor and outdoor ice-skating rinks, and several restaurants. A movie theater shows *Sun Valley Serenade,* a film about the resort, every day and first-run features in the evening.

Railroad magnate Averell Harriman launched Sun Valley as a way to draw passengers west, and he was quite successful. His vision of 'roughing it in luxury' is best demonstrated in the main lodge, where the lobby boasts rich oak paneling, a massive fireplace, and butter-soft leather couches. The opulent main dining room feels more like it belongs in a palace. The European-style Sun Valley Inn offers lovely rooms in a chalet atmosphere. For those who want more privacy, condos encircle the village.

Beyond the elegant fare and dazzling wine list of the dining room, six other restaurants offer fare ranging from a prime rib buffet to European pastries, pizza to fondue. A cafeteria offers well-prepared, affordable options.

INSIDER TIP Two of the three outdoor pools at Sun Valley Resort are heated for a rare winter swimming experience.

Services: Massage. **Swimming:** 3 pools. **Recreation:** Bowling, fishing, hiking, horseback riding, ice-skating, skiing, tennis, trap shooting.

▦ 146 lodge rooms, 114 inn rooms, 280 condos.

✕ Meals à la carte. Seven restaurants, from an elegant dining room to a cafeteria. **Sample Meals:** Mesquite-grilled chicken, grilled swordfish (dinner).

✑ Nightly rate $124–439 per room. Seasonal specials available. AE, D, DC, MC, V.

✉ *Sun Valley Resort, Sun Valley, ID 83353,* ☎ *208/622–4111, 800/ 786–8259,* FAX *208/622–3700. www.sunvalley.com*

ILLINOIS

THE HEARTLAND SPA

NUTRITION AND DIET

Filled with midwestern hospitality, the Heartland Spa is nestled on a tranquil dairy farm in the middle of Illinois farmland. Sophisticated diet and exercise programs, a limited number of guests, and easy access from Chicago make this a repeat destination for Midwesterners.

In this unpretentious environment the well-trained staff leads a wellness program that teaches you how to make health-enriching changes by teaching you about fitness, nutrition, and stress management. There are no rules or restrictions here; your day can be as structured as you please. You can choose to spend the afternoon in exercise classes and educational lectures or being pampered in the spa.

High-tech workouts and circuit-training sessions are held in a converted barn. The impressive three-level fitness center, which includes an indoor Olympic-size pool and spa-treatment rooms, is reached through an underground passage from the main house. There are 30 group exercise and relaxation classes, including aerobics, martial arts, and meditation. In addition, a challenging ropes course helps you work past self-imposed limitations and builds self-esteem.

INSIDER TIP The Heartland provides most of your clothing, including sweats, T-shirts, shorts, jackets, and robes. Leave your heels at home—there's no need to dress for dinner.

Equipment: Cross-country ski machines, elliptical trainers, free weights, stationary bikes, treadmills, weight-training circuit. **Services:** Aromatherapy, massage, mud wraps, sea-salt exfoliation, Vichy shower. **Swimming:** Indoor pool, lake. **Classes and Programs:** Adventure course, body-composition analysis, discussions on health-related topics, par course, nutrition evaluation. **Recreation:** Biking, fishing, hiking, tennis.

▣ 14 rooms.

✕ Meals included. Mostly vegetarian menu, supplemented with fish and poultry, with 1,200 calories for women, 1,500 for men. **Sample Meals:** Spinach pizza, turkey taco with unfried beans (lunch); homemade spinach ravioli with sage broth, teriyaki-grilled salmon (dinner).

▦ Nightly rate $380 double occupancy during week. 2-night weekend package $880, double occupancy. AE, D, DC, MC, V.

✉ 1237 E. 1600 North Rd., Gilman, IL 60938, ☎ 815/683–2182 or 800/545–4853, FAX 815/683–2144. www.heartlandspa.com

INDIANA

FRENCH LICK SPRINGS RESORT

LUXURY PAMPERING ∘ MINERAL SPRINGS

French Lick Springs Resort's claim to fame is its so-called Pluto Water. This sulfurous spring water has attracted a wealthy clientele since the 19th century. "When Nature won't," the old ads read, "Pluto will." The French Lick Springs Resort, built in the early 1840s, was ideally positioned to take advantage of the therapeutic mineral waters. The famous water is still used in the Pluto Bath, in the hotel's health club, but today those relaxing soaks can be complemented with challenging exercise classes and a wide range of skin-care treatments.

Though it has been renovated several times, the hotel retains its original Victorian elegance, with French doors, carved woodwork, and verandas that overlook formal gardens. Its 2,600 acres of lawns and rolling woodlands, set in the Hoosier National Forest, contain the largest tennis complex in the Midwest (18 courts, eight of them indoors), and two championship golf courses. Nearby are trails ideal for hiking and horseback riding. With all these recreation facilities at hand, one of the favorite pastimes is porch sitting, as guests spend summer evenings in rocking chairs gazing out onto the rolling hills.

Pluto Water, named for the god of the underworld, is murky, dense, and full of 22 trace minerals. The resort no longer bottles Pluto Water—it has a laxative effect if you drink too much of it—but you can still have a sip from a well beneath a historic gazebo. At the spa a Pluto Bath in a seven-jet private hot tub helps soothe your joints and renew your skin. No formal program of activities is offered, so you can set your own schedule.

INSIDER TIP For a true taste of southern charm, let a lantern-lighted carriage ride sweep you away to a romantic evening.

Equipment: Rowing machines, stair climbers, stationary bikes, weight-training circuit. **Services:** Aromatherapy, loofah body scrub, mud wrap, reflexology, seaweed wrap. **Swimming:** Indoor and outdoor pools. **Classes and Programs:** Personal training. **Recreation:** Biking, billiards, bowling, fishing, hiking, horseback riding, sailing, skiing. **Children's Programs:** Supervised day camp for children.

🛏 471 rooms and suites.

✕ Meals à la carte. Low-fat, low-calorie selections. Dinner buffet offers soups, salads, and entrees. **Sample Meals:** Romaine, red potato, and asparagus salad (lunch); salmon with mustard sauce (dinner).

✉ 1-night spa package $99 per person, double occupancy, includes lodging, spa treatments. 2-night spa package $189 per person, double occupancy, includes lodging, spa treatments. AE, D, DC, MC, V.

⊠ *8670 W. Hwy. 56, French Lick, IN 47432,* ☎ *812/936–9300 or 800/457–4042,* ☏ *812/936–2100. www.frenchlick.com*

IOWA

THE RAJ

HOLISTIC HEALTH ○ MEDICAL WELLNESS

The Raj is a self-contained world of quiet elegance dedicated to holistic philosophies of health and healing that have been practiced in India for centuries. You learn the secrets of ayurveda in a program designed to stimulate health and vitality.

Treatment begins with an assessment of your physiological makeup by a physician concerned with both physical and spiritual health. Skeptics are often amazed at how ayurvedic experts accurately diagnose body type, personality traits, and physical imbalances simply by feeling the pulse. Maharishi therapies, designed to restore balance in your body, are deeply relaxing. Traditionally known as panchakarma, treatments include warm herbalized-oil massages, herbal steam baths, and internal cleansing. In one relaxation treatment, oil is slowly poured across your forehead, letting your thoughts melt away. Aromatic oils are used to enliven your marmas (energy points) to create a feeling of well-being. For stress reduction and to expand inner awareness, you are introduced to transcendental meditation and given a mantra.

Developed by Rodgers Badgett and his wife, Candace, the program includes luxurious accommodations in suites or villas and three gourmet vegetarian meals a day. The facilities are limited, usually to groups of 10, and all treatments are in private rooms. Informal discussion groups often form in the living room, and guest speakers cover everything from attitudes toward beauty to prevention of chronic disorders. The daily session of yoga brings everyone together in a carpeted studio. Long walks in the rolling meadows and woodlands are a nice complement to the daily activities. If you require more serenity, the Raj offers a silent dining table and a "silence pin" that signals your wishes.

A few treatments here are focused less on your inner self. A three- to seven-day skin-rejuvenation program for women involves a medical consultation, followed by daily mud baths, milk baths, and massage. Called the Royal Skin Rejuvenation Program, it is a combines both ancient and contemporary philosophies that exemplify the goals of the Raj.

INSIDER TIP The Raj is more sanctuary than spa. Those wanting an activity-filled vacation will want to look elsewhere. The Raj offers a tranquil retreat for people seeking to cleanse the ama, or toxins, from their bodies and souls.

Equipment: Free weights, stair climbers, stationary bikes, treadmills.
Services: Aromatherapy, ayurvedic massage. **Classes and Programs:**

Health-related lectures, nutrition and diet counseling, sound therapy, stress management, transcendental meditation, yoga.

🖼 16 suites.

✕ Meals included. Vegetarian meals daily, prepared according to ayurvedic standards, served in dining room. **Sample Meals:** Indian dal soup, basmati rice, date and cilantro chutneys, dal with basmati rice and cilantro sauce, organic lemon broccoli or dilled green beans (lunch); fresh green peas in coconut milk, summer squash sauté, couscous pilaf and asparagus phyllo rolls (dinner).

🖼 Nightly rate $125 per couple. Royal Skin Rejuvenation Program $602 per day. Royal Beauty from Within program $597 per day. AE, D, MC, V.

✉ *1734 Jasmine Ave., Fairfield, IA 52556,* ☎ *515/472–9580 or 800/ 248–9050,* FAX *515/472–2496. www.theraj.com*

KENTUCKY

FOXHOLLOW

LUXURY PAMPERING ○ HOLISTIC HEALTH

Any description of the charms of Foxhollow has to begin with the fact that your hot-stone massage or paraffin body wrap takes place in the middle of a 1300-acre working farm on the western edge of Kentucky's Bluegrass region—there are Thoroughbreds grazing in a field outside the spa. The drive through the gently rolling landscape and up the dogwood-lined drive should relax and delight you before you get out of your car.

The Kentucky motif continues inside. Owner Mary Shands is an ardent collector and patron of Kentucky folk art, and the light, airy rooms throughout the lodgings, clinic, and spa are decorated with delightful pieces, from polka-dot wooden roosters to colorful quilts to hand-painted watermelon sections.

It isn't folk medicine going on here, however. The Foxhollow clinic, affiliated with Switzerland's Paracelsus Klinik, practices integrative biological medicine—an approach that synthesizes as Asian and European treatments.

The Manor House, built in 1837, is the main lodging and dining room (although there are also rooms in some of the white-clapboard cottages, trimmed in green, a short walk away). A large living room is stocked with health magazines and adventure books to read in front of the fireplace. Wander into the kitchen, and the chef offers you coffee, herbal tea, and freshly baked cookies. Guest rooms have warm comforters on the beds (king-size or double), a reading chair, and bouquets of fresh flowers. Most cottages have living rooms and fireplaces.

The Wetlands Wellness Spa, a short drive from the Manor House, is a turn-of-the-last-century farmhouse which offers a variety of spa treatments that support the clinic's work with body wraps, a Vichy shower, a hydrotherapy tub, and a number of massage techniques. The LaStone massage draws on different traditions from Hopi to Hindu, but at a more immediate level it involves being massaged with hot and cold rocks (there's also aromatherapy, with scents dropped on the rocks). When your therapist takes up the hot basalt rocks, it feels as if you're being worked over by someone with the power to turn his hand showerhead-hot. The freezer-stored marbles, used briefly to stimulate circulation, may be too cold for some people. A number of spa packages are available that combine massage and other treatments with facials, manicures, and other pampering services. You can also arrange to have lunch in a bright, open dining room.

There's plenty to do here: Stroll around the grounds, following a stream through the woods; enjoy a gourmet vegetarian dinner in the convivial dining room; or travel into Louisville, 25 minutes away, for big-city attractions such as Churchill Downs and its mesmerizing museum of horse racing. Whether you're looking to readjust your lifestyle or simply to enjoy a luxurious getaway, Foxhollow provides a stylish setting and expert counseling for it.

INSIDER TIP If you can't get away for long, Foxhollow also runs a spa in downtown Louisville.

Equipment: Free weights, stationary bikes, trampolines, treadmills, weight-training circuit. **Services:** Acupressure, hot stone therapy, hydrotherapy, reflexology, seaweed and herbal wraps. **Classes and Programs:** Meditation, personal training, Pilates, yoga. **Recreation:** Biking, golf, hiking, horseback riding.

🛏 19 rooms, 5 cottages.

✗ Meals à la carte. Mostly vegetarian menu served at Manor House and Wetlands Spa. **Sample Meals:** Spinach soup with garlic, tempeh salad with honey poppy-seed dressing, chocolate-tofu cake with fresh berries (lunch); wild-mushroom soup, spinach salad, seared tuna with red pepper sauce and quinoa, carob-almond tart (dinner).

💳 Nightly rate $55–$80 per room. Day spa package $327. AE, MC, V.

✉ *8909 Hwy. 329, Crestwood, KY 40014* ☎ *502/241–8621 or 800/ 624–7080,* FAX *502/241–3935. www.Foxhollowus.com*

MAINE

NORTHERN PINES HEALTH RESORT

NUTRITION AND DIET ○ HOLISTIC HEALTH ○ MEDICAL WELLNESS

In the more than 20 years that Northern Pines Health Resort has been operating, it has slowly evolved from a place that emphasized a rigid diet-and-exercise program to one where guests come to release stress. And no wonder, as the 68-acre lakefront retreat allows you to rough it in comfort, strolling among the evergreens and hardwoods, swimming in the shimmering lake, taking a class in music or art, or just taking it all in. Northern Pines offers an ever-changing assortment of courses designed to help you develop new ways of controlling your weight and learn to control the stresses in your life. The program is unregimented, as the transition to a healthier lifestyle is meant to be a gradual one.

Each day begins with meditation at 6:30 AM, followed by stretching exercises and a brisk walk through the woods. Each week has a different focus, and special classes offered may include anything from cooking and managing money to acupuncture and transcendental meditation. Always offered are classes in aerobics, acupressure, massage, and reflexology. Morning and afternoon yoga are optional, as are the two guided walks offered each day. Evenings are given over to more learning activities as well as the ever-popular 10-minute shoulder massage. About 15 guests are here at any given time, allowing for lots of personal attention from the staff.

The camp's lakeside log cabins date from the 1920s and provide total seclusion for couples. Newer lodge rooms and cabins with two bedrooms are on the hillside amid towering pines, spruce, and hemlock. There are also two-person yurts (earth-covered cabins) with carpeting and modern conveniences.

The informality and laid-back pace appeal to stressed-out professionals, who come here to rejuvenate and relax. For those who are in need of a little retail therapy, the L.L. Bean headquarters and scores of factory outlets are about 45 minutes away.

INSIDER TIP This is a great place for older people to get in shape. Campers range widely in age, but many are over 40.

Equipment: Cross-country ski machines, free weights, stationary bikes, weight-training equipment. **Services:** Acupressure, aromatherapy, body wrap, herbal wrap, reflexology. **Swimming:** Lake. **Classes and Programs:** Massage and yoga workshops. **Recreation:** Boating, canoeing, hiking.

⌶ 32 lodge rooms, 8 cabins, 2 yurts.

✕ Meals à la carte. Vegetarian buffet. Supervised fasts available. **Sample Meals:** Lentil and vegetable soup with green salad, chocolate-tofu dessert (lunch); pasta primavera with steamed vegetables, apple crisp with cinnamon yogurt sauce (dinner).

▥ Nightly rate $110–$149 per room. 1-week program $894–$1,194 per couple. AE, MC, V.

✉ *559 Webbs Mills Rd., Raymond, ME 04071,* ☎ *207/655–7624,* ℻ *207/655–3321. www.maine.com/norpines*

POLAND SPRING HEALTH INSTITUTE

MEDICAL WELLNESS ∘ MINERAL SPRINGS

An extended stay at the Poland Spring Health Institute is a cross between a holiday at a New England bed-and-breakfast and at one of Europe's old-fashioned spas. Poland Spring has been synonymous with healthy water for more than a century, and the institute draws its water from the same aquifer as the nearby commercial bottling plant. The water is used in all manner of healing treatments, including in the whirlpools and in the steam room, where you receive body wraps preceding a massage.

Just ten guests at a time are accommodated in the five simple rooms of a big farmhouse, where the average stay is two weeks. You work closely with specialists on ways to combat health problems such as diabetes and stress-related ailments. A nurse prescribes rigorous exercises and hydrotherapy treatments based on your physical condition. Everyone is expected to keep to a vegan diet.

This nonprofit, private wellness center was founded in 1979 and emphasizes Christian prayer. The 260-acre property is bordered by a lake surrounded with hiking and biking trails. In winter guests can cross-country ski and ice-skate.

INSIDER TIP Need help quitting the habit? A special two-week program for smoking cessation is offered each year.

Equipment: Stationary bikes. **Services:** Swedish massage. **Swimming:** Lake. **Classes and Programs:** Health-related lectures. **Recreation:** Biking, boating, canoeing, horseback riding.

▥ 5 rooms with shared bath.

✕ Meals included. Vegan buffet. **Sample Meals:** Baked potato, green beans, salad (lunch); lasagna with greens, corn chowder with crackers and fruit (dinner).

▥ 1-week program $750–$950 per room, includes meals, programs. No credit cards.

✉ *32 Summit Spring Rd., Poland Spring, ME 04274,* ☎ *207/998–2894,* ℻ *207/998–2164. www.tagnet.org/pshi*

MASSACHUSETTS

CANYON RANCH IN THE BERKSHIRES

LUXURY PAMPERING ○ HEALTH AND FITNESS ○ NUTRITION AND DIET ○
MEDICAL WELLNESS

Driving past formal gardens and an elegant mansion, you may think
you've arrived at a millionaire's mountain retreat. The centerpiece of
the 120-acre woodlands retreat is Bellefontaine, a mansion dating
from 1897 that is a replica of the Petit Trianon, in Versailles.

Once past the registration desk, however, the focus on fitness and
healthy living becomes quite apparent. The East Coast counterpart to
the original Canyon Ranch in Arizona adopts the same holistic approach.
Upon arrival you consult with a program coordinator and a nurse who
map out a plan of activities. You'll need the help, as there are more
than 250 daily classes, outings, and workshops from which to choose.

The resort has a 100,000-square-ft indoor fitness center unlike any other
in the Northeast, complete with cardiovascular and weight-training
rooms, racquetball, squash, and tennis courts, running track, and 75-
ft swimming pool. Skiers can get in shape before tackling cross-country trails, and executives can use the latest biofeedback systems to help
get rid of stress.

The main attraction for many guests is the opportunity to rest and rejuvenate with cutting-edge spa treatments. The latest body treatment,
a 100-minute session called Euphoria, combines an invigorating shower
with an aromatherapy scalp massage using fragrant rose-geranium
oil, a warm botanical body mask, immersion in a hydrotub scented with
citrus, and a full-body massage with warm oil. Instead of standard
Swedish massage, consider the craniosacral body alignment, an os-
teopathic technique that releases tension in the neck, cranium, and spine.
For total pampering try the signature Parisian body polish, which uses
crushed pearls to smooth and soften your skin.

The resort offers an extensive roster of packages designed to address
specific issues, such as weight loss, smoking cessation, and chronic pain
management. With the Basic Optimal Living Package, guests work with
a team of health professionals to broaden their awareness of health,
fitness, nutrition, movement, stress management, and creative expression. A variety of spiritual awareness classes, including yoga, tai
chi, and breathing and relaxation, are also offered.

Dining at the mansion, you won't feel deprived: Though the menu is
spa cuisine and includes calorie counts, it is also gourmet, with favorites
such as rack of lamb and lobster, a variety of pastas, and deserts such

as hot-fudge sundaes and cheesecake. Single guests seeking company can sit at the Captain's Table.

On either side of the mansion's elegant lobby are two floors of guest rooms. The rooms are more functional, contemporary–New England style with flowered fabric and big windows.

With diverse cultural attractions in the area—the Tanglewood Music Festival, the Jacob's Pillow Dance Festival, the Williamstown Theater—summer reservations must be made well in advance. Rates are lower in other parts of the year, so you may want to consider a stay during the fall or winter.

INSIDER TIP A major factor in the resort's success is its three-to-one ratio of staff to guests. Among the staff are physicians, psychologists, nutritionists, nurses, fitness instructors, and bodywork therapists.

Equipment: Cross-country ski machines, free weights, rowing machines, stair climbers, stationary bikes, treadmills, weight-training circuit. **Services:** Acupuncture, herbal wraps, mud wraps, reflexology, reiki, seaweed wraps, shiatsu, thalassotherapy. **Swimming:** Indoor and outdoor pools. **Classes and Programs:** Aerobics, aquaerobics, cooking classes, health and lifestyle lectures, holistic health counseling, line dancing, medical checkup and fitness evaluation, meditation, tai chi, yoga. **Recreation:** Basketball, biking, canoeing, hiking, kayaking, racquetball, skiing, squash, tennis, volleyball.

🛏 126 rooms, 24 suites.

✕ Meals included. Low-fat international fare in dining room. **Sample Meals:** Crab and avocado quesadilla, Filipino-style noodles, lentil dal with curried basmati rice (lunch); grilled artichoke and leek pasta, beef tenderloin with port-wine sauce, potato-crusted salmon with shallot Dijon sauce (dinner).

💳 3-night package $1,195–$1,460 per person, double occupancy. 7-night package $2,465–3,490 per person, double occupancy. AE, D, DC, MC, V.

✉ *165 Kemble St., Lenox, MA 01240,* ☎ *413/637–4100 or 800/742–9000,* FAX *413/637–0057. www.canyonranch.com*

KRIPALU CENTER FOR YOGA AND HEALTH

HOLISTIC HEALTH ○ MEDICAL WELLNESS

Yoga, meditation, exercise, and a bit of pampering are the paths to happiness—or at least to a feeling of well-being—at the Kripalu Center, one of the largest yoga-based retreat centers in the world. The accommodations are basic, but the location, high in the Berkshires, is beyond compare.

Kripalu, a nonprofit health retreat, is designed to help visitors achieve peace of mind and insights about healthy lifestyles based on ancient wisdom. Amrit Desai, who founded the first center in Pennsylvania in 1972, developed Kripalu yoga, a gentle practice that combines postures, breathing techniques, and meditation. The goal is to focus your mind's attention to discover what is blocking you from living joyfully.

The program at Kripalu combines yogic practices with contemporary wisdom about holistic health. Residents—who can number as many as 450 at a time—participate in a prescribed regimen of yoga and meditation, including workshops designed to fight stress and increase well-being. Mornings begin with yoga and meditation and are followed by a breakfast eaten in silence. Morning and afternoon workshops may include Kripalu DansKinetics—a unique blend of yoga and low-impact aerobic dance. Evening programs include concerts, lectures, and other entertainment.

As you get oriented to the daily yoga routine, you'll learn about optional classes such as "The Dance of Tennis"—a spiritual approach to improving your performance on the courts. You can sign up for Kripalu bodywork, including soothing, meditative massage, and Phoenix Rising yoga therapy based on body-posture training. In addition to the daily schedule, there are weeklong programs on topics such as meditation and improving self-esteem. One of the most popular programs, called Retreat and Renewal, allows guests to create their own schedules, picking and choosing from various activities.

The center, which opened here in 1983, is housed in a former Jesuit seminary on a 300-acre wooded site adjacent to the grounds of Tanglewood Music Festival. The four-story brick building has basic accommodations, most with shared bath. Making up for the lack of creature comforts are spectacular views of gardens designed by Frederick Law Olmsted, who was also responsible for New York City's Central Park. In summer you can swim in a lake on the property. In winter there's skiing at the nearby Butternut resort as well as cross-country skiing.

INSIDER TIP Teenagers can participate in the one-week Coming of Age outdoor camping program, which combines yoga and sports.

Services: Acupuncture, meditative massage, polarity therapy, shiatsu, reflexology. **Swimming:** Lake. **Classes and Programs:** Dance, meditation, yoga instruction. **Recreation:** Biking, hiking, skiing. **Children's Programs:** Activities for ages 5–12 and 9–19.

▦ 180 rooms without bath, 150 dormitory beds.

✕ Meals included. Vegetarian buffet. **Sample Meals:** Vegetable quesadilla, Mexican-style rice (lunch); vegetable-pesto pizza with rice and beans (dinner).

▧ 2-night rate $132–$252 per person. 6-night rate $342–$654 per person. Children's program $40 per day. MC, V.

✉ *Box 793, Lenox, MA 01240,* ☎ *413/448–3152 or 800/741–7353,* FAX *413/448–3384. www.kripalu.org*

THE KUSHI INSTITUTE OF THE BERKSHIRES

NUTRITION AND DIET ○ HOLISTIC HEALTH

At this former Franciscan abbey set on 600 acres of woodlands and meadows, you learn the macrobiotic way of life by living it. Cooking classes, lectures, and workshops are used by trained staff to guide you in the process of changing to a more balanced lifestyle. Founded by Aveline and Michio Kushi, the Kushi Institute has been in the forefront of macrobiotic research and education since 1979.

For newcomers to macrobiotics, a weeklong introductory course includes exercise and shiatsu massage. A monthlong career-training program prepares aspiring professional macrobiotic chefs, cooking teachers, lecturers, and health guides. Also scheduled are four or five days of instruction on preventing cancer and heart disease. Scheduled seminars vary from the weeklong macrobiotic program, offered three times a month, to four- and five-day spiritual retreats.

The daily activities begin with a session of do-in, stretching exercises that are simple and easy to learn. Periods of meditation alternate with lectures and workshops in food preparation. Couples and families often participate together.

Most guests stay in the main lodge, where seven of the ten plain but comfortable guest rooms share a bathroom. A dormitory building has additional rooms for participants in monthlong programs. Buffets, served at all three meals, are one of the highlights of a stay at the institute.

Children are welcome at Kushi and participate in a special youth program designed for specific age levels. Activities include arts and crafts, sports, cooking classes, and more.

INSIDER TIP Only 15 participants can be accommodated at any one time, so the mood at the Kushi Institute is serene.

Services: Acupressure, massage, shiatsu. **Swimming:** Lake. **Classes and Programs:** Diet and nutrition workshops.

▣ 10 rooms, 10 dormitory rooms.

✗ Meals included. 3 buffet-style macrobiotic meals daily. **Sample Meals:** Brown rice, lentil soup with carrots and onions, steamed broccoli and cauliflower with pumpkin-seed dressing (lunch); mashed millet and cauliflower with seitan (wheat gluten), sautéed string beans with sesame-seed dressing, steamed collard greens (dinner).

▨ 6-day Way to Health seminar $1,745, includes lodging, meals, classes. 1-month macrobiotic career-training program $3,750 per person. AE, MC, V.

✉ *198 Leland Rd., Box 7, Becket, MA 01223,* ☎ *413/623–5741 or 800/975–8744,* ℻ *413/623–8827. www.kripalushop.org*

MAHARISHI AYUR-VEDA MEDICAL CENTER

HOLISTIC HEALTH ○ MEDICAL WELLNESS

Eastern and Western medicine meet at the Maharishi Ayur-Veda Medical Center in treatments following ayurvedic principles. Based on an analysis of your dosha, or physical and emotional type, the physician-supervised program includes an organic vegetarian diet, massage with essential oils, and total relaxation.

The healing process of panchakarma begins with a physical examination and a thorough questionnaire to determine your type of dosha: vata (quick, energetic, movement prone), pitta (enterprising and sharp), or kapha (tranquil and steady). Therapy and diet are prescribed accordingly.

Although the medically supervised program tends to attract people with cancer and other chronic illnesses, many attend for preventive health care. The center's doctors and nurses are trained in both Eastern and Western medicine. A daily two-hour session to rid the body of impurities includes massage, heat treatments such as a steam bath or hot oil bath, and a gentle laxative. A yoga program is also offered. The combination of these treatments and meditation is said to be effective (by more than 600 published studies) in reducing stress and improving overall health.

Guests stay in a mansion built in the early part of the last century situated on 200 acres of private forest. Rooms overlook the mountains, the terraced gardens, or a beech grove. Meals can be taken in the dining room on the main floor, on the adjoining patio, or in their rooms.

INSIDER TIP This is a place dedicated to rejuvenation and enlightenment, rather than recreation.

Services: Aromatherapy, massage, steam bath. **Classes and Programs:** Meditation classes, physical examination, yoga.

⊡ 9 rooms, 3 suites.

✕ Meals included. **Sample Meals:** Lemon basmati rice, mung dal soup, sautéed fennel, roasted butternut squash, poached pear with mango sauce (dinner).

▧ 1-week program $3,290–$4,200 per person, includes lodging, meals, classes. AE, D, MC, V.

⊠ *679 George Hill Rd., Lancaster, MA 01523,* ☏ *978/365–4549 or 800/290–6702,* FAX *978/368–7557. www.lancasterhealth.com*

THE OPTION INSTITUTE

HOLISTIC HEALTH

The goal at the Option Institute, a 95-acre retreat in the Berkshires, is to nurture healthy attitudes toward life. Personal attitudes, beliefs, and feelings are examined to develop a fuller understanding of how to improve one's physical and mental health. Working in group and private sessions, participants are taught to be more accepting of themselves, to learn to find alternatives, and to form more loving relationships.

Founded in 1983 by Barry Neil Kaufman and Samahria Kaufman, who have written and lectured on interpersonal relationships, the Option Institute sets out to provide a stimulating environment for people from all walks of life—from young professionals to families of children with special needs. Guests come for weekends and intensive programs of up to eight weeks.

Along with a full-time staff of more than 60, the Kaufmans seek to teach the philosophy of their best-selling book *Happiness Is a Choice.* The process begins with guests sitting in a circle on the floor and discussing their personal beliefs. Participants say these sessions brought about a profound sense of energy and vigor that has empowered them to enjoy a happier life.

The retreat has simply furnished guest houses that use natural wood and lots of windows for a woodsy, rustic feel. Some kitchen-equipped units are available. Grassy meadows, forests, and streams abound—prime territory for meditation walks.

INSIDER TIP Hikers have access to the Appalachian Trail, and skiers can take advantage of the nearby Butternut and Catamount ski resorts.

Services: Private counseling. **Swimming:** Pond. **Classes and Programs:** Workshops on communication, health, personal relationships. **Recreation:** Hiking, skiing.

⊡ 35 rooms.

✕ Meals included. Vegetarian buffet. **Sample Meals:** Vegetarian lasagna, whole-grain casseroles (lunch); seasonal vegetables, Greek salad, pasta (dinner).

✉ 3-day package $650 per person, double occupancy, includes lodging, meals. 1-week Radical Authenticity package $1,495 per person, double occupancy, includes lodging, meals, programs. MC, V.

✉ *2080 S. Undermountain Rd., Sheffield, MA 01257,* ☎ *413/229–2100,* FAX *413/229–8931. www.option.org*

SMITH COLLEGE ADULT SPORT/FITNESS CAMP

SPORTS CONDITIONING

Do you long for those carefree days of summer camp? Smith College's one-week sports program brings it all back. It's an array of activities from waterskiing and sculling to swimming and skydiving. There's serious attention to stress management, nutrition, and general fitness.

This weeklong program is like a postgraduate course in wellness. The philosophy here is that a full, active lifestyle leads to healthy, happy, and productive people. The camp provides an environment where you can experiment with different sports and improve skills you already possess.

The three-building sports complex has first-rate facilities. You can receive instruction in more than 25 different sports and exercises. Open at all times to campers are two gymnasiums, a six-lane swimming pool with two diving boards, and a strength-training room. There are also indoor and outdoor tennis courts, squash courts, running tracks, and a 5,000-meter cross-country course that winds through woods and fields.

Each day's program varies, encouraging you to try new activities such as in-line skating, archery, or yoga. Workouts are scheduled before breakfast: You can join a group swim or take a tai chi class. A climbing wall and a ropes course tempt adventurous types, and a boathouse on the nearby Connecticut River provides equipment for rowing and other water sports.

Complementing the sports programs are fitness profiles involving flexibility and body composition tests, stress-control evaluations using biofeedback equipment, and sports medicine consultations with a certified athletic trainer.

The atmosphere is very low-key. You stay at Tyler House, a student residence during the academic year, in rooms that sleep either one or two persons.

INSIDER TIP You definitely won't feel left behind by the crowd here. The average age of participants is 50.

Equipment: Weight-training circuit. **Services:** Swedish massage. **Swimming:** Indoor pool, lake. **Classes and Programs:** Dancing, tai chi, yoga. **Recreation:** Basketball, boating, diving, fencing, fishing, golf, horseback riding, kayaking, squash, sky-diving, tennis.

🛏 50 dormitory beds in single and double rooms, all with shared bath.

✗ Meals included. American buffet. **Sample Meals:** Hamburgers, cold cuts (lunch); salmon fillet, pasta primavera, baked ziti (dinner).

✉ 6-night program: $825 per person, includes lodging, meals, activities. No credit cards.

✉ *Michelle Finley, Ainsworth Gymnasium, Smith College, Rte. 9, Northampton, MA 01063,* ☎ *413/585–3977,* FAX *413/585–2712.*

MINNESOTA

BIRDWING SPA

LUXURY PAMPERING ○ NUTRITION AND DIET

Birdwing Spa brings European treatments to a bucolic Minnesota setting. Personalized attention is perfectly balanced with unstructured time that allows you to explore the 300-acre country estate. Staff members are friendly and unpretentious—many have been here for years—and explain treatments for newcomers. No more than 25 guests may attend at a time, and owners Elisabeth Carlson, a registered nurse, and her husband, Richard, tailor the program for each group.

Once a working farm, Birdwing has 2½ mi of lakeshore and 12 mi of trails. Emphasizing outdoor activities, the spa has equipment for biking, canoeing, and cross-country skiing. Some fitness machines are provided for the habitual gymgoer, such as treadmills and elliptical trainers, which are easy-gliding indoor cross-country–skiing simulators.

An hour of yoga, a cooking demonstration, or a natural skin-care tutorial are scheduled around lunch, which may be taken outdoors on the lawn. Afternoons are good for a wildflower walk (be careful about ticks), perhaps a swim or a nap, and your choice of two hours of daily spa treatments, which may include the intensely exfoliating sea body polish or skin-care treatments for the back or legs.

In the chaletlike main building is the dining room, from which you can watch cardinals, jays, and hummingbirds flit around the feeders. Beauty-treatment facilities, a sauna, and a hot tub are downstairs. Guest rooms upstairs have Ethan Allen furnishings, draperies, and shared baths. The six suites in the renovated barn have hand-carved Georgian pine furniture seemingly straight from the pages of *Country Living* magazine, as well as huge private whirlpool baths; one also has a fireplace and steam bath.

INSIDER TIP It's worth paying a little extra for a sparkly champagne, oxygenating, or Vitamin C facial.

Equipment: Elliptical trainers, free weights, stationary bikes, treadmills. **Services:** Alpha-hydroxy facial, gel or herbal body wrap, massage, paraffin therapy, scalp massage, sea body polish. **Swimming:** Outdoor pool. **Classes and Programs:** Cooking classes, fitness evaluation, fitness instruction, nutritional counseling; guest speakers address stress, nutrition, and problems faced by career women; art and nature studies programs. **Recreation:** Biking, bird-watching, canoeing, skiing.

⌘ 8 rooms, 5 with bath, 6 suites.

✕ Meals included. **Sample Meals:** Feta-cheese pie, mesclun salad with tangerine vinaigrette (lunch); halibut over wild rice and asparagus (dinner).

▨ 1-day package $275–$325 per person, includes room, spa treatments. 2-day retreat $395–$550 per person, includes room, spa treatments. MC, V.

✉ *21398 575th Ave., Litchfield, MN 55355,* ☎ *320/693–6064 or 800/ 644–5541. www.birdwingspa.com*

THE MARSH

HOLISTIC HEALTH ○ MEDICAL WELLNESS

In her battle against lupus, Ruth Stricker discovered the philosophy that now governs her wellness center: achieving the balance of mind and body to promote health. In her efforts Stricker created the Marsh, the most comprehensive wellness center in the Midwest.

Set at the edge of a marshland near Minneapolis—you can't miss the silo-shape meditation tower—the 67,000-square-ft facility includes a modern spa, physical therapy center, fitness training center with a squadron of physical trainers, a 75-ft lap pool, and a 94°F therapy pool. More than 60 fitness classes are offered on land or in water, including various levels of aerobics, yoga or stretching therapies, tai chi (called ai chi in the water), and chi ball (a small rubber ball is used in light aerobic exercise). Every inch of the Marsh is accessible to wheelchairs, including the therapy pool with a ramp, and many programs cater to senior citizens and people living with illness or pain.

The Strickers, art collectors who've donated pieces to the Minneapolis Institute of Art, made sure an Eastern feeling permeated the center, from the Asian-style portico and decorative motifs in the guest rooms and lobby to the interconnection of the building with the tranquil wooden expanse behind it.

The full-service spa has a variety of body and massage treatments (including one for pregnant women) and facials (from acne-regulating to oxygenating) to serve a wide range of skin types and needs. Perhaps the best value among body treatments is the multifaceted body wrap, which begins with a steam shower, followed by an exfoliating scrub, and then a Swedish shower (with 12 magnificent jets) to rinse away debris. Then you're covered up to the neck in sea algae, wrapped in Mylar (a lightweight foil) and then in a heated blanket, which draws out toxins while you nap for 20 minutes.

The friendly and experienced therapists and technicians are specialists in their technique—a hair stylist will not be handling your pedicure, for example. In fact, the Spa Pedicure is so thorough, you'll have calluses and rough spots that other pedicurists ignore filed away and, by some mysterious brushing trick, the polish won't chip for weeks.

INSIDER TIP Bring a book to your spa treatments. Afterward, while lounging in your fluffy robe, you can read on the private deck (or in the spa's Great Room) overlooking the woods and marsh.

Equipment: Cross-country ski machines, rowing machines, stair climbers, stationary bikes, treadmills, weight-training circuit. **Services:** Acupuncture, acupressure, Alexander technique, body treatments, massage (medical and therapeutic). **Swimming:** Indoor pool, 2 therapy pools (1 with underwater treadmill). **Classes and Programs:** Aerobics, chi ball, nutritional counseling, personal training, physical therapy, Pilates, qigong, Spinning, tai chi, workshops on healthy pregnancy, self-defense, etc., yoga. **Recreation:** Hiking, walking. **Children's Programs:** Childcare and developmental activities for ages 6 weeks–6 years.

⛺ 6 rooms.

✕ Meals à la carte from café or Moon Terrace restaurant. **Sample Meals:** Mango-mesclun salad with shrimp and homemade bread, black-bean burritos (lunch); bok choy stir-fry with tofu or chicken, penne with pesto and wild mushrooms, grilled fish (dinner).

💳 Nightly rate $100–$115, double occupancy. All spa treatments are à la carte. AE, MC, V.

✉ *15000 Minnetonka Blvd., Minnetonka, MN 55345,* ☎ *612/935-2202,* FAX *612/935-9685. www.themarsh.com*

MISSOURI

THE ELMS RESORT & SPA

LUXURY PAMPERING ○ NUTRITION AND DIET ○ HOLISTIC HEALTH ○
MEDICAL WELLNESS ○ MINERAL SPRINGS

If Harry Truman or Al Capone turned down the magnificent, tree-lined
avenue leading to the Elms Resort & Spa today, they would undoubtedly feel as if little had changed since their days of retreat and
relaxation here. Careful renovations in the late 1990s restored the spirit
and grandeur that attracted health seekers to the Elms for more than
a century.

The mammoth main building, constructed of Missouri limestone, was
built in 1912 after fire destroyed the original structure. Original tile floors,
marble staircases, and stained glass grace the lobby, which gleams with
wood-burning fireplaces and elegant walnut and mahogany woodwork. It is now listed on the National Register of Historic Places.

The modern 10,000-square-ft spa facility spreads over two floors of the
main building. There are seven sound-proof massage rooms and "quiet"
rooms for treatments ranging from aromatherapy to hot stone massage.
Once in a dark corner of the lower level, the new swim track, filled with
mineral water, is enhanced with bright flowers and rest islands.

Native Americans called the region surrounding Excelsior Springs "the
Valley of Vitality" for the number of mineral springs that bubble up
here. Once the home of nearly 65 mineral bathhouses, only the Elms
and two smaller facilities remain (one of them, the Hall of Waters, boasts
the world's longest mineral water bar). Sights in the area include the
boyhood home of Jesse James, Harry Truman's birthplace, and numerous
attractions in Kansas City.

INSIDER TIP If you can only indulge in one spa treatment, make it the
rose petal and salt scrub, a signature item at the Elms.

Equipment: Free weights, stair climbers, stationary bikes, treadmills,
weight-training circuit. **Services:** Aromatherapy, lymphatic massage, milk
bath, mud and seaweed body wrap, paraffin body wrap, reflexology,
Vichy shower. **Swimming:** 2 pools. **Classes and Programs:** Acupuncture, meditation and stress reduction, nutrition and cooking, smoking
cessation, yoga. **Recreation:** Badminton, biking, boccie, croquet, horseshoes, hiking, volleyball.

🛏 108 rooms, 42 suites.

✕ Meals à la carte. Monarch Room and Dining Room serve American fare. Low-fat and kosher meals available. **Sample Meals:** Blue-corn

crepes, poached peaches, green-pea pancakes (breakfast); ostrich fillet, pheasant, tuna steaks, Kansas City strip steaks (dinner).

✉ Nightly rate $99–$179 per room. 1-night bed-and-breakfast package $119–$159 per couple. 2-night Weekend Getaway package $339 per couple. AE, D, DC, MC, V.

✉ *401 Regent Ave., Excelsior Springs, MO 64024,* ☎ *816/630–5500 or 800/843–3567,* FAX *816/630–5380. www.elmsresort.com*

TAN-TAR-A MARRIOTT RESORT

LUXURY PAMPERING

Nestled in the foothills of the Ozarks, the Tan-Tar-A Resort attracts those in search of outdoor adventure. Boating, fishing, and waterskiing are available on the pristine Lake of the Ozarks. On land you can try horseback riding, clay shooting, tennis on either the indoor or outdoor courts, or a round of golf on a 27-hole championship course surrounded by oak and gnarled cedar trees.

Established in 1960 as a 12-cottage lakeside resort, Tan-Tar-A now includes more than 930 guest rooms. The 185 suites include balconies and fireplaces, which are especially nice in the off-season. Nine restaurants and lounges serve everything from Ozark favorites to seafood.

A focal point of the property is the full-service Windjammer Spa, which underwent a $5 million renovation in 2000. The spa, connected to the resort's indoor swimming pool and fitness facility, overlooks a sandy beach. Everything from aromatherapy to hydrotherapy can be booked à la carte or as a part of eight different packages.

In addition to the numerous outdoor recreational options at the lake, a favorite activity is shopping at the 180-store Osage Beach Outlet Mall as well as the antiques and crafts shops in the area. Several of Missouri's most interesting caves are within minutes of Tan-Tar-A, including Bridal Cave, where you just might walk in on a wedding ceremony in progress, or Meramec Caverns, where Jesse James and gang once hid their treasures.

INSIDER TIP You'll find the Ozarks most crowded in the summer, particularly on holiday weekends. But Tan-Tara-A is often most enjoyable in the off-season. Tee times are easier to schedule, and spa services are less expensive.

Equipment: Rowing machines, stationary bikes, treadmills, weight-training circuit. **Services:** Aromatherapy, herbal linen wrap, paraffin body wrap, reflexology, sea-salt glow. **Swimming:** 3 outdoor pools, 1 indoor pool, lake. **Recreation:** Billiards, bowling, golf, ice-skating, jet skiing, miniature golf, tennis, waterskiing. **Children's Programs:** Supervised activities for children and teenagers.

🛏 930 rooms, 185 suites.

✗ Meals à la carte. 9 restaurants serve varied cuisine. No spa menu available. **Sample Meals:** Split king crab legs, steam-baked sea bass, 22-ounce Porterhouse steak in herb-butter sauce (dinner).

✉ Nightly rate $69–$179 per room. 1-night package $186–$310, includes breakfast, golf. Day spa package $167–$300. AE, D, DC, MC, V.

✉ *State Rd. KK, Osage Beach, MO 65065,* ☎ *573/348–3131 or 800/ 826–8272,* FAX *573/348–3206. www.marriotthotels.com/marriott/osbmo*

MONTANA

BOULDER HOT SPRINGS

MINERAL SPRINGS

Peace Valley derives its name from Native American tribes who designated this area a sanctuary where no fighting was allowed. That peaceful spirit still pervades the area as you enjoy the healing properties of the mineral-spring baths and hikes in the surrounding mountains.

Built in 1883, Boulder Hot Springs was the first permanent building in the area and one of Montana's earliest tourist attractions, hosting both presidents and power brokers. It occupies 274 pine-filled acres bordering the Deer Lodge National Forest.

The geothermal water, which ranges in temperature from 140°F to 175°F, is piped to indoor pools, where it is mixed with cold spring water. The water, free of added chemicals, is changed every four hours. Bathing suits are optional in the men's and women's bathhouses. Bathing-suit-clad guests of both genders and all ages are welcomed in the large outdoor pool.

The grand old hotel at Boulder Hot Springs has seven bed-and-breakfast rooms decorated in Arts and Crafts style, as well as five hotel-style rooms and 26 larger rooms used to accommodate groups. Breakfast is served every morning, and there's a Sunday brunch buffet (a soak is included in the price).

INSIDER TIP Boulder Hot Springs prohibits both alcohol and smoking on the premises.

Services: Massage. **Swimming:** Pool. **Recreation:** Hiking, fishing, skiing.

⌬ 33 rooms.

✕ Breakfast included for B&B guests. For other meals, numerous restaurants are a short drive away. **Sample Meals:** Banana-walnut pancakes and waffles, homemade biscuits and muffins, bacon, sausage, eggs, fresh fruit (breakfast).

▦ Nightly rate $60–$90 per room. MC, V.

✉ *Box 930, Boulder, MT 59632,* ☎ *406/225–4339,* FAX *406/225-4345. www.boulderhotsprings.com*

CHICO HOT SPRINGS RESORT

MINERAL SPRINGS

This rustic resort tempts many tourists to detour on their way to Yellowstone National Park for some time in the saddle and in its two hot-springs pools. About 30 mi from the park's northern gateway, the 150-acre Chico Hot Springs Resort offers pack trips into the Gallatin National Forest and the Absaroka Range of the Rocky Mountains.

Surrounded by spectacular mountain scenery, the open-air pools are fed by 110°F mineral water from several springs. As you soak, you just might spot deer on the nearby slopes. The pools are open to the public. There are places to change into your bathing suit, but bring your own towel if you're not staying at the lodge.

You can stay either in the cozy guest rooms of the turn-the-last-century main lodge or in a newer lodge that maintains the western feeling and boasts more spacious quarters. Also available are family-size suites and two log cabins for families or larger groups. Meals range from gourmet fare to lip-smacking barbecue, and the saloon features entertainment and western swing dancing.

With resident wranglers and a 35-horse stable, Chico Hot Springs has year-round programs for outdoor adventure. In winter there are cross-country skiing and dogsledding. Hikers and mountain bikers can head up to the Beartooth Mountains straight from the lodge. Staffers at the resort's activity center map trails to suit your fitness level. Anglers can test their skills in the resort's pond, and guides lead outings to the spring-fed creeks that run through the forest. A fitness center is also available.

For kids up to age 12, a day camp held from June through August offers a wide range of activities, from identifying animal tracks to outdoor safety.

....

INSIDER TIP Many resorts bill themselves as family establishments, but Chico Hot Springs Lodge extends its welcome to the furry members of your clan. The lodge prides itself on being dog-friendly.

....

Services: Deep-tissue massage, reflexology, shiatsu, Swedish massage. **Swimming:** Pool. **Recreation:** Biking, boating, fishing, hayrides, horseback riding, skiing, snowmobiling, trapshooting, white-water rafting. **Children's Programs:** Day camp June–Aug. for kids up to age 12.

⊞ 81 lodge rooms, 5 suites, 12 motel rooms, 1 2-bedroom and 1 5-bedroom log cabin.

✕ Meals à la carte. Elegant meals in dining room, casual fare in Poolside Grille and lodge saloon. **Sample Meals:** Grilled-beef sandwich with mushrooms and bell peppers, topped with Swiss cheese (lunch); beef Wellington with duck liver pâté, roast venison, grilled trout (dinner).

▥ Nightly rate $39–$189 per room. AE, D, MC, V.

⊠ *1 Chico Rd., Pray, MT 59065,* ☎ *406/333–4933 or 800/468–9232,* FAX *406/333–4694. www.chicohotsprings.com*

FAIRMONT HOT SPRINGS RESORT

MINERAL SPRINGS

Nestled near the Pintlar Wilderness, the Fairmont Hot Springs Resort combines striking modern architecture and western hospitality. The range of amenities and activities—horseback riding, fishing, golf, skiing, and more—makes it ideal for a family vacation in summer or winter.

Native Americans worshiped the "medicine water" of the natural hot springs. The mineral water, 160°F when it surfaces, is cooled to about 94°F for the two Olympic-size swimming pools. Smaller indoor and outdoor soaking pools run 100°F to 105°F for soaking weary muscles. There's a 350-ft warm-water slide to keep children busy.

Accommodations range from well-appointed rooms at the lodge to a fully furnished condominium apartment.

INSIDER TIP Fairmont is famed for its 18-hole golf course, which boasts a fifth hole that's the longest in the state.

Services: Salt-glow, Swedish, and shiatsu massage. **Swimming:** 2 outdoor pools, 1 indoor pool. **Recreation:** Fishing, golf, hayrides, horseback riding, skiing, tennis. **Children's Programs:** Hayrides, sleigh rides.

⌂ 152 rooms.

✕ Meals à la carte. American fare in the Dining Room. **Sample Meals:** Honey-smoked prawns, stuffed rainbow trout, tenderloin of beef, chicken Brie (dinner).

☎ Nightly rate $89–$109 per room. AE, D, MC, V.

⊠ *1500 Fairmont Rd., Anaconda, MT 59711,* ☎ *406/797–3241, 800/443–2381, or 800/332–3272 in Montana,* FAX *406/797–3337. www.fairmontmontana.com*

FEATHERED PIPE RANCH

HOLISTIC HEALTH

In the Rocky Mountains close to the Continental Divide, the Feathered Pipe Ranch sits on land that was once hallowed ground for Native Americans. Climbing to "sacred rocks" for meditation, you gain a panoramic view of the 110-acre ranch. Miles of hiking trails, a sparkling lake and stream, and the dry, clear air add to the experience.

For the past 25 years people from many backgrounds—from professionals in the healing arts to and novices taking their first yoga class—have been coming here to attend workshops led by world-renowned teachers and practitioners. Subjects range from astrology and shamanism to massage training and women's studies. The number of participants in each workshop ranges from 35 to 50, and some families attend with young children.

The log-and-stone buildings give it the look of a frontier outpost. Beyond the main lodge, a huge timbered structure, are a traditional sweat lodge and a cedar bathhouse that holds huge hot tubs, a sauna, and a massage room staffed by professional therapists. Lodging can be in tepees, Mongolian yurts, cabins, and basic tents.

INSIDER TIP Serious concentration is the norm here, so you will find little of the fun-and-fitness holiday atmosphere of other resorts.

Services: Massage. **Swimming:** Lake. **Classes and Programs:** Talks related to study programs. **Recreation:** Hiking, volleyball.

⌂ 6 cabins, 12 dorm beds, tents, tepees, yurts.

✕ Meals included. Vegetarian buffet. **Sample Meals:** Bean enchiladas, tuna salad with pita bread, pasta with vegetables (lunch); baked trout, eggplant and cheese casserole, zucchini baked with tomatoes (dinner).

▦ 1-week program $1,195–$1,445 per person, including lodging, meals, instruction. MC, V.

✉ *2409 Colorado Gulch, Helena, MT 59601,* ☎ *406/443–0430 or 406/442–8196,* FAX *406/442–8110. www.featheredpipe.com*

POTOSI HOT SPRINGS RESORT

MINERAL SPRINGS ◦ SPORTS CONDITIONING

Hikes in the Tobacco Root Mountains are the mainstay of the affordable program at Potosi Hot Springs Resort. A trek to nearby Potosi Peak, for example, takes you through grassy meadows to shimmering lakes and rocky ridges. Mountain biking is another option, especially since all your equipment is provided. And this being Montana, the fishing is great. The nearby Madison and Jefferson rivers are known for trout, but you may want to try one of the other creeks and ponds in the area.

The best part of a stay at Potosi comes at the end of an active day. Stroll a short distance up a side canyon behind the lodge, and you come to natural mineral-water soaking pools, one 90°F, another 102°F.

Guests sleep in four log cabins that face South Willow Creek. Each can accommodate up to six people, with a sleeping loft, kitchen, and living room with a wood stove and river-rock fireplace. There is no air-conditioning or phone, however. Most guests elect to head to the main lodge for family-style meals, which feature gourmet organic fare.

INSIDER TIP Don't worry that the hikes will be too much for you. Daily outings are planned based on the fitness level of each participant.

Services: Massage. **Swimming:** Pool, pond. **Recreation:** Biking, fishing, hiking, horseback riding.

▦ 4 cabins.

✕ Meals à la carte. Breakfast and dinner are served in the dining room, and box lunches accompany guests on their varied activities. **Sample Meals:** Fresh fish, elk tenderloin (dinner).

▦ Nightly rate $150 per person, double occupancy. 1-night package $200 per person, double occupancy, includes lodging, meals. MC, V.

✉ *Box 688, Pony, MT 59747,* ☎ *406/685–3330 or 888/685–1695,* FAX *406/685–3390. www.potosiresort.com*

NEVADA

AQUAE SULIS

LUXURY PAMPERING

Aquae Sulis, Latin for "waters of the sun," offers a full range of treatments and techniques, from a European-style "taking the waters" to a southwestern hot stone massage. It offers some of the most innovative treatments in Las Vegas, as well as a fitness center, full-service salon, and even a boutique.

The spa is part of the Regent Las Vegas, a fairly new resort built in a wealthy suburb of Las Vegas called Summerlin. The property includes two hotels, the Regent Grand Spa and the Regent Grand Palms. Surrounded by three championship golf courses, the Regent Las Vegas has an 11-acre garden and several upscale retail stores and gourmet restaurants.

Every 50-minute treatment begins with the Aquae Sulis Ritual. Based on the ancient Roman bathing tradition, you take hot and cold plunges, then a soak in a warm whirlpool and an outdoor therapy pool, and then a steam and sauna. After a shower guests are served drinks (tea, water, or juice) and fruit. Services range from acupressure to an aura-imaging consultation.

The gym, directly behind the lobby desk, is in a circular room with a vaulted ceiling. It includes complete cardiovascular and weight-training equipment (several pieces of equipment include their own televisions). The spa offers personal fitness training and nutritional and stress-management consultations.

INSIDER TIP You may have trouble choosing which treatment to try. The spa offers more than 20 types of massages and 13 kinds of facials.

Equipment: Free weights, stair climbers, stationary bikes, treadmills. **Services:** Acupressure, aromatherapy, deep-tissue massage, hot stone massage, hydromassage, reflexology, sandalwood body wrap, seaweed wrap, shiatsu. **Swimming:** Hotel pool. **Classes and Programs:** Personal trainer, kickboxing, tai chi, yoga. **Recreation:** Biking, golf, hiking, horseback riding, rock climbing.

⊞ 502 rooms and suites.

✕ No spa café, but meals can be ordered from hotel restaurants. The Parian restaurant serves international fare. **Sample Meals:** Ravioli with sweet summer peas, pearl onions, and farmer cheese, cardamom glazed quail on roasted eggplant, (lunch); grilled salmon on olive couscous with Moroccan pepper relish, linguini tossed with shrimp, scallops, and mussels, wok-seared pepper scallops on lemongrass and kaffir-lime risotto (dinner).

🛏 Nightly rate $195–$295 per room. No spa packages offered at press time. Day spa passes $42. AE, DC, MC, V.

✉ *221 N. Rampart Blvd., Las Vegas, NV 89145,* ☎ *702/869–7807, 877/869–5777,* ℻ *702/869–7772. www.resortatsummerlin.com*

CANYON RANCH SPACLUB

LUXURY PAMPERING

Even among the posh hotels on the Las Vegas strip, the Venetian has a reputation for opulence. You can indulge your passion for shopping in the stores lining a replica of the Grand Canal (or even take a ride in a gondola), sample the finest cuisine in restaurants such as Emeril Lagasse's Delmonico Steakhouse and Kevin Wu's Royal Star, and relax in sumptuous suites with every amenity. It's no surprise to find the Canyon Ranch SpaClub in one of the finest hotels in the city.

A 40-ft rock-climbing wall extends into the spa's lobby, adding to the Southwest-influenced decor of sandstone, simple white walls, and bronze artwork. A salon is also on this level, while a fitness center and treatment rooms are on the level below.

The SpaClub offers a wide range of services, from body wraps to ayurvedic treatments that combine herbs and oils to rejuvenate the skin. Signature services include the Rasul Ceremony, based on an ancient Middle Eastern ritual. Medicinal muds and steamed herbs are self-applied while sitting in a tile steam chamber. The treatment ends with a rain-shower rinse.

INSIDER TIP Lunch at the Canyon Ranch Café, right in the spa, is a must. It's menu is low in fat and calories, but you'd never know it.

Equipment: Cross-country ski machines, free weights, stair climbers, stationary bikes, treadmills. **Services:** Aromatherapy, balneotherapy, European peat body cocoons, lavender and lilac body scrubs, reflexology, reiki, shiatsu. **Swimming:** Pool. **Classes and Programs:** Body sculpting, kickboxing, yoga. **Recreation:** Golf.

🛌 3,036 standard suites, 318 deluxe suites.

✗ Meals à la carte. Canyon Café serves spa cuisine. Hotel restaurants serve varied cuisines. **Sample Meals:** Grilled shrimp with harissa (spicy North African condiment), seared Hawaiian ahi tuna with cinnamon plum dressing (dinner).

🛏 Nightly rate $119–$349 per suite. Spa packages $200–$590 per day, plus lodging. AE, DC, MC, V.

✉ *3355 Las Vegas Blvd. S, Las Vegas, NV 89109,* ☎ *702/414–3600, 877/220–2688.* ℻ *702/410–1100. www.venetian.com*

CASABLANCA RESORT

LUXURY PAMPERING

Mesquite began as a Mormon settlement in 1879. These days it's a tranquil community with a population of about 16,000. But this small town has some big-city entertainment: 10 casinos and five championship golf courses.

One of the best is the Casablanca Resort, a 500-room hotel with a lagoon-style pool with waterfall and water slide. The spa here offers a limited selection of services, but the price is right and the atmosphere divine.

All spa services include access to the mineral pools, eucalyptus steam room, and exercise room. Each spa package includes a choice of a Swedish massage, aromatherapy massage, mud body wrap, or European facial, manicure, and pedicure. For absolute indulgence you can book a couples massage in the spa's lovely gazebo.

Highly recommended is the Ultimate Body Glow. The three-step exfoliation process takes an hour. It's followed by a half-hour massage with a choice of scented lotion: lavender, rosemary, or citrus.

INSIDER TIP Want to get away from the crowds? Enjoy an affordable spa vacation in Mesquite, an hour north of Las Vegas.

Equipment: Free weights, stair machines, stationary bicycles, treadmills. **Services:** Aromatherapy, body wraps, hydrotherapy, reflexology, reiki, salt glow. **Swimming:** Pool. **Recreation:** Golf.

⊞ 500 rooms.

✕ Meals à la carte. Hotel has three restaurants that serve varied fare.

▱ Nightly rates $39–$89 per room. 1-night spa package $121, includes lodging, spa treatment. 2-night spa package $184, includes lodging, spa treatments. AE, DC, MC, V.

✉ *950 W. Mesquite Blvd., Mesquite, NV 89027,* ☏ *702/346–6760 or 800/459–7529,* FAX *702/346–6857. www.casablancaresort.com*

DAVID WALLEY'S HOT SPRINGS RESORT

LUXURY PAMPERING ∘ MINERAL SPRINGS

Early pioneers discovered the soothing thermal waters in Genoa. Now spa enthusiasts can take advantage of the six natural mineral-water pools, as well as a host of other services, at David Walley's Hot Springs Resort.

The resort, 25 minutes from South Lake Tahoe, provides a rejuvenating experience after days on the slopes and nights in the casinos. It offers 13 treatment rooms and classes ranging from aquaerobics to tai chi. Massage therapists create massages based on your individual needs. The spa doesn't offer specific types of massages, instead it offers blocks of time from 30 to 90 minutes.

Take a dip in one (or all) of the six mineral pools, where temperatures range from 98°F to 104°F. If you prefer, there's also a freshwater swimming pool. Tennis courts are available, but you should call ahead to reserve court space.

INSIDER TIP Try the salt-glow scrub. The 45-minute treatment, a specialty here, makes your skin feel soft and refreshed. It includes a massage with a choice of lavender or sandalwood oil.

Equipment: Cross-country ski machines, free weights, stair climbers, stationary bikes, treadmills. **Services:** Massage, mud and seaweed wraps, salt-glow scrub. **Swimming:** 6 mineral-water pools, 1 freshwater pool. **Classes and Programs:** Aquaerobics, tai chi. **Recreation:** Skiing, tennis.

⊞ 42 rooms, 2 cabins.

✕ Meals à la carte. DW Restaurant serves American fare. The Café serves brunch fare. **Sample Meals:** Mediterranean wrap with artichoke hearts, feta cheese, marinated eggplant, and balsamic vinegar, avocado club with sprouts, tomato, hard-boiled egg, Greek salad with wedges of pita (lunch); lobster medallions with a chardonnay beurre blanc, grilled swordfish with fresh ratatouille, linguini with pine nuts and tiger prawns (dinner).

▨ Nightly rate $105–$155 per room. Day spa packages $150–$220. AE, MC, V.

✉ *2001 Foothill Rd., Box 26, Genoa, NV 89411,* ☎ *775/782–8155, 800/628–7831,* ᖴᴬᕼ *775/782–2103.*

DESERT INN

LUXURY PAMPERING

For more than 50 years the Desert Inn has maintained an atmosphere of luxurious indulgence. Not to be outdone by the new, glitzier properties on Las Vegas Boulevard, this landmark recently underwent a $200 million renovation to ensure its place on the Strip.

Greek columns and marble statues may evoke the ancient baths, but the 20,000-square-ft Spa at Desert Inn is state of the art. A stunning glass-walled, floor-to-ceiling rotunda leads to therapy pools, hot- and cold-water plunges, and a big central hot tub. The spa has 20 treatment rooms (as well as two private VIP rooms), six whirlpools, six hydrotherapy tubs, two Finnish saunas, and two Turkish steam baths. You can relax in the spa's heated pool or take a dip in the hotel pool.

The spa offers typical spa treatments: body wraps, body scrubs, and therapeutic baths. Try one of the sea-salt baths. Soaking for 20 minutes in water scented with aromatic oils (pine or chamomile) will soothe aching muscles and moisturize dry skin.

The 2,000-square-ft fitness facility features traditional treadmills and free weights, as well as the newest in fitness technology: virtual reality bikes. Riders face a big screen and take a computerized ride through a variety of settings. Be careful on the curves, as the bike reacts just like a real one.

Guest quarters are spread among four buildings. Suites in the Palm Tower have oversize hot tubs. Three two-level suites have private swimming pools and patios. The nine villas that make up the Villas del Lago complex have three-bedroom suites and boast swimming pools and hot tubs on private patios, workout rooms, and butler service.

INSIDER TIP The spa here is quite popular, so book your treatments at least two weeks in advance.

Equipment: Free weights, rowing machines, stair climbers, stationary bikes, treadmills. **Services:** Aloe-vera revitalizer, aromatherapy, balneotherapy, deep-tissue massage, desert-clay body wrap, herbal body wrap, reflexology, shiatsu, salt glow, seaweed body wrap, thalassotherapy. **Swimming:** 2 pools. **Classes and Programs:** Aquaerobics, personal trainer. **Recreation:** Golf, tennis.

▤ 608 rooms, 107 suites.

✕ Meals à la carte. Ho Wan serves Asian food, Portofino serves Mediterranean-influenced fare, Monte Carlo serves French cuisine, and Terrace Pointe serves American food. **Sample Meals:** Mixed-vegetable fried rice, cashew chicken, spaghetti carbonara (lunch), tomato soup with roasted pumpkin oil, wild greens with balsamic vinaigrette, grilled veal medallions with olives and tomato-basil coulis (dinner).

Nightly rate $215–$275 per room. Spa packages $190–$395 per day. AE, DC, MC, V.

3125 Las Vegas Blvd. S, Las Vegas, NV 89109, ☎ 702/733–4444 or 800/634–6906, FAX 702/733–4437. www.thedesertinn.com

MANDALAY BAY

LUXURY PAMPERING

Spa Mandalay offers typical services in atypical surroundings. Like the rest of the Mandalay Bay resort, the spa reflects the opulence of India with the use of marble and rich, dark wood. The 30,000 square-ft facility is tucked away in the lower level of the hotel, not far from where you access the hotel's private beach.

Spa Mandalay offers three spa packages: The Sensory Journey lasts 1½ hours, the Island Experience lasts 2½ hours, and the ultimate indulgence, the Mandalay Day, offers more than three hours of pampering. Each package includes body wrap, massage, and facial, while the Mandalay Day package also includes a body scrub.

Highly recommended here is the aloe wrap, one of six types offered here. The wrap is an especially effective moisturizer for dry or damaged skin.

INSIDER TIP Ask for the scalp treatment. Peppermint is massaged into the scalp, leaving it feeling tingly and refreshed.

Equipment: Free weights, stair climbers, stationary bikes, treadmills. **Services:** Aloe, eucalyptus, salt-glow, volcanic dust, and kiwi body wraps, aromatherapy, deep-tissue massage, reflexology, shiatsu. **Swimming:** Pool. **Classes and Programs:** Personal trainers. **Recreation:** Golf.

3,700 rooms.

✕ Meals à la carte. Several restaurants serve varied cuisine.

Nightly rate $109–$209 per room. 1-day spa packages $128–$289. AE, DC, MC, V.

3950 Las Vegas Blvd. S, Las Vegas, NV 89109, ☎ 702/632–7220, 800/632–7777, FAX 702/632–7224. www.mandalaybay.com

THE MGM GRAND SPA

LUXURY PAMPERING

Low lighting, tile walls, and soothing music create an atmosphere of understated luxury at the MGM Grand Spa. The 30,000-square-ft facility, with 22 treatment rooms as well as two VIP treatment rooms, offers some of the best pampering in Las Vegas.

Along with massages, wraps, and scrubs, the spa offers full-service nail care. Try a personalized facial: A mixture of soothing ingredients is created just for you. As a bonus, you get to keep the excess, good for about two to three more applications. Also highly recommended is the Italian thermal mud body wrap. The spa uses imported Italian mud to detoxify and rejuvenate the skin.

The gym here is small, but it includes the latest in fitness equipment, including virtual-reality bicycles and treadmills with Internet-access screens.

The hotel won't be hard to find—it's the one with a 100,000-pound, 45-ft-tall brass lion perched on a 25-ft pedestal in front. There's plenty to do here besides the spa. The hotel has 16 restaurants, lounges, theaters, a theme park, a lion habitat, and more than a dozen retail stores.

....

INSIDER TIP Day packages are available during the week, but on the weekend the spa is the exclusive domain of hotel guests.

....

Equipment: Free weights, stair climbers, treadmills. **Services:** Aromatherapy, loofah scrub, milk-and-honey body wrap, sea-salt scrub, tropical seaweed wrap. **Swimming:** No spa pool. Hotel has 5 pools.

▣ 5,034 rooms.

✕ Meals à la carte. Hotel has 16 restaurants serving varied cuisine.

▧ Nightly rate $109–$209 per room. Spa packages $140–$550 per day. AE, DC, MC, V.

✉ *3799 Las Vegas Blvd. S, Las Vegas, NV 89109,* ☎ *702/891–3077 or 888/646–1203,* FAX *702/891–3549. www.mgmgrand.com*

NEW HAMPSHIRE

WATERVILLE VALLEY RESORT

SPORTS CONDITIONING

The first thing you'll notice at Waterville Valley is people on the move. There's so much to do at this 500-acre recreational megacomplex that guests never seem to stand still. In addition to downhill and cross-country skiing, hiking and horseback riding in the White Mountains, and golf at an 18-hole championship course, there are a year-round ice-skating rink, a mountain-biking center, and a sports center with 18 clay tennis courts.

Skiing gave this area its start, and it remains a major draw: 225 acres of ski terrain is crossed by more than 35 downhill trails ranked for beginner, intermediate, and advanced skiers. Snowmaking equipment assures good conditions from December to April. At the Cross Country Ski Center, 65 mi of trails lead into the heart of the White Mountain National Forest. In addition, miles of hiking trails are used for snowshoeing.

The White Mountain Athletic Club, open all year, has indoor and outdoor tennis, lap swimming, an indoor running track, racquetball, squash, a strength-and-toning room, and a cardiovascular room with views of the surrounding mountains. A coed sauna and steam room are available, in addition to separate facilities. You can also sign up for aerobics classes and aquaerobic sessions in the pool. Massage is the only bodywork available.

Accommodations are scattered throughout the valley, ranging from chalet-style inns to condominium apartments (reservations are made through a central lodging bureau). The resort has no central dining facility, but several restaurants are easily accessible.

INSIDER TIP One of the highlights of the summer is the annual chamber music festival, which features everything from classical to jazz.

Equipment: Free weights, rowing machines, stair climbers, stationary bikes, treadmills. **Services:** Swedish massage. **Swimming:** Indoor and outdoor pools, pond. **Classes and Programs:** Aerobics, aquaerobics. **Recreation:** Biking, golf, hiking, ice-skating, racquetball, sailing, skiing, squash, tennis, track.

🏨 4,000 beds in various lodges booked through Central Reservations (☎ 800/468–2553).

✕ No restaurants on the premises. Many restaurants in the area.

1-night Summer Unlimited packages $109–$225 per room, includes lodging at nearby hotels, boating and outdoor activities. 1-night Winter Unlimited package $80–$233, includes skiing and other winter activities. Day passes without lodging $15–$30. AE, DC, MC, V.

✉ *Box 540, Waterville Valley, NH 03215,* ☎ *603/236–8311 for ski and spa information, 800/468–2553 for lodging reservations,* FAX *603/236–4344. www.waterville.com*

NEW JERSEY

BALLY'S PARK PLACE

LUXURY PAMPERING

Escape the crowded beaches, noisy hotels, and glitzy casinos of Atlantic City by indulging in a relaxing massage or vigorous workout at the best spa and fitness facility on the New Jersey coast. Secluded on the eighth floor of a beachfront tower, the Spa at Bally's Park Place has lovely ocean views (especially from the outdoor deck), as well as spacious facilities and top-of-the-line equipment. It's possible to visit the spa and fitness center without ever setting foot in the casino. Most people working out in the weight room also exercise the one-armed bandits.

In the spa complex, light streams into a domed atrium surrounded by terraced gardens. A coed glass-walled sauna flanks the swimming pool (which often gets crowded with children and aquaerobics classes), seven whirlpool tubs, and two showers. Upstairs are Turkish bath, treatment rooms, and exercise equipment. The best value here is the day spa package, which includes lunch, salon treatments, and exercise classes such as low-impact aerobics, shaping with weights, and yoga.

Starting your day with a walk or jog on the boardwalk is the best antidote for a night at the slot machines. You can rent bikes at several places along the wooden walkway, which extends all the way to residential areas of Margate and Ventnor. Atlantic City has been the site of the Miss America Pageant since the 1920s, and during pageant week in September many contestants are seen working out at Bally's.

INSIDER TIP The ultimate relaxer, favored by high-rollers at the casino, is a private massage in the MVP Suite, which comes with its own marble whirlpool and steam shower.

Equipment: Cross-country ski machines, elliptical trainers, stationary bikes, stair climbers, treadmills, weight-training circuit. **Services:** Algae body masque, body polish, herbal wrap, loofah body scrub, sea-mud treatment. **Swimming:** Indoor pool, outdoor pool, beach. **Classes and Programs:** Aerobics, aquaerobics, yoga. **Recreation:** Biking, basketball, racquetball.

🛏 1,268 rooms, 110 suites.

✗ Meals à la carte. Buffet lunch available in Spa Café. Spa cuisine available in hotel's 10 restaurants. **Sample Meals:** Spinach salad, lentil soup (lunch); pan-seared scallops with saffron rice, steamed salmon with onions in balsamic vinegar sauce, lobster and shrimp casserole (dinner).

✉ Nightly rate $89–$275 per room. 2-night spa package $395 per person, double occupancy, includes lodging, spa treatments. 5 night spa package $795 per person, double occupancy, includes lodging, spa treatments. AE, DC, MC, V.

✉ *Boardwalk and Park Pl., Atlantic City, NJ 08401*, ☎ *609/340–4600, 800/772–7777, or 800/225–5977,* ☎ *609/340–4713. www.ballysac.com*

THE HILTON AT SHORT HILLS

LUXURY PAMPERING

Combining the amenities of a luxury hotel with the services of a European health spa has made the Hilton at Short Hills a popular hideaway for Manhattanites.

Occupying two floors of this award-winning hotel, the spa and fitness facilities offer a wide range of services. Secluded on the upper level are the treatment rooms, where all-natural products are used in body wraps, facials, scrubs, and massage. Try the four-layer facial, which uses seaweed to tighten and tone the skin. Two aerobics studios are on the floor below, with classes scheduled from morning to night. On the grounds are tennis courts lighted for nighttime action, as well as racquetball and squash courts.

Rooms and suites are in a seven-story glass-walled complex. For the ultimate escape stay in a spacious Hilton Tower suite, where you'll have access to concierge services and a private lounge with complimentary breakfast, snacks, and dessert. Dinner in the elegant Dining Room features American food with a French accent. For lunch you can opt to dine on low-fat fare on the swimming pool terrace.

....
INSIDER TIP Once you show up, you don't have to think about a thing. Even complimentary workout attire is provided.
....

Equipment: Free weights, rowing machines, stationary bikes, stair climbers, treadmills, weight-training circuit. **Services:** Aromatherapy, body polish, herbal wrap, sea-salt glow, shiatsu, Swedish massage. **Swimming:** Indoor and outdoor pools. **Classes and Programs:** Fitness assessment, computerized nutritional analysis, personal training. **Recreation:** Racquetball, squash, tennis.

🛏 300 rooms, 37 suites.

✗ Meals à la carte. Spa cuisine served poolside or in Terrace Restaurant. **Sample Meals:** Yellow tomato gazpacho with Cajun grilled shrimp, pan-seared yellowfin tuna Niçoise salad (lunch); pan-seared Chilean sea bass fillet with lemon thyme and sherry reduction, seared jumbo sea scallops with lemon-pepper linguine (dinner).

✉ Nightly rate $135–$300 per room. Day spa packages $215–$500, includes lunch, spa treatments. AE, D, DC, MC, V.

✉ *41 JFK Pkwy., Short Hills, NJ 07078,* ☎ *973/379–0100 or 800/455–8667,* ☎ *973/379–6870. www.hiltonatshorthills.com*

OCEAN PLACE RESORT

LUXURY PAMPERING

In the quiet central Jersey shore town of Long Branch, the Ocean Place Resort takes full advantage of its breathtaking seaside setting. The indoor and outdoor pools overlook the ocean, the latter with a sprawling deck for sunbathing and lounging. The 4-mi promenade along the beach is a great place to get in a cardio workout.

The hotel, which attracts many conferences, caters to those seeking a healthy getaway. All rates include use of the spa, which is on the second floor adjacent to the indoor pool. The spa offers a range of treatments, from traditional massages and herbal wraps to hydromassage and hot stone therapy.

Rooms and suites, all with their own balcony, are in a gleaming 12-story tower. Meals are served in the Palm Court Dining Room, whose dramatic glass wall faces the sea. The Captain's Quarters, an intimate pub, serves meals on an outdoor patio during the summer.

INSIDER TIP Most rooms don't face the water, so be sure to ask for one with a direct view of the ocean.

Equipment: Free weights, stationary bikes, stair climbers, treadmills, weight-training circuit. **Services:** Body polish, herbal wrap, hydromassage, reflexology, shiatsu, Vichy shower. **Swimming:** Indoor and outdoor pools. **Classes and Programs:** Personal training. **Recreation:** Racquetball, squash, tennis.

⊞ 254 rooms and suites.

✕ Meals à la carte. **Sample Meals:** Buffet featuring spinach salad with citrus fruit, sole with shrimp in a dill sauce (lunch); seafood chowder, grilled swordfish with tequila lime butter (dinner).

▨ 1-night Spa Escape $220–$275 per person, double occupancy, includes lodging, spa treatments. Day spa packages $135–$300. AE, D, DC, MC, V.

⊠ *1 Ocean Blvd., Long Branch, NJ 07740* ☎ *732/571–4000 or 800/ 411–6493,* ꜰᴀх *732/571–8974. www.oceanplace.com*

NEW MEXICO

OJO CALIENTE MINERAL SPRINGS

MINERAL SPRINGS

Ojo Caliente Mineral Springs bills itself as "the oldest spa in North America," and the claim would be hard to dispute. As far back as 1200, Native Americans built their pueblos on a mesa overlooking the mineral-rich waters of the natural hot springs hidden here in a secluded valley. But Ojo Caliente is also unique because it is the only place in the world where five types of mineral water—soda, arsenic, lithium, iron, and sodium—bubble to the surface in the same area. More than 100,000 gallons of the stuff pour out every day.

Ojo Caliente, which means "hot eye" for the center of the spring, was named by Spanish explorer Cabeza de Vaca when he visited here in 1535. "The greatest treasure I have found these strange people to possess are some hot springs which burst out of the foot of a mountain that gives evidence of being an active volcano," he wrote in his journal. "I believe I have found the Fountain of Youth."

Modern-day visitors draw similar conclusions about the restorative powers of the springs. The spa itself, built in the 1920s (no one knows the exact date), is a funky, no-frills establishment. The demands of 21th-century patrons have led to added services such as acupuncture, aromatherapy, facials, and mud wraps. Included in the nightly lodging rates are use of the mineral water pools as well as two Milagro Wraps (dry blanket wraps to induce the release of toxins).

The hotel, which was one of the original bathhouses, has accommodations that are decidedly spare but clean and comfortable, with cozy down comforters. The building is on the National Register of Historic Places. Also listed is the adjacent Round Barn, from which visitors can take horseback tours and guided hikes to the ruins of the ancient pueblo dwellings and petroglyph-etched rocks.

Ojo Caliente is the kind of place where you needn't feel self-conscious about your body. Ensconced in a rock-lined pool at the base of a sandstone cliff and inhaling the clean desert air, it's easy to imagine yourself one of the early pueblo dwellers who soaked here centuries ago.

INSIDER TIP Just over an hour from Santa Fe, Ojo Caliente can be a restful overnight trip. The remote rural setting enhances the sense of detachment and relaxation.

Services: Acupuncture, blue-cornmeal facial, herbal wrap, moor mud wrap, red-clay facial, salt glow, seaweed wrap. **Swimming:** Pool. **Recreation:** Biking, hiking, horseback riding, rafting, skiing.

🏠 19 rooms, 19 cottages.

✕ Meals à la carte. Poppy's Café & Grill serves casual American fare. **Sample Meals:** Chicken-mushroom-melt sandwich, Ojo club on a whole wheat tortilla, red or green chili with beans (lunch); chicken with charred-tomato salsa, pasta puttanesca (with tomatoes, olives, anchovies, and capers), New York strip steak, vegetable stir-fry (dinner).

💳 Nightly rate $100–$130 per room, includes lodging, spa treatments. AE, D, DC, MC, V.

✉ *Box 68, Ojo Caliente, NM 87549,* ☎ *505/583–2233 or 800/222– 9162,* 📠 *505/583–2464. www.ojocalientespa.com*

TEN THOUSAND WAVES

MINERAL SPRINGS

Perched on a hill overlooking Santa Fe and the spectacular Sangre de Cristo Mountains, Ten Thousand Waves brings a bit of Japan to the Southwest. Despite the dozens of people who often soak in the communal pool, a serene hush pervades the crisp desert air, especially at night.

Sybaritic rather than fitness-oriented, this resort has an esoteric menu of treatments. Choices include an ayurvedic massage with herbal oils and calamus-root powder. The Japanese hot stone massage uses hot lava rocks and cold marble stones to stimulate the circulation for an experience that is deeply relaxing yet revitalizing. Most bodywork takes place in breezy cedar-paneled rooms, and some accommodate couples.

The open-air soaking tubs (refilled after every use) resemble authentic Japanese baths. Nine tubs are available by the hour. The tile Imperial Ofuro holds 10 people and has a private bathroom and changing area plus two balconies. The Waterfall has a natural rock deck, warm tub, and cold plunge pool, and holds up to 12 people. The new Kojiro has a pebble bottom. All have access to cold plunge pools and saunas or a steam room. There are also two communal tubs, one for everyone and one just for women. Bathing suits are optional in the communal tub until 8:15 PM and in the women's tub at all times.

Clad in a cotton kimono and sandals issued at check-in, you follow paths from the pools to your room at the Houses of the Moon, which centers around a lantern-lighted garden. Furnished with hand-carved wooden fixtures and futons and beds with buckwheat husk pillows, most rooms accommodate up to four persons. One room has a tatami-mat floor in the style of a Japanese country inn. All come equipped with a fireplace for chilly nights.

INSIDER TIP Just 20 minutes from Santa Fe, this is a quick getaway for those who want to meditate and release stress naturally.

Services: Herbal wrap, massage, salt glow. **Recreation:** Hiking, horseback riding, rafting, skiing.

🏠 9 guest houses.

✕ No lunch or dinner available. Snacks and drinks for sale in the lobby.

💳 Nightly rate $205–$250 per room, includes breakfast. Day spa packages $99–$317. D, MC, V.

✉ *Hyde Park Rd., Box 10200, Santa Fe, NM 87504,* ☎ *505/982–9304,* 📠 *505/989–5077. www.tenthousandwaves.com*

TRUTH OR CONSEQUENCES

MINERAL SPRINGS

This funky, easygoing little town offers a taste of authentic New Mexico–style hot springs at bargain prices. Originally called Hot Springs, the town's odd moniker came about when the 1950s television game show of the same name offered fame and fortune to any town willing to rename itself. Classy it may not be, but the area does attract many artists and senior citizens in search of affordable alternatives to Santa Fe.

The downtown district is where the mineral water is easily tapped and available at bargain prices as low as $3.50 an hour for a good soak. But plans were in the works for more upscale offerings. A New York City business has announced plans to open a luxury spa called Sierra Grande Lodge at the site of a now closed bathhouse in the historic downtown area. For now, Truth or Consequences is still a down-home place with a low-key charm.

Among Truth or Consequences' many resorts are **Hay-Yo-Kay Hot Springs** (✉ 300 Austin Ave., ☎ 505/894–2228), one block south of Broadway. The complex, the largest in the area, offers five naturally flowing pools. In 2000 owner Steve Kortemeier was rebuilding the adjacent **Yucca Bathhouse,** which will mean the addition of two new pools. A half-hour soak here costs $4. Massages and reflexology sessions are available for $30 for a 30-minute session.

Riverbend Hot Springs (✉ 100 Austin Ave., ☎ 505/894–6183) is an extraordinarily user-friendly, ultracasual facility with clean but slightly dilapidated hostel accommodations. Three outdoor tanks once used for growing minnows for fish bait have been converted into hot tubs. You can soak in a hot Minnow Bath while being serenaded by the murmuring waters of the Rio Grande and gazing out at the changing shadows of Turtleback Mountain. In the evening guests gather for conversation around a fire pit. There's also a meditation area. Room rates are from $20 to $45, which include free access to the hot tubs.

Firewater Lodge (✉ 309 Broadway, ☎ 505/894–5555 or 505/894–3405) offers B&B-style lodging in a renovated motel with a horseshoe configuration. The parking lot has been converted to a courtyard for a quiet retreat. This is the only site in town where you can rent a room with its own private hot bath tapping into underground mineral waters. You'll find the popular Hot Springs Bakery at this site, with healthful offerings such as homemade whole-wheat and barley bread and tofu salad. There are also a vegetarian menu and diabetic-friendly treats. Three rooms are available for $45 to $75. The site also has three separate, private hot-bath rooms available free to guests and at $4 for visitors.

Ask for individual rooms with turtle, lizard, or Mimbres petroglyph themes at the **Marshall Hot Springs** (✉ 311 Marr, ☎ 505/894–9286). New Age music and incense enhance spiritual "good vibes" here. Owners Jane Ehrenreich and Gerald Liebovitz recently added lodging, with three rooms available for $45 to $80. A one-hour massage here costs $6, while $4 will buy you a half-hour session. Acupuncture treatments cost $25 for a 30-minute session. Natural skin-care and body products also are sold here.

At **Indian Springs** (✉ 218 Austin, ☎ 505/894–2018), seven modest rooms are available for $30. A special $135 weekly rate is also available. Guests have free access, twice daily, to two indoor hot baths.

At the **Artesian Bathhouse & RV Park** (✉ 312 Marr, ☎ 505/894–2684), camping is available for recreational vehicles along with access to a bathhouse with eight tubs in private rooms for $3.50 per hour ($2 for registered campers). Massage can be arranged for a price of $35 hourly.

The **Charles Motel & Bath House** (✉ 601 Broadway, ☎ 505/894–7154) has rooms with kitchenettes for $35 to $45. Massage, reflexology, holistic healing, tai chi, yoga, and other treatments are also available.

INSIDER TIP You might miss some of the modern conveniences at the spas in this town with a "Route 66" appearance, but you won't miss the higher prices. Low-cost lodgings and cheap eats make some people roost here indefinitely.

Swimming: Nearby lake. **Recreation:** Boating, fishing, hiking, tubing, windsailing.

🏨 See individual lodgings listed above.

✗ No restaurants at most bathhouse resorts. Dining options within walking distance.

✉ *Chamber of Commerce, Drawer 31, Truth or Consequences, NM 87901,* ☎ *505/894–3536.*

VISTA CLARA RANCH RESORT & SPA

LUXURY PAMPERING ○ HOLISTIC HEALTH

An up-to-the-minute health and fitness facility incorporating ancient Native American healing arts, Vista Clara occupies a former ranch in the Galisteo Basin amid soul-stirring mountains, rock formations carved with prehistoric petroglyphs, and inspiring high-desert vistas. The contrast of old and new is a recurring theme here. You can work out in a state-of-the-art fitness center or participate in a cleansing sweat-lodge ceremony. You can enjoy the latest massage techniques or attend the Ancestral Ways program, which explores Native American history, culture, and spirituality.

The setting is expansive, but the scale of the resort itself is intimate, almost cozy. Accommodations are spacious and decorated in southwestern style, with carved wooden furnishings and log-beamed ceilings; all have either a deck or patio. In a dining room that's part of the original historic ranch house, you'll be treated to the "Southwest Spa Cuisine" of award-winning chefs Steve and Kristin Jarrett. Their use of fresh local ingredients, many from the spa's own organic garden, makes each dish come alive with flavor—you won't have to worry about a diet of raw vegetables and sprouts, and you'll find their reverence for high-quality, organic ingredients is contagious.

In addition to spa staples such as massage, facials, and other beauty treatments (including organic hair coloring), you can take a dip in the chlorine-free swimming pool or soak in an outdoor hot tub with panoramic views of the valley. Other activities include horseback rides, daily guided hikes to historic sites, cooking and art classes, and tours to Santa Fe's famous galleries.

A typical day at Vista Clara begins with a gourmet breakfast, followed by a hike and a dance class. After a cooking demonstration by the resident chefs, a healthy lunch is served. The afternoon might include a massage and a body treatment or soothing craniosacral therapy. Finish up with a class in yoga or the ancient Chinese movement arts of tai chi or qigong.

INSIDER TIP Although astrology readings and various holistic therapies are available here, the atmosphere remains down-to-earth, with none of the New Age attitudes that pervade some spas.

Equipment: Free weights, stair climbers, stationary bikes, treadmills, weight-training circuit. **Services:** Aromatherapy, 4-handed massage, moor mud wrap, reflexology, shiatsu, Swiss shower. **Swimming:** Pool. **Classes and Programs:** Aerobics, aquaerobics, art and cooking classes, dance, meditation, personal training, qigong, tai chi, yoga. **Recreation:** Hiking, horseback riding.

⊞ Meals à la carte. The Ranch House serves southwestern cuisine. Low-fat food available. **Sample Meals:** Grilled beet and goat cheese quesadilla with branded onion salsa, habanero chicken sausage and vegetable tostada with apple salsa, Caesar salad with achiote marinated shrimp (lunch); grilled pork tenderloin with plum-basil sauce, Cornish hens with apricot glaze, sautéed salmon with chipolte cream sauce, roasted pork loin (dinner).

✗ 10 rooms.

▧ Nightly rate $225 per person, double occupancy. 5-night spa package $1,780 for two, includes lodging, spa treatments. Day spa package $315. MC, V.

✉ HC 75 Box 111, Galisteo, NM 87540, ☎ 505/466–4772, 888/663–9772, ℻ 505/466–1942. www.vistaclara.com

COPPERHOOD INN & SPA

LUXURY PAMPERING

Tucked beside Esopus Creek in the Catskill Mountains, the Copperhood is a intimate, European-style inn and spa that caters to both individuals and couples. Elizabeth Winograd is an extremely hands-on proprietor, and she and her small staff work with all her guests to create a daily schedule that caters to each person's needs and expectations.

The spa experience here is about capturing a "zest for life." Although meals are healthful, this is not necessarily a place to come to lose weight. Activities range from hiking to mountain biking on nearby nature trails. You can swim laps in the 60-ft indoor pool or play a few games of tennis. There are classes in everything from fencing to belly dancing, which illustrates the spa's philosophy that exercise should never be boring.

As all the therapists work on a freelance basis, all treatments must be discussed and booked in advance. Massage is a specialty at Copperhood, as is something called European Body Treatment. Two hours of complete indulgence begins with an almond scrub and ends with a Swedish massage.

The Copperhood is very much about the details. Guest rooms are comfortable and filled with antiques. The dining room has a central fireplace and wagon-wheel chandelier hanging above. Dinner is a set menu, and everything from the rolls to the salad dressing is prepared fresh. Winograd is never far away, and in the morning over a buffet breakfast of fresh fruit, pastries, and eggs, she will sit down with you to plan the rest of your day.

Equipment: Free weights, stair climbers, stationary bikes, treadmills, weight-training circuit. **Services:** Acupuncture, aromatherapy, body wraps, reiki, reflexology, salt glow, shiatsu. **Swimming:** Indoor pool, river. **Classes and Programs:** Belly dancing, fencing, meditation, personal training, strength training. **Recreation:** Biking, hiking, fishing, golf, jogging, skiing, tennis.

🛏 19 rooms.

✕ Meals included. Breakfast buffet; lunch and dinner served in the dining room. **Sample Meals:** Mesclun greens with balsamic vinaigrette, smoked trout with spicy yogurt dressing, fruit sorbet (lunch); leek-and-potato soup, free-range chicken breast in sun-dried tomato and tarragon purée with wild rice and braised fennel (dinner).

✉ Nightly rate $280 per person, double occupancy, includes room, meals, spa treatments. 2-night package $570 per person, double occupancy. Day spa package $279. AE, MC, V.

✉ *Rte. 28, Shandaken, NY 12480,* ☎ *914/688–2460,* FAX *914/688–7484. www.copperhood.com*

GURNEY'S INN

LUXURY PAMPERING ○ NUTRITION AND DIET

Thalassotherapy is the specialty at this spa on the tip of Long Island. At Gurney's Inn you can soak in seaweed baths, swim laps in a 60-ft heated seawater pool, indulge in a seaweed facial, and dine on seafood, all while enjoying a view of the sea. You can even arrange to go deep-sea fishing from a nearby marina.

Among the spa's many innovative uses of seawater are underwater massages in private Roman tubs and body scrubs using salt from the Dead Sea. Also popular are body wraps that mix mud with seaweed to create a mineral-rich gel said to promote balance and healing in the body while relieving many symptoms of arthritis.

Brisk morning walks along the shore usher in the daily program. After breakfast you can join an aquatic exercise class in the pool, take a tai chi or yoga class, join a group hike along the windswept dunes, or swim in the surf. For cardiovascular and strength training, a sea-view exercise room has personal trainers on hand to help you with the equipment. The spa's 60-person staff includes specialists in everything from traditional Swedish massage to craniosacral therapy, polarity, and reflexology.

Two of the inn's buildings face the beach. Another three buildings are set back behind the spa, though rooms in all five have ocean views. Four luxurious oceanfront cottages provide more private getaways. Guests dine either in the Café Monte or the more formal Sea Grill. Both restaurants have low-calorie options in addition to standard menus.

INSIDER TIP Book far in advance if you plan to visit during summer, the inn's busiest season. For peace and quite, schedule your visit for when the beach crowd goes home.

Equipment: Free weights, stair climbers, stationary bikes, treadmills, weight-training circuit. **Services:** Acupressure, craniosacral massage, fango, herbal wrap, loofah scrub, mud wrap, reflexology, reiki, seaweed wrap, shiatsu, thalassotherapy. **Swimming:** Indoor heated seawater pool, beach. **Classes and Programs:** Aerobics, aquaerobics, biofeedback, health and fitness consultation, health and nutrition lectures, kickboxing, personal training, tai chi, yoga. **Recreation:** Fishing, golf, hiking, horseback riding, jogging, tennis.

🛏 105 suites, 4 cottages

✗ Meals included. Café Monte and Sea Grill serve seafood, international cuisine. Low-calorie meals available. **Sample Meals:** Egg-drop soup, grilled salmon, whole wheat pasta (lunch); paella, vegetarian lasagna, chicken breast with asparagus (dinner).

✉ Nightly rate $145–$180 per person, double occupancy. 5-day package $1,400 per person, double occupancy, includes lodging, meals, spa treatments. Day spa package $197. AE, DC, MC, V.

✉ *Old Montauk Hwy., Montauk, NY 11954,* ☎ *516/668–2345 or 800/848–7639,* FAX *516/668–3203. www.gurneys-inn.com*

munal. But what keeps clients coming back year after year is the laid-back atmosphere. "It's a lot like an overnight camp, but the food is a lot better," says Paradise. "It's the kind of place you can let your hair down."

The days here are usually quite full, starting with a 7 AM hike, sometimes led by Paradise and her dogs, through woods teeming with deer. There is a choice of at least three exercise classes before lunch and several more before dinner. Of course, there is a variety of relaxing spa treatments from which to choose, from a four-hand massage to a moor mud wrap. The treatments are extremely popular, especially on the weekends, so book ahead. The indoor pool and hot tub area is a serene place to spend some free time, as are the sauna and steam rooms.

Buffet meals are served at set hours. Much of the organic food is grown on the property. The menu lists the calories for everything served, although if you want three servings of dessert, no one will stop you. After dinner there is usually a lecture, on topics ranging from meditation to diet to alternative healing methods.

INSIDER TIP Feeling adventurous? The resort's High Elements athletic course involves balancing on a log 30 ft above the ground, zipping down a wire on a pulley, and jumping to catch a trapeze from a pole 35 ft high.

Equipment: Free weights, stair climbers, treadmills, weight-training circuit. **Services:** Aromatherapy, body wraps, hydrotherapy, massage, reflexology. **Swimming:** Heated indoor and outdoor pools. **Classes and Programs:** Aerobics, muscle conditioning, meditation, stretch, yoga. **Recreation:** Hiking, skiing, snowshoeing.

✕ 38 rooms.

✕ Meals included. Three low-fat, low-sodium buffets are served. **Sample Meals:** Corn chowder, mesclun greens and vegetables, pasta primavera (lunch); white-bean soup, grilled salmon with mustard sauce (dinner).

▣ Nightly rate $156–$359 per person, double occupancy, includes meals, use of spa facilities, participation in programs. 5-night Mini-Week program $778–$1,795 per person, double occupancy. AE, DC, MC, V.

✉ *Rte. 55, Neversink, NY 12765* ☎ *914/985–7600 or 800/682–4348,* FAX *914/985–2467. www.newagehealthspa.com*

OMEGA INSTITUTE

HOLISTIC HEALTH ∘ MEDICAL WELLNESS

Part summer camp, part holistic health center, the Omega Institute is a roving program that takes place several times throughout the year in various parts of the country, including the U.S. Virgin Islands. On this 140-acre campus in the scenic Hudson Valley, campers of all ages—including singles, couples, and families—participate in more than 250 workshops on topics ranging from cooking to spirituality that are scheduled from May through mid-October.

The core program, a five-day Wellness Week, involves working with a small group in a structured workshop where you learn how to incorporate the latest findings on health, diet, and nutrition into your lifestyle. Most workshops and seminars last from two to five days, and each requires a separate registration fee.

Though there is no gym on the property, groups assemble for yoga and tai chi sessions each morning and afternoon. Massage is available, but bring your own towel and bathing suit as facilities are coed.

Guests have a choice of simple accommodations. There are 230 two-room cottages and seven dormitory-style facilities with two beds in each room. Several double-occupancy tent cabins on raised platforms have electricity but little else. For those who truly want to rough it, there are campsites near the lake or on a hill that share communal bathhouses. Whichever option you choose, prepare to go without television, phone, and air-conditioning.

Everyone comes together during mealtimes in the big, self-service dining room. Spontaneous discussion groups often form on the porch. In the evening you can take time out for a quiet walk down a country lane or a swim in the lake. Often there are performances of gospel music, chanting, and dance.

Children's programs are designed to open young minds to new ideas and the traditions of people around the world. For those under 12 there are programs in nature study, music, and movement. Two family weeks, one in July and one in August, include nature studies and creative games for children between the ages of 4 and 17, as well as workshops for adults.

INSIDER TIP The stress here is more on the spirit than the body, so come with an open mind. For some a week or even just a weekend here can be a life-changing experience.

Services: Massage. **Swimming:** Lake. **Classes and Programs:** Nutrition consultations, wellness workshops. **Recreation:** Basketball, canoeing, jogging, tennis, volleyball. **Children's Programs:** Ongoing programs for ages 4–12 and ages 12–17.

🏠 230 cabins, 7 dormitory-style rooms, 10 tent cabins. Campsites available.

✕ Meals included. Vegetarian buffet, with some fish and dairy. **Sample Meals:** Mushroom-barley soup, stir-fried greens with brown rice, cashew chili with cheddar (lunch); Pad thai (Asian noodle dish), salmon with wasabi glaze, Cajun catfish, fresh ravioli (dinner).

💳 2-day program $130–$260 per person, double occupancy, includes meals. 5-day Omega Wellness program: $290–$320, lodging and meals not included. MC, V.

✉ *260 Lake Dr., Rhinebeck, NY 12572,* ☎ *914/266–4444 or 800/ 944–1001,* FAX *914/266–4828. www.eomega.org*

SAGAMORE RESORT & SPA

LUXURY PAMPERING

Set on a 70-acre island surrounded by Lake George, the white-clapboard Sagamore Resort & Spa is an escape to a bygone era. The sprawling 350-room hotel—built in 1930 on the site of the original Sagamore Inn that opened in 1893—affords a stunning view of the Adirondack Mountains.

In addition to massage, facials, and body treatments, the specialties at the European-style spa include seaweed wraps, mud therapy (using natural mud in body wraps), and therapies to speed healing of sports injuries. You can wind down your treatment with a full-body rubdown using a mixture of sea salt and massage oil that leaves your skin tingling.

The resort includes a modern health club flooded with natural light, an indoor swimming pool, and indoor tennis and racquetball courts. Classes, from walks to water aerobics, are scheduled throughout the day. There are plenty of exercise machines in the fitness center and personal trainers on hand to help you learn how to use them.

Accommodations in the colonial-revival main house have views of the lake and gardens. The seven newer lodge buildings are right on the lake. Don't miss the beautiful par-70 championship golf course designed by Donald Rose, which is full of cross-country skiers in winter. Even if you don't ski, stop by the clubhouse for dinner.

....
INSIDER TIP Spa treatments are usually selected on an à la carte basis, but one of the flexible spa plans offers more for your money.
....

Equipment: Cross-country skiing machines, rowing machines, stair climbers, stationary bikes, treadmills, weight-training circuit. **Services:** Acupuncture, aromatherapy, body polish, body scrub, herbal wrap, mud wrap, reflexology, reiki, salt glow, seaweed wrap, shiatsu. **Swimming:** Indoor pool, lake. **Classes and Programs:** Aquaerobics, step aerobics, tai chi, yoga. **Recreation:** Boating, golf, hiking, horse-drawn sleigh rides, horseback riding, ice-skating, racquetball, skiing, sledding, tennis, tobogganing, water sports.

▦ 172 rooms, 178 suites.

✕ Meals à la carte. 5 restaurants serve American and international fare. All have low-calorie options. **Sample Meals:** Grilled vegetable sandwich, pecan-crusted chicken (lunch); roasted Maine lobster with vanilla fava-bean risotto, roast veal tenderloin (dinner).

▨ Nightly rate $125–$465 per room. 2- to 4-hour spa packages $109–$285, includes spa treatments only. 2- or 3-day Spa Getaway package $359, includes spa treatments only. AE, D, DC, MC, V.

✉ *110 Sagamore Rd., Box 450, Bolton Landing, NY 12814,* ☎ *518/644–9400 or 800/358–3585,* 𝖥𝖠𝖷 *518/644–3033. www.thesagamore.com*

SIVANANDA ASHRAM YOGA RANCH

HOLISTIC HEALTH

Stressed-out urbanites, take note: You can leave your worries behind when you reach the Sivananda Ashram Yoga Ranch, a rustic retreat on 80 wooded acres a few hours from New York City.

Morning and evening everyone here participates in classes devoted to traditional yogic exercise and breathing techniques. The dozen asana positions range from a headstand to a spinal twist, and each has specific benefits for the body. You will learn how proper breathing, or pranayama, is essential for energy control.

The days begin and end with meditation and chanting, followed by communal vegetarian meals (a large organic garden provides seasonal vegetables). Participation in the ashram's programs is mandatory, including various talks about yogic practice and philosophy. A coed sauna is the only spa facility available, although on the weekends it is possible to sign up for a massage or shiatsu session. There is no exercise equipment on the premises.

Accommodations, in a century-old farmhouse and a 50-year-old building that was once a hotel, are simple. Rustic rooms hold from two to four people. Tent space is also available.

INSIDER TIP To avoid driving in New York traffic, take advantage of the shuttle-van service that leaves from the city every Friday.

Services: Massage and shiatsu on weekends. **Swimming:** Pond. **Classes and Programs:** Chanting, lectures, meditation. **Recreation:** Hiking.

▤ 60 rooms, most without bath. Campsites available.

✗ Meals included. Vegetarian buffet is served in the main house. **Sample Meals:** Pancakes, granola, fruit (breakfast); lentil soup, basmati rice, tofu loaf (dinner).

▨ Nightly rate $45–$60 per person, includes lodging, meals. 5-day Yoga Vacation $250 per person, includes lodging, meals, yoga. 1-month work-study program $450. MC, V.

⊠ *Budd Rd., Box 195, Woodbourne, NY 12788,* ☎ *914/436–6492, 914/434–9242, or 800/783–9642,* ⅋ᴀ⅀ *914/434–1032. www. sivananda.org*

VATRA NATURAL WEIGHT LOSS SPA

NUTRITION AND DIET

Set on 23 wooded acres at the base of Hunter Mountain, the Vatra Natural Weight Loss Spa is surrounded by trails that wind through a nearby state park. It's a place to stroll along quiet country roads or amble past lonely ponds edged by cattails. This not a place for serious fitness buffs, however. Like the not-so-fancy "fat farms" of years past, Vatra strives to make everyone at home, with an unintimidating, supportive approach to shedding extra pounds.

Most people who come here follow a 750-calorie-per-day meal plan, though there's also a 1200-calorie-per-day alternative. No additions or variations are made without special arrangements, and no between-meal snacks are allowed. Guests start with a brief medical history to determine nutritional needs and fitness level. A computerized body-composition analysis may be recommended.

The program consists of two daily aquaerobics workouts and various exercise classes led by fitness instructors. Spa director George Borkacki sometimes leads the 6:30 AM yoga class and occasional walking excursions. Educational lectures on food and food products are offered from time to time, usually on weekends and during the summer.

Almost all activities take place in the main building, a renovated farmhouse. The dining room is a large, homey room with lots of windows and decorated with European collectibles. The workout room doubles as a lounge, with separate areas containing exercise equipment, mirrored exercise space, and a sofa and television. A heated swimming pool is housed in a separate building. A few spa treatments are offered upstairs, in former bedrooms.

The lodge has 25 simply furnished guest rooms and a large sundeck. Some upstairs rooms have sleeping lofts and skylights, and one has a whirlpool tub.

INSIDER TIP This is a place for serious weight loss. If you stick with the program, you are likely to see results in a week.

Equipment: Free weights, stair climbers, stationary bikes, treadmills. **Service:** Aromatherapy, body polish, reflexology, seaweed wrap. **Swimming:** Indoor and outdoor pools. **Classes and Programs:** Aerobics, aquaerobics, body-composition analysis, cholesterol testing, fitness consultation, stress management, yoga. **Recreation:** Basketball, biking, hiking, tennis, volleyball.

▦ 25 rooms.

✗ Meals included in packages. 3 750- or 1,200-calorie vegetarian meals served in the main house. **Sample Meals:** Spinach fettuccine primavera, carrot soup, stuffed peppers, Waldorf salad (lunch); zucchini lasagna, broiled eggplant, stuffed cabbage, grilled bean curd (dinner).

▨ Nightly rate $98 per room. 2-night weekend package $375 per person, double occupancy, includes meals, classes, spa treatments. 4-night package $680 per person, double occupancy, includes meals, classes, spa treatments. AE, MC, V.

✉ *Rte. 214, Box F, Hunter, NY 12442,* ☎ *518/263–4919 or 800/232–2772,* ℻ *518/263–4994. www.vatraspa.com*

DUKE UNIVERSITY DIET & FITNESS CENTER

NUTRITION AND DIET

The Duke Diet & Fitness Center, part of the Duke University Health System, has been helping individuals struggling with obesity for more than 30 years. Designed to help address the underlying causes of weight problems, the two- to four-week medically supervised and structured program is tailored to each individual.

Programs begins with full medical checkups, including a full physical, medical-history review, and an exercise test to help screen for cardiovascular disease and determine your fitness level. From this information the medical staff sets up a schedule based on your personal interests. An integral part of the experience is support—from the experienced staff as well as your fellow participants.

The program includes lectures, workshops, personal and group counseling, exercise sessions, cooking classes, as well as excursions to a supermarket and restaurant to help you learn how to choose healthier food. There are also weekend workshops in smoking cessation, stress management, and diabetes management as part of an overall weight-loss program. You also receive a thick binder full of tips on how to continue the regimen at home.

Housed in a former YMCA, the center is a 30,900-square-ft facility containing medical and administrative offices, classrooms, an indoor exercise pool, a fully equipped gym with cardiovascular and strength-training machines, and a dining hall.

Weekends and evenings provide opportunities to explore the area and take in sports events and entertainment. Downtown, the Carolina Theater houses a lively season of shows and concerts, while the old Bull Durham ball field hosts jazz concerts.

INSIDER TIP Many participants choose Duke because of the emphasis on comprehensive medical care. The staff carefully monitors medical conditions that are sensitive to the effects of diet and exercise, such as diabetes and hypertension.

Equipment: Elliptical trainers, rowing machines, stair climbers, stationary bikes, treadmills, weight-training circuit. **Classes:** Aerobics, stretching, tai chi, yoga. **Services:** Massage. **Swimming:** Indoor pool. **Classes and Programs:** Body-composition testing, career counseling, personal training, psychotherapy, swimming instruction. **Recreation:** Basketball, volleyball.

☎ Rooms available in nearby hotels.

✕ Meals included. Food low in calories, fat, and cholesterol served in cafeteria (vegetarian and kosher diets can be accommodated, within limits). **Sample Meals:** Seafood gumbo with rice, lamb stew, eggplant Parmesan (lunch); Italian baked fish, barbecued chicken, black-bean tortillas (dinner).

💲 1-week program $3,295 per person. 4-week program: $6,195 per person. Extended stay program $715 per person per week. AE, D, DC, MC, V.

✉ *804 W. Trinity Ave., Durham, NC 27701,* ☎ *919/688–3079 or 800/ 235–3853,* ᶠᴬˣ *919/684–8246. www.dukecenter.org*

STRUCTURE HOUSE

NUTRITION AND DIET

Structure House is one of the country's most successful centers for serious weight loss. The program, which combines nutritious food, enjoyable exercise, and behavioral therapy, allows you to continue your healthier lifestyle at home.

Director Gerard J. Musante developed his techniques while working as a clinical psychologist with the Duke University Medical Center. He noted that many obese patients who lost weight on supervised diets regained weight when they returned home. Musante reasoned that the patient must become aware of his or her relationship with food to gain long-term success. He applied this pioneering behavioral approach to weight management and founded Structure House in 1977.

Seventy-five health care professionals—including psychotherapists, exercise counselors, and nutritionists—focus on behavior modification and help you to understand and overcome obesity. They help you plan an individual diet-and-exercise regimen. If you have diabetes, hypertension, or cardiac problems, you are constantly monitored.

As a participant, you can take advantage of more than 70 classes, workshops, and activities each week. You will learn the details of good nutrition—how to shop for and prepare healthy meals and how to eat better in restaurants. You will learn what type of exercise is best for you. Most important, you will understand how to create a positive relationship with food that leads to a healthy lifestyle.

Housed in a large, Georgian-style building, participants often feel they're in a supportive, self-contained community. The environment is pleasant, and the grounds are attractively landscaped and well maintained.

INSIDER TIP Unlike some weight-loss centers, the clientele here is quite diverse. About 40% of participants are men.

Equipment: Cross-trainers, elliptical trainers, free weights, stationary bikes, treadmills, weight-training circuit. **Services:** Massage. **Swimming:** Indoor and outdoor pools. **Classes and Programs:** Diet and nutrition workshops, medical consultation, personal trainers. **Recreation:** Badminton, basketball, golf, Ping-Pong, tennis.

☎ 76 1- and 2-bedroom furnished apartments.

✕ Meals included. Menus follow American Heart Association guidelines. **Sample Meals:** Chef salad, tuna salad (lunch); grilled chicken, marinated pork chop (dinner).

✉ 1-week program $2,139 per person. 4-week program $7,396 per person. MC, V.

✉ *3017 Pickett Rd., Durham, NC 27705,* ☎ *919/493–4205 or 800/ 553–0052,* ℻ *919/490–0191. www.structurehouse.com*

WESTGLOW SPA

LUXURY PAMPERING ○ NUTRITION AND DIET

With the Blue Ridge Mountains just outside your door, you may find staying indoors difficult at the Westglow Spa, located on a gorgeous 20-acre country estate.

Westglow, built as a summer home by artist Elliot Dangerfield, got its name from the panoramic view of Grandfather Mountain to the west. Dangerfield's art studio became the spa when current owner Glynda Valentine converted Westglow into an intimate, polished country inn. Vintage furnishings, Oriental rugs, and a large library retain the mansion's classic southern elegance. The glow of radiant sunsets and gold-flecked sunrises brightens each room.

Bathed in light, the spa has an indoor swimming pool, nine treatment rooms, a salon, a fitness studio, an aerobics studio, and a poolside café. A daily schedule of classes is posted, though the staff will also do one-on-one training upon request.

Don't expect a hard-core schedule of advanced classes and activities. Devise your own plan and enjoy the glory of being here. Nearby Blowing Rock is a charming mountain village of unique shops and restaurants. Miles of forest provide an opportunity to hike or cycle. Mountain bikes can be rented in the area, and trails abound. You can also take a rafting trip in nearby whitewater rapids or go canoeing. Arrangements can be made nearby for horseback riding, golf, and, in winter, downhill skiing.

Attention has been paid to a healthy diet, not easily found in southern resorts. Valentine teaches low-fat cooking, and spa guests get to taste the results. Beautifully presented, each item is prepared to order and served on fine china. At night, climb the grand staircase to your room, settle into a white-linen-covered bed and enjoy the quiet.

INSIDER TIP Need more privacy? Two cozy and secluded guest cottages are equipped with kitchenettes and fireplaces.

Equipment: Free weights, stair climbers, stationary bikes, weight-training circuit. **Services:** Aromatherapy, body scrub, deep-tissue massage, herbal wrap, lymphatic drainage, reflexology. **Swimming:** Indoor pool. **Classes and Programs:** Fitness assessment, nutrition and diet consultation, personal training. **Recreation:** Biking, hiking, tennis.

🛏 6 rooms, 2 cottages.

✗ Meals included. Elliott's Restaurant serves low-fat fare. **Sample Meals:** Grilled Portobello mushrooms with sautéed spinach, smoked tomatoes, and creamy risotto, roasted 5-spice pork tenderloin with banana, apple, and yam confit, grilled marinated shrimp with grits and a spicy smoked tomato gravy (lunch); vegetarian platter, baked chicken, mountain trout with couscous (dinner).

✉ 2-night package $776–$1,064. 7-night package: $2,323–$2,772. Day spa package $120–$280, includes lunch, spa treatments. MC, V.

✉ *Hwy. 221 S, Box 1083, Blowing Rock, NC 28605,* ☎ *828/295– 4463 or 800/562–0807,* ℻ *828/295–5115. www.westglow.com*

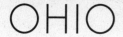

OHIO

KERR HOUSE

LUXURY PAMPERING ◦ NUTRITION AND DIET ◦ HOLISTIC HEALTH

The Kerr House is an antiques-filled Victorian manor in the historic canal village of Grand Rapids, 25 mi south of Toledo. It's a hideaway for those seeking privacy and quiet time devoted mainly to relaxation. With just six to eight guests in residence at a time, the facility takes on the atmosphere of a private club. Most guests are women, but many men stay here as well.

Yoga, the specialty of the house, is taught in a carpeted exercise room on the top floor; guests usually practice stretching and deep breathing for two hours in the morning and one hour in the afternoon. Sessions are followed by discussion of how to adapt what you've learned to a program you can do at home. Laurie Hostetler, the instructor, teaches from her own book of asanas, the exercise positions used in yoga. Other exercise options include low-impact aerobics, walking, and working out in the small exercise room.

Personal counseling makes this spa experience attractive for those who want to learn healthy habits. A good deal of time is spent discussing nutrition, self-esteem, and stress management. Body treatments include massage, baths, wraps, and more.

Guests at Kerr House share rooms; private accommodations are available for a supplemental charge. Copiously draped in linens and velvet, the rooms exude a warm aura of old-fashioned living, enhanced by the absence of televisions. The handsome, authentic antiques, furniture, and memorabilia are appropriately high-Victorian style, as the house dates from 1878. High-ceiling rooms accented by lace curtains, stained-glass windows, and massive wood doors reflect Hostetler's love of antique furniture and manners.

Each morning guests are served breakfast in bed on a wicker tray with fresh flowers and the schedule for the day. Lunch is served in a small café, and dinner is by candlelight in the dining room, most nights to the accompaniment of a harpist. Proper nutrition is emphasized at the Kerr House, which serves only what it calls "real food," which is always fresh and free of any additives, preservatives, or dyes. Hostetler has just published a new cookbook featuring more than 350 healthful recipes from the spa's kitchen.

If you're up for a little exploring, Grand Rapids is full of Americana. Near the Kerr House are hiking paths along the Maumee River, and the towpath of the historic Miami & Erie Canal. In the area you can visit studios of crafts artists, as well as a water-powered grist mill.

Equipment: Stationary bikes, treadmills. **Services:** Body wrap, herbal wrap, massage, mud bath, reflexology, shiatsu. **Swimming:** Pool nearby. **Classes and Programs:** Yoga. **Recreation:** Boating, hiking.

🖭 5 rooms.

✕ Meals included. Spa cuisine served in dining room. **Sample Meals:** Creamy mushroom soup, couscous with chicken and fresh vegetables (lunch); vegetarian minestrone soup, chicken with purple onions, baked bananas with raspberry sauce (dinner).

🖼 Nightly rate $295 per person, double occupancy. 3-day program $1,275 per person, double occupancy. 5-day program $2,375 per person, double occupancy. AE, D, MC, V.

✉ *17777 Beaver St., Grand Rapids, OH 43551,* ☎ *419/832–1733,* FAX *419/832–4303. www.hostetler.net/kerr.htm*

MARIO'S INTERNATIONAL SPA AND HOTEL

LUXURY PAMPERING ○ MEDICAL WELLNESS

Housed in an 1842 manor house that was once a fashionable stagecoach stop, this rustic-looking spa located between Cleveland and Akron is one of the most complete and sophisticated facilities in this part of the country. It offers an extensive selection of body treatments, massages, and beauty treatments.

In addition to a 13,000-square-ft spa building that combines a Roman look with the rough-hewn wooden accents of the original manor, the complex includes a hotel and conference center, restaurants, and the corporate headquarters of Mario's International, a line of beauty salons and spas owned and operated by Mario and Joanne Liuzzo.

The spa's lengthy list of more than 50 body and beauty treatments ranges from inexpensive procedures such as brow tinting and manicures to lavish five-day packages. Among Mario's signature services are Golden Spoons, a Kneipp procedure in which cold and hot spoons are alternately used to massage the face and neck to help stimulate blood circulation. Another favorite is the dulse scrub, in which seaweed powder and warm avocado oil are applied in a body-polishing treatment, followed by a loofah scrub and Vichy shower. A nearby building houses the spa sanctuary, a holistic center where yoga, tai chi, and other classes are offered in an atmosphere of flickering candles, trickling water, and tinkling chimes.

The restaurants, which feature dishes from the Italian region of Tuscany as well as traditional spa cuisine, are open to the public. A separate area is set aside for spa guests, who can relax over lunch wearing nothing but a fluffy white robe, as many of them do each day.

Services: Hydrotherapy, massage. **Programs:** Health and diet analysis, yoga. **Swimming:** Pool. **Recreation:** Biking, golf, tennis, horseback riding, skiing.

🖵 13 rooms, 1 suite

✕ Meals à la carte. Restaurants serve Tuscan fare. Spa cuisine available. **Sample Meals:** Roasted chicken on garden greens served with julienne vegetables with Dijon vinaigrette (lunch); sirloin steak with beefsteak tomatoes in balsamic reduction (dinner).

🎫 Half-day Teaser package $100. 1-night spa package $750 per couple, includes lodging, spa treatments. AE, D, DC, MC, V.

✉ *35 E. Garfield Rd., Aurora, OH 44202,* ☎ *330/562–9171 or 888/464–7721,* 🖷 *330/562–2386. www.marios-spa.com*

BREITENBUSH HOT SPRINGS RETREAT

HOLISTIC HEALTH ○ MINERAL SPRINGS

Breitenbush Hot Springs Retreat is a community of rustic cabins on the banks of the Breitenbush River, in the Willamette National Forest. The retreat is set in an 86-acre wildlife sanctuary. Like the Esalen Institute in California, Breitenbush is known for its workshops that focus on personal health and spiritual growth, and for its hot mineral springs, where a clothing-optional policy prevails.

The daily schedule begins with 7 AM meditation followed by stretching classes. Daily yoga sessions and therapeutic rituals and ceremonies take place in a pyramid-roof sanctuary and a Native American sweat lodge. Workshops on topics ranging from breathing to botany are scheduled throughout the year. Participation is optional, and there's no charge beyond the lodging fee.

Natural springs and artesian wells supply 180°F mineral water for the sauna and outdoor pools. At an idyllic spot in the woods, the water flows through four tiled tubs and a rock-lined pool. Each of the colorfully tiled, geothermally heated bathhouses (one for men, one for women) has all the usual amenities. Also naturally heated are the resort's 42 cabins.

About 90 mi from Portland, Breitenbush is surrounded by tall forests on the western slopes of Oregon's Cascades. Expect to encounter the high-minded environmentalism and slightly eccentric idealism of the '70s.

INSIDER TIP Bring your own blankets and towels. The bare-bones accommodations include only sheets for the beds.

Services: Craniosacral therapy, herbal wrap, hydrotherapy, reiki. **Swimming:** Pool, river. **Classes and Programs:** Counseling on health and healing. **Recreation:** Hiking, skiing.

⊞ 42 cabins, 20 tents. Campsites available.

✕ Meals included. Vegetarian meals served. **Sample Meals:** Vegetarian pizza, rice and green salad with sprouts (lunch); vegetarian lasagna, spinach pie with Greek salad and home-baked bread (dinner).

⌨ Nightly rate $55–$90 per person, double occupancy. Tent space $40–$55. MC, V.

✉ Box 578, Detroit, OR 97342, ☎ 503/854–3314, FAX 503/854–3819. *www.breitenbush.com*

KAH-NEE-TA RESORT

LUXURY PAMPERING ∘ MINERAL SPRINGS

The high desert provides an ideal setting for this outdoors-oriented resort. The Kah-Nee-Ta Resort, owned and managed by a confederation of tribes whose ancestors once worshiped at the springs, strikes a delicate balance between tradition and modernity. Guests are invited to tribal ceremonies and festivals and to a salmon-bake feast.

Spa Wanapine offers a full assortment of body treatments. An Olympic-size swimming pool filled with hot-springs mineral water attracts families. Bathhouses offer private soaks.

The imposing guest lodge sits atop a rocky ridge overlooking the Warm Springs River. Cedar-paneled guest rooms all have balconies, and many boast fireplaces and whirlpools. The lodge also houses the Indian Head Casino, with 300 slot machines, blackjack, and poker.

Trails for biking, hiking, and horseback riding fan out toward the distant Cascade Mountains on the 60,000-acre reservation. The Columbia River Gorge, famous for its windsurfing, and Mt. Hood, known for skiing and hiking, are both nearby. The Deschutes River is popular with white-water rafting enthusiasts.

....

INSIDER TIP Leave the umbrella at home. The Kah-Nee-Ta Resort boasts 300 days of sunshine in notoriously rainy Oregon.

....

Services: Aromatherapy, mud wrap, reflexology, reiki, Vichy shower. **Swimming:** Pool. **Classes and Programs:** Drumming and other Native American rituals. **Recreation:** Biking, fishing, golf, horseback riding, kayaking. **Children's Programs:** Day care for ages 3–14.

▦ 139 rooms, 21 tepees.

✗ Meals à la carte. American fare served in lodge dining room. **Sample Meals:** Salad with field greens, huckleberry vinaigrette, Oregon blue cheese, and candied pecans (lunch); boned Cornish game hen with wild juniper rice (dinner).

▨ Nightly rate $130–$150 per room. AE, DC, MC, V.

✉ *Box K, Warm Springs, OR 97761,* ☎ *541/553–1112 or 800/554–4786,* FAX *541/553–1071.*

LITHIA SPRINGS INN

MINERAL SPRINGS

This getaway in Oregon's Rogue Valley is part bed-and-breakfast, part hot springs. There are no communal tubs here—you enjoy the mineral water right in the privacy of your own room. Most accommodations feature a whirlpool bath.

Native Americans used the lithium-rich springs for health treatments. At the beginning of the 1900s the underground mineral springs began attracting visitors. This inn sits above those springs on 8 acres of gardens and country meadows, making it a great place to wander and reflect. Inside, you'll also find quiet—the rooms are soundproof.

In the morning a cooked-to-order breakfast is served. For lunch and dinner you're on your own. There's a paved path from the inn that's perfect for a stroll into town for a bite.

Nearby recreational activities include skiing and snowboarding at 7,500-ft Mt. Ashland (the slopes are open from November to April) and white-water rafting and kayaking down the Rogue River.

INSIDER TIP In the mood for some culture? Ashland's theater district, home of the Oregon Shakespeare Festival, is just down the road.

Services: Massage. **Recreation:** Hiking, rafting, skiing.

🖼 14 rooms and suites.

✕ Breakfast included. For other meals, several restaurants are nearby.

🖾 Nightly rate $115–$125 per room.

✉ *2165 W. Jackson Rd., Ashland, OR 97520,* ☎ *541/482–7128, 800/482–7128,* FAX *541/488–1645. www.ashlandinn.com*

DEERFIELD SPA RESORT

NUTRITION AND DIET

Housed in an attractive white-clapboard farmhouse dating from the 1930s, Deerfield Spa Resort is a homey place in which to unwind and shape up. Here your daily activities range from classes in aerobics and yoga to guided hikes in the Pocono Mountains and on the Appalachian Trail.

Programs, scheduled from April through mid-November, are tailored to individual needs. Participation is limited to 33 men and women who learn about exercise, diet, and nutrition from a 30-member staff. Lectures on spirituality and health from visiting experts often become discussion sessions among guests.

Workout equipment at Deerfield Spa Resort is minimal, and no activity is required. You can, however, opt for ambitious programs such as Total Fitness, which involves selecting a menu according to your personal goals.

INSIDER TIP A familylike feeling tends to develop among guests, many of whom are repeat visitors.

Equipment: Cross-country ski machines, free weights, stair climbers, stationary bikes, treadmills. **Services**: Aromatherapy, facials, reflexology, reiki, sea-salt body buff, seaweed body wrap, shiatsu. **Swimming**: Pool. **Classes and Programs**: Cooking demonstrations, health-related lectures, tarot readings. **Recreation**: Golf, horseback riding, ice-skating, in-line skating, tennis.

▥ 22 rooms.

✕ Meals included. Low-fat meals served in dining room. Vegetarian meals available. **Sample Meals**: Grilled chicken, chef's salad (lunch); baked orange roughy with herbed bread crumbs, baked salmon in white wine sauce (dinner).

▤ Nightly rate $340–$380 per person, double occupancy. Weekly rate $799–$970 per person, double occupancy. MC, V.

✉ *650 Resica Falls Rd., East Stroudsburg, PA 18301*, ☎ *717/223-0160 or 800/852-4494*, ⟨FAX⟩ *570/223-8270. www.deerfieldspa.com*

THE HIMALAYAN INSTITUTE

HOLISTIC HEALTH

One of the world's leading centers for the healing of mind, body, and spirit, the Himalayan Institute of Yoga Science and Philosophy was founded by Sri Swami Rama, who played a major role in bringing the teachings of yoga to the attention of physicians, psychologists, and researchers in this country. At this 400-acre retreat, you'll learn how yoga, along with breathing, diet, and nutrition, can help you develop healthy habits and overcome illness.

During his tenure as a research consultant to the Menninger Foundation Project on Voluntary Control of Internal States in 1970, the Indian-born Rama reportedly stopped his heart for 17 seconds, showing the human ability to control the body. The institute operates on the philosophy that individuals who learn to train the mind may be able to prevent and overcome illness and accelerate healing.

At the Center for Health and Healing, your counselor custom-designs an ayurvedic program for you. Based on a holistic health assessment, three levels of training and treatments are available, addressing problems such as low energy, high blood pressure, ulcers, arthritis, headaches, and stress-related disorders. Therapies may include one- to two-week sessions of homeopathy, biofeedback, acupuncture, massage, yoga, and meditation. For healthy people interested in a refresher, 3- to 10-day courses are offered. Cooking classes, scheduled during longer programs, focus on organic vegetarian cuisine.

The institute's wooded campus in the rolling foothills of the Pocono Mountains is a perfect setting in which to focus on achieving inner calm. (To enhance this inner tranquillity, guests are asked to maintain silence from 5 to 6:30 PM and from 10 PM until 8 AM.)

The three-story main building has 100 rooms that have few amenities besides a sink and one or two beds. Communal bathrooms are on each floor. A limited number of deluxe rooms with private bathroom are available. For extra comfort consider upgrading to an apartment in one of the nearby chalets. Each two-bedroom split-level unit has a bathroom, sitting area with sofa bed, and access to a central cathedral-ceiling lounge.

INSIDER TIP Recovering from illness? Special care is provided here for people who have had chronic illnesses, operations, and accidents.

Equipment: Rowing machines, stationary bikes, stair climbers. **Services:** Massage. **Swimming:** Pond. **Classes and Programs:** Medical and psychological consultations, meditation, vegetarian cooking classes, yoga. **Recreation:** Basketball, handball, hiking, ice-skating, skiing, tennis. **Children's Programs:** Supervision for ages 3–9.

⊞ 54 rooms, 4 with bath, 4 guest houses.

✕ Meals included. Vegetarian buffet. **Sample Meals:** Vegetable stir-fry with basmati rice, lentil dal and homemade bread (lunch); butternut-squash soup, hummus, apple-raisin couscous, spinach-tofu bake (dinner).

▦ Nightly rate $100–$110 per person, double occupancy. 3-day program $680 per person, double occupancy. 10-day program $2,850 per person, double occupancy. Weekend seminar tuition $140–$150. MC, V.

✉ R.R. 1, Box 400, Honesdale, PA 18431, ☎ 570/253–5551 or 800/822–4547,℻ 570/253–9078. www.himalayaninstitute.org

NEMACOLIN WOODLANDS

LUXURY PAMPERING ◦ SPORTS CONDITIONING

Atop a scenic bluff in the Laurel Highlands of southwestern Pennsylvania stands the Nemacolin Woodlands Resort. Once a private hunting reserve, it has become one of the country's best resorts. Its 32,000 square-ft spa, constructed of wood, glass, and native stone, is the best equipped this side of the Allegheny Mountains.

Back at the Woodlands Spa, an animated sculpture of Chief Nemacolin welcomes you to his tribal land. The range of bodywork available here is exceptional—scrubs and wraps using sea salts, oils, mud, and herbal mixtures. After relaxing in the steam room or the sauna, you can sink into a whirlpool and enjoy the view of woods and distant mountains. Upstairs are 28 treatment rooms, spacious and airy and warmed in winter by a stone fireplace. Body care includes a vitamin facial, which combines moisturizing with hydroxy-acid exfoliation. The water path, which combines walking through pools of water at 55°F and 105°F with alternating hot and cold showers and a warm saltwater tub, is designed to stimulate circulation and improve immune functions while enhancing energy and a feeling of well-being.

Downstairs is devoted to exercise: There are stationary bikes, treadmills, and stair climbers with video monitors, a weight room, a four-lane indoor lap pool, and a mirrored aerobics studio with a spring-cushioned wood floor that can hold groups of 40 or more. Fitness classes range from high-impact aerobics to tai chi. Personal training, as well as a fitness evaluation with body-composition analysis, can be part of your program.

The pace here is as relaxed or intense as you want it to be. Treatments and optional spa meals are included in packages of from one to six days, or booked à la carte.

There are plenty of indoor and outdoor activities at this 1,000-acre resort. You'll find an indoor equestrian center, outdoor tennis courts, a shooting academy course with 30 stations, and trout fishing in a stocked lake. In winter trails are groomed for cross-country skiing and snowmobiles, and the iced-over lake is filled with skaters. Downhill skiers can take advantage of a gentle 325-ft slope with three runs, lifts, and a snowmaking system. In summer golfers are challenged by Pete Dye's par-72 Woodlands course and the par-70 Mystic Rock course. Video analysis of your swing is offered at the Golf Academy, or you can drive balls indoors at a simulated course in the recreation center.

Your appetite sharpened by the mountain air and exercise, you can sample spa cuisine at Seasons in the Woodland Spa. Among the other nine restaurants, the elegant Golden Trout dining room and the Restaurant Lautrec have low-fat, low-cholesterol menus. Afterward, retire to an art deco English- or French-country-style room in the lodge, where tea is served daily, or settle into your spacious bedroom or terrace suite at the palace-style Chateau Lafayette.

INSIDER TIP Architecture fans, take note: Frank Lloyd Wright's Fallingwater and Kentuck Knob are both a short drive away.

Equipment: Free weights, stair climbers, stationary bikes, treadmills, weight-training circuit. **Services:** Aromatherapy, body-composition evaluation, body wrap, loofah body polish, reflexology. **Swimming:** Indoor and outdoor pools. **Classes and Programs:** Fitness assessment, stress-management program, personal training. **Recreation:** Badminton, biking, boating, croquet, fishing, golf, horseback riding, miniature golf, Ping-Pong, shuffleboard, tennis. **Children's Programs:** Children's playground, petting zoo, and family activities center.

🛏 220 rooms, 54 town houses.

✕ Meals à la carte. Lunch served at spa or in café. **Sample Meals:** Southwestern corn chowder, spinach and arugula salad (lunch); shrimp cocktail with cilantro-lime chili sauce, molasses-and-walnut-crusted lamb, wok-seared salmon in a coconut curry broth (dinner).

💳 Nightly rate $150–$250 per room. Day spa package $125–$430. AE, DC, MC, V.

✉ *1001 Lafayette Dr., Farmington, PA 15437,* ☎ *724/329–8555 or 800/422–2736,* 𝖥𝖠𝖷 *724/329–6177. www.nwlr.com*

HILTON HEAD HEALTH INSTITUTE

MEDICAL WELLNESS ○ NUTRITION AND DIET

It's hard to imagine a better setting for a wellness-oriented resort than the Hilton Head Health Institute. The perfect climate, the dozen miles of sandy beaches, and the walking and biking trails through local nature preserves go far to enhance and renew the spirit.

Since 1976 the courses here have taught participants how to change their daily lives and work habits, maintain their weight, stop smoking, or manage stress. With a maximum of 40 participants, the program allows you to stay as long as needed to gain control of problems.

This isn't a vacation, however. Health education begins with an understanding of your body. Lectures, workshops, and exercise classes are held in the institute's main building, a short walk from your living quarters. The effect of nutrition and exercise on the body's metabolism and the effect of stress on productivity and health are taught by a team of psychologists, nutritionists, and physical fitness specialists.

Other activities center on a campuslike cluster of cottages, which have traditional furniture, fine fabrics, a private porch, and color televisions. Most participants have a private bedroom and bath and share the living room and fully equipped cooking and laundry facilities. Private accommodations are also available. The Total Nutrition Plan, featured by the institute, is a structured and nutritionally balanced meal plan.

INSIDER TIP The medically supervised programs here are intended for those who have reached a point in their lives where change is necessary.

Equipment: Stair climbers, stationary bikes, treadmills. **Services:** Facials, massage. **Swimming:** Pool, beach. **Recreation:** Hiking, biking.

⌂ 40 villas.

✗ Meals included. **Sample Meals:** Pasta primavera with raw vegetables (lunch); chicken enchilada with salsa and brown rice (dinner).

▱ 7-night program $2,395–$2,695 per person. MC, V.

✉ *Box 7138, Hilton Head Island, SC 29938,* ☎ *843/785–7292 or 800/ 292–2440,* FAX *843/686–5659. www.hhhealth.com*

WESTIN RESORT

SPORTS CONDITIONING

Beachfront fitness clubs are hard to find in the Carolina lowlands, but the Westin Resort stands among lush landscaping on 24 acres of a nature preserve.

In the health club you can train for specific sports on a strength-training system. Mornings may begin with a beach walk, led by a staff member. Invigorated by sun, sea, and air, you can join an exercise group in step aerobics, aquaerobics, or muscle flexibility training. Comprehensive fitness testing is available by appointment. There are three swimming pools on the beach, including one that is glass-enclosed for year-round swimming and aquaerobics classes.

Dining choices in the ocean-view Barony Restaurant range from seafood specialties to a selection of low-cholesterol items spiced instead of salted. The Carolina Cafe buffet serves breakfast, lunch, and dinner.

Refreshed after recent renovations, the hotel's 412 guest rooms—with balconies, separate dressing areas, and large baths—reflect the glow of ocean light. Furnishings and architecture are reminiscent of grand Southern homes. Staying at the hotel's Royal Beach Club gives you extra amenities and access to a well-stocked lounge.

INSIDER TIP Want to practice your swing? The resort also sports three PGA championship golf courses.

Equipment: Cross-country ski machines, free weights, rowing machines, stair climbers, stationary bikes, weight-training circuit. **Services:** Massage. **Swimming:** 3 pools, beach. **Classes and Programs:** Fitness testing, golf and tennis clinics. **Recreation:** Croquet, golf, tennis, volleyball, water polo. **Children's Programs:** Supervised activities.

▥ 382 rooms, 30 suites.

✕ Meals à la carte. Low-fat meals available at two restaurants. **Sample Meals:** Charleston she-crab soup with aged sherry, Caesar salad, poached salmon with dill cream and cucumber salad (lunch); free-range chicken with black-pepper pasta and chanterelle mushroom sauce, sautéed shrimp Provençal over angel-hair pasta (dinner).

▧ Nightly rate $240–$380 per room. AE, DC, MC, V.

✉ *2 Grasslawn Ave., Hilton Head Island, SC 29928,* ☎ *843/681–4000 or 800/228–3000,* FAX *843/681–1087. www.westin.com*

BLACK HILLS HEALTH AND EDUCATION CENTER

HOLISTIC HEALTH

Nestled in a beautiful pine-clad canyon, the Black Hills Health and Education Center provides a holistic approach to medicine that combines a vegetarian cuisine with a prescribed exercise plan. The center's highly structured 13- to 20-day programs attract people of all ages who want to learn how to live a healthier life.

The medically supervised programs at Black Hills are designed to teach healthy habits to those who suffer from diabetes, arthritis, hypertension, heart problems, and obesity. Each person's lifestyle is analyzed and a suitable regimen of exercise and diet prescribed. The center, established in 1978, has a staff that includes two doctors, a registered nurse, dietician, physical therapist, exercise physiologist, and massage therapist.

The program begins with a complete physical examination, blood tests, and medical counseling. Hydrotherapy (included in the program fee) and massage may be recommended; the lodge is equipped with a whirlpool, a steam cabinet, and a shower that alternates hot and cold water from six sprays. Once or twice a week an excursion takes participants to a fitness center and a swimming pool fed by warm springs.

Though lectures cover stress control and nutrition, the central philosophy is one of learning by doing. Everyone joins in bread-making and cooking classes, and outings to a supermarket and restaurant are led by staff members who demonstrate how to shop for and order nutritious foods.

Run by Seventh-Day Adventists as an affiliate of the Black Hills Missionary College, the Healing Center draws on the campus for services. On Friday evening students and guests traditionally gather around the big stone fireplace in the lounge and join in a music program. The campus is set in the scenic Banana Belt of the Black Hills, so named for the temperate climate and sunny days that prevail even in winter.

INSIDER TIP The mood is informal and down-to-business: Some guests even bring along a baby-sitter so they can concentrate on the program.

Equipment: Rowing machines, stationary bikes, treadmills, weight-training circuit. **Services:** Hydrotherapy, massage. **Swimming:** Pool. **Classes and Programs:** Medical consultation, personal training, medical lectures. **Recreation:** Gold panning, rock collecting, skiing.

⊞ 11 rooms. Campground with RV hookups.

✕ Meals included. Low-fat buffet. **Sample Meals:** Steamed vegetables, vegetarian lasagna with nondairy cheese (lunch); vegetarian taco salad, baked tofu, cashew chow mein.

▣ Nightly rate $45 per room. 5-day program $450 per person, double occupancy. D, MC, V.

✉ *Box 19, Hermosa, SD 57744,* ☎ *605/255–4101 or 800/658–5433,* FAX *605/255–4687. www.bhhec.org*

TENNESSEE FITNESS SPA

NUTRITION AND DIET

Get back to nature and back in shape at this no-frills mountain camp. The Tennessee Fitness Spa combines organized activities such as aerobics and weight training with walks through the Tennessee Hills in a program designed to help you to lose weight.

A weekly class on nutrition and a cooking demo are held in the natural-stone dining hall, where the resort's chef demonstrates how to cook meals that are low in fat, sodium, and sugar. Most guests are concerned with weight management, and some come for several months to develop a workable weight-loss regimen they can continue at home.

Guests, who range in age from 16 to 90, join a group leader for an 8 AM hike. The daily schedule rotates between aerobic exercise, strength training, and lectures. Cross training can be followed by a volleyball game or a soak in the 10-person hot tub.

Accommodations are in two-story wooden chalets and a lake-view lodge. All are simply furnished and provide a choice of a full-size or twin beds. Phones are available on request for a small fee.

INSIDER TIP The friendly staff is one reason to come to Tennessee Fitness Spa. They are noted for fostering camaraderie among guests, which adds to the fun as you shed pounds together.

Equipment: Free weights, stair climbers, stationary bikes, treadmills, weight-training circuit. **Services:** Manicure, massage, pedicure. **Swimming:** Pool. **Recreation:** Bingo, hiking, fishing, racquetball, volleyball.

⊞ 32 rooms, 1 4-bedroom house.

✗ Meals included. Food low in fat, sodium, and sugar. **Sample Meals:** Vegetarian pizza, black beans and rice, pasta salad (lunch); salmon, chicken enchiladas, turkey burgers, Dijon chicken, lasagna (dinner).

▨ Nightly rate $595 per person, includes meals, program. AE, D, MC, V.

✉ *299 Natural Bridge Park Rd., Waynesboro, TN 38485,* ☎ *931/722-5589 or 800/235-8365,* FAX *931/722-9113.* www.tfspa.com

TEXAS

COOPER AEROBICS CENTER

MEDICAL WELLNESS ∘ NUTRITION AND DIET

At first glance the guest lodge of the Cooper Aerobics Center looks more like a country club than a health center. However, the stately redbrick mansion is not a place for relaxation. A recognized leader in the study of the medical value of exercise, the center helps you to achieve permanent changes in your lifestyle, whether for weight loss, smoking cessation, or stress control.

Pampering takes a backseat to getting—and staying—healthy at this posh north Dallas complex. The father of aerobics, Kenneth H. Cooper, M.D. founded this establishment in 1970 and still plays a vital role in its day-to-day operations.

Approximately 90% of guests begin their stay with a comprehensive physical examination. This can add anywhere from $418 to $2,900 to the cost of the program, though health insurance may pick up some or all of the tab. Men over age 40 and women over age 50 are required to undergo a treadmill stress test or provide medical documentation of testing within the previous year. The medical report determines the exercise program recommended for you.

Multiple exercise sessions are part of each day's program. You can jog on paved and lighted trails that wind through the 30-acre wooded estate or swim laps in either of two outdoor pools. A gymnasium has basketball courts and a three-lane running track. The four outdoor lighted tennis courts are equipped with automatic ball machines. Other fitness equipment includes strength-training equipment, free weights, and a full range of cardiovascular machines, such as stair climbers, rowing machines, and stationary bikes. Those who prefer a more social workout can opt for classes in step aerobics, yoga, or Pilates.

After a full day of exercises and lectures, participants are invited to relax in the facility's whirlpool, sauna, or steam room or indulge in spa treatments. The spa, which opened in August 1998, offers skin care (facials, glycolic-acid peels), body treatments (massage, waxing, body polishes and wraps) and salon services (manicures, pedicures) at prices ranging from $15 for a brow wax to $120 for a 70-minute black moor-mud body envelopment.

Limited to groups of no more than 22, the program appeals to high-powered executives who have lost control of their health. Here they work with a team of 16 physicians, nutritionists, and personal trainers. The combination of a supportive environment, state-of-the-art equipment, and the professional staff helps many guests here see significant results in lowering of their cholesterol levels in only two weeks.

INSIDER TIP You don't have to learn on an empty stomach. You'll enjoy a breakfast, lunch, and dinner at some of the finest local restaurants as you learn how to order heart-healthy fare.

Equipment: Free weights, rowing machines, stair climbers, stationary bikes, weight-training circuit. **Services:** Aromatherapy, body polishing, glycolic-acid peels, salt glow. **Swimming:** 2 pools. **Classes and Programs:** Aerobics, medical testing and evaluation, personal diet/exercise/fitness counseling, and exercise, Pilates, tai chi, yoga. **Recreation:** Basketball, martial arts, tennis. **Children's Programs:** Summer youth camp for ages 5–12.

▦ 50 rooms, 12 suites.

✕ Meals included. 3 calorie-controlled meals served daily. **Sample Meals:** Tossed salad with low-calorie dressing, Hawaiian chicken with potatoes and baked tomato (lunch); beef Burgundy on a bed of pasta (dinner).

▨ Nightly rate $120–$130 per person. 4-day program $2,095, includes meals, programs. AE, MC, V.

✉ *12230 Preston Rd., Dallas, TX 75230,* ☎ *972/386–4777 or 800/ 444–5192,* ⓕⓐⓧ *972/386–0039. www.cooperaerobics.com*

FOUR SEASONS RESORT AND CLUB

LUXURY PAMPERING ○ SPORTS CONDITIONING

Big in every way, the Four Seasons Resort and Club is the best little spa in Texas. Services range from massage and aromatherapy to herbal wraps and hydrotherapy to facials and waxing. A recently added—and highly recommended—treatment is the herbal body polish, a gentler version of a salt glow. Vitamin-rich minerals leave skin smooth and rejuvenated, while soothing aromatherapy oils relax the mind as well as the body.

The centerpiece of this 400-acre resort is the four-level Sports Club, which is connected to the spa by an underground tunnel. Two championship golf courses (including the Tournament Players Course, site of the annual GTE Byron Nelson Classic), indoor and outdoor tennis courts, squash courts, racquetball courts, and indoor and outdoor jogging tracks, as well as indoor and outdoor swimming pools, complete the picture.

There is truly something for everyone at the Four Seasons' Sports Club. More than 40 exercise classes a week cater to hard bodies devoted to numerous aerobics offerings, while more solitary types can feel the burn on high-tech cardio equipment. Guests needing personal training or private instruction will find one-on-one services at the club, and those with children can take advantage of the resort's many kid-friendly attractions— including a children's pool, child-care center, and playground.

Seven miles from Dallas/Fort Worth International Airport, the resort features 312 rooms and suites in the main nine-story tower or 50 golf villas set between a free-form swimming pool, the golf course, and the Sports Club. Rooms in the towers have private balconies, while villa accommodations feature a patio.

INSIDER TIP Less than a half hour from downtown Dallas, the Four Seasons Resort seems a world away from the hustle and bustle of urban life.

Equipment: Cross-country ski machines, free weights, rowing machines, stair climbers, stationary bikes, treadmills, weight-training circuit. **Services:** Aromatherapy, herbal body polishes, herbal wraps, hydrotherapy, loofah salt glows. **Swimming:** Indoor lap pool, 3 outdoor pools. **Classes and Programs:** Aerobics, body sculpting, fitness evaluation, personal training. **Recreation:** Basketball, golf, racquetball, softball, squash, tennis. **Children's Programs:** Playground, child-care center (ages 6 months–8 years), activity center (ages 5–13 years).

▥ 348 rooms, 14 suites.

✕ Meals à la carte. 3 restaurants feature food low in cholesterol, fat, calories, sodium. **Sample Meals:** Broiled chicken, Mexican chicken enchilada (lunch); grilled salmon, roast quail with fresh berry sauce (dinner).

▱ Nightly rate $195–$395 per room. 2-night spa package $1,940–$2,110 per couple. AE, DC, MC, V.

✉ *4150 N. MacArthur Blvd., Irving, TX 75038,* ☏ *972/717–0700 or 800/332–3442,* ⅁ᴬˣ *972/717–2550. www.fourseasons.com*

THE GREENHOUSE

LUXURY PAMPERING ∘ NUTRITION AND DIET

Privacy and freedom from stress are precious commodities to the harried young executives and spotlight-dodging celebrities who check into the Greenhouse for a week of physical and emotional rejuvenation. A destination for the knowledgeable spa set since 1965, the elegant enclave continues to lavish attention on its guests. At the same time it has expanded its programs to appeal to the ever-changing needs and desires of guests. Repeat visitors make up more than 75% of the clientele.

Airy, bright, and expensively furnished, the Greenhouse has the look of a semitropical hideaway. The skylighted, marble-floor atrium that encloses the pool and the luxurious bedrooms are very much a part of the therapy. The overall camaraderie of the women, particularly by the end of a week together, is akin to friendships formed in a sorority house.

From the airport you'll be whisked in a chauffeured limousine to the Greenhouse, set amid gardens and fitness trails. Upon arrival you'll be assigned a personal aesthetician, hairdresser, manicurist, and masseuse for the week. A resident exercise physiologist, a nurse, and other staff members will plan a schedule to help you achieve your goal, whether it be weight loss or simply relaxation. No need to fret about your spa wardrobe—freshly laundered leotards, tights, sweats, T-shirts, and shorts are stocked daily.

Meals are creative and, for the most part, low in calories and fat. One evening each week the spa's executive chef plays host to an informal cooking class, preparing signature dishes and providing recipes so you can make them at home. You can opt to take all your meals in your room, though most choose to enjoy the refined elegance of the dining room, where the exquisite fine-china table settings change nightly. You will want to pack a couple of dressier outfits or make use of the tasteful caftan hanging in your closet, as dressing for dinner is a tradition here.

Each day begins around 7 with breakfast in bed. Your daily schedule comes on the tray. A brisk guided walk through the garden is followed by exercise classes. The Greenhouse trainers study your fitness profile and work with you at your own pace. Lunch is served poolside, followed by a daily massage and serious pampering in the spa. Evenings begin with hors d'oeuvres in the drawing room, followed by dinner in the formal dining room. An in-room "tuck-in" foot or shoulder massage ends each day.

A once-a-week shopping excursion shuttles guests to the tony Stanley Korshak boutique. Other off-premises excursions may be arranged individually.

....

INSIDER TIP Want to feel truly pampered? The staff outnumbers the guests here by more than four to one.

....

Equipment: Cross-country ski machines, free weights, stair climbers, stationary bikes, treadmills, weight-training circuit. **Services:** Acupuncture, aloe-vera and algae mask, aromatherapy, craniosacral therapy, hot rock therapy, loofah-scrub, lymphatic drainage, reflexology, thalassotherapy. **Swimming:** Indoor and outdoor pools. **Classes and Programs:** Cooking classes, health and nutrition lectures, kickboxing, makeup and beauty lectures, personal training, Pilates, stress and wellness lectures, tai chi, yoga. **Recreation:** Tennis, jogging.

▦ 37 rooms, 2 suites.

✗ Meals included. Choice of 1,000–1,200 or 1,500 calories a day. **Sample Meals:** Vegetarian pizza with baby greens salad, shrimp empanadas with savory cabbage salad and peanut-ginger dressing (lunch); Cornish hens with ratatouille, broiled lobster tail with spaetzle and citrus sauce (dinner).

▨ Weekly rate $5,250–$6,500 per person. AE, MC, V.

✉ Box 1144, Arlington, TX 76004, ☎ 817/640–4000, ℻ 817/649–0422. *www.thegreenhousespa.com*

LAKE AUSTIN SPA RESORT

LUXURY PAMPERING ○ NUTRITION AND DIET

A kaleidoscope of color thrives in the curvy, lake-filled canyon that cradles the Lake Austin Spa. Butterflies float among the wildflowers while white-tailed deer wander among the cacti and cedar and mesquite trees in the nature preserve that surrounds this laid-back 19-acre retreat. It's no wonder that at this resort, easily accessible from "Silicon Corridor," daily nature hikes and lakeside workouts combine with pampering treatments and outdoor relaxation.

The resort continues to undergo a complete makeover that began with the installation of formal limestone boxed gardens overflowing with native plants and flowers. Herbs, lettuces, and other greens are snipped daily from plantings overseen by a resident horticulturist. Red-gravel pathways capped by vine-covered trellises connect the cedar-and-stone lodges on the hillside. Some command superb lake views, others overlook the central garden and pool, and many open onto private Japanese meditation spaces. Inside, slipcovered headboards in muted floral patterns accompany fluffy duvets and pillows in oatmeal-colored linens. A comfy reading chair and deep soaking tub affirm that relaxation is a priority here. Bulky towels, monogrammed robes, aromatherapy toiletries, and nightly turndown service add an air of luxury.

Activities range from early morning walks to all-day canoe outings complete with gourmet picnics. Fitness classes fill time slots from morning to late afternoon. Choose to shape up with salsa or step classes, Pilates or yoga. The glass-walled gym, which seems to float on the edge of the lake, is stocked with up-to-date equipment: a weight-training circuit, Spinning bikes, treadmills, stair climbers, and free weights. Interspersed in the schedule are cooking classes lead by the spa's noted chef as well as presentations on gardening, humor, nutrition, and relaxation. Did you just want to relax? Chuck the whole schedule of events and snag a hammock stretched beneath a shade tree. You run your own agenda here.

The Healing Waters Spa, housed in a multilevel lake house, offers top-quality treatments in limited space (plans are on the drawing board for an expanded spa facility). Stroll uphill to the white cottage for facials, massages, and other personal services. The Blue Lagoon, a signature treatment here, is most popular. The skin is gently cleansed with an exfoliating brush, then smothered in a warm seaweed clay mask. Wrapped in a thermal blanket, you receive a heavenly craniosacral massage. You rinse off, then return to the treatment room for a heated oil massage that leaves your body and soul restored.

Meals creatively designed by a chef lauded by *Cooking Light* magazine help you maintain a balanced diet. The à la carte menu offers a number of Mexican- and Asian-inspired dishes all accompanied by calorie and fat-gram notations. Come to the dining room straight from a spa treatment or workout in your robe and sandals or exercise clothes. If you enjoy a glass of wine with your meal, the attentive staff will provide glasses and cooler for the vintage you brought with you.

INSIDER TIP Ask for the Ladybird Suite, an expansive lodging with a private garden and hot tub, named in honor of the flora-loving former first lady.

Equipment: Elliptical trainers, free weights, rowing machines, stair climbers, stationary bikes, treadmill, weight-training circuit. **Services:** Aromatherapy, body brushing, body polish, herbal wrap, hot rock massage, hydrotherapy, moor mud therapy, reflexology, seaweed body mask, shiatsu. **Swimming:** Indoor and outdoor pools. **Classes and Programs:** Cooking demonstrations, kickboxing, meditation, Neuromuscular Integrative Action (NIA), personal fitness and nutrition consultations, smoking cessation, Spinning, tai chi, yoga. **Recreation:** Canoeing, kayaking, sculling, tennis.

🏠 14 rooms, 11 suites, 15 cottages.

✗ Meals included. **Sample Meals:** Parmesan-encrusted trout with steamed Texmati rice and asparagus spears, grilled vegetable tacos and quesadillas (lunch); pad Thai, grilled chicken and fennel sausage with pomegranate marmalade and mint-lemon-walnut orzo, pork tenderloin grilled with rum-cola glaze and orange mashed sweet potatoes (dinner).

💳 Nightly rate $400 per person, double occupancy. 3-night refresher package $1,280 per person, double occupancy, includes lodging, meals, spa treatments. AE, D, MC, V.

✉ *1705 S. Quinlan Park Rd., Austin, TX 78732,* ☎ *512/372–7300 or 800/847–5637 (Canada 800/338–6651),* FAX *512/266–1572. www.lakeaustin.com*

OPTIMUM HEALTH INSTITUTE OF AUSTIN

NUTRITION AND DIET ○ HOLISTIC HEALTH ○ MEDICAL WELLNESS

Set in the rolling countryside near Austin, the Optimum Health Institute is an educational center for individuals who want to rid themselves of stress, toxins, and bad habits. The program, designed to restore the body's natural balance, uses the consumption of wheat-grass juice and raw foods to produce a "cellular detox."

The first week of the program is challenging. You probably will not feel good for several days as your body is sloughing off waste and adjusting to the diet of only raw fruits and vegetables. The quiet, low-activity environment is helpful to those new to cleansing and experiencing the affects of withdrawal from caffeine, sugar, and processed foods. As the week progresses, a breakthrough generally occurs accompanied by a surge of energy and feeling of rejuvenation.

The center has a professional and nurturing staff, but don't expect to be pampered or reminded of your next treatment. You manage your own schedule of classes, appointments, and activities. You will garner the support of others in the program as you build camaraderie through meditative circles, group hugs, and spiritual exercises.

The two-story Spanish-style facility is in a decidedly rural setting. A great hall with its soaring ceiling and massive stone fireplace is an inviting space where groups gather for informal chats on the Southwestern-print sofas. Oak furniture and quilted spreads outfit the soft-hued guest rooms.

A variety of guests come to the Optimum Health Institute, from the fit and well to the seriously health challenged. The institute operates as a part of the Free Sacred Trinity Church, which helps to keep fees low. While honoring all beliefs and religions, references to the Bible and Christian beliefs permeate in the presentations.

....

INSIDER TIP Those with environmental sensitivities appreciate that an allergen-free environment is maintained by specialized filtration and ventilation systems.

....

Equipment: Free weights, stair climbers, treadmills. **Services:** Energy consultation, massage, chiropractic and colonic therapy. **Swimming:** Pool. **Classes and Programs:** Classes in mind/body connection, mental and emotional detoxification, self-esteem, relaxation, food selection and preparation, pain management. **Recreation:** Ping-Pong.

▦ 28 guest rooms, some with shared baths.

✗ Meals included. Family-style meals served around oak tables overlooking pool and patio. **Sample Meals:** Cream of asparagus soup, wild rice salad, quinoa salad, "spaghetti" with tomato sauce (lunch and dinner).

▧ 1-week package $550–$650 per person, double occupancy, includes lodging, meals, class instruction and counseling. AE, D, MC, V.

✉ *R.R. 1, Box 339-J, Cedar Creek, TX 78612,* ☎ *512/303–4817,* FAX *512/332–0106. www.optimumhealth.org*

HOUSTONIAN HOTEL, CLUB & SPA

LUXURY PAMPERING ∘ SPORTS CONDITIONING

Peacefulness envelops you as leave the jammed freeway and drive under the pines at this 18-acre luxury resort near Houston. Arriving at the Houstonian Hotel feels more like returning to a private home than a hotel.

As you enter the spa, housed in a refined 1930s art deco mansion, a harpist serenades you. Upstairs, mineral baths soothe tired muscles and weary minds with scents of rosemary, chamomile, eucalyptus, and lavender. A full menu of massages—from aromatherapy to shiatsu—leave you feeling rejuvenated. Other body treatments include salt scrubs and seaweed and moor mud body masks, as well as facials and other skin treatments. The busy salon downstairs polishes appearance with hair, nail, and makeup services.

The staff here devises a customized plan to your specifications. In addition, there are medical and nutritional consultants on staff to assist. The fitness facility—a membership club where hotel guests are afforded unlimited access—is in a modern athletic hall. With more than 200 pieces of exercise equipment, indoor and outdoor tracks, a multilane lap pool, and even a boxing ring, there is no excuse for leaving without experiencing energizing workouts.

Nattily appointed guestrooms along a ravine boast floor-to-ceiling views. Most are quiet and restful, though large groups in adjoining rooms can compromise the atmosphere. Two of the resort's four restaurants provide menus that advise of calorie and fat counts: Olivette, an upscale tasty Mediterranean bistro, and the Manor House, which once served as former president George Bush's private residence. Quick meals between appointments can be taken at the fitness club's juice bar and poolside grill.

INSIDER TIP Go ahead and bring the kids. This family-friendly resorts lets Mom and Dad enjoy themselves while the kids revel in specifically designed activities.

Equipment: Elliptical trainers, treadmills, stair climbers, stationary bikes, weight-training circuit. **Services:** Aromatherapy, body polish, reflexology, salt glow, seaweed and moor mud body masks. **Swimming:** 3 pools. **Classes and Programs:** Aerobics, boxing, cardio-conditioning, fitness and nutrition consultation, kickboxing, martial arts, meditation, Pilates, smoking cessation, tai chi, weight-management consultation, yoga. **Recreation:** Golf, racquetball, rock climbing, running, squash, tennis.

⊞ 277 guest rooms, 9 suites.

✕ Meals à la carte. 4 restaurants serve varied cuisine. **Sample Meals:** Grilled salmon with sweet-corn risotto and red-bell-pepper pesto, 7-vegetable tagine (Moroccan stew) with couscous, chickpeas, and spicy harissa (hot sauce), Japanese barbecued tuna steak with gingered Japanese noodles and steamed bok choy.

▤ Nightly rate $139–$269 per room. Day spa packages $195–$350. AE, D, DC, MC, V.

✉ *111 N. Post Oak La., Houston, TX 77024,* ☎ *713/680–0626 or 800/231–2759,* ℻ *713/680–2992. www.houstonian.com*

UTAH

GREEN VALLEY SPA & TENNIS RESORT

LUXURY PAMPERING ∘ NUTRITION AND DIET

In the dry desert of southern Utah, the Green Valley Spa & Tennis Resort is something of an oasis. Here, amid some of the most breathtaking vistas, you'll enjoy an intriguing blend of Native American and New Age traditions. A certain color will be used to activate your senses each day. On a red day, for instance, the staff will surround you with red flowers, red-tinted baths, and even red dishes.

Begin your day with the 7 AM group hike, covering up to 8 mi over trails in nearby state parks. Passing through sandstone ravines and volcanic and red-rock canyons, you often come upon 1,000-year-old petroglyphs left by Native American tribes like the Anasazi. You can also take a trip by van to Zion National Park, where the dry desert air is scented by fresh sage.

With a maximum of 60 participants per week, the staff physiologists and nutritionists can give you personalized attention. They will help create a workout program to help you reach your goals. Tennis and golf buffs can take a few lessons at Vic Braden's Tennis College or the Golf Digest School.

Filled with Native American and Southwestern art, the 25,000-square-ft spa draws on indigenous healing traditions. Featuring treatments with indigenous herbs and flowers, the spa provides an introduction to Native American cultures. Among specialties are treatments with volcanic clay and herbs.

Rooms in the Coyote Inn contains either a king-size four-poster featherbed or two queen-size feather beds, plus three TVs (one to watch meditation videos while you're soaking in the tub), a microwave, a refrigerator, a private patio, a two-line direct-dial phone, and a fax machine. Amenities include terry robe, slippers, spa outfit, and Starbucks coffee.

INSIDER TIP Learning ways to prepare healthier food is part of the program. Exchanging recipes with the chef during cooking demonstrations is encouraged.

Equipment: Free weights, stair climbers, stationary bikes, treadmills, weight-training circuit. **Services:** Acupuncture, hot stone therapy, massage, mud and herbal wraps, powdered-pearl body rub, reflexology, reiki. **Swimming:** 5 outdoor pools, 1 enclosed heated pool. **Classes and Programs:** Bread baking, health and nutrition lectures, Native American culture, personal weight-loss counseling, stress management.

Recreation: Basketball, racquetball, tennis, volleyball. **Children's Programs:** Summer camp for children.

⊞ 38 rooms.

✕ Meals included. Low-fat food served in dining room. **Sample Meals:** Turkey burger and fries, pizza, chicken pita sandwich (lunch); salmon with seasonal vegetable and rice (dinner).

⊞ Nightly rate $400 per room. 7-day Spa Vacation package $2,950 per person, double occupancy, includes lodging, meals, golf and tennis instruction, use of resort amenities. AE, D, MC, V.

✉ *1871 W. Canyon View Dr., St. George, UT 84770,* ☎ *435/628–8060 or 800/237–1068,* ℻ *435/673–4084. www.greenvalleyspa.com*

THE LAST RESORT

NUTRITION AND DIET ∘ HOLISTIC HEALTH

Yoga, meditation, and a diet based on natural foods are used as vehicles for rejuvenating the body and mind at the Last Resort, a mountain retreat in southern Utah that accommodates up to 10 guests. At 8,700 ft above sea level, the resort enjoys spectacular mountain views. It's a suitably majestic environment for the spiritually oriented program.

A seven-day retreat includes two yoga workouts and two meditation sessions daily, which leaves plenty of free time for walking and reading. Every evening there are videos and discourses on nutrition and related topics. Each session includes a full day of silence, plus a visit to the Pah Tempe Hot Springs and other spectacular canyons in the area.

In addition, there's a natural-foods cooking course that teaches meal planning and preparation of tofu, tempeh, and other healthy ingredients. A special "spring cleaning of the body" retreat includes four days of juice fasting and bowel cleansing. A relationship workshop teaches partners how to bolster communication skills.

INSIDER TIP The spectacular scenery encourages outdoor activities. Marked trails draw backpackers in warmer months. In winter the powdery snow makes conditions ideal for cross-country skiing.

Swimming: Nearby lakes. **Classes and Programs:** Cooking classes, meditation instruction, nutrition lectures, yoga. **Recreation:** Cross-country skiing, hiking.

⊞ Dormitory beds and private rooms, all with shared bath.

✕ Meals included. Vegetarian buffet. **Sample Meals:** Steamed fresh vegetables, whole grains, rice, casseroles (lunch/dinner).

⊞ 7-day retreat $750 per person, includes lodging, meals. 5-day cooking course $495, includes lodging, meals, instruction. No credit cards.

✉ *Box 707, Cedar City, UT 84727,* ☎ *435/682–2289.*

RED MOUNTAIN SPA & FITNESS RESORT

NUTRITION AND DIET

Spectacular desert scenery makes Red Mountain Spa & Fitness Resort an intriguing destination. That's undoubtedly why one of the prime attractions here is exploring some of the most glorious canyons in the West. Often called the "walking spa," the program allows hikers of every skill level to hit the trails. At daybreak, guided groups hike more than 30 trails in nearby Snow Canyon State Park. Along the way are lava caves and ancient Native American petroglyphs. Some return later in the day, while other camp for several days.

Hiking is not the only activity here. In summer you can take a course in kayaking and rock climbing. In winter you can try cross-country skiing and snowshoeing. All year you can join an aerobics class or engage a personal trainer for some serious workouts in the fitness center.

Although vigorous outdoor exercise is a primary focus for the resort, its spa is available to soothe weary bodies. Participants can choose a range of masks, wraps, and massages. Try the 50-minute High Desert package, which includes a mint salt glow, facial, and mud wrap.

Red Mountain also concentrates on healthy eating; programs include nutrition and cooking classes. Three nutritionally balanced meals are offered each day. Many guests report seeing their blood pressure and cholesterol levels drop after staying at Red Mountain.

INSIDER TIP Visit in the winter, when the weather is dry and invigorating.

Equipment: Cross-country ski machines, free weights, stair climbers, stationary bikes, treadmills, weight-training circuit. **Services:** Aromatherapy, body polish, deep-tissue massage, hot stone therapy, mud wrap, reflexology, salt glow. **Swimming:** 2 indoor pools. **Classes and Programs:** Cooking classes, health and nutrition workshops, Tai chi, yoga. **Recreation:** Hiking, tennis.

▦ 112 rooms.

✕ Meals included. Breakfast and lunch buffet; dinner served in dining room. **Sample Meals:** Black barley and roasted vegetable strudel with a pink-lentil puree and balsamic drizzle, oven-roasted baby potatoes and seared pork tenderloin, Southwestern seasoned blackened chicken served with a black bean cake, baby vegetables dressed with a sweet corn broth (dinner).

▤ 4-day package $835 per person, double occupancy, includes lodging, meals, outings. Day spa packages $225–$325. AE, D, MC, V.

✉ *1275 E. Red Mountain Circle, Ivins, UT 84738,* ☏ *435/673–4905, 888/444–4230 or 800/407–3002,* ⊠ *435/673–1363. www.redmountainspa.com*

SNOWBIRD RESORT

LUXURY PAMPERING ○ SPORTS CONDITIONING

A penthouse spa with alpine views is just one of the attractions at the sports-oriented Snowbird Resort. In summer there are rock-climbing classes, overnight backpacking trips, bike tours, and guided treks to the peaks of the Wasatch Cache National Forest. In winter helicopters whisk skiers to the upper peaks, where 1,900 acres of groomed ski slopes await.

Tennis players can take advantage of the 23 tennis courts (10 indoor) at the Canyon Raquet Club, 10 mi from the resort. The 11-acre club also has racquetball and squash courts, spa and fitness facilities, and an outdoor Olympic-size pool. Golfer can enjoy the championship course at Jeremy Ranch.

The Cliff Spa itself is a two-story complex on the top floors of the hotel's east wing, with a 60-ft outdoor lap pool and a giant outdoor whirlpool with glorious mountain views. The same views can be enjoyed from the fitness center, which has an aerobics studio with a suspended wooden floor, as well as a full line of weight-training equipment. There are 20 treatment rooms and a café with healthy snacks and drinks.

There's plenty for children to do while their parents exercise or pamper themselves. There are ski lessons available for children ages 3 to 15. Those who prefer to ski with their children enjoy a break on lift tickets: Children 12 and under ski free when accompanied by adults. There's also a day-care center, nursery, and evening parties that allow parents to slip away for a romantic dinner.

INSIDER TIP Challenge yourself by enrolling in one of several courses at Snowbird's Adventure Park. They combine hiking with exploration aided by a map and compass.

Equipment: Rowing machines, stair climbers, stationary bikes, treadmills, weight-training circuit. **Services:** Acupressure, alpine salt glow, aromatherapy, balneotherapy, body glow, herbal wrap, mud bath, polarity therapy, shiatsu, thalassotherapy. **Swimming:** 3 pools. **Classes and Programs:** Aerobics, aquaerobics, stretching, guided nature hikes and mountain treks, personal training, tai chi. **Recreation:** Biking, hiking, racquetball, rock climbing, skiing, snowboarding, squash, tennis. **Children's Programs:** Day-care center, nursery, ski instruction for ages 3–15.

🖼 532 rooms and suites.

✗ Meals à la carte. 12 restaurants serve varied cuisine. **Sample Meals:** Wild-mushroom enchiladas, pineapple-habanero chile shrimp (lunch); crab lasagna, skinless breast of duck with Sicilian date-almond sauce, lobster over pasta (dinner).

💷 Nightly rate $109–$289 per room. 4-night Cliff Retreat package $991 per person, double occupancy. AE, D, DC, MC, V.

✉ *Little Cottonwood Canyon Rd., Snowbird, UT 84092,* ☎ *800/232–9542 or 800/453–3000,* 🖷 *801/933–2225. www.snowbird.com*

VERMONT

THE EQUINOX

LUXURY PAMPERING ○ SPORTS CONDITIONING

Outdoor adventure distinguishes this handsome Green Mountain hostelry overlooking historic Manchester Village. Fly-fishing, golf, tennis, snowshoeing, biking, hiking, horseback riding, and even Land Rover driving are among the many sports options available at this resort in the shadow of 3,800-ft Mt. Equinox.

But the major attraction for those is search of pampering is the fitness spa, which offers a full complement of services such as herbal wraps, salt-glow scrubs, and essential oil treatments. When you arrive, a staff member will tailor an individual exercise schedule for you, based on a computerized body-composition analysis. You will then participate in an informal discussion on exercise physiology, nutrition, and stress management. Advance planning with the spa director will help you focus on your goals, be they weight loss, stress management, or behavior modification.

After a day of sports, you can relax in luxury accommodations. The 230-year-old Equinox has hosted such notables as Mary Todd Lincoln, Ulysses S. Grant, and Theodore Roosevelt. The dining room preserves part of a 1769 tavern, once a gathering place for Vermont's revolutionary Green Mountain Boys. Additional guest rooms are scattered throughout separate buildings in many different architectural styles. Rooms have a fresh but historic style, with Audubon prints and Vermont country charm.

In the heart of Vermont's arts circuit, the resort is close to major summer music and theater festivals as well as historic Hildene, home of Robert Todd Lincoln. If your idea of exercise is shopping till you drop, just drive to nearby Manchester Center, one of New England's largest outlet centers.

INSIDER TIP Take a hands-on lesson in British falconry. A bird and all necessary equipment are provided.

Equipment: Cross-country ski machines, free weights, rowing machines, stair climbers, stationary bikes, weight-training circuit. **Services:** Body scrub, herbal wrap, massage, reflexology, reiki, seaweed wrap. **Swimming:** Indoor and outdoor pools. **Recreation:** Biking, canoeing, croquet, fishing, golf, hiking, horseback riding, ice-skating, tennis, snowshoeing.

⌂ 154 rooms, 29 suites, 10 3-bedroom town houses.

✕ Meals à la carte. Three restaurants serve seafood and New England specialties. **Sample Meals:** Seviche of sole with cilantro, grilled medallions of beef with shallots, chilled asparagus with seasoned wild rice (lunch); herbed pasta with mushrooms, poached salmon, veal medallions (dinner).

🛏 Nightly rate $189–$339 per room. 3-night spa package $833 per person, double occupancy, includes lodging, meals, spa treatments. AE, DC, MC, V.

✉ *Rte. 7A, Manchester Village, VT 05254,* ☎ *802/362–4700 or 800/ 362–4747,* 🖷 *802/362–1595. www.equinoxresort.com*

GOLDEN EAGLE RESORT

SPORTS CONDITIONING

Toning up the body is what Golden Eagle Resort does best. The sprawling complex has winter and summer activities as well as a health complex that includes outdoor and indoor pools, a giant whirlpool, and a fitness center with a wide range of equipment.

The resort's 80 acres include a well-developed walking and nature trail. A brochure available at the front desk details a self-guided tour with descriptions of local flora and fauna (staff members will accompany guests on walks if requested). For longer hikes and bike rides, try the Stowe Recreation Path, a 5½-mil scenic route through the valley and out toward the Mt. Mansfield ski area.

Two ponds at the resort are stocked for fishing (poles can be rented). The activity desk has tennis rackets available for free use on the clay tennis court. In-line skates and bicycles (some with child carriers) can be rented from local sporting-goods stores. There's an alpine slide just up the road at nearby Stowe Mountain Resort.

The guest rooms—individually decorated in a country-casual style— all have private bathroom, refrigerator, and coffeemaker. Larger accommodations have more extensive cooking facilities. Some rooms have a whirlpool or a fireplace.

INSIDER TIP The Golden Eagle is a perfect getaway spot for the whole family, near summer and winter activities at Stowe Mountain Resort.

Equipment: Free weights, rowing machines, stair climber, stationary bikes, treadmills, weight-training circuit. **Services:** Aromatherapy, reflexology, reiki. **Swimming:** Indoor and outdoor pools. **Recreation:** Biking, fishing, skiing, snowshoeing, tennis. **Children's Programs:** Supervised activities for ages 4–12.

🛏 71 rooms, 18 suites.

✕ Meals à la carte. Low-fat selections on breakfast and dinner menus. **Sample Meals:** Seafood mixed grill, broiled Atlantic swordfish, steamed vegetables and fish on bamboo (dinner).

🛏 Nightly rate $89–$169 per room. AE, D, DC, MC, V.

✉ *Box 1090, Mountain Rd. (Rte. 108), Stowe, VT 05672,* ☎ *802/ 253–4811 or 800/626–1010,* 🖷 *802/253–2561. www.stoweagle.com*

GREEN MOUNTAIN AT FOX RUN

NUTRITION AND DIET ∘ SPORTS CONDITIONING ∘ MEDICAL WELLNESS

Green Mountain, billed as the country's first residential lifestyle program for women, was established more than 25 years ago. It teaches guests how to eat, not starve, to reach weight and health goals. Whether you want to lose 10 or 100 pounds, spend a weekend or a month, this woodland retreat has a program for you.

For women who are serious abut losing weight and changing their relationship with food, coming to Green Mountain at Fox Run is a commitment to change. The difference is not just a new diet or vigorous exercise, but a new lifestyle based on healthy habits. The program provides a practical approach to eating, exercise, stress management, and behavioral change that can ensure long-term success.

One of the first lessons you learn here is that diets make you fat and eating can make you thin. You learn how to normalize your eating habits, thus decreasing a tendency to binge. Guests are shown that being more active can be as pleasant as taking a walk down a country lane. For women who have unsuccessfully attempted to manage their weight with extremely low-calorie diets, there is a special program to overcome negative effects and resume a livable and enjoyable approach to eating.

Working with a team of registered dietitians, nutritionists, and behavioral therapists with specialties in nutrition, metabolism, and stress management, you develop a personalized weight and health program that becomes part of your daily routine. A follow-up program helps you to maintain this routine at home. Tuition costs cover individual nutrition/dietary counseling and exercise prescription and modification. Massage therapy, facials, aromatherapy, body treatments, personal training, and one-on-one behavioral counseling are available at an additional expense.

Facilities include a range of weight-training equipment, an outdoor heated pool, tennis courts, and some off-site indoor pools for aquaerobics classes. Daily exercise classes (aerobics and resistance and circuit training), walking, hiking, biking, and in winter, cross-country skiing and snowshoeing fill most of the day.

Common areas include a cozy lounge with a wood stove and televisions and a high-ceiling dining room with rafters. Guest rooms have mission-style wooden furniture and Vermont-country accents.

....
INSIDER TIP The aerobic dance sessions here teach that exercise can be something fun that fits easily into everyday life.
....

Equipment: Cross-country ski machines, free weights, rowing machines, stair climbers, stationary bikes, treadmills, weight-training circuit. **Services:** Acupressure, body polish, herbal wraps, reflexology, salt glow. **Swimming:** Indoor and outdoor pools. **Classes and Programs:** Cooking classes, golf and skiing instruction, personal training, private counseling, tai chi, yoga. **Recreation:** Biking, golf, horseback riding, snowshoeing, tennis.

▦ 26 rooms.

✕ Meals included. 1,400-calorie menu served in dining room. **Sample Meals:** Sesame chicken, vegetarian roll-up, pizza (lunch); shrimp and vegetable stir-fry over basmati rice, eggplant Parmesan, grilled salmon, swordfish kebabs (dinner).

▱ 1-week session $1,080–$2,180 per person, includes lodging, meals, seminars. MC, V.

✉ *Fox La., Box 164, Ludlow, VT 05149,* ☎ *802/228–8885 or 800/448–8106,* FAX *802/228–8887. www.fitwoman.com*

NEW LIFE HIKING SPA

NUTRITION AND DIET ◦ HOLISTIC HEALTH

The alpine valleys of Vermont's Green Mountains are the main attraction at the New Life Hiking Spa, though the program also involves a comprehensive shape-up including exercise programs, cooking demonstrations, and nutritional counseling.

Launched in 1978 by Jimmy LeSage, a former professional cook and hotel manager, New Life operates from May through October at the Inn of the Six Mountains, just down the road from the ski resort of Killington. Programs, limited to a maximum of 25 participants, include a morning hike guided by staff members. The diverse terrain of the Appalachian Trail and Vermont's Long Trail challenges those of all skill levels. The advanced hikes scale the second-highest peak in Vermont, continue to neighboring Pico Peak, and end with an exuberant ride down the alpine slide.

Afternoon exercise classes are held in a tent with a specially designed floor. Yoga and stretching classes relax and invigorate the body. Other options, including aquaerobics classes, are available at the fitness center, which includes a lap pool, whirlpool, and heated outdoor swimming pool.

Healthy eating complements the vigorous physical activity. LeSage's philosophy on nutrition and meal preparation is published in his book *The New Life Guide to Healthy Eating,* which is given to each guest. For those who want to learn more, LeSage teaches cooking classes in the hotel kitchen. Wholesome, tasty meals are served in a cheery room with mountain views. Fresh fruit, herbal teas, decaffeinated coffee, and spring water are always on hand in the hospitality lounge.

Accommodations at New Life are furnished with twin or king beds and have private baths. The pine-paneled lobby has a lounge with fireplaces and comfy chairs.

INSIDER TIP These hikes are no walk in the park, so make sure to bring a good pair of hiking boots.

Services: Facial, massage. **Swimming:** Indoor and outdoor pools. **Classes and Programs:** Aquaerobics, body toning, cooking demonstrations, meditation, tai chi, yoga. **Recreation:** Hiking, tennis.

⬚ 100 rooms.

✗ Meals included. Food low in fat and high in complex carbohydrates served in dining room. **Sample Meals:** Corn chowder with pita pizza, chicken curry salad (lunch); salmon with dill sauce, spinach-rice casserole with string bean amandine (dinner).

▨ 3-night sampler $659 per person, double occupancy, includes lodging, meals, programs. 5-night program $1,099 per person, double occupancy. MC, V.

✉ *Inn of the Six Mountains, Box 395, Killington, VT 05751,* ☎ *802/422–4302 or 800/228–4676,* FAX *802/422–4321. www.newlifehikingspa.com*

TOPNOTCH AT STOWE

LUXURY PAMPERING ∘ NUTRITION AND DIET ∘ SPORTS CONDITIONING

Set in Vermont's Green Mountains in the ski resort town of Stowe, Topnotch is a classic country resort that combines a 23,000-square-ft European-style spa and fitness center with a highly rated sports program, including one of the country's top rated tennis academies.

The spa—with a staff of more than 80 treatment therapists, fitness instructors, personal trainers, and professional lifestyle and health consultants—boasts 20 treatment rooms. You can choose from 105 treatments, including a selection of massages, body wraps, and facials. There's a full roster of classes, including aerobics, yoga, meditation, tai chi, and instruction in outdoor sports such as snowshoeing and cross-country skiing.

A skylighted solarium houses a hot tub and 60-ft indoor pool, which are ideal for easing sore muscles. Even more indulgent is a shoulder massage under a cascading waterfall. The facilities also include state-of-the-art aerobics, weight-training, and cardiovascular studios.

At the beginning of your stay, a physiologist puts together a fitness profile based on strength, flexibility, and blood tests and plans an exercise program. Outfitted with a daily issue of shorts, T-shirt, robe, and slippers, you have a choice of group sessions or one-on-one cardiovascular and strength-training sessions with a personal trainer.

Topnotch has 10 outdoor tennis and 4 indoor tennis courts, and downhill skiing at Mt. Mansfield and cross-country skiing on 15 mi of groomed trails. Three- to seven-day programs include instruction as well as time on the courts and slopes.

Though Topnotch is minutes from the bustling village of Stowe, mountain views make it feel worlds apart. A massive fireplace warms the high-ceiling main lounge, where guests often enjoy a cocktail by the fire. Rooms are more like an English country house than a ski lodge. The formal dining room serves "New Vermont cuisine," with dishes such as locally caught fish, filet mignon, and free-range chicken, as well as heart-healthy cuisine.

....

INSIDER TIP Many products used at the spa are made with Vermont wildflowers and herbs. You can even buy some to take home.

....

Equipment: Elliptical trainers, free weights, rowing machines, stair climbers, stationary bikes, treadmills, weight-training circuit. **Services:** Acupressure, aromatherapy, herbal wrap, hydrotherapy, loofah body scrub, reflexology. **Swimming:** Indoor and outdoor pools. **Classes and Programs:** Aerobics, aquaerobics, nutrition seminars, tennis instruction, yoga. **Recreation:** Biking, billiards, croquet, horseback riding, table tennis, tennis. **Children's Programs:** Supervision for ages 5-12. Babysitting available.

▦ 80 rooms, 10 suites, 25 1- to 3-bedroom town houses.

✕ Meals à la carte. **Sample Meals:** Mushroom-barley soup with salad of asparagus and roasted red peppers, whole wheat pizza, chicken breast in cilantro-mint sauce (lunch); seafood pasta in three-mustard sauce, grilled chicken (dinner).

▨ Nightly rate $80–$188 per person, double occupancy. 3-night tennis/spa package $396 for two. AE, DC, MC, V.

✉ *4000 Mountain Rd., Box 1458, Stowe, VT 05672,* ☎ *802/253-8585 or 800/451-8686,* FAX *802/253-9263.* *www.topnotch-resort.com/spa*

WOODSTOCK INN & RESORT

LUXURY PAMPERING ○ SPORTS CONDITIONING

Picture the perfect New England town: the county courthouse and library facing an oval green, a covered bridge leading to immaculate farms and a Colonial inn. Add a full-service health-and-fitness center, more than 200 downhill trails, and one of New England's top golf courses, and you have the Woodstock Inn & Resort.

The current inn, the fourth on the site, spreads from the historic town green to the sports center, which includes the 18-hole championship golf course and croquet lawn, outdoor and indoor swimming pools, and tennis, racquetball, squash, and volleyball courts. A little over a mile south of the inn is the health-and-fitness center with first-rate strength training and cardiovascular exercise equipment, a heated indoor pool, an aerobics studio, and regularly scheduled classes in everything from aerobics to yoga. Massage services, available seven days a week, include deep-tissue work.

Ski resorts surround Woodstock; some of the best are Suicide Six, Killington, Ascutney Mountain, and Okemo Mountain. Cross-country skiers and snowshoers can use the facilities of Woodstock Ski Touring Center, with 37 mi of trails surrounding the village, or opt for one of the other nearby scenic routes, including 12 mi of woodland trails on Mt. Peg, and 18 mi of century-old carriage roads at the base of Mt. Tom. The touring center also offers professional instruction, equipment rental, and a heated trailside log cabin.

Time seems to have stood still in this classic New England village, with its white-steeple church and redbrick county government buildings. Appropriately, there's a dress code in the inn's dining room, where hearty New England fare is a throwback to pre-health-spa days. Rooms are equally traditional, with New England antiques and patchwork quilts on the beds. The nearby Billings Farm Museum has exhibits of early New England farm life and a prize-winning dairy barn.

....

INSIDER TIP Depending on your interests, this old-fashioned inn can be a romantic getaway, a family fun spot, or a luxurious spa. Best of all, it can be all of these at the same time.

....

Equipment: Free weights, rowing machines, stationary bikes, treadmills, weight-training equipment. **Services:** Massage. **Swimming:** Indoor and outdoor pools. **Classes and Programs:** Aerobics, aquaerobics, personal training, tennis instruction, yoga. **Recreation:** Croquet, horseshoes, nature walks, racquetball, sleigh rides, squash, tennis, volleyball; cross-country skiing, downhill skiing, horseback riding nearby. **Children's Services:** Baby-sitting available.

▦ 144 rooms, 7 suites, 3 houses.

✕ Meals à la carte. The dining room serves American fare, while the Eagle Café and Richardson's Tavern serve casual fare. **Sample Meals:** Tricolor cheese-filled tortellini, roast Vermont turkey breast, Boston baked scrod (lunch); oven-roasted Chilean sea bass with artichoke and sun-dried-tomato risotto and smoked-tomato-tarragon coulis (dinner).

▨ Nightly rate $169–$545 per room. AE, MC, V.

✉ *14 The Green, Woodstock, VT 05091,* ☎ *802/457–1100 or 800/ 448–7900,* ℻ *802/457–6699. www.woodstockinn.com*

VIRGINIA

HARTLAND WELLNESS CENTER

MEDICAL WELLNESS ○ NUTRITION AND DIET

Motivation through diet, exercise, and prayer is the prescription for wellness at this Hartland Wellness Center. The retreat's long-established 10- to 18-day program teaches you how to overcome physical and emotional obstacles to a healthy lifestyle through nutritional instruction, private and group counseling, and physical therapy.

Heart disease, arthritis, cancer, diabetes, obesity, addictions, and digestive disorders are among the diseases addressed by the team of specialists. Their specific recommendations for diet take into account your physical condition, nutritional requirements, and personal goals. Doctors and other staff members are all Seventh-Day Adventists, although the program is nondenominational.

Your personalized schedule begins with a daily check of blood pressure and weight, followed by breakfast. Group exercises and lectures, individual counseling sessions, and cooking classes round out the day. Meals at the center are vegan. Lunch is the largest meal of the day, followed by a light dinner.

Accommodations, in an elegant two-story building near Hartland College, have antique furnishings and cherrywood furniture. There is an indoor swimming pool and limited exercise equipment for your free time.

INSIDER TIP Because it's on a 760-acre estate in the foothills of the Blue Ridge Mountains, the Hartland has extensive nature trails for you to explore.

Equipment: Stationary bikes, treadmills, weight-training circuit. **Services:** Hydrotherapy, massage. **Swimming:** Indoor pool. **Classes and Programs:** Cardiac and cancer rehabilitation, exercise counseling, spiritual guidance, smoking-cessation, stress-management classes, vegetarian cooking instruction, weight-control counseling. **Recreation:** Hiking.

☖ 15 rooms.

✕ Meals included. 3 vegan buffet. **Sample Meals:** Vegan lasagna (lunch); banana smoothie, fruit salad (dinner).

✉ 10-day program $1,995 per person, includes lodging, meals, programs. No credit cards.

✉ Box 1, Rapidan, VA 22733, ☎ 540/672–3100 or 800/763–9355, FAX 540/672–2584. www.hartland.edu

THE HOMESTEAD

LUXURY PAMPERING ○ MINERAL SPRINGS

Step back to an era of gracious Southern hospitality, when high society arrived by private train to take the waters. The mineral springs that made the Homestead famous as long ago as 1766 still pour forth. In the 1840s bathing here was advertised as a panacea for just about anything that ailed you. Such claims fell out of fashion, but the Homestead endures.

Arriving in the Great Hall, which is flanked by 16 stately Corinthian columns, you are treated to afternoon tea as a trio entertains with music of a kinder, gentler era. You can easily picture Thomas Jefferson rejuvenating himself in the warm springs pool, simultaneously concocting plans for a wooden covering and for the nation's independence. Even today, despite the resort's rambling size and erstwhile conventions, the Homestead makes you feel at home.

Furnished with 1920s-style wicker furniture and flowered-chintz draperies, the spa still has huge marble tubs for mineral-water soaks, plus an indoor swimming pool dating from 1903. Light pours in from giant windows, creating an airy greenhouse effect. Hot springs continually circulate water, so the temperature hovers around 88°F. For those who want to work out, a new fitness center upstairs offers aerobics, an array of cardiovascular and weight-training equipment, and a spectacular view of the grounds.

Relaxation therapy begins with a private soak in one of the marble tubs. The naturally heated thermal water, high in sulfur, magnesium, and 16 other minerals, reaches your tub at 104°F. After a few minutes in the sauna or steam room (the men's side also has a Turkish bath), you're led to a marble slab for a rubdown with coarse salt. After you shower, you're treated to a massage by a real pro. The treatment, which originated here more than 100 years ago, is called Dr. Goode's Spout Bath and costs $35.

Two recently added spa treatments incorporate indigenous wildflowers. The Allegheny Raspberry Relaxer features a raspberry scrub followed by an application of fragrant raspberry oil. The Mountain Laurel Bath Soak is a mineral bath scented with mountain laurel. Other spa services, from aromatherapy to hairstyling, are available in the fourth-floor health and beauty salon.

Three golf courses and 12 tennis courts, playable most of the year, are big outdoor attractions. Sam Snead describes the Cascades Course as "America's finest mountain course." Other recreation includes horseback riding, mountain trout fishing, archery, and trapshooting. Surrounded by a 15,000-acre mountain preserve, the Homestead has miles of hiking trails. In winter, snowmaking equipment prepares slopes for downhill skiing, and trails are groomed for cross-country skiing.

By day's end you may well be exhausted, but there's still a dinner dance in the capacious old dining room as well as a multicourse menu that will put a serious dent in your diet. As he has for nearly four decades, executive chef Albert Schnarwyler designs meals to attract the vigorous, if not the particularly adventurous, diner. Finally, you can retreat to your room, either in the main section (the best are in the tower) or in the newer south wing. Furnishings include mahogany bedsteads, writing tables, lounge chairs, and lacy white curtains. Some rooms have fireplaces, walk-in closets, and French doors that open onto a private balcony or screened porch.

INSIDER TIP The choicest rooms are in the tower, with views of the surrounding Blue Ridge Mountains.

Exercise Equipment: Free weights, rowing machines, treadmills, weight-training circuit. **Services:** Aromatherapy, herbal wrap, loofah body scrub, mineral tub, therapeutic whirlpool. **Swimming:** 2 pools. **Recreation:** Archery, falconry, fishing, golf, hiking, horseback riding, ice-skating, lawn bowling, skeet and trapshooting, skiing, tennis. **Children's Programs:** Kids Club for ages 3–12.

▥ 432 rooms, 81 suites.

✕ Breakfast and dinner included. **Sample Meals:** Virginia ham stuffed with greens, roast beef with farm produce (lunch); sautéed whole trout (dinner).

▤ Nightly rate $205–$230 per person, double occupancy, includes lodging, breakfast and dinner. 2-night makeover package $351, includes lodging, breakfast and dinner, spa treatments. AE, D, DC, MC, V.

✉ *Box 2000, Hot Springs, VA 24445,* ☎ *540/839–1766 or 800/838–1766,* ℻ *540/839–7670. www.thehomestead.com*

KINGSMILL RESORT

LUXURY PAMPERING ∘ SPORTS CONDITIONING

Bring your golf clubs, your tennis racket, and your kids because fun and fitness are on tap in equal measure at this resort. Nestled amid lush, green woodlands on the banks of the historic James River, Kingsmill Resort makes an ideal base from which to explore area attractions such as Busch Gardens, Colonial Williamsburg, and the scenic Tidewater area.

Built and managed by Anheuser-Busch, the 2,900-acre resort is part of a gated residential community, complete with marina and the state's largest golf resort. Golfers play the Woods Course, designed by Tom Clark and Curtis Strange; the River Course, designed by Pete Dye; the Plantation Course, designed by Arnold Palmer; or a nine-hole course.

The Sports Club provides a light-filled environment for workouts on state-of-the-art cardiovascular and weight-training equipment, one-on-one training, and laps in indoor and outdoor swimming pools. There are racquetball courts, saunas, steam rooms, and whirlpools. Spa services are scheduled à la carte or as part of day or half-day packages.

Staying in one of the two-story lodges that border the river and golf courses, you gain access to a world of upscale pleasures. Villas have one to three bedrooms with king- or queen-size beds, and some have a complete kitchen and living room with fireplace. Dining ranges from formal, at the river-view Bray Dining Room, to casual, at the Sports Club's grill and a tavern at the country club.

INSIDER TIP The atmosphere is more residential than resort. If you enjoy planning your own program, the elements are all here.

Equipment: Cross-country ski machines, free weights, rowing machines, stair climbers, stationary bikes, treadmills, weight-training circuit. **Services:** Massage, mud treatments, seaweed wrap. **Swimming:** 4 pools. **Classes and Programs:** Aerobics, aquaerobics. **Recreation:** Billiards, golf, racquetball, shuffleboard, tennis. **Children's Programs:** Kamper summer program for ages 5–12.

▥ 400 rooms and suites.

✕ Meals à la carte. Sports Club and Bray Dining Room serve American cuisine. **Sample Meals:** Crab cakes, Brie and red-pepper soup, Michelob shrimp (lunch); honey-glazed salmon with corn cakes and asparagus, seafood stew in spicy wine-tomato sauce, pecan-encrusted breast of duck, rack of lamb with smoked Gouda and spinach (dinner).

✉ Nightly rate $134–$184 per room. 2-night spa package $549–$684, includes lodging, spa treatments. AE, D, DC, MC, V.

✉ *1010 Kingsmill Rd., Williamsburg, VA 23185,* ☎ *757/253–1703 or 800/832–5665,* FAX *757/253–8237. www.kingsmill.com*

TAZEWELL CLUB

LUXURY PAMPERING ○ SPORTS CONDITIONING

Since there wasn't much pampering in 18th-century America, one of the few places in Colonial Williamsburg that isn't a living museum is the Tazewell Club. Despite being housed in a building that was once a patriot's home, the mood at this inn is contemporary. Nonetheless, a stay at the Tazewell Club means you can learn about Colonial soap-making techniques during the day, then be pampered by their modern equivalents by night.

The Tazewell Club is a short walk from Colonial Williamsburg, offering easy access to anyone interested in touring the many 18th-century shops and restored homes or just strolling down the cobblestones on Duke of Gloucester Street.

Designed for newcomers as well as fitness buffs, the facilities include strength-training equipment and an aerobics studio. The swimming pool, which opens onto a sundeck, is popular with families, but certain hours are reserved for lap swimmers. Nearby are two Robert Trent Jones golf courses, eight tennis courts, a croquet court, a bowling green, and two outdoor swimming pools.

The Tazewell Club is available to anyone staying in the Williamsburg Lodge. Admission to the club is also complimentary to those staying in any of the five hotels—such as the famous Williamsburg Inn, a few steps away—or in the restored Colonial houses operated by the Colonial Williamsburg Foundation.

INSIDER TIP Spa services, such as the loofah body scrub or massage, are traditional rather than trendy, making up for in dependability what they lack in innovation.

Equipment: Rowing machines, stationary bikes, treadmills. **Services:** Massage, loofah scrub, herbal wrap. **Swimming:** 2 pools. **Classes and Programs:** Aquaerobics. **Recreation:** Badminton, biking, croquet, golf, lawn bowling, miniature golf, tennis, volleyball.

▣ 25 Tazewell Club rooms and 2 suites in Williamsburg Lodge, 235 rooms in Williamsburg Inn, 85 rooms in Colonial homes.

✗ No meals at Tazewell Club, but dining room at Williamsburg Lodge is in the same bldg.

✉ Nightly rate $195–$235 per room in Tazewell Club. AE, D, DC, MC, V.

✉ *Williamsburg Lodge, 310 S. England St., Williamsburg, VA 23187,* ☎ *757/229–1000 or 800/447–8679,* FAX *757/221–8797. www. history.org*

YOGAVILLE

HOLISTIC HEALTH

The name says it all: At Yogaville, meditation and yoga provide the central focus of daily life. In the beautiful James River valley near Charlottesville, the ashram welcomes people of all faiths and backgrounds to study and practice yoga under the guidance of Sri Swami Satchidananda, a native of India who became a figure in the counterculture movement in the United States in the 1960s. Although he is not always in residence, Satchidananda leads the Saturday-night meditation when available.

At Yogaville the body-mind connection of Integral Yoga (a version of hatha yoga) is strengthened through in-depth workshops in asana (physical posture) and pranayama (breathing technique). Participants work at their own rate, with thoughtful supervision from the staff.

Guests are free to participate or observe, and special yoga training is available for beginners. Classes begin at 6:30 AM. Courses offered during the day focus on meditation techniques. The ashram also offers a variety of two- to five-day workshops, retreats, and teacher certification programs. A special curriculum for children ages 6–12 is also available.

Services include physician-administered acupuncture, treatment with Chinese herbs, and massage therapy, but you should call in advance to check on availability. Chiropractic care and therapeutic massage are available at the Integral Health Center. In addition, the center offers courses in stress management and support groups for those with heart disease and those who want to avoid it.

The ashram campus is dominated by the dome-shape Lotus Shrine, used for group meditation, and its reflecting pool. Grounds and buildings are decorated with hand-painted symbols of inner peace. Unlike trendier yoga programs, Yogaville has a traditional feel. Here you won't find the high-energy aerobic workout of "power yoga."

Guest accommodations range widely. A two-story wooden lodge, the Lotus Inn, has a health-food café and private rooms, each with kitchenette. A two-story dormitory includes classrooms as well as guest rooms with four to six beds sharing communal baths. Tent campsites, some with platforms, are in a wooded area near the dormitory and have shower and laundry facilities. Motor homes can also be parked on the grounds of the 750-acre retreat.

The main meal is lunch, served in a communal hall. A vegetarian diet emphasizes whole grains, protein sources such as tofu and legumes, fresh fruit, and vegetables. Breakfast and supper buffets are light, made up of cereals, herbal tea, yogurt, low-fat milk, and the like. Those who volunteer for work in the organic garden, kitchen, or other areas earn free meals.

INSIDER TIP Although you should reserve in advance for special programs, the ashram can sometimes accommodate last-minute arrivals if you want to drop in for a weekend sampler.

Services: Massage. **Swimming:** River. **Classes and Programs:** Courses in heart health, sketching and drawing, creative spirituality. **Recreation:** Gardening, hiking.

⊞ 6 private rooms, 25 dorm rooms, 8 campsites.

✗ Meals included. Vegetarian buffet. **Sample Meals:** Baked tofu, brown rice, steamed vegetables (lunch); miso soup, millet (dinner).

🖾 Nightly rate $80–$95 per couple in private room, $40–$45 per person in dormitory, includes meals, program. MC, V.

✉ *Rte. 604, Buckingham, VA 23921,* ☎ *804/969–3121 or 800/858–9642,* ℻ *804/969–1303. www.yogaville.org*

WASHINGTON

ALTA CRYSTAL RESORT

LUXURY PAMPERING

Some visitors to this luxurious mountain resort claim that it's actually the cathedral majesty of nearby Ohanapecosh, with its 1000-year-old trees, that helps them relax and renew their spirit. Some maintain it's the views of the 14,411-ft-high volcanic dome of Mt. Rainier that does it. Others say they just like to sit and listen to the rushing waters of Deep Creek and to the chatter of the birds.

Of course, accommodations at Alta Crystal Resort have all the civilized amenities a spoiled urbanite could wish for in the wilderness. Sprawling over 22 forested acres, just outside the northeast entrance to Mt. Rainier National Park, this resort has miles of hiking and mountain-biking trails through the old-growth national forest (which become snowshoe trails after the white stuff falls).

But this is one resort where you don't have to exert yourself at all: all rooms have fireplaces, fully equipped kitchens, VCRs, and telephones with data ports. Or you could swim a few laps in the heated pool, laze in the hot tub, or play horseshoes, croquet, or volleyball.

INSIDER TIP Bring your mountain bike to explore the miles of trails surrounding the resort.

Swimming: Pool. **Recreation:** Biking, croquet, fishing, hiking, horseshoes, Ping-Pong. **Children's Programs:** Nighttime bonfire.

⊞ 24 rooms, 1 cabin.

✗ No restaurant.

▣ Nightly rate $129–$199 per room. AE, MC, V.

✉ *68317 SR 410 East, Greenwater, WA 98022,* ☎ *360/663–2500 or 800/277–6475,* ℻ *360/663–2556. www.altacrystalresort.com*

BELLEVUE CLUB

LUXURY PAMPERING

You'd expect to find all the latest exercise equipment at a hotel that started out as an athletic club. What may come as a surprise to first-time guests, however, is the utter luxury, as well as the beauty of the surroundings, at the Bellevue Club Hotel.

The Bellevue Club hotel has won all sorts of awards for its architecture and for the design of its rooms, which run to warm, comforting earth tones (which are supposed to create the illusion of sunshine even when it's raining outside) and are decorated with original Northwestern art work. The warm colors are further enhanced by cherrywood furniture and raku pottery. All rooms have large, comfortable armchairs, as well as spa-size baths with deep soaker tubs and separate showers. Many have private landscaped patios.

The club's exercise and spa facilities are just a short walk away. There are an Olympic-size pool, racquetball, squash, and tennis courts, and a full range of classes from aerobics to yoga.

As far as recreational activities go, you can try boating on nearby Lake Washington, hiking Sammamish River Trail and Snoqualmie Valley Trail, or exploring Cougar Mountain Park. There's also skiing in the Cascade Mountains, to the east.

INSIDER TIP Ask for a room with views of Mt. Rainier, which looms to the south.

Equipment: Free weights, stair climbers, stationary bikes, treadmills, weight-training circuit. **Classes and Programs:** Aerobics, dance, karate, yoga. **Swimming:** Pool. **Recreation:** Biking, hiking, skiing. **Children's Programs:** Kids' camp, gymnastics programs.

🏠 64 rooms, 3 suites.

✕ Meals à la carte. 3 restaurants serve varied cuisine. **Sample Meals:** Albacore tuna salad sandwich, barbecued duck stir-fry with soba noodles and shiitake mushrooms, coriander-and-pumpkin-seed-crusted sea bass (dinner).

✉ Nightly rate $235–$295 per room. AE, CB, MC, V.

✉ *11200 S.E. 6th St., Bellevue, WA 98004,* ☎ *425/454–4424,* FAX *425/ 688–3101. www.bellevueclub.com*

CARSON HOT MINERAL SPRINGS RESORT

MINERAL SPRINGS

The claw-foot tubs are characteristic of the old-fashioned friendliness bathers enjoy at the Carson Hot Mineral Springs Resort. The bathhouses here, on the banks of the Wind River near where it meets the mighty Columbia River, date from 1876. Proud of using "the same bath methods for over 100 years," the management strives to remain unpretentious and comfortable.

The oldest remaining structure on the property, a three-story wooden hotel, was built in 1897 to accommodate bathers who traveled by steamboat from Portland, Oregon. The Hotel St. Martin still houses guests in nine simple rooms. Nearly two dozen rustic cabins were built in the early 1920s.

Taking the waters is a simple two-step procedure: A tub soak is followed by the traditional sweat wrap, in which an attendant covers bathers in sheets and heavy blankets to induce a good sweat. The 126°F mineral water is piped directly into the tubs (eight for men, six for women), which are drained and refilled after each use. Chemical analysis shows the water to be high in sodium and calcium, similar to springs at principal European spas. The crowning touch is the hour-long massage or herbal wrap.

INSIDER TIP If taking a dip isn't your thing, there's also a golf course on the premises.

Services: Massage. **Recreation:** Fishing, golf, hiking.

▦ 9 rooms, 23 cabins.

✕ Meals à la carte. Hotel restaurant serves American fare. **Sample Meals:** Club sandwich, pasta salad, beef lasagna (lunch); prime rib, vegetable burger, grilled salmon (dinner).

▧ Nightly rate $40–$60 per room. MC, V.

✉ *Box 1169, Carson, WA 98610,* ☎ *509/427–8292 or 800/607– 3678,* FAX *509/427–7242. www.ohwy.com/wa/c/carminhs.htm*

NOTARAS LODGE

MINERAL SPRINGS

Notaras Lodge, with the slogan "luxury in logs," has long been this small resort town's main attraction. It once had a regional reputation for its theme rooms, dedicated to such locally beloved stars as Norma Zimmer, the "bubble lady" on *The Lawrence Welk Show.* The theme rooms burned down a few years back, but the therapeutic waters of nearby Soap Lake are still on tap in the remaining rooms, which are large and comfortable. If the waters alone don't suffice to heal your aching muscles, you can always get a massage.

Two-mile-long Soap Lake straddles the lower end of the Grand Coulee, fed by mineral-rich groundwater bubbling up from cracks in the basalt bedrock. Because the lake has no outlet, its waters are high in minerals—and are thought to be of therapeutic value. The lake gets its name from the soapy texture of the water, created by 16 naturally occurring chemical salts (including sodium, carbonate, bicarbonate, and sulfate) which make the water slippery to the touch and salty to the tongue. Never mind its supposed healing qualities—you want to try it for the unique tactile experience it provides.

The lodge has 14 guest rooms in the hand-hewn log cabins. Each room has a kitchenette with microwave and refrigerator and a choice of fresh or Soap Lake mineral water for your bath. Five rooms also offer in-room whirlpools.

Don's Restaurant (under the same ownership) is popular with locals for its steaks and Greek food. Order with care: the huge portions cater to the appetites of Columbia Plateau farmers and ranchers and easily overwhelm urban visitors (don't look for spa cuisine in Soap Lake.) At night the lounge has country-and-western entertainment.

INSIDER TIP Visit the Soap Lake Businessman's Club, next door to the Notaras Lodge. It's possibly the state's last members-only "bottle club," a throwback to post–Prohibition-era blue laws.

Services: Massage. **Swimming:** Lake. **Recreation:** Boating, fishing, golf, hiking.

▦ 10 rooms.

✕ Meals à la carte. Don's Restaurant serves steaks and Greek food. **Sample Meals:** Steak, lamb chops, pasta, veal, seafood (dinner).

▧ Nightly rate $58–$65 per room. MC, V.

✉ 236 E. Main St., Soap Lake, WA 99851 ☎ 509/246–0462, FAX 509/246–1054. www.notaraslodge.com

ROSARIO RESORT

LUXURY PAMPERING

As you arrive by ferry or floatplane, the natural beauty of this peaceful cove in the San Juan Islands may take you by surprise. Orcas Island, with its stands of towering trees, is an obvious choice for relaxation and renewal.

The Rosario Resort is certainly not a huge high-rise hotel. The centerpiece is the 1909 mansion constructed by shipbuilding magnate Robert Moran. From here, and from many of the guest cottages on the nearby hills, you have an unobstructed view of Cascade Bay.

The mansion's public rooms have a nautical look; portholes and other parts salvaged from old ships pop up in the room that houses the indoor swimming pool and in other unexpected places. The mansion's focal point is an Aeolian pipe organ that graces a music room with cathedral ceilings and stained-glass windows. Daily concerts are held in the summer.

Extensive spa treatments are available at Rosario's Natural Wellness Center. In addition, there's an aerobics studio where the daily schedule might consist of yoga, aquaerobics, and conditioning classes.

Outside the spa, simple pleasures include hunting for driftwood on the 2-mi beach and hiking to the lookout over the San Juan Islands from the top of Mt. Constitution. The Canadian Rockies are a few hours' drive north.

INSIDER TIP If you take a floatplane, getting there will be half the fun. Three different companies have flights to the island.

Equipment: Cross-country ski machines, free weights, rowing machines, stair climbers, stationary bikes, weight-training circuit. **Services:** Aromatherapy, reflexology, salt glow, shiatsu. **Swimming:** 3 pools, beach, mountain lake. **Recreation:** Boating, hiking, kayaking, tennis, whale-watching.

⊡ 127 rooms, 8 suites.

✗ Meals à la carte. The Orcas Room and Compass Dining Room serve American fare. **Sample Meals:** Green salad dressed with fruit juice and cayenne pepper, chicken baked in romaine lettuce, beer-steamed Lopez Island mussels (lunch); grilled salmon with a peppercorn/basil/red pepper sauce, veal topped with crab and asparagus, carpaccio of yellowfin tuna with baby greens and braised Washington lingcod (dinner).

🖃 Nightly rate $108–$241 per person, double occupancy. 2-night spa package $333 per person, double occupancy, includes lodging, spa treatments. AE, DC, MC, V.

✉ 1 Rosario Way, Eastsound, Orcas Island, WA 98245, ☎ 360/376–2222 or 800/562–8820. www.rosario-resort.com

SALISH LODGE & SPA

LUXURY PAMPERING

This Asian-influenced health retreat looks out on the magnificent scenery of the Cascade Mountains. The airy, wood-and-glass pavilion evokes the feeling of a bathhouse at a Japanese hot spring. Seaweed treatments, shiatsu, and Pacific Rim–style cuisine add to the experience.

Viewers of the TV series *Twin Peaks* might recognize the four-story lodge, which is perched at the crest of a waterfall taller than Niagara. Guest rooms all have a wood-burning stone fireplace, rough-hewn furniture, and either a balcony or window seat. Large bathrooms have oversize whirlpool tubs. Those who prefer spending time in public spaces can sip complimentary morning coffee or afternoon tea by the fireplace in the lodge's library.

The spa's most spectacular feature is a pair of hydrotherapy pools set in natural rock and joined by a waterfall. In addition, there are four private rooms for massage and bodywork, plus a wet-treatment room with a Vichy shower. For privacy you can arrange a fireside massage in your room. Although there are no organized exercise programs, a small fitness center has a good range of equipment.

For adventure-minded guests, there are hiking in Snoqualmie Falls Park, mountain biking, white-water rafting, and horseback trail riding. The lodge can arrange it all.

INSIDER TIP Try the Falls Refresher, which includes a 30-minute aromatherapy massage, a facial, and a sea-salt deep-cleansing hand-and-foot polish. You also get a spa snack.

Equipment: Free weights, rowing machines, stair climbers, stationary bikes, treadmills, weight-training circuit. **Services:** Body scrub, mud wrap, seaweed wrap, reflexology, shiatsu, Vichy shower. **Recreation:** Biking, horseback riding, white-water rafting.

🛏 91 rooms, 4 suites.

✕ Meals à la carte. The Dining Room serves seafood as well as spa cuisine. **Sample Meals:** Spinach fusilli, cashew-crusted sea bass with dried-current polenta (lunch); confit of Northwest king salmon, roasted venison chop, mushroom risotto (dinner).

💳 Nightly rate $275 per room. AE, DC, MC, V.

✉ *U.S. Hwy. 202, Box 1109, Snoqualmie, WA 98065,* ☎ *425/831–6500 or 800/826–6124,* 🖷 *425/888–2420. www.salishlodge.com*

SKAMANIA LODGE

LUXURY PAMPERING

The mighty Columbia River welcomes visitors to the Skamania Lodge, built on a ridge in the Gorge National Scenic Area, 45 minutes from Portland. This area is great for hiking, and the blustery winds that blow through the gorge make it perfect for sailboarding.

This is Chinook tribe territory, and Skamania Lodge's architecture reflects the area's rich heritage. Creating the casual, calming interior are Native American–style rugs, handwoven fabrics, and mission-style wood furnishings. A stone fireplace dominates the three-story great room.

The spa and fitness center have great views of the surrounding forests. The spa includes a hydrotherapy pool, as well as indoor whirlpools and an outdoor hot tub. You can also take advantage of the 60-ft lap pool, complete with its own waterfall.

Also on the grounds is an 18-hole golf course that winds through the forest. Golfers warm up on a driving range, putting green, and practice bunker before tackling this challenging course. Guided trail rides on horseback are reserved through the lodge's guest-services desk. In winter, trails are groomed for cross-country skiing.

INSIDER TIP Take one of the popular guided treks to the area devastated by the eruption of Mt. St. Helens in 1980.

Equipment: Rowing machines, stair climbers, treadmills, weight-training circuit. **Services:** Massage. **Swimming:** Indoor pool. **Recreation:** Golf, hiking, mountain biking, tennis, volleyball.

⊞ 195 rooms.

✕ Meals à la carte. The Dining Room serves Pacific Northwest cuisine. **Sample Meals:** Trail-wagon burger (lunch); plank-roasted salmon with chardonnay-butter sauce, roast leg of venison with wild-berry relish (dinner).

🍽 Nightly rate $139–$239 per room. 1-night spa package $319–$389, includes lodging, breakfast and dinner, spa treatments for two. AE, DC, MC, V.

✉ *Box 189, Stevenson, WA 98648,* ☎ *509/427–7700 or 800/221–7117,* FAX *509/427–2547. www.dolce.com/properties/skamania*

SOL DUC HOT SPRINGS RESORT

MINERAL SPRINGS

Here's the place to bring the family for a soak after a hike in Olympic National Park. Operated by the Department of the Interior, the Sol Duc Hot Springs Resort is open from May through October.

Accommodations here are decidedly rustic. There are 32 minimally outfitted cabins and 20 sites for recreational vehicles. The Springs Restaurant serves casual yet healthy fare.

The real draw here, though, is the mineral spring–fed pools. Park visitors can use the public and private pools for a fee, while overnight guests use them for free. Piped in at a temperature of 123°F, the mineral water is cooled for use in three large outdoor soaking pools. The water's continuous flow into the pools makes chlorination unnecessary.

INSIDER TIP The grocery store here is a great place to shop for provisions.

Swimming: Pool. **Classes and Programs:** Lectures by park rangers. **Recreation:** Fishing, hiking. **Children's Programs:** Ranger-led nature walks for children ages 5–15.

⊞ 32 cabins, 20 RV sites.

✕ Meals à la carte. Springs Restaurant serves low-fat meals. **Sample Meals:** Vegetarian sandwich with roasted red peppers, cucumbers, tomatoes, sprouts, and cheddar cheese (lunch); baked cod with mushrooms, stuffed acorn squash with wild-rice pilaf and tarragon beurre blanc.

🍽 Nightly rate $98–$165 per room. AE, D, MC, V.

✉ *Soleduc River Rd., Olympic National Park, WA; Reservations: Box 2169, Port Angeles, WA 98362,* ☎ *360/327–3583. www. northolympic.com/solduc*

SUN MOUNTAIN LODGE

LUXURY PAMPERING

Perched atop a mountain ridge, this resort on 3,000 acres of meadow and forest slopes has everything: spectacular views (the snowcapped peaks looming to the south, west, and east rise to heights of 7,000–8,000 ft), comfortable rooms, a regionally famous restaurant, and just about every spa treatment you could wish for.

The lodge and the other buildings are scattered across the property, making the place seem more intimate. The lodge has a secluded library with a fireplace and a dining room with a panoramic view of the jagged North Cascades. There are 102 guest rooms, some with balcony or patio. Several have gas or wood fireplaces, and some have whirlpool baths. More than a dozen lakefront cabins have fireplaces and space for up to six people.

The award-winning Dining Room serves American fare with an emphasis on Pacific Northwest specialties. If you want to accompany your reveries with a glass of wine, you can choose from more than 3,000 bottles in the lodge's cellar.

The spa features treatments found in all the best facilities: masks, massages, and wraps of all types. Especially tantalizing is the river-rock massage, which uses heated stones to relieve sore muscles and aching joints. There's also a facial using similar techniques.

Best of all, this is a very laid-back place. No one pressures you into doing anything. If you come here to get away from it all, soak up the mountain air, smell the wildflowers, and take a stroll now and then, that's all you need to do.

INSIDER TIP Try the Sun Mountain Facial, the spa's signature treatment, which combines cleansing and exfoliating the skin with lymphatic drainage.

Swimming: 2 pools. **Classes and Programs:** Body wraps, river rock massage, reflexology. **Recreation:** Fishing, hiking, horseback riding, ice-skating, mountain biking, skiing, sleigh rides, snowshoeing, tennis, white-water rafting. **Children's Programs:** Playground.

⊞ 102 rooms.

✗ Meals à la carte. Regionally renowned Dining Room serves Pacific Northwest fare. **Sample Meals:** Chili-roasted chicken wings, roasted vegetable and garlic-herb wrap (lunch); steamed scallops, citrus-cured spring-run chinook salmon, steamed chicken and roasted pepper wrap, seared cold-water prawns with tomatoes, artichokes, capers, preserved lemon, and arugula (dinner).

▱ Nightly rate $155–$310 per room. AE, DC, MC, V.

✉ *Box 1000, Winthrop, WA 98862* ☏ *509/996–2211 or 800/572–0493,* FAX *509/996–3133. www.sunmountainlodge.com*

WEST VIRGINIA

BERKELEY SPRINGS STATE PARK

MINERAL SPRINGS

Spartan and old-fashioned by today's standards, the facilities at Berkeley Springs State Park offer a down-home brand of healing. Bargain prices and a sense of history are the main draws.

Berkeley Springs, billed as "the country's first spa," rests at the foot of the mountain named Cacapon, a Native American word meaning "healing waters." In the mid-18th century, the town was named Medicine Springs. In 1776 George Washington's family and friends incorporated the town of Bath, named after the resort town in England. That is still the town's official name.

Ever since George and Martha Washington took the waters here, this secluded town has attracted healers and promoters. A museum atop the Roman baths documents the area's development. The town has attracted bodyworkers and therapists, and a bottling plant exports the spring water. At the Bath House on Fairfax Street, you can shop for health products and spa guides, make appointments for therapeutic treatments, and take yoga and tai chi classes. The new Atasia Spa, on Congress Street, offers a range of massages, facials, wraps, and other treatments. Nearby is Homeopathy Works, a full-service homeopathic pharmacy where exhibits trace the development of homeopathy.

Tari's Premier Café, on Washington Street, next door to the venerable Star Theatre, serves up a mix of low-fat vegetarian, seafood, and meat specialties for lunch and dinner and hosts weekly live music jams. Inspirations is a new breakfast and lunch spot on Washington Street, while Lot 12 Public House on Warren Street serves seasonal contemporary cuisine for dinner. The town is home to many antiques shops that will entertain window-shoppers. In winter in the state park the town hosts an international water-tasting event and a special celebration of George Washington's bathtub. Autumn features the popular Apple Butter Festival.

The West Virginia Division of Natural Resources operates the bathhouses, which are in the center of town just off busy Washington Street. The original building dates from 1815 and has eight 750-gallon public pools that can accommodate four people each. Another building, dating from the 1930s, has separate men's and women's facilities; in the women's bath heated mineral water spurts from enormous pipes into two 3-ft-deep tile plunge pools where patrons soak in privacy. A public swimming pool is open throughout the summer. Bathhouses are open daily from 10 to 6.

The park doesn't have accommodations, but you can spend the night at any number of nearby inns, hotels, and bed-and-breakfasts. The 1930s

Country Inn (☎ 304/258–2210 or 800/822–6630), next door to the state park, is also a beauty salon and full-service spa with mineral-water whirlpools. The inn's budget-price accommodations and two restaurants offer a taste of country traditions. In addition, there are several bed-and-breakfasts in town or nearby. **The Highlawn Inn,** on Market Street (☎ 304/258–5700 or 888/290–4163), a hilltop Victorian mansion, has antiques-filled rooms; some have whirlpool and fireplace, as does the carriage-house suite. **Inspirations Café and Bakery** also has a small B&B in a recently renovated Victorian home (☎ 304/258–2292).

INSIDER TIP History buffs will enjoy hiking along the C & O Canal or strolling through Harpers Ferry National Historical Park.

Services: Massage, Roman bath, steam bath. **Swimming:** Pool.

🚺 None in Berkeley Springs State Park. For a list of area accommodations, see www.berkeleysprings.com

💲 Roman bath $10 per person. Bath and massage $55–$60 per person.

✉ *121 S. Washington St., Berkeley Springs, WV 25411, ☎ 304/258–2711 or 800/225–5982. www/berkeley_springs.html*

COOLFONT RESORT

NUTRITION AND DIET ∘ HOLISTIC HEALTH

Bring your jeans and hiking boots to this informal family-run spa set on a 1,300-acre retreat in the foothills of the Appalachian Mountains. Although the resort itself is like a summer camp rather than a luxury spa, the Spa at Coolfont offers a wide array of treatments and activities. The beautiful setting and relaxed atmosphere are perhaps what draw guests back.

The spa has 23 private rooms for a wide range of bodywork, a full-service salon, and an aerobics studio. Instructors are well trained and attentive to guests. The spa also features an indoor spring-fed pool and exercise room with limited cardiovascular and strength-training equipment. A full range of scheduled classes is available to resort guests for a modest fee.

For those who want to immerse themselves in wellness education, members of the resident staff combine expertise in physical fitness, nutrition, massage, and holistic health in regularly scheduled programs. Guest instructors lead workshops on natural nutrition, creative problem solving, and stress reduction. The spa also regularly offers a weekend of massage instruction for couples and a weeklong smoking-cessation program.

In summer Coolfont's spring-fed lake provides family recreation. The retreat runs its own stables, and golf greens are nearby. The retreat and surrounding area include miles of trails (bring your own bike). In winter the resort offers snow tubing, cross-country skiing, and skating, and there's downhill skiing at the Whitetail Recreation Area, in Pennsylvania.

Guests can choose to stay either in private vacation homes, a three-story lodge, or rustic log cabins. The Manor House, listed on the National Register of Historic Places, also has several well-appointed bedrooms. Most popular are the 31 chalets with whirlpool baths, wood-burning stoves, and decks. Set on a hillside, the chalets are a healthy hike from the spa and restaurant, so bring walking shoes. Unfortunately, outdated furnishings and fluorescent lighting fill many rooms. Private vacation homes might be a better choice for guests seeking more updated accommodations.

INSIDER TIP Wild Women's Weekends draw eclectic groups of women for drumming, journaling, hiking, and spiritual explorations.

Equipment: Free weights, rowing machines, stair climber, stationary bikes, treadmills, weight-training circuit. **Services:** Acupuncture, craniosacral therapy, herbal wrap, loofah body scrub, reflexology, shiatsu. **Swimming:** Indoor pool, lake. **Classes and Programs:** Fitness evaluation, nutrition consultation. **Recreation:** Boating, hiking, horseback riding, ice-skating, skiing, tennis. **Children's Programs:** Supervised camp for children ages 4–10.

🛏 19 lodge rooms, 31 chalets, 4 log cabins, 32 vacation homes. Tent sites, RV hookups available.

✕ Meals included. Treetop House restaurant serves low-fat fare. **Sample Meals:** 5-onion soup, pan-seared salmon (lunch); Portobello scallopini picatta, sage-marinated free-range chicken (dinner).

💳 Nightly rate $69–$139 per person, double occupancy. 2-night Spa & Fitness package $310–$390 per person, double occupancy. Day spa package $150. AE, DC, MC, V.

✉ *1777 Cold Run Valley Rd., Berkeley Springs, WV 25411,* ☎ *304/258–4500 or 800/888–8768. www.coolfont.com*

THE GREENBRIER

LUXURY PAMPERING ◦ NUTRITION AND DIET ◦ MEDICAL WELLNESS ◦ MINERAL SPRINGS

The Greenbrier remains the grande dame of spa resorts. Its genteel air envelopes guests and sweeps them to a bygone era. The hotel's guest roster has included its share of royalty and celebrities, none of whom seemed capable of resisting the Greenbrier's old-world opulence.

The neoclassic hotel with Georgian colonnades is surrounded by formal gardens. Amenities include an international cooking school and therapies utilizing 200-year-old thermal waters. Parts of the resort are older, as reflected in the family cottages built by plantation owners for the social season. There are 71 guest houses and cottages on the grounds. Guest suites are large, with parlors and walk-in closets. Rooms, suites, and common areas are punctuated by the hotel's signature colors: pink and green.

The lavishly tiled indoor swimming pool is filled with springwater and flanked by a juice bar, wicker lounge chairs, and potted plants. Just steps away are the spa, salon, exercise-equipment room, and aerobics studio. The staff includes university-trained physiology specialists with a knack for making newcomers comfortable. The signature treatment, called the Greenbrier, involves being submerged in a private tub filled with sulfur water as underwater jets do battle with tension. Then it's on to the steam or sauna room before heading for a Swiss shower. The treatment is followed by a 25-minute massage. Spa director Kathryn Tuckwiller suggests making appointments prior to arrival. Each package is customized, and the staff will discuss your priorities.

Afternoon tea is served and is usually accompanied by a pianist and violinist. Of course, you'll dress for dinner. The chandeliered dining room in the central section of the hotel dates from 1913. In keeping with old-world tradition, hot rolls and breads are passed constantly, and between courses you're entertained by a string ensemble. Spa cuisine options are available.

The Greenbrier stands among 6,500 acres of Allegheny Mountain woodlands and boasts three 18-hole championship golf courses, all of which begin at a clubhouse where you can enjoy lunch and dinner. Recreational activities include tennis, horseback riding, skeet and trapshooting, fly-fishing, and even falconry. Two new activities—a Sam Snead

Golf Academy and a Land Rover driving school—were recently added to the resort's offerings.

INSIDER TIP Probably the most unique feature of the resort is an underground bunker built in 1959 to accommodate Congress in the event of a nuclear attack. Never used, of course, it has been preserved, and tours are now offered.

Equipment: Free weights, stationary bikes, stair climbers, treadmills, weight-training circuit. **Services:** Herbal wrap, massage, mineral or herbal bath. **Swimming:** Indoor and outdoor pools. **Classes and Programs:** Aerobics, fitness evaluation, personal exercise program, personal training. **Recreation:** Biking, bowling, carriage rides, croquet, fishing, golf, hiking, horseback riding, skeet and trapshooting, tennis. **Children's Programs:** Daily activities for ages 3–12.

🛏 637 rooms, 71 guest houses, 46 suites.

✕ Breakfast and dinner included. American fare plus low-calorie alternatives at breakfast and dinner in the main dining room. **Sample Meals:** Thai shrimp salad, vegetable stir-fry with white sticky rice (lunch); seared Chilean sea bass, grilled yellowfin tuna with saffron-tomato broth (dinner).

💳 Daily rate $196–$347 per person, double occupancy. 5-day spa package $2,866 per person. AE, D, MC, V.

✉ *White Sulphur Springs, WV 24986,* ☎ *304/536–1110 or 800/624–6070,* FAX *304/536–7854. www.greenbrier.com*

LAKEVIEW SCANTICON RESORT

LUXURY PAMPERING ○ SPORTS CONDITIONING

Surrounded by Appalachian woodlands, the Lakeview Scanticon Resort offers two championship golf courses and a broad range of outdoor activities. There's also a full-service spa that was added during recent renovations.

Massage, aromatherapy, and other services are offered in the new spa. Lunch is available at the spa juice bar. The fitness center features two racquetball courts, 50-ft lap pool, climbing wall, indoor walking track, and cardiovascular and weight-training equipment. Nearby are two indoor and four outdoor tennis courts and an outdoor pool. Registered guests have access to all facilities.

INSIDER TIP Bring the kids. A children's activities center now provides full and half-day programs for youngsters up to age 12.

Equipment: Rowing machines, stair climbers, stationary bikes, treadmills, weight-training circuit. **Swimming:** 2 pools. **Classes and Programs:** Dancing. **Recreation:** Biking, boating, climbing, fishing, golf, horseback riding, racquetball, tennis, waterskiing.

🛏 187 rooms, 55 2-bedroom condos.

✕ Meals à la carte. Light fare in the Sportsview Grille. **Sample Meals:** Vegetable pita sandwich (lunch); pasta with vegetables, chicken salad, grilled salmon filet (dinner).

💳 Nightly rate $89–$199 per room. AE, DC, MC, V.

✉ *1 Lakeview Dr., Morgantown, WV 26505,* ☎ *304/594–1111 or 800/624–8300,* FAX *304/594–9472. www.lakeviewscanticon.com*

WISCONSIN

ABBEY RESORT

LUXURY PAMPERING

The first thing you notice at the Fontana Spa is the friendly atmosphere. Here's a getaway without the fuss of some fancy facilities. Convivial chatter can be heard among the terry-robed patrons and the friendly staff.

Though the Abbey Resort has a country-lodge feel, the Fontana Spa is airy and modern, with muted earth tones designed to soothe the soul. Fontana provides treats for all the senses: The aroma of herbs and oils from the imported Phytomer skin-care products wafts through the treatment rooms as skilled technicians soothe and stimulate your skin with a range of spa services.

In addition to the treatments, there's a range of exercise classes and a room of cardio equipment, as well as individualized fitness assessments. Pitchers of fresh juice and baskets of fruit are kept brimming. You can lunch comfortably in your robe by the pool (on weekends there's a low-fat buffet) or opt for room service.

....

INSIDER TIP Try the sea-foam cocoon wrap, in which mud and seaweed are applied to your body. After it is rinsed away, your skin is moisturized with a hydrating lotion.

....

Equipment: Rowing machines, stair climbers, stationary bikes, treadmills, weight-training circuit, free weights. **Services:** Body scrubs, fango mud treatments, herbal wrap, hydrotherapy, lymphatic drainage, reflexology, shiatsu. **Swimming:** 3 pools, lake. **Classes and Programs:** Aerobics, aquaerobics, fitness evaluation, personal training. **Recreation:** Biking, boating, parasailing, tennis, volleyball. **Children's Programs:** Kids Kapades for ages 4–12.

🛏 321 rooms, 13 suites.

✕ Meals à la carte. 3 restaurants offer healthy meals. **Sample Meals:** Beef fajita salad, turkey roll-ups (lunch); char-grilled swordfish with tropical fruit salsa, stir-fried shrimp (dinner).

🛏 1-night Spa Spree $255–$272 per person, double occupancy, includes lodging, lunch, spa treatments. 2-night Spa Escape package $252–$303 per person, double occupancy, includes lodging, meals, spa treatments. Day spa facility fee $23. AE, D, DC, MC, V.

✉ *Hwy. 67/Fontana Blvd., Fontana, WI 53125,* ☎ *262/275-9751 or 800/772-1000,* 📠 *262/275-5948. www.theabbeyresort.net*

THE AMERICAN CLUB

LUXURY PAMPERING

When it was built in 1918 as housing for immigrants working at a factory producing plumbing fixtures, this structure symbolized a new way of life for the town's residents. These days the American Club is accessible to anyone seeking a luxurious and healthful escape in the heart of the Midwest.

The Kohler Waters Spa, which opened in 2000, emphasizes the therapeutic benefits of water. The spa occupies two floors of the Carriage House, a separate structure just east of the main building. Of the 13 treatment rooms, four are designed for therapeutic water services. One, the RiverBath, is an oversize whirlpool for two with a cascading waterfall that is reached by walking along a path of heated stones. Taking the water theme even further, spa treatments such as the Great Lakes hot stone massage use marine-based products. The lower level has a central pool for exercise classes, as well as hot and cool dip pools, sauna, and steam room.

Down the road, the Sports Core fitness center has six indoor and six outdoor tennis courts, with top instructors from Peter Burwash International. You'll also find two indoor pools (one for lap swimmers and one for families), racquetball courts, exercise rooms, an aerobics studio, and a salon.

Golfers delight in four challenging 18-hole courses, including the acclaimed Blackwolf Run (site of the 1998 U.S. Women's Open), and the rugged Whistling Straits (site of the 2004 PGA Championship), each designed by Pete Dye and carved out of the natural environment. The resort also includes River Wildlife, a private 500-acre wilderness preserve that offers 25 mi of woodland trails along with fishing, hunting, and trapshooting. Cross-country skiing, canoeing, and horseback riding are also available.

The Tudor-style buildings of the American Club bring to mind a grand manor house in the countryside. Each guest room has down comforters and luxurious Kohler whirlpool baths. For the ultimate in luxury, several suites have whirlpools for two set on glass-covered terraces and in mirrored baths, while others have a Kohler MasterShower Tower or the powerful BodySpa, which functions like a 10-jet vertical whirlpool.

INSIDER TIP Try a soothing bath in a copper tub that was handcrafted by the same metalsmiths who refurbished the Statue of Liberty's torch.

Equipment: Cross-country ski machines, free weights, rowing machines, stair climbers, stationary bikes, weight-training circuit. **Services:** Aromatherapy, hot stone massage, hydrotherapy, reflexology, seaweed wraps, thalassotherapy. **Swimming:** 2 indoor pools, lake. **Classes and Programs:** Aerobics, fitness consultations, kickboxing, NIA, Pilates, Spinning, tai chi. **Recreation:** Biking, canoeing, fishing, golf, handball, hiking, racquetball, skiing, snowshoeing. **Children's Programs:** Child care for children ages 18 months–7 years.

▦ 215 rooms, 21 suites.

✕ Meals à la carte. 9 restaurants serve varied cuisine. Some spa selections. **Sample Meals:** Turkey pita club with applewood-smoked bacon, fresh dill and citrus walleye sandwich (lunch); grilled Atlantic salmon with white-bean cassoulet, grilled vegetables with orzo and Portobello mushrooms (dinner).

✉ Nightly rate $160–$900 per room. 2-night Wisconsin Experience package $319–$849 for 2, includes lodging, 1 dinner. Day spa packages $290. AE, D, DC, MC, V.

✉ *Highland Dr., Kohler, WI 53044,* ☎ *920/457–8000 or 800/344–2838,* FAX *920/457–0299. www.americanclub.com*

GRAND GENEVA RESORT & SPA

LUXURY PAMPERING

From its peaceful atmosphere you'd never know the Grand Geneva Resort & Spa was originally built in 1968 as the Playboy Resort and Country Club and featured entertainers such as Sammy Davis Jr. and Sonny and Cher. The bunnies have long been banished (though some of the original staff still works here) and the resort is now a family-friendly destination.

Nestled among 1,300 acres of beautiful Wisconsin countryside, the resort offers an escape in all seasons, with indoor and outdoor pools, horseback riding, two 18-hole golf courses, miles of cross-country skiing trails, and 12 downhill runs.

At the resort's Spa & Sport Center, you can compete on indoor and outdoor tennis courts or work out on the weight-training equipment or in the cardio room. When you're finished working, it's time to start pampering yourself with spa treatments designed to relax and rejuvenate you. Facials customized to meet your skin's needs include a soothing massage of face, neck, and scalp.

INSIDER TIP The friendly, knowledgeable staffers make it their business to help you relax so you can take your mind off of your business.

Equipment: Free weights, stair climbers, stationary bikes, treadmills, weight-training circuit. **Services:** Body polish, herbal wraps, hot stone therapy, lymphatic massage, mud masks, thalassotherapy, Swiss shower. **Swimming:** Indoor pool. **Classes and Programs:** Aerobics, body sculpting, fitness consultations, kickboxing, personal training, Spinning, yoga. **Recreation:** Bicycling, boating, golf, horseback riding, ice-skating, skiing, tennis, volleyball. **Children's Programs:** Day care for ages 6 weeks–4 years; Kids Club for ages 4–12.

🖼 304 rooms, 51 suites.

✗ Meals à la carte. Spa menu available for lunch and dinner. **Sample Meals:** Oriental chicken salad, smoked turkey Reuben, grilled Portobello mushrooms with roasted vegetables (dinner).

✉ 1-night spa package $446.71–$545.21 per couple, includes lodging, spa services. Day-use spa fee $12. AE, D, DC, MC, V.

✉ *7036 Grand Geneva Way at Hwys. 50E and 12, Box 130, Lake Geneva, WI 53147,* ☎ *262/249–4750 or 800/246–5468,* FAX *262/249–4734. www.grandgeneva.com*

WYOMING

ANTELOPE RETREAT AND EDUCATION CENTER

HOLISTIC HEALTH

An isolated ranch in the Wyoming foothills, the Antelope Retreat and Education Center is a haven where guests can slow down and step away from life's demands. The center will not fill your time with a long list of activities. Instead, the focus here is on freeing yourself from the need to be occupied, allowing you the space to relax and reflect.

John Boyer, who grew up on the ranch and founded the retreat center in 1986, says his goal is to share the inner peace that can be accessed by being in touch with the land. The center offers special programs such as creativity development, nature-awareness training, and a wilderness quest based on American teachings (there's even a traditional sweat lodge on the grounds).

The ranch is in the lush Savery Creek Valley amid miles of rolling sagebrush hills, bordered on the east by the Sierra Madre and on the west by the breathtaking Red Desert. The facility is centered around an 1890s log house and a huge white barn. Accommodation include private rooms in the main house and other refurbished ranch buildings. Camping also is available in many secluded sites on the 500-acre ranch. You are welcome to help with gardening, ranch chores, and preparation of healthy meals.

INSIDER TIP The ranch is available in the winter for writers and others seeking quiet isolation. Blanketed in snow, the facility offers unmatched seclusion and winter splendor.

Swimming: River. **Classes and Programs:** Life coaching, nature awareness, personal growth activities, sacred hoop. **Recreation:** Fishing, gardening, skiing, swimming.

⊞ 4 rooms, camping available.

✕ Meals included. Low-fat meals served family style. **Sample Meals:** Salad, sandwiches on homemade bread (lunch); barbecued chicken, grilled fish, tofu burritos, vegetable stir-fry, rhubarb pie (dinner).

▨ Nightly rate $80–$200 per person. 1-week program $560–$1,400 per person. No credit cards.

✉ *Box 156, Savery, WY 82332,* ☎ *307/383–2625 or 888/268–2732.*

HOT SPRINGS STATE PARK

MINERAL SPRINGS

Resting on the lazy banks of the Big Horn River, the town of Thermopolis claims to have the world's largest mineral hot spring. Long before explorers discovered the spring, it was a bathing place for the Shoshone and Arapahoe tribes. When the land was purchased by the federal government in 1896, the deed stipulated that the spring remain open and free to all. Accordingly, the State Bath House still has private and group pools that are free to the public.

The water here wells from the earth at a temperature of 135°F and spills down a series of mineral-glaze terraces on its way to the Big Horn River. Some of the flow is diverted to the state-run facility as well as privately operated bathhouses such as those at Tepee Spa, the Star Plunge, the Fountain of Youth RV Park, and the Holiday Inn of the Waters.

Facilities in the area are patronized by families en route to Yellowstone National Park and by senior citizens from a nearby retirement home. Those who wish to spend the night have several options. The Holiday Inn on the banks of the Big Horn River has the most amenities, including exercise facilities, private mineral water tubs, and an outdoor freshwater pool.

The area is brimming with family adventures. You can take a whitewater rafting trip on the Wind River. The Wyoming Dinosaur Center treats visitors to an active dig site, as well as a hands-on museum. Indoor and outdoor commercial pools with waterslides and steam caves are nearby.

INSIDER TIP Grab the camera because at Hot Springs State Park you can still spot bison roaming on a 1,000-acre preserve.

Equipment: Free weights, stair climbers, stationary bikes, treadmills. **Services:** Massages. **Swimming:** Pool. **Recreation:** Fishing, golf, skiing, snowmobiling.

⊞ 80 rooms.

✕ Meals à la carte. Safari Club Restaurant serves American fare. **Sample Meals:** Western steaks and chicken, grilled fish, baked mountain trout (dinner).

⌨ Nightly rate $61–$115 per room. AE, D, DC, MC, V.

✉ *Thermopolis Chamber of Commerce, 700 Broadway St.,*

Thermopolis, WY 82443, ☎ *307/864–3192.* www.thermopolis.com

✉ *Holiday Inn of the Waters, Box 1323, Thermopolis, WY 82443,* ☎ *307/864–3131 or 800/465–4329,* FAX *307/864–3131. holidayinn-thermopolis.com*

CANADA

The phrase "getting away from it all" means something totally different in Canada. If you are headed to Hollyhock for some holistic healing, for example, the only way to get to the island resort in the Pacific Ocean is by floatplane or ferry. The Wickaninnish Inn, on the extreme western edge of Vancouver Island, is in the middle of an ancient rain forest. The Banff Springs Hotel is set amid the spectacular scenery of the Canadian Rockies.

Splendid scenery is an essential part of a fitness vacation in many areas of Canada, and hiking, horseback riding, kayaking, and mountain biking abound. Looking for a great round of golf? Gray Rocks, in Québec, has two challenging courses, *La Belle* (The Beauty) and *La Bête* (The Beast). Tennis, anyone? The Inn at Manitou, in Ontario, lets you play indoors or outdoors and even has instructors to help you perfect your serve. How about skiing? Some of the best downhill slopes on the continent are at Château Whistler, a mountain resort in British Columbia.

But all the fun isn't outdoors, as Canadian resorts offer some state-of-the-art spas. Thalassotherapy is the specialty of small resorts along the Gaspé Peninsula, such as the Auberge du Parc Inn. At the Inn at Manitou, in Ontario, oxygen facials are new to the repertoire. At Club Tremblant, in Québec, the signature treatment is a body polish that combines sea salts, almond oil, gentle massage, and jets of water to leave the skin incredibly soft.

And did we mention the food? The French-influenced cuisine at the Aerie Resort, in British Columbia, relies almost exclusively on organic products from local farmers. Le Manior Richelieu, in Québec, is renowned for its gourmet cuisine and unique regional specialties, such as Charlevoix veal, Migneron cheese, and the rare blue potatoes.

Canadian spas offer more than a change of pace; since the currency exchange rate enhances the value of the U.S. dollar, there are substantial savings. (As this book went to press, $1 in United States currency was worth about $1.50 in Canadian currency.) Remember to bring identification papers for Canadian customs: a passport isn't required for U.S. citizens, but having one will get you over the border without a hassle. Hotel rates in Canada may include a room tax as well as a Goods & Services Tax. The GST is refundable to visitors upon departure, so save receipts from retailers.

Calling resorts in Canada is no problem, as you can simply dial "1" followed by the area code and number. All prices in this chapter are in U.S. dollars.

ALBERTA

BANFF SPRINGS HOTEL

LUXURY PAMPERING ○ MINERAL SPRINGS

After a long day of hiking, skiing, or horseback riding in the Canadian Rockies, there's no better place to rejuvenate than at the Solace Spa at Banff Springs Hotel. Built at the turn of the last century to accommodate people coming to "take the waters," Banff Springs Hotel remains a bastion of traditional hospitality.

Opened in 1888, the turreted hotel—the largest in Canada west of Toronto—looks like a castle out of Camelot. It's equally majestic inside. Although many of the 770 rooms and suites are decorated with antiques, they also boast most modern conveniences. If money is no object, a three-story suite features a private glass elevator, sauna, whirlpool, and lap pool. For maximum privacy and luxury, reserve one of the suites in the towers above the spa; the views of the valley are priceless.

The impressive 35,000-square-ft Solace Spa features a state-of-the-art strength-training room with glass walls that overlook the Bow River valley. The next level down is devoted to a skin care boutique and beauty salon. There are 16 treatment rooms (two specially designed for wet bodywork) where you can indulge in a variety of massages, scrubs, and wraps. Due to heavy demand for appointments, it is wise to book spa services in advance of your arrival at the resort.

Designed to mimic the sulfur-rich waters of historic Banff Springs, the spa's indoor mineral pool contains therapeutic crystals from Sarvar Springs, in Hungary. Underwater music adds to the relaxing effect of this mineral bath. Refresh yourself by enjoying the three surrounding waterfall massage pools. You can also swim laps in the 32-meter indoor saltwater pool or the 20-meter heated outdoor pool.

The natural attractions of Banff National Park include glaciers, alpine meadows, and cool canyons where you might spot elk, deer, bear, bighorn sheep, and mountain goats. Bird-watching and wildlife photography are popular in the summer. Rebuilt by Parks Canada, the spring-fed pools on the mountainside are open to the public. It's worth a hike for an inexpensive, meditative soak in misty sunlight amid the lodgepole pines.

The Banff Springs Hotel is big and brawny, practically a city unto itself, and its enduring popularity is built on serving just about every interest imaginable, from golf to river rafting. The hotel has 14 restaurants, from the formal Banffshire Club to a sushi bar. There is also the Solace Lite Restaurant, the spa's café, where healthy breakfasts, lunches, and dinners are available every day.

INSIDER TIP Golfers shouldn't miss the hotel's championship 27-hole course. You may have to jostle with an elk on the green, but the beauty of Banff National Park is unforgettable.

Equipment: Free weights, stair climbers, stationary bikes, treadmills, weight-training circuit. **Services:** Acupressure, body scrub, body wraps, hydrotherapy, massage, reflexology, shiatsu. **Swimming:** Indoor and outdoor pools. **Classes and Programs:** Fitness training, nutritional consultation. **Recreation:** Biking, bowling, golf, hiking, tennis, skiing, skating, dogsledding, helicopter tours, horseback riding, and white-water rafting nearby.

🛏 770 rooms and suites.

✕ Meals à la carte. Japanese, Italian, and other cuisines available in 14 restaurants. Spa café open daily.

📧 Nightly rate $128–$450 per room, $228–$1,012 suites. 3-night Ultimate Retreat spa package $1,450 per person. Day spa package $101–$202. AE, MC, V.

✉ *Box 960, Banff, Alberta T0L 0C0,* ☎ *403/762–2211 or 800/441–1414, 403/762–1772 (spa), 800/404–1772,* FAX *403/762–5755, 403/762–1766 (spa). www.cphotels.com/banff*

MOUNTAIN ESCAPE AT LAKE LOUISE INN

LUXURY PAMPERING ○ HOLISTIC HEALTH

The Mountain Escape Program at Lake Louise Inn is available for five weeks each spring and fall. The program, for women only, is devoted to improving body and soul, and the warm and supportive atmosphere leads to many repeat visitors.

This isn't roughing it, however, and nobody is going to make you give up your morning cup of coffee at this resort. Lectures on healthy eating and fitness guidance from qualified staff members introduce you to the benefits of a healthy lifestyle. Special weeks focus on yoga, tai chi, and self-defense. Challenge Week is a more advanced fitness program.

From the sunrise eye-opener walk to an afternoon stretch-and-tone session, the emphasis is on personal development and learning how to set realistic health goals. A team of instructors works with you in small, compatible groups. Activities are geared to the general energy of the group rather than to individual peak performance.

Breathtaking mountain peaks come into view on walks around Lake Louise, and snow-covered Victoria Glacier is mirrored in its aqua blue water. While one group does high-energy aerobics, another learns aquatic exercises in the pool. Two hour-long classes are scheduled each morning, and yoga is practiced before dinner.

INSIDER TIP If you've been itching to try reflexology or reiki, this is a great place to do so. The rates are very reasonable, and you'll leave in a stress-free state.

Equipment: Free weights. **Services:** Acupressure, aromatherapy, mud wraps, reflexology, reiki, shiatsu. **Swimming:** Indoor pool. **Classes and Programs:** Aerobics, aquaerobics, yoga. **Recreation:** Biking, hiking, horseback riding, skiing.

⊡ 232 rooms.

✕ Meals included. **Sample Meals:** Pita wrap with apple-squash soup, vegetarian stew with corn bread, noodles with vegetables and peanut sauce (lunch); pork tenderloin with apricot sauce, poached salmon with ratatouille, St. Lucia chicken, wild rice with turnip and apple puree (dinner).

🖃 6-night program $472–$503 per person, double occupancy. Condensed 4-night program $364 per person, double occupancy. AE, MC, V.

✉ *Box 209, Lake Louise, Alberta T0L 1E0,* ☎ *403/522–3791,* ℻ *403/ 522–2018.*

THE AERIE RESORT

LUXURY PAMPERING

The Aerie Resort's two Mediterranean-style villas cling to a forested hillside on southern Vancouver Island, offering striking views of the Olympic Mountains, Georgia Strait, and outlying islands. Popular for the past decade with couples seeking a romantic retreat, a new spa makes it a popular choice for those seeking a little rejuvenation as well.

The Aerie Wellness and Beauty Centre, a small white space flooded with natural light, offers a range of spa treatments, body wraps, and massage using Aveda products. The priority here is relaxation, though knowledgeable staff can also provide advice on everything from skin care to wellness. Several of the services are also available in the guest rooms: the most popular treatment (in keeping with the resort's reputation for romance) is an in-room massage for two.

A glassed-in pool (equipped with water jets so swimmers can work out against the current) and an outdoor hot tub occupy a deck overlooking the ocean. A sauna and another hot tub are available inside. Don't expect a full gym, however; a single weight station is the extent of the exercise equipment. Active visitors opt for a game on the resort's tennis court, golf on one of three championship courses in the area, or a hike in one of the nearby provincial parks.

Dining is an important part of the experience at the Aerie Resort. The French-influenced cuisine relies almost exclusively on organic produce, meat, and fish available from local farmers. Guests can sample the island's salmon, ostrich, forest-foraged mushrooms, organic herbs, and locally made cheeses in elegant multicourse meals. A good option is the chef's seven-course tasting menu, based on what's fresh and available that day. A five-course vegetarian menu, suitable for ovo-lacto vegetarians, is available, and special diets can be catered to with advance notice. Though there is no special spa menu, the chefs keep things light with limited use of fats and oils. Interested guests can join the chef each afternoon for a briefing on the day's menu and the kitchen's philosophy.

The owner, Maria Schuster, is originally from Austria and built her resort in a European style, with whitewashed walls and red-tile roofs. Inside, the rooms and suites are furnished in an eclectic, slightly theatrical mix of hand-painted furniture, Persian rugs, and curtained four-poster beds. Each room is unique, though virtually every one has a view and a private balcony or deck. The pricier rooms include whirlpool tubs and fireplaces. The atmosphere here is one of graciousness and pampering: Belgian chocolates and fresh flowers are delivered to the rooms at check-in, and a basket of fruit and muffins and a morning paper arrive at your door each morning.

Nearby, the attractive seaside city of Victoria is filled with quaint shops, stunning gardens, and excellent museums. Besides golf, you can try hiking, sailing, fishing, horseback riding, cycling, and kayaking, as well as whale-watching tours.

INSIDER TIP The Aerie Resort is extremely popular. If you plan to come in the summer, it's good to book a room at least three months ahead and to reserve your spa treatments at the same time.

Equipment: Weight training machine. **Services:** Aromatherapy, body exfoliation, body mask, body polish, massage. **Swimming:** Indoor pool with swim jets. **Classes and Programs:** Wellness and alternative health workshops for groups of 12 or more. **Recreation:** Tennis.

⌂ 27 rooms, 2 suites.

✕ Breakfast included in the room rates, lunch and dinner are à la carte. Vegetarian and other special diets available with advance notice. **Sample Meals:** Salad greens with warm goat-cheese croutons, forest mushroom ravioli (lunch); herb-braised pheasant breast, white bean and potato *brandade* (puree), salmon with ragout of mussels (dinner).

🛏 Nightly rate $171–$306 per room. 1-night Gourmet Getaway package $178–$239 per person. 2-night Romantic Hideaway package $521–$669 per couple. AE, DC, MC, V

✉ *600 Ebedora La., Box 108, Malahat, British Columbia V0R 2L0* ☎ *250/743–7115 or 800/518–1933,* ℻ *250/743–4766. www. aerie.bc.ca*

CHÂTEAU WHISTLER RESORT

LUXURY PAMPERING ○ SPORTS CONDITIONING

Some of the best skiing on the continent is in the vicinity of Château Whistler, a mountain resort that draws an international clientele year-round. Château Whistler offers downhill skiing on North America's greatest vertical rise in winter and spring, water sports and glacier skiing in summer, and alpine hiking, fishing, tennis, and horseback riding in summer, spring, and fall. Golfers can play five courses in the area, including Château Whistler's 18-hole course designed by Robert Trent Jones II.

The baronial 12-story Château Whistler, the largest hotel in Whistler, is a family-friendly, ski-in/ski-out resort with its own spa, health club, golf course, and tennis courts. Though relatively new (it was built in 1990) it has much of the old-world ambience of its sister hotel, the Château Lake Louise. The cathedral-ceiling lobby is filled with folk art and rustic Canadiana. Overstuffed couches gather around a grand stone fireplace, and tall windows offer unobstructed views of Blackcomb Mountain's slopes. Guest rooms, decorated in rich burgundies and turquoises, are comfortably furnished and have mountains views. Rooms and suites on the Entrée Gold floors have fireplaces, whirlpool tubs, and their own concierge and private lounge.

The spa off the hotel's lobby offers a range of ayurvedic treatments, based on the ancient Indian philosophy of health care. Services in the 14 treatment rooms range from hydrotherapy to shiatsu, as well as pre- and post-workout sports massages. At the resort's elegant health club, there's a weight room with cardiovascular equipment, and tennis and fitness training is available by appointment.

INSIDER TIP Don't feel like skiing? You can watch skiers glide down the slopes from one of the outdoor hot tubs or swim laps to underwater music in the new 60-ft outdoor pool.

Equipment: Free weights, rowing machines, stair climbers, stationary bikes, treadmills, weight-training circuit. **Services:** Aromatherapy, ayurvedic therapies, body wraps, exfoliation, massage, mineral baths, shiatsu, Vichy shower. **Swimming:** Indoor/outdoor pool, outdoor lap pool. **Classes and Programs:** Tennis lessons and camps. **Recreation:** Golf, tennis, skiing. **Children's Programs:** Ski and snowboard programs for children 18 months to 17 years are available.

☷ 502 rooms, 56 suites.

✗ Meals à la carte. The Wildflower Restaurant serves fresh seafood, wild boar, and venison in season. The Portobello delicatessen offers lighter, more casual fare. **Sample Meals:** Seafood chowder with mussels, clams, salmon, shrimp, and potatoes (lunch); grilled vegetable tower layered with goat cheese, pan-seared Pacific red snapper with Atlantic mussels and saffron sauce (dinner).

▨ Nightly rate $235–$471 per room. 1-night spa package $148–$280 per person. 3-night ski & spa package $154 per person per night. AE, D, DC, MC, V.

✉ 4599 *Château Blvd., Whistler, British Columbia V0N 1B4,* ☏ *604/ 938–8000 or 800/606–8244, 800/401–4018 for spa reservations, 800/ 441–1414 for golf packages,* ℻ *604/938–2055. www.cphotels.com*

ECHO VALLEY RANCH

LUXURY PAMPERING ○ NUTRITION AND DIET ○ HOLISTIC HEALTH

In the remote wilderness of Cariboo Country is Echo Valley Ranch Resort and Spa, a 10,000-acre resort. It's also a working ranch with 170 head of cattle, 46 horses, and numerous chickens, turkeys, and rabbits.

Owners Norm and Nan Dove began their ranch in 1990 as a weekend retreat from their home in Vancouver. Echo Valley has evolved into one of Canada's premiere wilderness resorts. In 1999, it was awarded first prize in the Canadian Tourism Commission's competition for best winter travel package.

The spa opened in 1997 under the direction of Mehraneh Mehr, who will gladly accompany you on an early morning jog and work through the kinks afterwards. Here you can relax in the outdoor hot tub or indoor sauna while enjoying the panoramic views. Mehraneh works closely with Nan, a native of Thailand, to bring their vision of "East Meets West" to fruition on the ranch. A new Thai Barn, designed by world-renowned architect Pinyo Suwankiri, opened in 2000 to accommodate the growing services centering on their unique approach to wellness.

The gifts of nature evident in every component of Echo Valley include organic cuisine prepared by Danish chef Kim Madsen. He takes responsibility for planting and maintaining the vegetable, herb, and berry garden. The chicken, turkey, and rabbit that are the centerpiece of most dinners are raised at the ranch. The well water served with all meals has received perfect ratings from the Canadian health officials.

In addition to the accommodations and services at the ranch, guests may choose to sleep a few nights under the stars or in a tepee. Outdoor barbecues are regular features in the warm months, along with an occasional line dancing or square-dancing.

INSIDER TIP The aromatherapy facials are among the spa's most popular service. You'll understand why if you request yours by spa director Mehraneh Mehr.

Equipment: Free weights, rowing machines, stair climbers, stationary bikes, treadmills. **Services:** Aromatherapy, body scrubs, herbal wrap, hydrotherapy, paraffin wrap, reflexology, sea mud wrap. **Swimming:** 1 indoor pool. **Classes and Programs:** Roping, riding, yoga. **Recreation:** Billiards, biking, bird-watching, darts, fishing, horseback riding, horseshoes, nature walks, snowshoeing, white-water rafting.

▨ 3 cabins, 2 lodges with 16 rooms.

✗ Meals served family style in the main lodge. **Sample meals:** Shiitake mushroom soup, roast pork (dinner).

▨ 3-night package $615 per person, includes lodging, meals, spa treatments, activities. 7-night package $1370 per person, includes lodging, meals, spa treatments, activities. MC, V.

✉ *Echo Valley Ranch Resort., Box 16, Jesmond, Clinton, British Columbia, VOK 1KO,* ☎ *250/459–2386 or 800/253–8831,* FAX *250/459–0086. www.evranch.com*

ECOMED NATURAL HEALTH SPA

HOLISTIC HEALTH ◦ MEDICAL WELLNESS

On the grounds of Vancouver Island's Pacific Shores Nature Resort, EcoMed Natural Health Spa features nature trails and a beach on one of British Columbia's warmest swimming bays. A bird sanctuary and a nature reserve are adjacent to the property. Spa guests have access to the resort's facilities, including a fitness center with a pool, a sauna, and indoor and outdoor hot tubs.

Founded and directed by Stefan Kuprowsky, a naturopathic physician who has studied with alternative medicine pioneer Deepak Chopra, the spa offers comprehensive diagnostic services and treatments including allergy testing and treatment, blood cell analysis, acupuncture, oxygen therapies, and nutritional counseling. The focus is treating conditions such as arthritis, allergies, chronic fatigue syndrome, diabetes, and immune deficiencies, but many guests visit for simple relaxation and wellness retreats.

Cleansing the body of toxins is the basis of healing retreats that range in length from a week to a month. Shorter programs are devoted to health workshops, nature walks, relaxation, and inner cleansing. Spa and aesthetic services are on an à la carte basis or included in program packages. A hydrotherapy tub for herbal soaks, facials with products developed by Canadian skin care specialists, aromatherapy, and massage are available. At press time, plans were underway to double the size of the spa facilities in 2001.

Guests stay in a cluster of contemporary beachfront condos decorated with local artwork and modern furnishings. Rooms have either a garden view or a patio overlooking the bay. Suites have living rooms with fireplaces, whirlpool baths, and kitchens. Vegetarian meals, included in the daily program fee, feature fresh produce from nearby organic farms.

Equipment: Free weights, stair climbers, stationary bikes, treadmills, weight-training equipment. **Services:** Acupressure, aromatherapy, herbal wraps, hydrotherapy massage, shiatsu. **Swimming:** Indoor pool, beach. **Classes and Programs:** Allergy testing, blood testing, nutritional consultation, psychological counseling, wellness workshops. **Recreation:** Biking, boccie, canoeing, fishing, horseback riding, kayaking, sailing.

▦ 6 rooms, 6 suites.

✗ Meals included. Vegetarian and seafood meals served family style. **Sample Meals:** Cold kale-cucumber soup, curried pumpkin soup, smoked salmon with artichoke hearts and arugula salad, fresh fruit crumble (lunch); tropical-fruit cocktail, brown-rice sushi, shallots with roasted red pepper–tofu sauce, buckwheat noodles with shiitake mushrooms, lemon silken pie, carob-tofu mousse (dinner).

▨ Nightly rate $101–$135 per person, double occupancy. 2-night retreat $320–$387 per person, double occupancy. 1-week Spa Rejuvenation $871–$1,110 per person, double occupancy. MC, V.

✉ *515–1600 Stroulger Rd., Nanoose Bay, British Columbia V9P 9B7,* ☎ *250/468-7133,* FAX *250/468-7135. ecomedspa.com*

FAIRMONT HOT SPRINGS RESORT

MINERAL SPRINGS

The hot mineral pools are only one of the attractions at this family-oriented vacation complex in the Rocky Mountains. Surrounded by mountain forests, the Fairmont Hot Springs Resort has two 18-hole golf courses, tennis courts, and recreation ranging from skiing to horseback riding.

The historic mineral baths on the premises, which are a constant 118°F, were used as sweat lodges by the area's early Native peoples. The resort has a large outdoor swimming complex, open to day visitors as well as to hotel guests, that includes a hot soaking pool, a lap pool, and a larger pool equipped with high and low diving boards. There's also a heated pool exclusively for hotel guests. Be forewarned: The facilities can be crowded with tourists during holiday periods.

The spa on the premises provides a wide range of skin care and beauty services, sold either in packages or à la carte.

Accommodations are varied here. You can choose from the 140 rooms in the rustic main lodge or from one of five cottages. There is also a 311-site trailer park on the premises, for those who like to rough it a bit.

Services: Aromatherapy, mud wrap, seaweed and peppermint body polish, seaweed bath, seaweed wrap. **Swimming:** Outdoor pools. **Classes**

and Programs: Aquaerobics. **Recreation:** Golf, hiking, horseback riding, tennis, skiing.

☎ 86 rooms, 48 suites, 5 cottages, 311 RV sites.

✕ Breakfast included. **Sample Meals:** Cold cucumber soup, red cabbage and apple salad, curried chicken with yogurt dressing, fillet of sole with braised leeks (lunch); veal cutlet with wild mushrooms, chicken breast stuffed with lobster, red snapper fillet with curry sauce (dinner).

🖼 Nightly rate $66–$169 per room. 2-night spa package $121–$167 per person. AE, MC, V, D, DC.

✉ *Box 10, Fairmont Hot Springs, British Columbia V0B 1L0,* ☎ *250/ 345–6311 or 800/663–4979,* FAX *250/345–6616. www.fairmontresort.com*

THE HILLS HEALTH RANCH

MEDICAL WELLNESS ○ SPORTS CONDITIONING ○ NUTRITION AND DIET

Saddle up for a western-style workout replete with horseback riding and line dancing at the Hills Health Ranch, in the heart of British Columbia. Encompassing 20,000 acres of lakes, mountains, and forest, the resort offers a range of programs, including stress management and weight control regimens, in a homey, informal setting.

Here you'll find the usual facials, body scrubs, and herbal wraps (using rose-hip oil and other products made at the ranch), but you'll also find old-fashioned hayrides and sing-alongs that the whole family will enjoy. Workshops in everything from music to horse whispering (a method of training equines) round out a program that emphasizes fitness in both mind and body.

Opened in 1985, the resort's Canadian Wellness Centre provides medically based programs in healthy living. Affiliated with the University of British Columbia, the facility conducts lifestyle research and offers special programs for rehabilitation after injury or surgery. The emphasis is on nutrition, long-term behavioral changes, and the link between mental attitude and physical health. Several programs focus on the needs of older persons, including tips on maintaining a healthy heart through exercise and nutrition.

If you choose one of the many wellness packages, you'll participate in exercise, nutrition, and stress-management sessions. After a fitness evaluation you'll join a variety of scheduled activities: morning power walks, daily guided hikes, aerobics and step classes, line dancing, aquaerobics in the indoor pool, circuit and weight-training, and stretching/relaxation classes.

Woodsy A-frame chalets and two-story lodges fan out from the log-sided main building, where the spa, fitness center, and dining room are located. Accommodations are standard hotel rooms; each has modern furniture, a private bath, and a shared veranda, and some have expansive mountain views. For families and groups, the basic but comfortable chalets have three bedrooms, kitchen, and living room. Dogs are welcome in the chalets.

A new lodge called the 1871 (for the year British Columbia became part of Canada) offers a number of options for the evenings: an antiques-decorated tearoom is a place for quiet contemplation, a saloon offers microbrewed beers in a more social setting, and the 1871 restaurant serves up Swiss-style meals, including low-fat fondue.

Three hearty meals are served daily in the lodge's dining room. The menus are personalized based on each guest's goals and preferences, though all feature attractive low-fat cuisine. The ranch is justifiably known for the quality of its low-calorie, heart-healthy meals.

INSIDER TIP The 93 mi of groomed trails make the resort a prime spot for cross-country skiing, and a snow tubing run is fun for adults and kids.

Equipment: Free weights, rowing machines, stair climbers, stationary bikes, treadmills, weight-training circuit. **Services:** Acupuncture, clay and herbal wraps, hydrotherapy, reflexology. **Swimming:** Indoor pool. **Classes and Programs:** Aerobics, belly dancing, horseback-riding lessons, line dancing, stretching, skiing lessons, workshops on nutrition, wellness, music, and horse care. **Recreation:** Biking, canoeing, hiking, horseback riding, ice-skating, snow boarding, sleighing, tobogganing. **Children's Programs:** Horseback riding, swimming, skiing instruction.

⊡ 26 rooms, 20 chalets.

✕ Breakfast included in rate. Spa cuisine or ranch-style meals served à la carte. Low-fat menu served in the lodge's dining room. **Sample Meals:** Chicken stir-fry on seven-grain pilaf, turkey fajita and fresh asparagus soup (lunch); salmon in phyllo pastry with lemony wild rice; stuffed sole fillets, orzo pilaf with mushrooms, leeks, and sun-dried tomatoes (dinner).

▧ Nightly rate $34–$45 per person, double occupancy. 5-night Horseback Holiday $714 per person, double occupancy. 10-night weight loss program $2,092 per person, double occupancy. AE, MC, V.

⊠ *Box 26, 108 Mile Ranch, British Columbia V0K 2Z0,* ☏ *250/791–5225,* FAX *250/791–6384. www.spabc.com*

HOLLYHOCK

HOLISTIC HEALTH

On a secluded island in the Pacific and accessible only by plane or ferry, Hollyhock seems far removed from the real world. Yet from April through October the resort teems with activity. Since 1982 specialists in alternative therapies and spiritual health have drawn inspiration from each other in this island setting.

More than 90 three- to six-day workshops are offered here on subjects ranging from healing to shamanism, as well as intensive month-long programs in such topics as herbal medicine and yoga. There are tai chi instruction and a range of creative writing, music, and art programs, as well as professional development courses for holistic practitioners.

Though most guests are involved in at least one of the workshops, space is sometimes available for those who simply want to enjoy the peaceful surroundings. Kayaking and sailing excursions are organized for more adventurous visitors. Bodywork, aromatherapy, and skin care services are also available. If you'd rather just soak in the hot tub overlooking the shore, that's fine, too.

You enter Hollyhock through gates fashioned from driftwood. The 48-acre site, amid stands of towering fir trees, is made up of a seaside lodge, cabins, dormitories, and session houses (circular structures where meetings are held). Paths lead to Smelt Bay, a favorite place for watching the pink-rimmed sunset over Vancouver Island, and to the Body-work Studio, where a craniosacral massage eases tension and might release emotions. An organic garden, a ¼-acre showplace, produces flowers and vegetables for the dining room.

Accommodations range from single rooms to dormitory-style rooms with three to six beds. Tent sites are also available. The two-story main lodge has a small library upstairs, kitchen and dining room on the first floor, and a deck facing the Strait of Georgia. Refreshments are available at all times of the day: a decaf ice tea, a refreshing tisane (a naturally decaffeinated herbal mixture), or perhaps an iced latte.

....
INSIDER TIP Arriving at Cortes Island by floatplane is a dazzling introduction to some of the most stunning natural scenery on the continent. The entire area is a glacier-carved collection of coves, capes, and fjord-like passages.
....

Services: Aromatherapy, craniosacral therapy, reflexology, reiki, shiatsu. **Swimming:** Beach. **Classes and Programs:** Guided bird walks, meditation, wilderness interpretation tours, yoga. **Recreation:** Kayaking, sailing, walking trails. **Children's Programs:** Kids 5–12 and 14–18.

▦ 25 rooms, 17 with shared bath, 3 dormitory rooms, 14 tent sites.

✗ Meals included. International buffet, mostly vegetarian with some seafood. There's also a weekly oyster barbecue at the beach. **Sample Meals:** Vegetarian casserole Provençale with sourdough baguette, Thai fish soup with homemade bread, Greek salad (lunch); barbecued oysters, grilled salmon (dinner).

▦ Nightly rate $80–$103 per person, double occupancy. Tuition fees range from $64 to $663, depending on program. Closed Nov.–Apr. MC, V.

✉ Box 127, Manson's Landing, Cortes Island, British Columbia V0P 1K0, ☎ 250/935–6576 or 800/933–6339, FAX 250/935–6424. www.hollyhock.bc.ca

MOUNTAIN TREK FITNESS RETREAT & HEALTH SPA

HOLISTIC HEALTH ∘ NUTRITION AND DIET ∘ SPORTS CONDITIONING

To get in shape, stay in shape, or significantly improve your level of fitness, head to the Mountain Trek Fitness Retreat & Health Spa, in the beautiful Kootenay Mountains of southwestern British Columbia. Set on 34 lakeside acres of forest, this 12-room cedar lodge is a comfortable base from which to explore high country trails. You can picnic in pristine meadows, soak in the hot springs, or embark on overnight camping trips in the mountains.

Hiking and snowshoeing are the core activities here. There are six treks per week, with all equipment included. You'll tackle the Whitewater Glacier Trail, which once attracted miners searching for gold and silver. You may see grizzlies, deer, mountain goats, and marmots as you explore alpine slopes, expansive flower meadows, and temperate forests. The lead-and-shepherd guide system allows you to go at your own pace. There are more than 20 other trails within an hour's drive of the lodge that will challenge beginner, intermediate, and advanced hikers.

Workouts in the main lodge are scheduled before and after hikes. Yoga sessions are held in a wood-floor studio with views of the mountains and lake. A separate weight-training room has a selection of machines and free weights. A natural thermal-spring bath is a five-minute walk, and there is an outdoor hot tub next to the lodge's sauna. Health checkups and lectures by physicians are included with the minimum stay of six days.

The lodge features rooms with private baths, but this is not a luxury getaway. There is no television, telephone, or air-conditioning. But exercise clothes, robes, and knapsacks are provided, and there's a full-service laundry room.

INSIDER TIP It's early to bed, early to rise at Mountain Trek, but the gorgeous hiking trails and the mountain air are worth getting up for. The knowledgeable guides let you set a comfortable pace.

Equipment: Free weights, weight-training circuit. **Services:** Aromatherapy, colonic irrigation, hydrotherapy, massage, reflexology. **Swimming:** Hot springs nearby. **Recreation:** Biking, hiking, kayaking, snowshoeing. **Classes and Programs:** Fasting, spa cuisine cooking, weight loss, yoga.

🛏 12 rooms.

✕ Meals included. Spa cuisine buffet. **Sample Meals:** Szechuan vegetable noodle salad with date-nut bar and fruit, millet burger, whole wheat pita sandwich (lunch); ginger-beet soup, vegetarian shepherd's pie, poached wild salmon with lemon rice pilaf and asparagus (dinner).

🔖 3- to 7-night hiking or snowshoeing program $900–$2,030 per person. 4- to 7-night hiking, biking, and kayaking program $1,265–$2,153 per person. 7-night fasting program $650 per person. MC, V.

✉ Box 1352, Ainsworth Hot Springs, British Columbia V0G 1A0, ☎ 250/229–5636 or 800/661–5161, FAX 250/229–5246. www.hiking.com

OCEAN POINTE RESORT HOTEL & SPA

LUXURY PAMPERING

With a charming harbor-front location and a full-service European-style spa, the Ocean Pointe Resort attracts vacationers, businesspeople, and local residents in search of a vacation retreat or a just few hours enjoying the view from the glassed-in pool.

The Spa at Ocean Pointe offers a wide range of facials, herbal wraps, and beauty treatments. It uses and sells a variety of product lines, including Phytomer's seaweed products and Aveda's natural hair- and skin care line. You can indulge in mineral baths and massages or try the hot stone therapy, in which smooth hot and cold stones are used to massage the body. The couple's massage, where each partner enjoys a 45-minute massage while the other learns the techniques, is popular for romantic getaways. For complete relaxation try the 1½-hour Himalayan body wrap. It starts with a full body gommage (exfoliation), follows with a wrap using Himalayan mud, and finishes with a body massage and a Vichy shower. Spa services book up quickly, so it's a good idea to reserve your treatments two to four weeks ahead.

The hotel's fitness center has trainers experienced in working with seniors as well as younger people. One-on-one workouts and fitness assessments are available. Scheduled classes in aerobics and aquaerobics plus a series of lectures on nutrition and health round out the program. Those on working vacations can take a jog before morning meetings or play a game of squash or racquetball at lunchtime.

Ocean Pointe also makes a convenient base from which to explore the byways of Ainsworth Hot Springs as well as the beaches on the Pacific side of Vancouver Island. Take a scenic day trip on the E&N Railroad, which departs from its terminal near the hotel. The mild climate enjoyed most of the year makes the island a mecca for those enjoying golf, sailing, fishing, and scuba diving. You can schedule your tee time at a nearby golf course or court time on one of the hotel's two tennis courts.

The hotel is comfortable and finely decorated. In the lobby, couches are set before fireplaces and expansive ocean-view windows. Many of the modern guest rooms are large and feature views of the harbor and distant Olympic Mountains. The apartment-size suites have kitchenettes and separate living and dining areas.

You can enjoy a private lunch in the spa, or opt for a casual meal at the hotel's Boardwalk Café, where tables spill out onto a seaside terrace during the summer. For dinner the hotel's romantic Victorian Restaurant is one of the city's finest dining rooms, with candlelight, ocean views, an extensive wine list, and dishes featuring local ingredients. The chefs can cater for most special dietary needs with a few days' notice.

....

INSIDER TIP To get an up-close look at whales and other marine life, ask the concierge to book you on an excursion aboard one of Seacoast Expeditions' 12-passenger boats, which depart from the hotel's dock.

....

Equipment: Rowing machines, stair climbers, stationary bikes, treadmills, weight-training circuit. **Services:** Algae wraps, aromatherapy, cellulite treatment, hydrotherapy, mineral baths, mud wraps, reflexology, shiatsu, Vichy shower. **Swimming:** Indoor pool. **Classes and Programs:** Aerobics, aquaerobics. **Recreation:** Racquetball, squash, tennis.

▥ 212 rooms, 34 suites.

✕ Meals à la carte. Meals available in the Boardwalk Café, the Victorian Restaurant, and in the spa. **Sample Meals:** Vegetarian sandwich with olive bread, hummus, roasted tomatoes, cucumber, carrots, and *bocconcini* (bite-size pieces of mozzarella), tandoori chicken breast (lunch); rack of lamb with maple and juniper glaze, baked macadamia nut–crusted salmon fillet and lobster (dinner).

▤ Nightly rate $199–$495 per room. 2-night Pacific Sea Delight package $449–$552 per person, double occupancy. 3-night escape package $726–$918 per person, double occupancy. Day spa packages $74–$218. AE, DC, MC, V.

✉ 45 Songhees Rd., Victoria, British Columbia V9A 6T3, ☎ 250/360–2999 or 800/667–4677, ℻ 250/360–1041. www.oprhotel.com

THE WICKANINNISH INN

LUXURY PAMPERING

The extreme western edge of Vancouver Island, with its crashing Pacific surf and a backdrop of old-growth rain forest, is one of the most striking settings on the continent. It's here, near the tiny village of Tofino, that Dr. Howard McDiarmid, the local general practitioner, built his weathered cedar inn. Though it only dates to 1996, the inn is already an institution in this part of the world and has played a major role in redefining this out-of-the-way region as a major ecotourism destination.

The Wick, as it's known to locals, lets you enjoy the wilderness in comfort. The three-story building, set on a promontory at the ocean's edge, holds rustically elegant guest rooms, a full service spa, and one of western Canada's most innovative dining rooms.

The mile-and-a-half expanse of hard-packed, driftwood-strewn sand has plenty of room for solitary jogs, meditative walks, beachcombing, and enjoying the almost spiritual setting of ancient rain forest against open ocean. The Pacific Rim National Park, just down the road, has an extensive network of hiking trails, and the whole region is a popular destination for fishing, kayaking, scuba diving, and surfing. The staff at the inn can also arrange games of golf and excursions to nearby forested coves and islands, including one with a natural hot springs-fed pool. Whale-watching is also popular here, especially during the gray whales' February to May migration down the coast from Alaska to Mexico.

The Ancient Cedars Spa offers soothing details such as heated tile floors and woven rattan slippers for each guest. Every treatment starts with a 15-minute consultation in which you choose the essential oils that best resonate with your mood, followed by a fireside foot bath in aromatic oils. A signature treatment is the hot stone massage, in which warmed stones are used to massage the body. The Sacred Sea thalassotherapy treatment starts with a full body exfoliation, followed by a soak using algae products and essential oils in a 144-jet hydrotherapy tub. The final touch is a body wrap and massage.

The guest rooms, decorated in soothing neutral shades, echo the seascape outside. The beauty here is in the thoughtful details, from the rustic driftwood chairs to bathtubs set before ocean-view windows. The rooms are large, and each has a fireplace and a private balcony.

The glass-enclosed Pointe Restaurant sits on an outcrop over the sea and offers views of the crashing surf. It's also one of Canada's most renowned Pacific Northwest restaurants, making the most of such local delicacies as oysters, gooseneck barnacles, wild mushrooms, Dungeness crab, and Pacific salmon. The meat is all free range, and the chef selects the seafood himself at the Tofino docks. There's no separate spa menu, and little need for one, as a four-course vegetarian selection using local ingredients is a permanent feature on the seasonally changing menu. The maitre d' can match your entrée selection with a good wine—many are locally produced and hard to find elsewhere.

INSIDER TIP Book well ahead for the Wick—even in winter it's popular, as people come to watch the dramatic storms that play out on the coast; in spring they come to watch the whale migrations.

Services: Acupressure, aromatherapy, body exfoliation, hot stone massage, hydrotherapy, reflexology, shiatsu, Vichy shower. **Recreation.** Golfing, fishing, hiking, kayaking, scuba diving, surfing.

▥ 46 rooms.

✗ Meals à la carte. International cuisine available at the Pointe Restaurant. **Sample Meals:** Grilled wild sockeye salmon sandwich, sun-dried tomato ravioli (lunch); steamed Dungeness crab, spinach and roasted garlic risotto (dinner).

▤ Nightly rate $155–$287 per room. 2-night spa package $589–$723 per person. AE, DC, MC, V.

✉ *Osprey La. at Chesterman Beach, Box 250, Tofino, British Columbia V0R 2Z0,* ☎ *250/725–3100 or 800/333–4604,* ℻ *250/725–3110.* *www.wickinn.com*

ONTARIO

THE INN AT MANITOU

LUXURY PAMPERING ∘ SPORTS CONDITIONING

Nestled on the shores of Lake Manitouwabing near Parry Sound, the Inn at Manitou is part summer camp, part European-style spa. Tennis clinics have been a staple here since the early 1960s, but it is also a popular retreat for guests seeking peace and seclusion. It's also a destination for gourmands, who come for the award-winning cuisine.

Open from May to October, the tiny but elegant spa has 11 private treatment rooms (two designed for wet therapies like mud masks, body wraps, and loofah scrubs) and a hydrotherapy tub with 47 underwater jets and a hand-operated hose. Personal trainers are on hand to provide one-on-one instruction or lead groups in Pilates and yoga. Two regularly scheduled aerobics classes are held daily—either high- or low-impact, step, or stretching—in the bright, well-equipped exercise room with the "floating" maple floor. Enjoy tennis? There's an indoor court as well as 12 outdoor ones. Want to improve your swing? There's a new golf academy.

The menu of treatments is extensive, from aromatherapy to reflexology. Hot rock massage and oxygen facials are new to the repertoire. Body wraps use mud imported from France, said to enable detoxification as the minerals and other active ingredients are absorbed by the body. Used by monks during the 14th and 15th centuries to cure everything from rheumatism to depression, the mud is said to contain 3,000 organic ingredients.

The inn has chalet-style rooms, most on the lakefront and each with a log-burning fireplace. Suites have a sunken living room, antique marble fireplace, dressing room, bathroom with whirlpool tub, private sauna, and sundeck. For those who need more room, a three-bedroom house is available.

INSIDER TIP With 12 French chefs rising to the gastronomic challenge, spa cuisine takes on a new flavor and elegance here. Celebrate a win on the tennis court with a wonderful guilt-free meal.

Equipment: Cross trainers, free weights, stair climbers, stationary bikes, treadmills, weight-training circuit. **Services:** Aromatherapy, body mask, body polish, herbal wraps, mud wraps, reflexology, scalp massage, shiatsu. **Swimming:** Pool. **Classes and Programs:** Fitness consultation, golf academy, Pilates, tennis consultation. **Recreation:** Billiards, boating, fishing, golf, hiking, horseback riding, mountain biking, tennis, water sports.

▣ 33 rooms, 11 suites.

✕ Meals included. Choice of French or spa cuisine is served in the restaurant or on the terrace. **Sample Meals:** Seafood pasta with citrus-oregano sauce, warm white asparagus with blood-orange sabayon, pizza with marinated goat cheese (lunch); grilled breast of guinea hen with sesame seeds, paper-baked Georgian Bay trout with peaches, roast Maine lobster with smoked-potato mousse and whiskey sauce (dinner).

▣ Nightly rate $167–$334 per person, double occupancy. 1-day spa sampler package $169. AE, DC, MC, V.

✉ *McKellar, Ontario P0G 1C0,* ☎ *705/389–2171 or 800/571–8818,* FAX *705/389–3818. Winter:* ✉ *77 Ingram Dr., Suite 200, Toronto, Ontario M6M 2L7,* ☎ *416/245–5606,* FAX *416/245–2460. www.manitou-online.com*

LANGDON HALL

LUXURY PAMPERING

Built in Cambridge in 1853 as a private home for an heir to legendary financier John Jacob Astor, Langdon Hall has been beautifully restored to its former glory. Here you can experience a taste of what life must have been like for the privileged few of that era. All your creature comforts are taken care of by the friendly staff at this secluded inn. If you leave your shoes outside your door in the evening, they'll be shiny by the morning.

Visiting the spa is a perfect way to begin your foray into self-indulgence. The Cleopatra Wrap is a good introduction to the facilities. After a body scrub, the therapist applies a mixture of milk, citrus, green clay, and blended oils to your skin and cocoons you in bunting. While this mixture is nourishing your skin, the therapist massages your face and neck. You are rinsed with a warm Vichy shower, then rubbed with moisturizer. If that isn't enough indulgence, you can choose from a wide variety of massages, hydrotherapy treatments, and beauty services.

The spa facilities have been recently expanded but still maintain an intimate feel. Between treatments you can visit the sauna, steam bath, and whirlpool or just relax with a magazine and an herbal tea or munch on a spa luncheon. Although there are no scheduled classes, a personal trainer is available on request. The exercise facility is compact but well-equipped, and each piece of equipment has its own television.

Stroll around the grounds and you'll come across orchards, gardens, and a lily pond that is home to a family of ducks. The cooperation between gardener and chef is apparent. Extensive gardens supply the chef with a wide variety of fresh vegetables and herbs that are turned into award-winning cuisine.

Each of the 40 guest rooms and 12 suites has a different feel. Most have a fireplace and are decorated with period antiques. The feather beds are renowned for their comfort and are dressed in crisp white linens.

The pace of life is very relaxed at Langdon Hall. Whether your idea of a lovely afternoon is playing croquet and then retiring to the side porch for afternoon tea, or enjoying a rousing game of tennis, you can find just the thing to help you unwind.

INSIDER TIP If you have been looking to treat yourself or a loved one, this is the perfect spot. Indulgence is the key word here.

Equipment: Free weights, rowing machines, stair climbers, stationary bikes, treadmills, **Services:** Aromatherapy, body polishing, deep-tissue massage, fango wrap, herbal wrap, hydrotherapy, lymphatic massage, myofacial massage, reflexology, reiki, seaweed wrap, shiatsu. **Swimming:** Heated outdoor pool. **Classes and Programs:** Personal training. **Recreation:** Biking, billiards, croquet, hiking, tennis, volleyball.

⊞ 40 rooms, 12 suites.

✕ Breakfast included in room rate. Vegetarian and pub fare available. **Sample Meals:** Lobster salad, cold poached salmon and asparagus with caviar and chardonnay dressing (lunch); risotto of wild mushrooms and black truffles, pheasant with foie gras *mousseline* (dinner).

▤ Nightly rate $174–$444 per room. 1-day Romance Spa package from $266 per couple. AE, D, MC, V.

✉ *R.R. 33, Cambridge, Ontario N3H 4R8,* ☎ *519/740–2100 or 800/ 268–1898,* ℻ *519/740–8161. www.relaischateaux.fr/langdon*

MILLCROFT INN

LUXURY PAMPERING

With a 40-minute drive you can escape from the hustle and bustle of Toronto to the peace and quiet of the Caledon Hills. Go farther still off the beaten track and you will find the historic Millcroft Inn tucked away beside the Credit River.

Originally a knitting mill dating from 1881, the main building is now home to 22 well-appointed guest rooms. The adjacent manor house looks and feels like a private home and features 10 larger rooms, each with its own hot tub. Across a small bridge there are 20 two-story cottages, all with fireplaces and three with private outdoor hot tubs. None of the rooms at the inn is equipped with television, so be sure to visit with someone interesting.

The spa facilities are away from the main building, near the outdoor pool. Although on the smallish side, the spa is nicely laid out, with well-equipped treatment rooms. A variety of massages and wraps are offered here, as well as a wide range of beauty services. The facials are a specialty here and are very effective in combating stress as well as the aging process. Arrange your treatments when making your reservations, as weekend appointments fill up quickly.

The gym, in its own small building beside the main house, is bright and airy. It contains the usual treadmills, stair climbers, and stationary bikes, as well as a weight-training circuit and free weights. Cycling or cross-country skiing are other exercise options, and bicycles or skis are available. This can be a romantic getaway for two, as the scenery here is lovely.

Dining at the Millcroft is a memorable experience. Chef Reinhard Scheer-Hennings's presentations are spectacular, with a mingling of flavors that is inspired. Even if you would normally skip dessert, indulge this time. The pastry chef's work is very creative, and you will find your eyes straying as other diners' dessert plates arrive.

....
INSIDER TIP Choose to soar up, up, and away in a hot-air balloon or dine in "the pod," a glass dome overlooking the river. There is a spectacular view from either vantage point.
....

Equipment: Free weights, stair climbers, stationary bikes, treadmills, weight-training circuit. **Services:** Aromatherapy, body wrap, reiki. **Swimming:** Outdoor pool. **Recreation:** Billiards, boating, canoeing, cross-country skiing, fishing, hiking.

⊞ 42 rooms, 10 suites.

✕ Breakfast included in room rate. Lunch and dinner à la carte. **Sample Meals:** Double-baked goat cheese soufflé, pan-seared halibut with summer berry sauce (lunch); grilled veal tenderloin and sweet breads, fettuccine pasta with Caribbean lobster and pink oyster mushrooms (dinner).

▨ Nightly rate $151–$191 per room. Golf package from $229 per person per night. Romantic getaway package from $154 per person per night. Day spa packages from $131 per person. AE, D, MC, V.

✉ *55 John St., Alton, Ontario L0N 1A0,* ☎ *519/941–8111 or 800/383–3976,* ℻ *519/941–9192. www.millcroft.com*

PILLAR AND POST INN

LUXURY PAMPERING

Originally an 18th-century canning factory, the Pillar and Post Inn has retained the look of yesteryear. The wooden rafters and brick walls remain, and there's an abundance of comfortable furnishings in the main lobby and dining room. Guest rooms are just as cozy, with flowered chintz draperies, canopy beds, and fireplaces.

The inn's soothing atmosphere is enhanced by the 100 Fountains Spa, whose treatment rooms are like movie sets, transporting you to exotic locales—China, Japan, Italy, France, Greece, Turkey, Sweden, and India. Here you will find all the standard treatments, such as facials, wraps, and massages, and Dead Sea mud wraps. The spa is staffed by well-trained aestheticians and registered massage therapists (some qualified for medical treatments). You can join aquatic exercise classes, swim laps in the pool, or soak in the whirlpool.

With the Pillar and Post now under the umbrella of Vintage Inns, you are free to use the facilities at any of the Vintage Inns' other four properties in the area. They range in style from the historic and opulent Prince of Wales Hotel to the cozy and charming Oban Inn. They are all within the town of Niagara-on-the-Lake, so it's no trouble to hop from one to another.

The Secret Garden Spa, at the newly renovated Prince of Wales, is aptly named, as you feel that you've stumbled into your own personal oasis. Although smaller than the 100 Fountains Spa, it is equipped with top-of-the-line treatment facilities. The pace here is unhurried, and the treatments are indulgent. The fitness area, which possesses a pristine elegance of its own, has a full range of workout equipment and a weight-training circuit.

Exploring the quaint village is the main order of the day. Founded by those loyal to the British crown who fled north during the American Revolution, the town was burned to the ground by an invading militia in 1813. Rebuilt in Victorian style, many of the residential and commercial streets haven't changed since. This green and pretty town is battling to preserve its traditions even as the Shaw Festival, held from April to September, attracts busloads of tourists.

Bike, jog, or drive along the Niagara Parkway to view the falls and vineyards. Winery visits allow a taste of Canadian vintages. At the Inniskillin estate, a self-guided tour explains environmental effects of the soil and cliffs forming the Niagara escarpment, considered beneficial to production of fine wines. The nearby Hillebrand Estate offers a variety of tours as well as wine tastings. About 9 mi away, Niagara Falls can be viewed from the Canadian side of the border.

INSIDER TIP While in town, take an elegant step back in time and visit the Prince of Wales drawing room for high tea served on Royal Crown Derby china.

Equipment: Free weights, stationary bikes, treadmills, weight-training equipment. **Services:** Aromatherapy, algae body wrap, herbal wrap, mud wrap, reflexology, shiatsu. **Swimming:** Indoor and outdoor pools. **Classes and Programs:** Aquaerobics, fitness consultation.

▦ 91 rooms, 32 suites.

✗ Meals à la carte. International fare served in the main dining room, with an optional menu of lighter fare. **Sample Meals:** Romaine hearts in roasted-garlic Parmesan dressing and spicy pancetta, pizza with spiced Italian sausage, Asiago cheese, oregano, coal-roasted peppers, and tomato coulis (lunch); rack of lamb with grilled corn, "smashed" potatoes, New Brunswick lobster and spinach cannelloni, grilled pork loin chop with ancho stone-fruit glaze, sweet-potato tamale, young leek sauté (dinner).

▧ Nightly rate $74–$469 per room. 1-night 100 Fountain spa package from $179 per person.

✉ *48 John St., Box 1011, Niagara-on-the-Lake, Ontario L0S 1J0,* ☎ *905/468–2123 or 800/361–6788,* ℻ *905/468–3551.*

STE. ANNE'S COUNTRY INN & SPA

LUXURY PAMPERING

A charming country estate about an hour from Toronto, Ste. Anne's Country Inn & Spa provides a comforting mix of luxury pampering and pure relaxation. Women of all ages, as well as the occasional couple, can be found socializing in the comfortable common rooms. White fluffy robes are the wardrobe here, worn even for breakfast and lunch. Days are unstructured, allowing you to book spa treatments, work out, play a few rounds of golf, or explore the countryside. You can even simply sink into a wing chair to read a book from an eclectic collection in the parlor.

Redolent of herbs, woodsy fireplaces, and fresh flowers, the inn could be a castle in Scotland. Set in rambling, stone-walled wings, guest rooms—ranging from cozy to deluxe—are appointed with antiques, fireplace, and twin or king-size beds. Suites have cathedral ceilings and whirlpool tubs, and some have four-poster beds.

The new Lifestyle Pavilion has wide-plank pine flooring, country-style windows, and a fresh, invigorating feeling. It also provides a panoramic view of the rambling 570-acre estate. The classes offered here daily are very popular, so reservations are recommended.

Soothe your muscles with a visit to the skylighted cedar-lined eucalyptus steam room. Nip outside for a relaxing soak in the hot tub or to take on the challenge of the 15-ft lap pool with adjustable current. These facilities are available day and night, year-round. In the summer months massages and other treatments are available in a private outdoor gazebo overlooking a spring-fed pool.

The signature treatment at Ste. Anne's is the moor mud bath. Here you sink into a rich mixture of Saskatchewan clay and mud dug from a lake formed by Canadian glaciers. This treatment can be followed by a sea-salt scrub or an herbal body polish, then a shower in a deluge of spring water with a high-pressure hose. The mud bath, effective for soothing aching muscles, is best experienced when you have a couple of hours available for a post-treatment nap.

....

INSIDER TIP After a leisurely train ride to the lush Northumberland Hills, you can travel to Ste. Anne's in style in a limousine. The hotel staff will be happy to arrange it.

....

Equipment: Stationary bikes, treadmills. **Services:** Acupressure, aromatherapy, herbal wrap, lomi lomi, lymphatic drainage, mud bath, reflexology, reiki, seaweed body wrap. **Swimming:** Pool. **Classes and Programs:** Aquaerobics, low-impact cardio, stress management, tai chi, yoga. **Recreation:** Mountain biking, tennis.

▥ 7 rooms, 3 suites.

✕ Breakfast included in room rate. Spa cuisine, vegetarian meals in dining room. **Sample Meals:** Louisiana crab cakes, roast vegetable wrap (lunch); pecan and dried cranberry-stuffed pork roast, steamed herb-crusted salmon (dinner).

▨ Nightly rate $76–$93 per room. 2-day stress maintenance package $476, includes spa treatments. Day spa package $111–$146, includes lunch and spa treatments. AE, D, DC, MC, V.

✉ *R.R. 1, Grafton, Ontario KOK 2GO,* ☎ *905/349–2493 or 888/ 346–6772,* ꜰᴀx *905/349–3531. www.steannes.com*

WHEELS COUNTRY SPA AT WHEELS INN

LUXURY PAMPERING

A family-oriented motel close to Detroit, Wheels Inn is an indoor resort with 7 acres of entertainment and recreation facilities under one roof. Cavort with the kids on the water slides at the pool, or drop them off at the supervised day-care center and Wild Zone amusement park on the premises. You can try some of the 42 revitalizing services in the European-style spa.

Taking a serious approach to shape-ups, staff members have credentials for cardiovascular and muscular testing. They conduct basic body measurements, a wellness profile, and one-on-one training in a well-equipped fitness center. Runners and joggers can set courses passing the town's Victorian mansions and modern marina. There are 15 routes mapped out, ranging from 1.8 to 13.5 mi.

Aerobics classes are scheduled according to your fitness level, from beginner to advanced. You can join a group doing aquaerobics in the fitness pool or a program designed for those with arthritis and circulatory problems. Then relax in the whirlpool and steam baths.

The wide variety of revitalizing body and skin treatments offered here is unique for Canada. Feel your stress melt away in the hands of registered massage therapists. You can schedule a reflexology session or be cocooned in a fragrant herbal wrap. Therapeutic Swedish massage or an invigorating sea-salt scrub can also be part of your package.

INSIDER TIP If escaping for some peace and quiet while on a family vacation sounds like an impossible dream, visit Wheels Inn. With something for everyone, they won't even notice you're missing.

Equipment: Free weights, rowing machines, stair climbers, stationary bikes, treadmills, weight-training equipment. **Services:** Aromatherapy, herbal wraps, hydrotherapy, loofah body scrub, massage, reflexology. **Swimming:** Indoor and outdoor pools. **Recreation:** Bowling, racquetball, squash, water slides. **Children's Programs:** Supervised day care from newborn to 8 years. In-room baby-sitting.

▣ 350 rooms.

✕ Meals à la carte. **Sample Meals:** Tossed salad, poached salmon with vegetables, cold tuna plate (lunch); cold grilled chicken breast with olive-cucumber relish, brochette of shrimp and scallops on rice, fresh fruit and yogurt (dinner).

▨ Nightly rate $80 per room. 1-night package $184 per person, includes meals and spa treatments. 2-night package $363 per person, includes meals and spa treatments. Day spa package $127, includes lunch and spa treatments. AE, MC, V.

✉ *Box 637, Chatham, Ontario N7M 5K8,* ☎ *519/351–1100, 519/436–5505 (spa), 800/265–5257,* FAX *519/436–5541. www.wheelsinn.com*

QUÉBEC

AUBERGE DU PARC INN

LUXURY PAMPERING

European-style pampering amid Victorian elegance is the order of the day at this tranquil inn perched on a hill overlooking the water of the picturesque Baie des Chaleurs. Soft music wafts throughout the spa as you are coddled with daily massages and cocooned in body wraps— a regimen that drains away stress and leaves you with a look of dreamy contentment. Thalassotherapy treatments with fresh seawater from the bay and algae imported from France take about three hours a day, which leaves time to play a round of tennis, curl up with a good book, or explore the scenic Gaspé coast.

Owner Jeanette Lemarquand doesn't believe in dictating to her guests, so gourmands needn't worry. The cuisine is as light or as luxurious as you want, with lower-calorie and vegetarian options available at every meal. Smoking is restricted to a separate dining room and lounge.

Although there are many opportunities to seek out exercise, there are no organized fitness classes. There is only a very modest exercise room with older equipment.

Accommodations are in 32 modern motel-style rooms set amid landscaped gardens, a short walk from the nearly 200-year-old country manor. Because the inn accepts only 40 guests at a time—nearly half are repeat visitors—the grounds never feel crowded. Although French is most commonly spoken, the staff is bilingual and welcoming.

INSIDER TIP Looking for a relaxing getaway? With three hours of treatments in a single block, you only have to check your watch once a day.

Services: Algae body wrap, lymphatic drainage, massage, pressotherapy, reflexology, thalassotherapy. **Swimming:** Indoor seawater pool, outdoor pool, beaches nearby. **Recreation:** Billiards, cycling, golf, hiking.

▦ 32 rooms.

✕ Meals included. International cuisine using local seafood and produce served in two dining rooms. **Sample Meals:** Fresh vegetable salad with cold salmon, oven-baked fillet of sole with steamed vegetables, guinea fowl conserve on spinach salad with raspberry vinegar (lunch); smoked shrimp with cucumber chutney, scallops with hazelnuts, baked breast of duck in Madeira wine sauce with candied gold raisins (dinner).

✉ 2-day package $337 per person, double occupancy, includes meals and treatments. 7-day package $846–$961 per person, double occupancy, includes meals and treatments. MC, V.

✉ *C.P. 40, Paspebiac, Québec G0C 2K0,* ☎ *418/752–3355 or 800/ 463–0890 in Québec,* 🖷 *418/752–6406. www.aubergeduparc.com*

CENTRE DE SANTÉ D'EASTMAN

HOLISTIC HEALTH

Nestled in the rolling countryside about an hour's drive southeast of Montréal, the Centre de Santé d'Eastman is a low-key retreat for anyone looking for a relaxing, rejuvenating getaway. There is no obligation to follow a tightly structured regimen. Resident owner-director Jocelyna Dubuc encourages guests to learn healthy habits that can be worked into their daily schedule at home.

A new $3 million pavilion with a panoramic view of nearby Mont Orford provides state-of-the-art spa facilities. It has allowed Eastman to offer watsu, as much an experience as a massage. As you float in a 4-ft-deep pool with water heated to 96°F, a therapist cradles you or moves your body through a series of dancelike movements designed to relax you.

Another of Eastman's specialties is its oxygen bath, said to increase vitality and leave your eyes looking brighter and your vision clearer. Encased below the neck in what looks like a white cocoon, you are surrounded by steam mixed with carbon dioxide to open your pores. You are then surrounded by oxygen for about 15 minutes, followed by the application of essential oils such as rosemary, eucalyptus, and pine.

Exercise is optional and not strenuous. Three guided walks are held daily along the spa's 9 mi of wooded trails—an early morning fitness walk, an "antistress" walk later in the morning, and an after-dinner walk. Daily classes offer you a chance to try yoga and tai chi. Personal training programs are also available.

Nine buildings house the spa facilities and room for up to 90 guests. Rooms in outlying buildings are comfortably furnished with country motifs. Slightly more expensive but more convenient rooms in the main building have a Zen-inspired decor, with white duvets and wrought-iron accents forged by local artisans. None of the rooms has television or telephone.

INSIDER TIP Want to take home your spa experience? The staff shows you how to incorporate exercise, better diet, stress reduction, and other healthier habits into your everyday routine.

Equipment: Stair climbers, stationary bikes, weight-training equipment. **Services:** Body scrub, body wrap, colonic irrigation, hydrotherapy, pressotherapy, reflexology, reiki, shiatsu, watsu. **Swimming:** Two pools. **Classes and Programs:** Daily exercise classes, stress reduction lectures, tai chi, yoga. **Recreation:** Hiking.

🛏 42 rooms, 1 cottage.

✗ Meals included. Mostly ovo-lacto vegetarian menu with some seafood and poultry served in dining room. **Sample Meals:** Corn-and-cucumber soup, salads, raw vegetables (lunch); Chinese stir-fry, eggplant Parmesan, whole wheat fettuccine (dinner).

✉ 1-day health and relaxation package $192 per person, double occupancy, includes meals and spa treatments. 2-day fitness package $206–$320 per person, double occupancy. 7-day Health Relaxation package $836–$1,244, double occupancy. AE, MC, V.

✉ *895 Chemin des Diligences, Eastman, Québec J0E 1P0,* ☎ *450/297–3009 or 800/665–5272,* FAX *450/297–3370. www.spa-eastman.com*

CLUB TREMBLANT

LUXURY PAMPERING ○ SPORTS CONDITIONING

For decades it has been a haven for skiers and hikers, but the resort area of Mont-Tremblant is also a destination for those seeking to get away from it all. From the wooden deck of Spa-sur-le-Lac, the full-service spa at Club Tremblant, you can see the ski slopes on the opposite shore of Lake Tremblant. You may even spot deer grazing in the gardens below.

The rustic ambience of the club's main lodge, dating from 1930, contrasts that of the new spa. Designed to complement the existing indoor swimming pool and exercise room, the spa's natural-wood trim, wrought-iron accents, and terra-cotta tiles create a warm and elegant atmosphere. The Spa-sur-le-Lac's relaxation lounge is a haven of peace and tranquillity where you can lie back and watch the clouds drift over the tree-covered mountaintop.

The spa offers a skin-care regimen that helps repair damage after a day on the slopes; it's particularly popular with men. The spa has the area's first hydrotherapy tub, installed in a private room. Its signature treatment, however, is the Spa-sur-le-Lac Body Polish, which combines sea salts, almond oil, a gentle massage, and jets of water, leaving the skin incredibly soft. Although a wide range of treatments offered, not all therapists are on hand each day, so call ahead to discuss your personal needs.

Mont-Tremblant, a huge, rumpled rock that since 1938 has attracted skiers, climbs to 3,001 ft. Currently, 92 runs descend the north and south faces. For those who are less athletic, a gondola ride to the mountain peak provides extraordinary views. Club Tremblant operates its own professional ski school, with equipment rentals on-site.

The buildings of Club Tremblant climb a hillside and resemble an alpine village. Guests stay in one- or two-bedroom condos with fully equipped kitchens, dining areas, living rooms with fireplaces, and balconies with views of the lake. Rustic wood furniture and contemporary bed coverings add ambience.

Club Tremblant's all-inclusive packages let you combine outdoor sports, spa therapies, and fitness facilities (although the gym's equipment is somewhat limited). Family-oriented programs, such as a supervised summer camp for kids, make it easy to sneak away for a massage. The club's shuttle bus provides free transportation to the mountain village in winter, where there is a colorful assortment of shops and entertainment year-round.

INSIDER TIP For adventure-minded guests, the hotel's concierge can arrange a day of dogsledding or snowmobiling on Mont-Tremblant, or a floatplane tour of the area.

Equipment: Free weights, rowing machines, stair climbers, stationary bikes, treadmills, weight-training equipment. **Services:** Algae wrap, body exfoliation, hydrotherapy, lymphatic drainage, pressotherapy, reflexology, shiatsu, Vichy shower. **Swimming:** Indoor and outdoor pools. **Classes and Programs:** Aquaerobics, tennis clinic. **Recreation:** Badminton, boating, canoeing, croquet, hiking, horseshoes, kayaking, tennis, volleyball, waterskiing. **Children's Programs:** Supervised activities for ages 2–16 in summer.

▦ 100 1- and 2-bedroom condos.

✗ Some meals included. Spa cuisine and French fare served in three dining rooms. **Sample Meals:** Ham-and-Brie sandwich, chicken sandwich on French bread (lunch); mesclun with sliced smoked duck, cold zucchini soup with mint, roast venison with berries, ostrich with pink peppers and mandarin oranges (dinner).

▨ 2-night package $399–$687, includes meals and treatments. 3-night package $660–$993. 5-night package $1,025–$1,580.

⊠ *121 rue Cuttle, Mont-Tremblant, Québec J0T 1Z0,* ☎ *819/425-2731 or 800/567-8341,* ⬛ *819/425-5617. www.clubtremblant.com*

GRAY ROCKS

SPORTS CONDITIONING

Built in 1906 as a hunting lodge, Gray Rocks opened the area's first Austrian-style ski school in 1938. The owners have focused on maintaining the lodge's old-fashioned comfort while constantly upgrading the facilities. They have spiffed up the accommodations, expanded the classic ski-week program, and now have two golf courses, *La Belle* and *La Bête* (The Beauty and The Beast).

Le Spa is a modest amenity in the main lodge, where an hour-long massage is a bargain at $37. There is a good variety of exercise equipment and classes such as aerobics and stretching. A personalized exercise program is available at an extra charge. The ozonated swimming pool is excellent for swimming laps, but it can be busy with kids during the day and evening.

The Gray Rocks domain is vast, encompassing a mountain with 22 ski trails, the largest outdoor tennis complex in Canada, a lake with a beach and a marina, and a ranch for horseback riding. Think of it as a university of sports. Certified instructors teach golf and tennis clinics, and *Ski* magazine chose the ski and snowboarding school as one of the top 10 in North America in 1999.

Accommodations are in one- to three-bedroom condos and are fully equipped with kitchens, washer-dryers, microwaves, dishwashers, TVs, and fireplaces. Although there are kennels on-site, pets are also allowed in the rooms. Minutes from the Mont-Tremblant, Gray Rocks provides complimentary transportation to the village so you can take advantage of the shopping and restaurants. But you may not want to leave, as the resort offers plenty of activities to keep your family busy, such as paddleboat trips and sleigh rides.

INSIDER TIP If your French doesn't extend beyond the menu you needn't worry, as Gray Rocks offers a survival course in conversational French.

Equipment: Cross-country ski machines, free weights, rowing machines, stair climbers, stationary bikes, treadmills, weight-training equipment. **Services:** Massage. **Swimming:** Pool, beach. **Classes and Programs:** Aerobics, skiing, stretching. **Recreation:** Biking, canoeing, golf, hiking, horseback riding, kayaking, skiing, snowboarding, snowmobiling, snowshoeing, tennis. **Children's Programs:** Daycare for children 6 months to 2 years, ski lessons for children 3–5. Kids Club for ages 3–17. 2-week golf and tennis camps for teenagers.

▦ 105 rooms and suites, 56 condominiums.

✕ Meals à la carte. **Sample Meals:** Hot and cold buffet including an assortment of salads (lunch); tomato and spinach soup, chicken livers on brioche, chicken supreme with mango sauce, shrimp, scallops, and chicken brochettes with Cajun spices (dinner).

▧ Nightly rate $69–$117 per person, double occupancy. 6-night package $768–$397–$677 per person, double occupancy, includes meals. AE, DC, MC, V.

✉ *525 Chemin Principal, Mont-Tremblant, Québec J0T 1Z0,* ☎ *819/ 425–2771 or 800/567–6767,* ℻ *819/425–9156. www.grayrocks.com*

LE CHÂTEAU BROMONT

LUXURY PAMPERING

Tucked away at the foot of a large ski slope amid the gently rolling hills of the Eastern Townships, Le Château Bromont has undergone a metamorphosis in recent years. Now catering more to corporate retreats, the hotel's limited gym, racquetball court, and indoor and outdoor pools testify to an earlier era when it was dedicated to serious shape-ups. However, the SpaConcept program remains, giving guests the chance to enjoy European-style treatments.

Offered here are body peeling, body wraps, and an unusually wide choice of massages—from soothing Swedish to shiatsu. Other specialties include lymphatic drainage, polarity therapy, and baths with algae, mud, or essential oils. Lunch is served just outside the spa area in an indoor courtyard, but there's only a metal divider and a few plants to separate spa customers in robes from hotel guests.

Only an hour from Montréal, the Château Bromont is a good choice for a quick getaway in a country setting. Rooms have been redone in an elegant English country style decor, and many feature wood-burning fireplaces.

INSIDER TIP Try a four-hand massage, developed here, which features two therapists working together in harmony, with one mirroring the movements of the other. There's also a special massage for pregnant women.

Equipment: Facials, free weights, stationary bicycles, weight-training circuit. **Services:** Algotherapy, aromatherapy, balneotherapy, colonic irrigation, lymphatic drainage, massage, polarity therapy, pressotherapy, reflexology, shiatsu, Vichy shower. **Swimming:** Indoor and outdoor pools. **Recreation:** Biking, horseshoes, racquetball, volleyball.

▦ 146 rooms, 6 suites.

✕ Meals included. **Sample Meals:** Duck galantine, roast beef with wine sauce (lunch); duck with garlic, beef filet in a pastry crust with port sauce, salmon with a honey sauce (dinner).

▧ 1-night package $201 per person, double occupancy. 3-night package $523 per person, double occupancy. 5-night package $924 per person, double occupancy. AE, MC, V.

✉ *90 rue Stanstead, Bromont, Québec J2L 1K6,* ☎ *450/534–2717 or 800/567–7727 (in Canada),* 🖷 *450/534–0599. www.spaconcept.qc.ca*

MANOIR RICHELIEU

LUXURY PAMPERING ○ SPORTS CONDITIONING

Former U.S president William Howard Taft once described the air of Québec's Charlevoix region as intoxicating as champagne without the headache in the morning—an assessment every bit as true today as it was at the turn of the last century, when pillars of high society in New York, Montréal, and Toronto flocked to what was then known as Murray's Bay.

One of the places they visited was Le Manior Richelieu. Perched atop a cliff overlooking the St. Lawrence River, the hotel has peaked roofs and landscaped gardens that make it resemble a French château. Constructed in 1899, the resort has been restored to its former grandeur.

One of the key areas renovated was the Relaxarium spa, where each of the 22 treatment rooms, including balneotherapy rooms for couples, features different decor by local artisans. The spa's philosophy is simple: if you can't ingest it, you shouldn't be putting it on your body. Consequently, it uses only natural products, including cold-pressed oils from France. Treatments often start with a reflexology session conducted by Roger Arbour, a professional reflexologist who, by massaging your feet, can tell you not only about your body but a lot about your life. After each treatment you are escorted back to a relaxation lounge where you are tucked into a comfy chair and offered juice or herbal tea while you listen to soothing music.

With 212 acres of land, Le Manior Richelieu offers a wide variety of sports for almost every taste—golf, hiking, tennis, and horseback riding are at the hotel, while downhill skiing is at the nearby Le Massif. The hotel is also a good base for exploring the Charlevoix region. The region is also a haven for artists and is renowned for its gourmet cuisine and unique regional specialties such as Charlevoix veal, Migneron cheese, and its rare blue potatoes.

....
INSIDER TIP For those with families, Manoir Richelieu is the most guilt-free spa imaginable. Drop the children off at the Kids Club, send your spouse off for a game of tennis, then settle in for a day of pampering that will leave you ready to face the world again.
....

Equipment: Free weights, stair climber, stationary bikes, treadmills, weight-training equipment. **Services:** Aromatherapy, balneotherapy, body wraps, exfoliation, hydromassage, lymphatic drainage, pressotherapy, reflexology, reiki, Vichy shower. **Swimming:** Indoor and outdoor saltwater pools. **Recreation:** Biking, croquet, dogsledding, golf, hiking, horseback riding, horseshoes, miniature golf, shuffleboard, skating, sleigh rides, snowmobiling, snowshoeing, tennis, volleyball. **Children's Programs:** Kids Club for children ages 4–12.

🛏 370 rooms, 35 suites.

✕ Meals included. The St. Laurent restaurant features buffet meals. Le Charlevoix, open only for dinner, offers innovative French and regional cuisine. Vegetarian options available. **Sample Meals:** Crab and shrimp on a bed of mesclun, fresh fruit platter with cottage cheese and honey sauce (lunch); trout tartar, pear salsa and fried leeks, filet of caribou in *grand veneur* sauce, fillet of Charlevoix veal with Migneron cheese (dinner).

✉ 1-night package $185 per person, double occupancy, includes meals and treatments. 3-day Spa Cure package $669 per person, double occupancy, includes meals and treatments. AE, D, DC, MC, V.

✉ *181 rue Richelieu, La Malbaie-Pointe-au-Pic, Québec G0T 1M0,* ☎ *418/665–3703 or 800/441–1414,* FAX *418/665–7878. www.fairmont.com*

SIVANANDA ASHRAM

HOLISTIC HEALTH

Although there are a number of resorts that pamper your body, Sivananda Ashram is one place that pampers your soul. The spartan lifestyle, coupled with yoga and meditation, provides an environment that allows you to feel rejuvenated. The change of seasons alters the atmosphere of the year-round camp, with the activity-filled days of summer giving way to a quieter, more reflective time in the fall, winter, and spring.

Campers revel in the natural beauty of 250 acres of unspoiled woodland. At dawn you are called to meditation, followed by asanas to stretch and invigorate the body. Breakfast comes at midmorning, and supper follows the afternoon asana session. In between you are free to take a dip in the pool or explore the countryside. Sunset meditation and looking at the stars conclude most days, and in summer there are often programs of Indian music and dance.

Based on five principles for a long and healthy life prescribed by Swami Vishnu Devananda, the program teaches how to properly breathe, relax, and exercise and how to combine diet with positive thinking and meditation. As the headquarters of a worldwide community, the ashram is dedicated to teaching yoga to people of all ages and backgrounds.

Introducing children to the principles of yoga is the focus of the month-long Kids Camp, held here since 1972. Designed for children 7–12, the program combines outdoor adventure, creativity, and discovery. Living in cabins with experienced counselors, kids participate in many of the same programs as adults, as well as cooking classes, sports, and arts and crafts. There's even a show for parents at the end of the month.

Built in 1995, the main guest lodge is constructed with straw-bale insulation between earth-tone plaster walls supported by wooden post-and-pole beams. There are two two-story lodges with dormitories and private rooms (most with private bath). Furnishings are simple, and linens are provided. Tent space is available on the grounds. A large hall with a heated floor is used for yoga and dining. Nearby is a huge wooden pavilion used in summer for yoga classes.

INSIDER TIP If you want to learn yoga, this is a good place to start. The program is flexible enough so that experts don't feel frustrated by a slow pace and newcomers don't feel left behind.

Swimming: Pool, lake. **Classes and Programs:** Traditional Indian music and dancing, yoga. **Recreation:** Biking, canoeing, hiking, rock climbing, skiing, volleyball, white-water rafting. **Children's Programs:** Month-long Kids Camp for ages 7–12.

⊞ 22 rooms with 62 dormitory beds, more than 100 campsites.

✕ Meals included. Vegetarian buffets served in large hall. **Sample Meals:** Hot grain cereal, vegetable soup, baked tofu, salad (lunch); lentil loaf, baked casserole of seasonal vegetables (dinner).

▨ Nightly rate $44 per person, double occupancy, includes meals and yoga instruction. Tent space $24. AE, MC, V.

⊠ *673 8th Ave., Val Morin, Québec J0T 2R0,* ☎ *819/322–3226 or 800/263–9642 in Canada,* ℻ *819/322–5876. www.sivananda.org/camp*

MEXICO

The concept of "taking the waters" is nothing new in Mexico. It can be traced back as far as the Aztecs, who bathed and worshiped spirits at the country's numerous natural springs. Other Native peoples also believed the waters had curative powers. The Huichol tribe revered a meandering, steaming river of hot mineral water in Jalisco. The name of the Temascaltepec Valley in the Sierra Madre came from the Nahuatl tribe, which combined the words *temazcali* (house of baths) and *tepac* (hill).

Throughout Mexico today these *balnearios* (mineral water baths) and *baños termales* (thermal hot-spring baths) are a bargain, offering mud wraps, relaxing massages, and warm hospitality. The largest and most luxurious of them is Hotel Ixtapan, in Ixtapan de la Sal, a two-hour drive southeast of Mexico City. At the other end of the spectrum is a more rustic retreat called Río Caliente Spa, secluded in a national forest about an hour from Guadalajara.

Tradition mixes with modern technology at Mexican spas. Try the *temazcal,* an Aztec sauna, at Spa Pre-Hispánico in Oaxaca's Puerto Escondido or at Misión del Sol in Cuernavaca. Fango body wraps are now common at spas around the world, but at the Qualton Club & Spa in Puerto Vallarta, the mineral-rich mud is gathered from a volcanic source in the state of Michoacán.

A very different experience, and a success since it opened 60 years ago, is the Rancho La Puerta, in Baja California. This is the action-oriented counterpart to the Golden Door in California; its holistic health program and vegetarian meals, all in the stress-free environment of the Sierra Madre, blend into a seamless vacation experience.

A few words of advice: Don't expect the types of organized exercise programs you'd find at spas in the United States. Aside from Rancho La Puerta, which offers dozens of classes daily, most resorts focus on relaxation. Any physical training will likely be one-on-one instruction from a personal trainer. And those who don't speak Spanish would be wise to pick up a phrase book and learn a few terms, as many of the employees at these resorts, especially the smaller ones, speak little English.

The country code for Mexico is 52 and must be dialed before the telephone and fax numbers listed below. In Mexico the prefix 01 is used with area codes. All prices in this chapter are in U.S. dollars.

BAJA CALIFORNIA

RANCHO LA PUERTA

LUXURY PAMPERING ○ NUTRITION AND DIET

Since 1940 Rancho La Puerta has set the standard for American health resorts. The formula for fitness may have changed somewhat in the past 60 years, but unchanged is the personalized service, with more than 300 employees seeing to the needs of up to 150 guests. Also the same are the nearly perfect year-round climate (an average of 341 sunny days), the natural beauty of the 575 acres of lush gardens surrounded by purple foothills and impressive mountains, and the mostly vegetarian diet.

Still managed by members of its founding family, Rancho La Puerta has a high number of repeat guests. The required seven-day stay fosters a group camaraderie. Friendships form easily in classes, during breaks taken on shaded patios, and at big round tables in the dining hall. Serious bonding takes place when the intensity of the exercise increases over the course of the week.

Mornings here begin with a hike—a slow jaunt on even terrain for beginners or a trek up sacred Mt. Kuchumaa for those with more experience. Then there are the more than 60 daily exercise classes, as well as such special programs as African dance, from which to choose. Gyms dot the landscape; some are open-air, others are enclosed for cool days. No sign-up is required for any of the numerous classes, including aerobic circuit training, the back-care workshop, and self-defense seminars. A specialty here is mind/body exercise, including intense yoga work. Those seeking spiritual renewal should try walking the new meditation labyrinth or participating in the Native American medicine-wheel ceremony.

Rancho La Puerta has a beautiful new health center, as well as the original health center; both offer bodywork and skin care at very reasonable prices. There is a full range of massages, body wraps, and facials available. New treatments include the Tipai hands and feet massage using paraffin wax and reflexology, designed specifically to relieve the stress on legs and ankles that hikers endure.

Accommodations vary from studiolike rancheras to luxury haciendas and villas decorated with handmade furniture and rugs. Many feature tile floors, fireplaces, and kitchenettes. There is no air-conditioning, television, or telephones. Although all guests enjoy equal access to activities, staying in a villa entitles you to have breakfast delivered to your door and to the option of an in-room massage. Come prepared for cool evenings and sunny, dry days. There are plenty of outdoor hammocks for a siesta, and you can warm up in front of the fireplace in the lounges.

INSIDER TIP Sign up early for breakfast at the ranch's organic gardens, where chef Bill Wavrin demonstrates cooking all-natural vegetarian cuisine.

Equipment: Free weights, stair climbers, stationary bikes, treadmills, weight-training circuit. **Services:** Aromatherapy herbal wrap, massage, seaweed wrap. **Swimming:** 3 pools, 1 heated for aquatic exercise classes. **Classes and Programs:** Aerobics, aquaerobics, circuit training, gardening, self-defense, swimming, tai chi, yoga. **Recreation:** Basketball, hiking, Ping-Pong, tennis, volleyball.

▥ 85 cottages.

✕ Meals included. Meals are ovo-lacto vegetarian, with fish served twice a week. Dinner is served in the dining room; breakfast and lunch are buffet. **Sample Meals:** Baked golden apples with granola and yogurt (breakfast); baked butternut squash with cinnamon and oranges, roasted corn tamale pie with garden vegetables; pesto tuna salad (lunch); Tecate bread, sea bass tacos with papaya chili salsa (dinner).

▤ 1-week minimum stay. 7-night package $1,590–$1,985 per person, double occupancy. MC, V.

✉ *Km 5, Carretera Federal Tijuana, Tecate, Baja California, Mexico,* ☎ *6/654–1155; reservations in U.S.:* ✉ *Box 463057, Escondido, CA 92046,* ☎ *760/744–4222 or 800/443–7565,* ⊠ *760/744–5007.* *www.rancholapuerta.com*

CABO REAL RESORT

LUXURY PAMPERING

Luxury comes in many packages at this huge resort near the tip of Baja California. Stretching for several miles along the coast where the Sea of Cortez meets the Pacific Ocean, the Cabo Real Resort is made up of four distinctive hotels. Staying at one hotel gives you access to spa facilities in the others—not that you'll want to leave, as each is a world unto itself.

Two 18-hole championship golf courses attract visitors from around the world. Rising dramatically from the beach to mountain slopes, the emerald green fairways were designed by golf legends Robert Trent Jones II and Jack Nicklaus. Jones's 15th hole sits right next to the surf between the Melia Cabo Real Beach & Golf Resort and Las Ventanas al Paraíso, allowing you to watch the action while dining or lounging by the pool. Down the beach, Casa del Mar Golf Resort & Spa has rooms clustered around a grand hacienda. Next in line is the Melia Los Cabos Beach & Golf Resort, an all-suites hotel offering the largest indoor spa on the coast.

But there's more to the Cabo Real Resort than golf. Nature lovers head for craggy desert trails where the dusty, sun-scorched landscape reveals cacti of every variety: cholla cactus with long chains of fruit, cardon cactus with arms held high, and fat barrel cactus. Amid vegetation such as prickly pear and yellow morning glory, birders may spot white-winged doves, hermit warblers, plovers, and yellow and vermilion flycatchers. The most impressive sight, however, is the annual migration of California gray whales, which can be witnessed from January to March. Whale-watching tours are easily arranged at the hotels.

The sea is integral to life at Los Cabos. Although the pounding surf might seem to rule out swimming, there is a protected cove where you can take a dip. Fishing fans marvel at the size of the marlin caught here. Local tour operators offer canoeing and kayaking excursions, but you can also rent a boat right on the beach.

INSIDER TIP The name of the game here is relaxation. Try a yoga class in an air-conditioned studio or on a flower-bedecked terrace.

Casa del Mar Golf Resort & Spa. In Casa del Mar's grand hacienda, the airy Baja Spa offers a wide range of skin care, hydrotherapy, and a salon for hair and nail care. Guests can choose from a variety of massages, including one for golfers that targets areas of the body most affected by your game—hands, arms, shoulders, and lower back ($91 for 45 minutes). The spa also offers a special massage designed to ease tensions brought on by the physical changes of pregnancy ($100 for 50 minutes).

Several signature treatments are available by appointment only. The Baja Desert Cleanse starts off with a purification ritual called "smudging," in which desert sage is burned to cleanse the mind and bring about inner calmness. Guests are painted with a blend of herbs and desert clay, then massaged with an aloe vera gel. Also available is a crystal healing massage.

Intriguing mixtures are available from an elixir menu, with potions offering relaxation, detoxification, and romance. You can mix and match the various types and take home a bottle ($15). There are also herbal mixtures that you can buy to put in your bath ($15–$22).

All the standard amenities are offered: a steam room, sauna, hot tub, and a fitness center. Some of the usual extras are not included, however. For example, there is an additional charge for juice.

The guest rooms, all suites with minimal furniture, contribute to the restful atmosphere here. All have showers and hot tubs, marble floors, and a screened balcony or terrace.

Equipment: Free weights, stationary bikes, treadmills, weight-training equipment. **Services:** Aromatherapy, massage, mineral salt scrub, reflexology, sea-mud wrap, shiatsu. **Swimming:** 9 pools, beach. **Recreation:** Golf, horseback riding, paddle tennis, tennis.

▣ 56 suites.

✕ Meals à la carte. Mexican food served at the Dining Room restaurant or on the terrace. **Sample Meals:** Seafood cocktail, seviche of marinated sea bass and shrimp, chicken with fine herbs, chilies rellenos, grilled beef fillet with rice and beans (lunch); Caesar salad with shrimp, seafood rellenos, sea bass in cilantro sauce, lobster (dinner).

▧ Nightly rate $250–$370 per room. Day spa packages $100–$190. AE, MC, V.

✉ *Km 19.5 Carretera Transpeninsular, San José del Cabo, Baja California Sur, CP23410,* ☎ *114/400–30, or 800/221–8808,* ℻ *114/40–034. www.mexonline.com/casamar.htm*

Las Ventanas al Paraíso. Tucked away in lush gardens, the two-level spa at Las Ventanas al Paraíso has both indoor and outdoor facilities. Some of the 12 treatment areas include patios for private massages. You'll find a beachfront pavilion equipped with a machine spraying a cool mist while you enjoy a variety of relaxing treatments.

The spa is known for having the latest, most innovative treatments: hot stone therapy, crystal massage, and Javanese lulur ritual. In-room treatments are offered for many of the spa's services, including private yoga instruction. The spa, with a focus on restoration and rejuvenation of the entire self, is popular year-round, so you should make appointments for treatments as soon as you make your reservations.

The hotel opened in July 1997, but an addition in 1999 doubled its size. One- to three-bedroom suites are lavishly appointed with Mexican ceramics, carvings, fabrics, and wrought iron. All suites have terraces, telescopes, and fireplaces, which you will want to use December–March, when temperatures dip to the mid-50s.

Equipment: Free weights, stair climbers, stationary bikes, treadmills, weight-training equipment. **Services:** Aromatherapy, algae body wrap, exfoliation, massage, moor mud wrap, reflexology. **Swimming:** Pool, beach. **Classes and Programs:** Personal training, yoga instruction. **Recreation:** Boating, fishing, golf, hiking, horseback riding, snorkeling, tennis, windsurfing.

▥ 61 suites.

✕ Meals à la carte. Continental cuisine served at the Restaurant, fish at beachfront sea grill. Room service available. **Sample Meals:** Seafood enchilada, black bean soup (lunch); seafood chowder, organic greens, poached sea bass (dinner).

▨ $525–$750 for junior suite, $2,000–$3,500 for luxury suite. Discovery Spa package for two $2,900–$7,250 for 3 nights, includes meals and spa treatments. Pure Romance package for two $5,500–$15,650 for 7 nights, including champagne upon arrival, meals, golf, and spa treatments. AE, DC, MC, V.

✉ *Km 19.5 Carretera Transpeninsular, San José del Cabo, Baja California Sur, CP23400,* ☎ *114/40–300, or 888/767–3966,* ℻ *114/40–301. www.lasventanas.com*

Melia Cabo Real Beach & Golf Resort. The Avanti Spa, smaller than its sister spa in the Melia Los Cabos, is on the third floor of this resort hotel. The spa has 10 therapists, and their forte is massage. The Moon and Stars, a relaxing massage given in one of the palm huts by the pool, is the most appealing.

Mayan carvings adorn the walls in the guest rooms, all of which have beautifully landscaped terraces. The feel is fresh and airy, with marble floors and attractive wooden furniture.

Equipment: Free weights, stair climbers, stationary bikes, weight-training circuit. **Services:** Aromatherapy, massage, mud wrap, seaweed wrap. **Swimming:** 2 pools, beach. **Recreation:** Boat tours, fishing, golf, scuba, table tennis, volleyball, water sports.

▥ 287 rooms, 15 suites.

✕ Meals à la carte. International cuisine at La Terraza restaurant. Room service available. **Sample Meals:** Minestrone soup, broiled chicken breast, tossed salad (lunch); broiled beef, broiled fish, spinach salad (dinner).

▨ Standard room $215–$235, single or double occupancy; suites $495–$775. Day spa package $175. AE, MC, V.

✉ *Km 19.5 Carretera Transpeninsular, San José del Cabo, Baja California Sur, CP23410,* ☎ *114/40–000, or 800/336–3542,* ℻ *114/40–101. www.solmelia.es*

Melia Los Cabos Beach & Golf Resort. The spa at this hacienda-style hotel, which opened in late 1998, includes all the usual amenities. Boasting the only hydrotherapy tub in the area, you can try an underwater massage or seaweed treatments. You can also enjoy the hot tubs with ocean views. The exercise equipment, however, is found in the fitness center, in another part of the hotel.

The high-rise hotel offers variously sized suites, many with ocean views, that feature marble floors and wooden furniture. All have balconies or patios.

Equipment: Free weights, stationary bikes, treadmills, weight-training equipment. **Services:** Aromatherapy, body scrub, body wrap, hydrotherapy, massage. **Swimming:** 3 pools, beach. **Recreation:** Horseback riding, tennis, water sports.

🛏 176 suites.

✗ Meals à la carte. Continental meals are served in two restaurants. Room service available. **Sample Meals:** Shrimp cocktail, grilled vegetables with goat cheese, grilled fish (lunch); pasta with sautéed shrimp, charcoal-grilled beef with fresh rosemary sauce, sea bass fillet (dinner).

💷 $185–$510 per room, single or double occupancy. 3-treatment spa package $165–$205. AE, MC, V.

✉ *Km 18.5 Carretera Transpeninsular, San José del Cabo, Baja California Sur, CP23410,* ☎ *114/40–202,* 🖷 *114/40–058. www.solmelia.es*

HOTEL COMANJILLA

MINERAL SPRINGS

A convenient base from which to explore some of Mexico's most interesting colonial towns, the Hotel Comanjilla is a restful and quiet retreat. Pathways shaded by canopies of pine trees lead to an Olympic-size pool filled with mineral water, ideal for swimming a few laps. You might opt for a relaxing soak in a smaller pool, said to be fed by 48 springs.

Lush gardens surround the quaint two-story Spanish colonial hotel, which houses an elegantly old-fashioned restaurant that serves up traditional Mexican fare. Many honeymooners and retirees come here for the well-appointed guest rooms. All the rooms have a balcony or patio with a view of the forest or pool.

People come for the hot springs, so the spa facilities are limited. Massage and other treatments, such as mud baths, are inexpensive (about $25), but appointments must be made well in advance. Medical and nutritional consultation is available in Spanish only. There's a gym, and exercise programs are organized upon request.

On the Pan-American Highway, the hotel is minutes from the Bajio Regional Airport, in León, a town noted for leather goods and worth a shopping trip for shoes and clothing. Also nearby is Guanajuato, a fascinating and beautiful university town that grew up around Spanish silver mines. Another colonial treasure, popular with retired Americans, is San Miguel de Allende, 52 mi east of León.

INSIDER TIP If you'd like to indulge yourself, reserve one of the suites that feature step-down tubs fed by the mineral springs.

Equipment: Free weights, stationary bikes. **Services:** Massage, steam bath. **Swimming:** 2 pools. **Classes and Programs:** Medical evaluation. **Recreation:** Biking, billiards, horseback riding, table tennis, tennis.

116 rooms, 5 suites.

✕ Meals à la carte. Traditional Mexican food at the restaurant. Food for vegetarian or other special diets can be arranged in advance.

Nightly rate $100–$150 per room, single or double occupancy. No spa packages available.

✉ *Carretera Panamericana 45, Km 385, León, Guanajuato, CP36100,* ☎ *47/14–6522,* FAX *47/14–6582. www.ciatex.mx/empressa/hotelcomanjilla*

JALISCO

QUALTON CLUB & SPA PUERTO VALLARTA

LUXURY PAMPERING

Some of the best bodywork this side of the Sierra Madre can be had at the Qualton Club & Spa, in Puerto Vallarta. Guests at this seaside resort are pampered with a range of treatments using natural extracts and herbs. Even the clay in the fango treatments has a history: It is gathered from a volcanic source in the state of Michoacán for exclusive use here.

This budget-price property has the area's largest fitness center. A full circuit of strength training equipment is in use day and night. Fitness evaluations are conducted in specially equipped examination rooms. Staff members test your aerobic capacity, strength, flexibility, and blood pressure prior to starting you on a schedule of exercise.

In the air-conditioned aerobics studio, certified aerobics instructors teach classes nonstop from 7 AM to 9 PM. The daily schedule of classes offered free to hotel guests includes step aerobics, water aerobics, and yoga. Popular new additions to the roster are Tae-Bo and merengue dance classes.

Set amid beautiful gardens, the 14-story hotel is a quiet, self-contained complex facing the blue waters of the Bay of Banderas. And at this all-inclusive resort, your meals, drinks, and admission to the fitness facilities are included in the daily rate. Puerto Vallarta discos lure guests with complimentary admission passes, but the resort's own nightly entertainment and theme shows are hard to beat.

INSIDER TIP Everything here is included in the room rate, so make sure to grab a surfboard or take an introductory scuba lesson.

Equipment: Free weights, stair climbers, stationary bikes, treadmills, weight-training circuit. **Services:** Acupressure, aromatherapy massage, fango, herbal wrap, loofah body scrub, massage, reflexology. **Swimming:** Pool, beach. **Classes and Programs:** Meditation, scuba lessons, step aerobics, tennis clinic, water aerobics, yoga. **Recreation:** Golf, horseback riding, tennis, water sports.

▦ 214 rooms, 4 suites.

✕ Meals included. International cuisine served at restaurants. **Sample Meals:** Vegetarian chili, grilled fish, sautéed vegetables (lunch); chicken fajitas, pasta primavera, baked snapper, broiled chicken Florentine with steamed vegetables (dinner).

✉ $80 per person, double occupancy. 7-night relaxation package $950 per person, includes 12 spa treatments. 7-night Slimming package $958 per person, includes 12 spa treatments. Daily spa pass $10.

✉ *Km 2.5, Av. Las Palmas, Puerto Vallarta, Jalisco, CP48300,* ☎ *322/ 43–216 or 322/43–308,* 𝖥𝖠𝖷 *322/44–447. www.qualton.com*

RÍO CALIENTE

NUTRITION AND DIET ○ HOLISTIC HEALTH ○ MINERAL SPRINGS

For thousands of years the Huichol tribe has revered the healing qualities of the meandering, steaming river of hot mineral water that gives the Río Caliente Spa its name. This rustic retreat, on 24-acres of pine-forested land, continues to attract an eclectic mix of guests from all over the world in search of stress relief, rest, and relaxation. Whether it's the water (pumped into many of the guest rooms), the reasonable rates (about $100 a day), or the lack of pretension (clothing is optional in the plunge pools), devotees return year after year, often for a month or more at a time.

As you enter the resort's bathhouse, you encounter a 20-ft wall of volcanic rock, in front of which are benches where guests relax while enjoying a sweat. In the Aztec steam room, a stream of steaming mineral water snakes through. Open 24 hours a day, the pools and steam room are places to commune with nature. Try soaking under the stars as steam rises off the pool.

Classes in meditation, tai chi, and yoga are scheduled for all guests who want to participate. Guides lead guests on nature hikes and ecoexpeditions on horseback. Lectures cover everything from bird-watching to local history. For those who are more spontaneous, spur-of-the-moment events are frequently announced on the blackboard outside the dining room.

Spa services are provided by a well-trained staff at prices ranging from $11 for mud wraps to $38 for a massage. A physician supervises treatments to combat aging and stress. It's not luxury pampering here, but the regulars don't seem to care.

The main building houses handsome, comfortable cabanas and rooms, all with fireplaces. There is no air-conditioning, but handcrafted beds and chairs and colorful fabrics woven by local artisans make you feel at home. Once the resort had no phone, but today there is a phone, fax, and computer terminal so guests can keep in touch with the outside world. There's still no address (the resort is in the middle of a forest), but taxis will know how to make the 45-minute trip.

INSIDER TIP Take advantage of the organized shopping trips to the famed crafts market in nearby Guadalajara.

Services: Acupuncture, homeopathy, massage, reflexology, reiki. **Swimming:** Outdoor pool, separate clothing-optional pools for men and women. **Recreation:** Hiking, horseback riding, shopping.

🛏 49 rooms, 2 suites.

✗ Meals included. Vegetarian buffet, including tropical foods like guava, jicama, *zapote,* and *guanabana.* **Sample Meals:** Organic raw greens, raw and cooked vegetables, soups (lunch); salads, home-baked bread and grain casseroles, tropical fruit (dinner).

✉ Nightly rate $92–$106 per person, double occupancy. 7-night package $675 per person, double occupancy. 10-night Stress-Buster package $960 per person, double occupancy. No credit cards.

✉ *Primavera, Mexico*, ☎ *650/615–9543, 800/200C2927 (U.S. reservations)*, ℻ *650/615–0601. www.riocaliente.com*

MEXICO

AVANDARO GOLF & SPA RESORT

LUXURY PAMPERING ○ NUTRITION AND DIET

Golf is the primary attraction at the Avandaro Hotel, and even in the aerobics studio you have a view of golfers strolling leisurely around the 18-hole championship course designed by Percy Cliff. But the Temascaltepec Valley of the Sierra Madre is best known for the curative properties of its waters.

When checking in at the spa, make sure you receive a thorough orientation, as the women's and men's facilities are almost identical. Exercise shorts and T-shirts are provided, and bathrobes and slippers are waiting for you in the locker rooms. In the sunlit atrium, a cold cascade gushes into a whirlpool beside a bubbling hot tub. Nearby are a sauna, a steam room, and a relaxation lounge where you can serve yourself juice and fruit while awaiting a therapist.

The focus of the spa is on stress reduction and anticellulite treatments, which many people believe make a visible difference after a week. Other options include a nonsurgical face-lift and antistress treatments, which use electrodes to promote relaxation.

Accommodations are in Spanish colonial–style villas and motel-style cabins. Suites have pretty seating areas, dining tables, and balconies or terraces. All rooms have wood-burning fireplaces, which come in handy in the winter, when temperatures at night can drop below freezing.

Valle de Bravo's unique attraction is the monarch butterfly migration, when millions of the colorful insects flock here from November through March. Guided hikes of the butterfly sanctuaries provide a close-up view. Hikers are cautioned to tread carefully on the wooded trails so as not to disturb the delicate monarchs.

For a change of pace head into town. The hotel is a mere 15 minutes from the picturesque 16th-century town of Valle de Bravo. Named for local patriot Nicholas Bravo, the town has become something of an artists' colony. Restaurants of all types crowd the cobblestone streets, where galleries, boutiques, and even the odd jazz club now compete with the numerous shops selling imported athletic equipment.

INSIDER TIP Ask for European-trained therapist Rosario Mojico, who—in addition to expertise in facials, massage, and reflexology—offers explanations and advice about all the treatments the spa offers.

Equipment: Free weights, rowing machines, stair climbers, stationary bikes, treadmills, weight-training equipment. **Services:** Aromatherapy, herbal wrap, loofah salt glow, massage, reflexology, shiatsu. **Swimming:** Pool, children's pool. **Classes and Programs:** Personal training, yoga. **Recreation:** Wilderness hiking.

▦ 22 rooms, 44 suites.

✗ Meals à la carte. Spa cuisine in Las Terrazas restaurant; Japanese food available weekends. **Sample Meals:** Spinach soup, baked trout, apple sorbet (lunch); artichoke vinaigrette, vegetable couscous (dinner).

▨ Nightly rate $126–$214 per person, double occupancy. 2-night Anti-Aging package $1,727 per person, double occupancy. 3-night Anti-Stress package $2,015 per person, double occupancy. AE. MC, V.

✉ *Vega del Río, s/n Fraccionamiento Avandaro, Valle de Bravo, CP51200,* ☎ *726/60–366, or 800/223–6510,* 🖷 *726/60–905.*

BALNEARIOS

MINERAL SPRINGS

A vast volcanic zone cuts all the way through the central part of the country from the Gulf of Mexico to the Pacific coast. Hundreds of hot springs dot the region, and one state—Aguascalientes—has been named for the hot waters.

Offering little more than rustic accommodations and a relaxing soak in public pools, the balnearios in this region are a time-honored tradition in Mexico. Although most of the springs are in their natural state, some have spas built around them that are popular with families getting away for the weekend. The splashing and cavorting of children at these spas creates a cheerful atmosphere.

This region includes some of Mexico's most dramatic mountain scenery, which makes the balnearios popular for nature lovers. It's not uncommon for people to go hiking in the morning, then return for a relaxing mud bath. Below are some of the balnearios where "taking the waters" can be enjoyed year-round.

Agua Hedionda. Close to the city of Cuernavaca, Agua Hedionda fills two public pools and eight private pools with its sulfuric water. Facilities include showers and dressing rooms, and the resort houses a restaurant with dancing on weekends. Across the road, Hotel Villasor offers 60 rooms, 3 suites, and a restaurant with vegetarian selections. Rooms are $45.

✉ *Av. Progreso s/n, Cuautla, Morelos, Mexico, CP62743,* ☎ *735/25–521,* 🖷 *725/70–067.*

Las Estacas. Towering stands of bamboo and royal palms shade the volcanic spring that serves as the centerpiece of this nature preserve. The spring known as El Borbollón, or "the bubbling one," spews forth more than 2,000 gallons of water per second. Clear and refreshingly cool, the river created by the spring is popular with families who swim, dive, and float along in tire tubes. Overnight accommodations are in 14 nicely maintained cabins for couples and 31 larger cabins for families and groups. Visitors relax under *palapas* (thatch-roof, open-air huts) as the children play on the painted slides and swings adjoining a concrete swimming pool. Popular pastimes include horseback riding and scuba lessons. About 45 minutes from Cuernavaca, the park is on a former ranch where Tarzan and 300 other movies were filmed. The area retains its idyllic charm.

✉ *Km 6, Carretera Tlaltizapán, Cuautla, Tlaltizapán, Morelos, CP62770,* ☎ *734/50–077,* FAX *734/50–350.*

Hotel Aldea del Bazar. While surfers congregate on the Pacific beaches, you can retreat to a tropical garden at the Hotel Aldea del Bazar. In the Spa Pre-Hispanico you can try a *temazcal,* the traditional steam bath that Native people used for hundreds of years before the Spanish arrived. Start with a body scrub and massage under the palm trees, then sit in one of the marble-wall temazcals (one for groups, one solo) as herbal water is poured on hot rocks. Try a facial with mud from volcanic ash. Connected to the beach by a long walkway, the white-wall hotel's 46 deluxe rooms and two suites create a Moorish fantasy, commanding top prices for the area, about $130 a night. A modest restaurant is adjacent to the huge swimming pool. For nature lovers, a marine ecology center dedicated to the protection of sea turtles called Centro Mexicano de la Tortuga is about an hour's drive down the coast.

✉ *Av. Benito Juárez Lote No. 7, Puerto Escondido, Oaxaca, CP71980* ☎ *95/82–0508.*

Hotel Balneario Atzimba. Adjacent to a popular water park, this rustic 19-room resort and campground is about 40 minutes from Morelia, capital of Michoacán. There are 82°F thermal water baths, a small restaurant, and lots of space for unwinding. Hikers may want to head to the nearby butterfly sanctuaries during the mating season, from November to March.

✉ *Av. Lázaro Cárdenas s/n, Zinapécuaro, Michoacán, CP58930* ☎ *435/50–042,* FAX *435/50–050.*

Hotel Balneario de Lourdes. An old hacienda converted into a spa, Hotel Balneario de Lourdes boasts water so healthful that it is bottled next door. Thirty-three miles south of the attractive colonial city of San Luis Potosí, the hotel features a heated pool and a whirlpool filled with the famous water. Guests can relax with squash, Ping-Pong, volleyball, or even horseback riding. The restaurant offers ordinary fare, and vegetarian meals tend to be simply the standard meals without meat. Any of the 33 rooms costs about $40 for two, including meals.

✉ *Reservation office: Libramiento Sur 240A, Fraccionamiento Las Cumbres, San Luis Potosí, Mexico,* ☎ *48/25–1434.*

Hotel Balneario La Caldera. Private baths filled with 169°F thermal mineral water, two swimming pools, an outdoor whirlpool, two tennis courts, and extensive gardens are features of the 116-room Hotel Balneario La Caldera. All rooms have private bath, television, and air-conditioning. Rates are about $95. A good restaurant, popular on weekends, is on the premises. The hotel is on Highway 110, 40 minutes west of Irapuato, Mexico's strawberry center.

✉ *Km 29 Libramiento, Carretera Abasolo, Abasolo, Michoacán, CP36970,* ☎ *469/30–020 and 469/30–021.*

Hotel Taninul. Time seems to stand still in this once-glamorous tropical hideaway a few hours south of the Texas border. Tour groups from the United States head here for the hot sulfur pool that has often been referred to as a fountain of youth. Fifty-five miles from Tampico, the three-star hotel has 132 air-conditioned rooms and 12 suites. Overnight accommodations cost about $40.

✉ *Km 15 Carretera Cd. Valles, Tampico Ciudad Valles, San Luis Potosí, CP76000,* ☎ *138/20–000,* FAX *138/24–414.*

⊞ **Hotel Tepozteco.** About 45 minutes east of the city of Cuernavaca, the sulfuric thermal springs at the Hotel Tepozteco were a favorite retreat of the 16th-century Aztec ruler Montezuma. They are still popular today, and the vast spring-fed swimming pools are alive with locals on weekends. Part of the vast Oaxtepec Vacation Complex, the 40-room hotel provide overnight accommodations for about $50.

✉ *Centro Vacacional Oaxtepec, Morelos, CP62738,* ☎ *735/60–101,* FAX *735/60–093 or 735/60–097.*

Las Termales de Atotonilco. Two spring-fed pools, several wading pools, and a restaurant enhance this public spa. Dressing rooms and lockers are also available. There are also tennis and basketball courts, as well as a game room for more sedentary pursuits such as chess and dominoes.

✉ *Atotonilco s/n, Jonacatec, Cuautla, Morelos, CP62925,* ☎ *735/50–820.*

IXTAPAN RESORT & SPA

MINERAL SPRINGS

In the 16th century, Aztec ruler Montezuma was known to bathe at the thermal springs at Ixtapan de la Sal. Today he has been followed by the multitudes who come to the Ixtapan Resort & Spa, the largest thermal-springs resort in Mexico.

Opened in 1942, the art deco hotel has long attracted visitors to the huge lake filled from a spring in an extinct volcano. But the crowd here is often a noisy one, making this a less than desirable choice for those who want peace and quiet.

The hotel's spa includes many programs that take advantage of the spring, including aquaerobics in an outdoor thermal-water pool. The spa also has a marble whirlpool, where you can relax while awaiting a facial or massage in private cubicles. Therapists here are friendly and offer an acceptable range of services, including fresh cucumber and tomato facials, but the exercise equipment is minimal.

Younger visitors will probably want to set their own schedule. Mountain bikes are available, and you can hike in the nearby desert. There are appealing sightseeing tours to the colonial city of Cuernavaca and the narrow winding streets of Taxco, where silver shops compete for your attention with baroque churches and chapels.

The hotel is a family-orientated establishment, and it offers train rides, horse-drawn carriage rides, and a bowling alley. Although the facilities are constantly being refurbished (a new dining room was recently unveiled), the carpeting and decor manage to retain a drab air of bygone better days. But if budgetary constraints are your prime concern, this is the choice for combining fun and fitness.

INSIDER TIP If you are seeking romance, you will be delighted by the luxurious cabins that hold two-person Roman baths fashioned from mottled green and brown marble.

Equipment: Free weights, rowing machines, stair climbers, stationary bikes, treadmills, weight-training circuit. **Services:** Acupuncture, herbal wraps, massage, mud wraps, reflexology, yoga. **Swimming:** Indoor and outdoor pools. **Recreation:** Golf, horseback riding, paddle tennis, tennis.

⚏ 167 rooms, 50 villas.

✕ Meals included. Full menu available in dining room or spa. Spa menu available. **Sample Meals:** Chicken with mushrooms, tuna platter (lunch); fresh trout, omelet, cheese plate (dinner).

⌨ Nightly rate $185, double occupancy. 7-night Classic spa program $1,271 per person, includes meals, salon treatments, spa treatments, and golf. AE, MC, V.

⊠ *Ixtapan de la Sal, Mexico, CP51900* ☏ *714/30–021, or 800/638–7950,* FAX *714/30–856. www.spamexico.com*

MORELOS

HOSTERIA LAS QUINTAS

LUXURY PAMPERING

This delightful spa is in the gardens of a hotel right in the heart of Cuernavaca, a city long known for its delicious climate that seems like perpetual spring. Nearly seven years old, the facilities have graduated from being a beauty salon to having been designated one of the Top 25 destination spas in North America (one of only two in Mexico). It fully merits its growing reputation.

Las Quintas prides itself on being the first spa to develop ecotour programs as part of its services. Adventure travelers might not be excited about the these outings, but spa goers may enjoy the challenge of scaling a pyramid instead of using a stair climber. Outings include a visit to the town of Tepoztlan, where a steep, rocky trail leads to a mountaintop pyramid. How about an "aerobic shopping tour" to Taxco, where silver sellers outnumber the tourists? Guests, the majority of whom come from the United States, are well taken care of by English-speaking guides.

The most welcoming of the noteworthy spas in Morelos, Las Quintas is infused with light and comfort. The waiting area affords a view of the spa's pool and rock cascade, while fresh air wafts in from the lush gardens. Guests can help themselves to juice and fruit as they await treatments. The 10 therapists—including two men—are prompt and professional.

In addition to the spa treatments, there are 10 organized classes included in a spa package, including aerobics, dance, and reiki. There is no better way to start the day than the 8 AM yoga classes offered by Enrique Castells. After spreading your towel on thick springy grass, you can't help but relax to the feeling of the sun on your skin, the scent of tropical flowers, and the trickle of nearby fountains.

Accommodations, mostly two-story suites, are in colonial-style buildings enveloped in deep pink bougainvillea. Reception can be a little hectic, especially if there is a convention, and there are no seats to rest on while you are waiting, but once you pass through to the gardens you have embarked on a restful experience.

INSIDER TIP The specialty here is the sensory-deprivation flotation tank—the only one in Latin America. It can send you to sleep or offer you a pure space for concentrated thinking.

Equipment: Cross-country skiing machines, free weights, stair climbers, stationary bikes, treadmills, weight-training equipment. **Services:** Body scrub, hydromassage, mineral mud wrap, pressotherapy, reflexology, shiatsu, thalassotherapy. **Swimming:** 2 pools (1 heated). **Classes and Programs:** Aerobics, dance, meditation, reiki, yoga. **Recreation:** Daily ecotours to pyramids and other archaeological sites.

▼ 60 suites.

✕ Meals included. International and low-calorie menu served in same restaurant. **Sample Meals:** Mixed crepes, salmon and endive salad (lunch); chicken liver pâté, black-bean cream soup, rack of lamb (dinner).

🕾 Nightly rate $195 per room. 2-night Stress Relief program $559–$665. 4-night Supreme Pampering package $1,035–$1,247. 7-day Slim Down, Shape Up program $2,135–$2,506.

✉ *Blvd. Diaz Ordaz 9, Colonia Cantarranas, Cuernavaca, Morelos, CP62440,* ☎ *7/318–3949 or 888/772–7639,* FAX *7/318–3895. www.hlasquintas.com*

HOTEL HACIENDA COCOYOC

LUXURY PAMPERING

Discovering a former sugar plantation comes as a surprise when you enter the ancient walls of the Hacienda Cocoyoc. The 22-acre complex includes a 17th-century chapel, an aqueduct that is still in use, and a family mansion filled with heirlooms. Secluded from the outside world of noisy truck traffic and sugar-cane farming, this is quintessential old-fashioned Mexico.

Set amid lawns and vast swimming pools, the spa building is a separate enclave with New Age music, a little loud for the taste of some guests who prefer to listen to the birds. There are separate wings for men and women, each with steam bath, sauna, showers, wet-treatment rooms, and private massage rooms. As sunlight streams into the lounges, where you await treatments in the robes and sandals provided by the spa, attendants hand you lime-water refreshers.

With a wide range of treatments available à la carte, the spa concentrates on relaxation, detoxification, and revitalization. The spa environment itself, all polished stone and wood in golden tones, is conducive to releasing stress. Shaded walkways lined by ancient banyan trees lead from the spa to the guest rooms. Standard Mexican fare is available at four restaurants, where informality is the rule and calories aren't counted.

Spa services can be combined with golf at an 18-hole course about 15 minutes away or at the 9-hole course adjoining the spa. Although the workout room, which has Nautilus equipment, is small, trainers are on hand to help with workouts or lead aquaerobics classes. Guests can also play tennis or go horseback riding.

Accommodations are in high-ceiling suites in the mansion and in private casitas, neither with air-conditioning. Staying in one of the colonial-style casitas that border the gardens adds a romantic touch. Each casita comes with a walled garden where a pool big enough for two provides for a refreshing dip in the morning or evening. In the bathrooms hand-painted tiles cover the walls and step-down shower.

INSIDER TIP History buffs, take note: there are dozens of archaeological sites within 45 minutes of Hotel Hacienda Cocoyoc. One of the closest is Pantitlan, an Aztec site that is home to ten pyramids.

Equipment: Stair climbers, stationary bikes, treadmills, weight-training equipment. **Services:** Body composition analysis, fango wrap, hydromassage, loofah scrub, massage, pressotherapy, reflexology, salt glow. **Swimming:** 4 pools. **Classes and Programs:** Water aerobics. **Recreation:** Golf, jogging, tennis.

▭ 183 rooms, 24 suites.

✕ All meals à la carte. 4 restaurants serving various cuisines open on different days. **Sample Meals:** Spinach crepe, enchiladas (lunch); stuffed chicken breast, grilled fish fillet with steamed vegetables (dinner).

▨ 2-night Tranquility package $420 per person, double occupancy. 4-night spa and golf package $966 per person, double occupancy. AE, MC, V.

✉ *Carretera Federal Cuernavaca Cuautla Km 32.5, Cocoyoc, Morelos, CP62739,* ☎ *735/622–11, or 735/612–11,* ⅢⅩ *735/612–12. www.cocoyoc.com*

MISIÓN DEL SOL

LUXURY PAMPERING ○ HOLISTIC HEALTH

With crystals studding the grounds to absorb bad and impart good energy, the Misión del Sol is the most New Age of Mexico's spas. Opened at the end of 1996, it aims to be a "center for human awareness."

No cars are allowed, so you are escorted by golf cart to the reception lounge. There you are greeted at a massive *mandala,* or symbol of the universe, created by Tibetan monks. People speak quietly and dress in soft cotton clothing to keep up the air of serenity. Priests and gurus of differing persuasions give conferences here, trading words of wisdom for small fortunes.

More retreat than resort, the Misión del Sol offers programs that blend many philosophies and religions, seeking universal truth. Creature comforts are deluxe, however, with accommodations in two-story lodges and family-size villas. The well-lighted rooms have high ceilings and huge mirrors in the shape of a sun.

Secluded on the grounds are a meditation pavilion, built around a Zen sand garden, the spa complex with soaking pool tiled in zodiac signs, and a beautiful temazcal (Aztec steam room). The staff is bilingual, and the guests are an interesting mix: pensive Europeans, stressed-out Mexico City professionals, and mothers bonding with daughters at a special retreat. The food is vegetarian and very good indeed, but you have to endure New Age music almost everywhere you go.

INSIDER TIP If you aren't into New Age philosophy, this might not be the place for you. The somewhat precious atmosphere isn't to everyone's taste.

Equipment: Free weights, stair climbers, weight-training equipment. **Services:** Aromatherapy, body scrub, chromotherapy, craniosacral therapy, crystal therapy, mud body wrap, polarity therapy, reflexology, reiki, seaweed body wrap, shiatsu. **Swimming:** Pool. **Classes and Programs:**

Aerobics, aquaerobics, various workshops. **Recreation:** Biking, hiking, tennis, volleyball.

🛏 90 rooms, 10 suites.

✕ Meals included. Mostly vegetarian meals served at Restaurante del Sol. **Sample Meals:** Beet soup, salad, vegetarian burrito (lunch); vegetarian lasagna, tamales (dinner).

🎟 1-night Full Moon package $258–$264 per person, includes meals and spa treatments. 2-night health package $525–537 per person, includes meals and spa treatments. MC, V.

✉ *Av. Gral. Diego González 31, Col. Parres, Cuernavaca, Morelos, CP62550,* ☎ *732/10–999, 800/999–9100, or 800/448–8355,* FAX *732/ 11–195. www.misiondelsol.com.mx*

NAYARIT

PARADISE VILLAGE BEACH RESORT

LUXURY PAMPERING

Bring the family for a beach vacation while you luxuriate at one of the fanciest spas in Mexico. Set on a peninsula between the beach and marina, the spa at Paradise Village Beach Resort is a modern Mayan temple of glass and marble devoted to health, fitness, and beauty.

Inside this cool oasis are separate wings for men and women, each equipped with private hydrotherapy tubs, whirlpools, saunas, and steam rooms. The coed cardiovascular and weight training rooms have state-of-the-art equipment and views of the ocean. Aerobics classes are scheduled throughout the day in a mirrored studio. There's an indoor lap pool, so you can escape the sun and the kids at the outdoor pool.

Spa director Diana Mestre, an old hand in these parts, brings together ancient healing arts and the latest electronic equipment. Start with a computerized diagnosis of your fitness level, then set up a personalized program of preventive and rejuvenation treatments. Workouts with a personal trainer can help you get started on an exercise program. Therapy selections are extensive, from sea fango for tired and swollen feet to a milk bath that rehydrates your entire body. You are then escorted to a private marble-wall room for a massage, a facial, and wraps.

Accommodations in the eight-story beachfront tower have two or three bedrooms, full kitchens, living rooms, and private terraces. The hotel features a pool complete with rocky grottoes, flowing waterfalls, and a Mayan-style temple. There is an 18-hole golf course at the resort, and guests have access to another nearby.

Completely self-contained, the resort provides lots of recreation options. Outdoor adventures begin steps from the spa, where sailing courses, speedboat excursions, and deep-sea fishing are offered at the marina. Bike tours are organized for basic and advanced bikers.

Eight miles north of the old cobbled streets of Puerto Vallarta, there are numerous shopping and nightlife options. For privacy head north to the town of Bucerías, then follow the bend of Banderas Bay past several small and pristine beaches. You can attend bullfights from November to April on Wednesday at 5 PM at a modest Plaza del Toros.

INSIDER TIP Want to see more of the area? Kayaking is the best way to explore Banderas Bay and its marine estuaries.

Equipment: Free weights, stationary bikes, treadmills, weight-training circuit. **Services:** Aromatherapy, facial, herbal wrap, loofah body scrub, paraffin body treatment, reflexology, shiatsu, thalassotherapy, Vichy shower. **Swimming:** Indoor and outdoor pools, beach. **Classes and Programs:** Aerobics, fitness evaluation. **Recreation:** Fishing, golf, horseback riding, kayaking, tennis, windsurfing.

⊞ 265 apartments.

✕ Meal included. Choice of spa menu or regular restaurant.

🖭 3-night Renewal package $550–$727 per person, double occupancy. 7-night Stress Reducer package $890–$1,180 per person, double occupancy. Day packages $45, includes lunch. AE, MC, V.

✉ *Av. de los Cocoteros 001, Nueva Vallarta, Nayarit, CP63731,* ☎ *322/66–770 or 800/995–5714,* 🅵🅰🆇 *322/66–726. www.paradisevillage.com*

MELIA CANCUN RESORT & SPA

LUXURY PAMPERING

When you want it all—luxury accommodations, sybaritic spa, archaeological sites to explore, nightlife to celebrate—this is the place to fulfill fantasies of Mexico. Set amid the strip of high-rise hotels for which Cancún is renowned, the Melia is perched on a spectacular white-sand beach overlooking the turquoise waters of the Caribbean. Enjoying massages poolside is the prescription for relaxation, and outdoor treatment cabanas let you enjoy the sea air without the sun. At night torches illuminate the cabanas, contributing to the romantic mood.

Secluded in an atrium garden, the spa provides a cool respite from the beach. Compact and coed, the 10,000-square-ft facility boasts a well-equipped, air-conditioned fitness center and 11 treatment rooms, including one where couples can be massaged together.

The spa charges a daily fee for use of the facilities, which is waived when you book a treatment. Because the spa lacks an aerobics studio, exercise classes are held on the pool terrace and in the swimming pool. Specialties here are the Mayan clay mask, sea-salt loofah scrub, and aromatherapy massage.

Rising nine stories above the spa, the hotel calls to mind Mayan temple design. Guest rooms are comfortable and modern, and most have a balcony facing the sea. An attentive bilingual staff provides information on local events and attractions. Bus and boat tours to Mayan sites are scheduled daily.

....

INSIDER TIP At the end of a long day, try the spa's aloe spritzer—a body shampoo followed by a cooling aloe body gel.

....

Equipment: Free weights, stair climbers, stationary bikes, treadmills, weight-training equipment. **Services:** Aloe body wrap, aromatherapy massage, hydrating facial, loofah body scrub. **Swimming:** 3 pools, beach. **Classes and Programs:** Exercise classes. **Recreation:** Golf, tennis, water sports.

🏨 800 rooms, 250 suites.

✕ Meal plan optional. International menus in five restaurants; spa meals served in the Spa Caribe. Poolside service for lunch. **Sample Meals:** Grilled grouper, vegetarian burrito, salads (lunch); fresh pasta, grilled chicken, vegetarian plate (dinner).

🖾 Nightly rate $290–$350 per room. Daily spa package $100–$237. AE, MC, V.

🖂 *Km 16.5 Blvd. Kukulkan, Zona Hotelera, Cancún, Quintana Roo, CP77500,* ☎ *988/111–00 or 800/336–3542,* FAX *988/51–263. www.solmelia.es*

ROYAL HIDEAWAY PLAYACAR

LUXURY PAMPERING

Located on the Yucatán Peninsula about 40 mi south of Cancún, the Royal Hideaway Playacar was the first Mexican resort to feature French thalassotherapy treatments. Other therapies that use seaweed and seawater are still very popular here.

Designed to resemble a Spanish colonial village, the resort includes 11 villa-type buildings with two- and three-story rooms and suites. Things are a bit more formal here than in other Mexican resorts. You might want to bring dressier clothes for the evening meal, which features live entertainment.

Facing the Caribbean, the spa has a cream-and-green color scheme accented by warm-tone woods. The facility is known for its wide range of specialized massages. Therapists will administer facials, body wraps, and relaxing hydrotherapy treatments. Spa service is à la carte, and clients can design their own programs according to their needs.

Peak season is from November to April, but recreation at the resort is nonstop. Guests have unlimited use of kayaks and snorkeling gear. Organized activities include basketball and croquet. Special fees apply for golf, horseback riding, scuba diving, and deep-sea fishing.

The hotel tends to attract young couples and families with children, so things can get a bit noisy. Ferries from Cozumel dock nearby, and cruise-ship passengers come ashore here, adding to the crowds at certain times.

....
INSIDER TIP The lovely landscaped grounds of the hotel make it popular for weddings. Honeymooners also seem to love this upscale hideaway.
....

Equipment: Free weights, stationary bikes, treadmills, weight-training equipment. **Services:** Aromatherapy, body wraps, hydrotherapy. **Swimming:** 2 outdoor pools, 6 spa pools. **Recreation:** Basketball, bikes, billiards, chess, croquet, golf, horseback riding, shuffleboard, tennis, water sports.

🏠 200 rooms, 6 suites.

✕ Meals included. Thai, Italian, Mexican, and international cuisine at four restaurants. **Sample Meals:** Grilled fish and chicken, vegetarian burger, vegetarian pizza, seafood salad (lunch); pasta, vegetarian lasagna, grilled salmon and swordfish, Caesar salad (dinner).

🖾 Nightly rate $400 per room. 2-day spa package $360. Day packages $120–$234. AE, MC, V.

🖂 *Lote Hotelero No. 6, Desarollo Playacar, Playa del Carmen, Quintana Roo, CP77710,* ☎ *988/52–987,* FAX *988/52–987. www.royalhideaways.com/playacar*

THE CARIBBEAN,
THE BAHAMAS,
BERMUDA

S pas are nothing new in the Caribbean. After all, French king Louis XIV built baths in the 17th century for his troops at the hot springs on St. Lucia. A century later British admiral Lord Horatio Nelson sailed to Nevis for the restorative baths.

It's still possible to hit the island hot springs. On Guadeloupe you can take an excursion to Bouillante (which literally means "boiling") and bathe in the aromatic thermal springs. The nearby spa at Espace Santé de Ravine Chaude still uses waters emanating from a dormant volcano for therapeutic purposes.

Today Caribbean spas offer so much more than just a few years ago. Many focus on European spa treatments that you may not be able to find in the United States. Ionithermie treatments, which use electrical stimuli to firm and tone skin and help rid the body of cellulite, are available at Cambridge Beaches in Bermuda. French balneotherapy, which uses seawater and seaweed, is a draw at Privilege Resort & Spa on St. Martin.

In the Caribbean you'll find some of the most opulent pleasure palaces around, from the hillside Jalousie Hilton Resort & Spa, in St. Lucia, where you arrive via helicopter, to the sprawling Wyndham El Conquistador Resort & Country Club, where you can gaze down from a 300-ft bluff to where the Atlantic Ocean meets the Caribbean Sea. But there are less expensive alternatives as well. The Bahamas has the no-frills Sivananda Ashram, on Paradise Beach in Nassau. St. John, in the U.S. Virgin Islands, is the winter outpost for the New York–based Omega Institute's personal-growth programs. And in Puerto Rico the rain forest provides a backdrop for meditation at La Casa de Vida Natural.

Today the Caribbean spa experience is most likely a mixture of fun and fitness. You'll be disappointed if you expect a self-contained spa with structured programs. Things are laid-back at most resorts, but that doesn't mean there isn't anything to do. You can go scuba diving at the Harbour Village Beach Resort, in Bonaire; play tennis at Half Moon Golf, Tennis, & Beach Club, in Jamaica; or hit the links at the Four Seasons Resort, on Nevis.

All prices in this chapter are in U.S. dollars.

ARUBA

HYATT REGENCY ARUBA

LUXURY PAMPERING

Set on a 12-acre strip of beach, the Hyatt Regency Aruba Resort & Casino focuses on water sports. An 8,000-square-ft, three-level swimming pool with cascading waterfalls and secluded lagoons faces a powdery white beach. A 50-ft luxury catamaran takes you out for sunset cruises, and two dive boats ferry you to coral reefs and sunken shipwrecks. You can also head out on your own in canoes or sailboats.

If you don't want to get wet, there's still plenty to do. Hike on the rugged coast near Boca Prins to Andicouri for a romantic picnic on a secluded beach surrounded by a coconut plantation. Aruba's volcanic origins are revealed at Casi Bari, a rock garden of giants, and at tall, unusual rock formations called Ayo. Nearby Arikok National Park is the place to spot iguanas, hares, wild goats, and the rare wayaca tree.

After all that hiking you'll need some R&R. The Hyatt Regency Aruba Spa is a full-service facility offering massage, facials, and hydrotherapy using Pevonia products. The fitness facilities—including exercise room, outdoor whirlpool, and sundeck for aerobics classes—overlook the sea and are open to all hotel guests.

Golfers gain a new perspective on the island's desert landscape of cacti, wind-shaped divi-divi trees, and rock formations at the Tierra Del Sol Golf & Country Club. The 18-hole, par-71 course designed by Robert Trent Jones II is open to the public.

Rooms and suites are in a nine-story tower and in two wings of four and five stories. The Regency Club has 27 deluxe rooms, with lounge and concierge service. All rooms have a balcony. Children under 12 stay free with parents.

Four restaurants offer heart-healthy menu options, including vegetarian dishes. The snack bar in the health spa sells herbal teas, protein drinks, and fruit. A poolside restaurant fashioned out of native coral stone is good for lounging.

INSIDER TIP Take some time to explore the island. Besides the glitzy casinos of Palm Beach, it has colorful Dutch colonial villages, a historic fort, and caves covered with ancient petroglyphs.

Equipment: Free weights, rowing machines, stair climbers, stationary bikes, treadmills, weight-training circuit. **Services:** Acupressure, massage, reflexology, shiatsu. **Swimming:** Pool, ocean beach. **Recreation:**

Biking, tennis, water sports. **Children's Programs:** Camp Hyatt schedules activities for ages 3–12.

▣ 342 rooms, 18 suites.

✕ Meals à la carte. Four restaurants serve Caribbean, Continental, Italian, and Spanish cuisine. Low-calorie options available. **Sample Meals:** Salads, sandwiches (lunch); custom-made pizzas, fajitas, paella for two, tapas (dinner).

▦ Nightly rate $205–$430 per room. AE, DC, MC, V.

⊠ *85 Juan E. Irausquin Blvd., Aruba,* ☏ *297/86–1234 or 800/233–1234,* ℻ *297/86–1682. www.hyatt.com*

SANDALS ROYAL BAHAMIAN RESORT AND SPA

LUXURY PAMPERING

This all-inclusive couples-only resort is a private oasis of luxury with what might be the best spa in the Bahamas. You can work out on weight-training equipment in an air-conditioned penthouse with ocean views or get your feet wet trying one of the numerous water sports.

The spa, which is accessible for those with disabilities, is adjacent to the manor and swimming pool. The facilities include a Vichy shower, hydrotherapy tubs, plunge pools, and seven treatment rooms. Among the sophisticated therapies are an herbal bath and a face masque with spirulina, a type of algae. There is a beauty salon for hair and nail care. Beachside aerobics and aquaerobics classes are scheduled daily, but there are no indoor facilities for group exercise. Guests from other hotels and cruise ships are accommodated on a space-available basis.

Spread over 23 acres of landscaped gardens and beach, the resort includes a sports complex with croquet, tennis, and volleyball. Sun worshipers can retreat to Sandals Cay, a private offshore island, and enjoy a secluded beach, then eat lunch at a breezy bar or take a dip in a freshwater pool and whirlpool. Water-sports equipment is complimentary at a dockside pavilion, where guests can take a free scuba course. Scuba trips for certified divers are included, with equipment at no charge.

Guests stay in the beachfront towers or deluxe garden cottages featuring a separate pool complex. Beachfront suites provide private balconies with sweeping ocean views. Honeymooners gain added privacy in garden villa suites. Opened in 1948 as the Balmoral Club, a private reserve for the rich and titled, the six-story manor was joined in 1998 by the 210-room Windsor wing of luxury suites. Facing a powdery sand beach, the twin towers frame vast swimming pools, where waterfalls massage your shoulders, a water mist sprays cooling vapors, and the open-air bar has swim-up service.

INSIDER TIP To feel really pampered, treat yourself to gourmet cuisine in the Crystal Room, where white-glove dinner service must be reserved in advance.

Equipment: Free weights, stair climbers, stationary bikes, treadmills, weight-training circuit. **Services:** Aromatherapy, body scrubs, herbal wrap, hydrotherapy, massage, mud bath, reflexology. **Swimming:** Pools, beach. **Recreation:** Billiards, boating, canoeing, croquet, karaoke, kayaking, scuba diving, shuffleboard, snorkeling, tennis, volleyball, waterskiing, windsurfing.

⚏ 196 rooms, 27 suites.

✕ Meals included. 8 restaurants serve cuisines from Caribbean to Continental. All offer heart-healthy options. **Sample Meals:** Conch fritters, seafood salad, grilled grouper (lunch); mousse of Bahamian conch and scallops baked in saffron sauce, grouper in pastry with sabayon sauce, roasted rack of lamb with herbs (dinner).

⚏ $325–$610 per person, double occupancy. 7-night package $2,740–$3,050 per person, double occupancy. AE, MC, V.

⚏ *Box C.B. 13005, Cable Beach, Nassau, Bahamas,* ☎ *242/327–6400 or 800/726–3257,* FAX *242/327—1894. www.sandals.com*

SIVANANDA ASHRAM YOGA RETREAT

HOLISTIC HEALTH

Even those who are out of shape are soon doing shoulder stands at this retreat on one of the finest beaches in the Bahamas. That's the point, since the Sivananda Ashram attracts an eclectic group of yoga devotees ranging from beginners to experts. Equal parts spiritual retreat and tropical holiday, the ashram operates educational programs that are practical and affordable.

Casuarina pines and palm trees shade the retreat and lend privacy from the holiday crowd at nearby Club Med. Although huge luxury hotels (including the sprawling Atlantis property) are a short walk away, the environment here is quiet and suffused with a mystical quality. The main house, once the beachfront refuge of a wealthy family, has been leased to the ashram, in appreciation for healing services, since 1967. The structure might have sunk into the sand long ago without the volunteer labor of members of the ashram.

Based on the teachings of Swami Vishnu Devananda, the yogic discipline and vegetarian diet here are identical to other Sivananda facilities in California, New York, and Québec. The regimen is intensive, and attendance at classes and meditations is mandatory for all guests. Mornings begin at 6 with meditation, chanting, and study. Yogic exercises, or asanas, designed to stretch and invigorate the body, are held at 8 AM and 4 PM. Between these sessions you can enjoy brunch and then a romp on the beach or a relaxing massage.

Meals are a communal affair, with buffets of steamed vegetables, lentils, and salads. The food is fairly bland, as no spices, onion, or garlic are used. After meals guests wash their own plates and utensils and dry them on open-air racks. For snacks there is a boutique that also provides books and yogic gear. There's no air-conditioning at this retreat, but a water-filtration system provides plenty of cool, chemical-free drinking water.

Lodging is in dormitories and cabins furnished with bare essentials. Each room has one to four beds and comes with linens and towels. The showers, toilets, and laundry facilities are communal. Transportation to Nassau is provided by the ashram's boat or, for a few dollars each way, the Paradise Island Ferry runs frequently.

INSIDER TIP Don't want to stay in one of the ashram's cabins? Many guests prefer to bring their own tent and camp among the tropical shrubbery.

Services: Massage, reflexology, shiatsu. **Swimming:** Beach. **Classes and Programs:** Personal counseling, yoga workshops. **Recreation:** Tennis, volleyball. **Children's Programs:** Yoga instruction for children.

▣ 103 beds in dormitory rooms and cabins with shared baths, 50 campsites.

✗ Meals included. Two vegetarian buffets served daily. **Sample Meals:** Lentil loaf, spinach, wheat bread (lunch); tofu stir-fry with rice, steamed vegetables, green salad, basmati rice, greens (dinner).

▧ Nightly rate $55–$70 daily per person in dormitory rooms, $60–$90 per person in cabin. Tent spaces $50–$64 per person. MC, V.

✉ *Box N7550, Paradise Island, Nassau, Bahamas,* ☎ *242/363–2902 or 800/783–9642,* FAX *242/363–3783. www.sivananda.org/paradise.htm*

BELIZE

THE SPA AT CHAA CREEK

LUXURY PAMPERING

The Spa at Chaa Creek is the newest addition at Chaa Creek Cottages, a resort focusing on ecotourism on a 330-acre private reserve in the mountainous rain forest of the Cayo District. The spa was the brain-child of Bryony Fleming, a licensed aesthetician whose parents own the lodge. Fleming has created a wonderful retreat, combining the serenity of the surrounding rain forest with her menu of therapeutic treatments. The result is a complete mind and body rejuvenation experience.

Upon entering the spa, relaxation and contentment set in. Cream-color gauze wafts in the breeze; local artwork and elegant furnishings are just the beginning. The facility is spotlessly clean and staffed by highly trained therapists who are licensed in their fields of expertise. The spa is fully appointed with state-of-the-art Pevonia equipment, including a hydrotherapy tub and a Vichy shower.

For relaxation a variety of massages is on the menu, including polarity therapy. Lulled by meditative music, you are eased into a peaceful state of mind with the calming scents of eucalyptus and rosemary. Afterward, gentle manipulation of your limbs and key pressure points helps to realign your body and invigorate your mind. Among the body treatments offered are wraps, scrubs, and body polishing. An extensive list of facial treatments and masks will amaze you with immediate results. Guests are welcome to laze the day away between treatments, lounging on the deck or in hammocks.

Lodging at Chaa Creek is a true experience, with thatch-roof cottages set among the gardens at the edge of the rain forest. All rooms have private baths and are decorated with regional textiles and objets d'art and lighted by kerosene lamps—there are no phones, television, or air-conditioning. Pavilions house the bar and restaurant. On-site activities that will prime you for the comforts of the spa include hiking and bird-watching along a network of trails, horseback riding, swimming, and canoeing. Expand these adventures with off-site excursions to local archeological sites as well as the Mayan ruins of Tikal in Guatemala.

Normally, lodging packages can be booked three to four weeks in advance, but for holiday periods book six months ahead. Spa treatments can be booked when you reserve your room. The lodge and its activities have long been popular with families. Children six years and up are also welcome at the spa when accompanied by a parent.

INSIDER TIP Come prepared for tropical weather. December and January have highs of 80°F–85°F, while the rest of the year temperatures are closer to 90°F. At night temperatures drop to 55°F–70°F.

Services: Aromatherapy, body polish, hydrotherapy, polarity therapy, massage, salt glow, seaweed wrap, Vichy shower. **Swimming:** River. **Recreation:** Biking, bird-watching, canoeing, horseback riding.

⊡ 19 cottages, 2 garden suites.

✕ Meals à la carte. Restaurant is open 6:30 AM–11 PM, serving three meals daily. Most special diets can be accommodated with advance notice. **Sample Meals:** Caesar salad, vegetable burritos (lunch); Grilled vegetable *crostini,* arugula salad, fish fillet with cilantro pesto, fresh fruit phyllo cup (dinner).

▨ Nightly rate $115–160 per room, $215–$365 per suite. 1-night spa package $296 per person, double occupancy, includes breakfast and dinner, spa treatments. 4-night package $948 per person, double occupancy, includes breakfast and dinner, spa treatments. Day spa packages $195–$279 per person. AE, MC, V.

⊠ *Box 53, San Ignacio, Cayo, Belize, Central America,* ☎ *501/92–2037,* FAX *501/92–2501. www.chaacreek.com*

BERMUDA

CAMBRIDGE BEACHES

LUXURY PAMPERING

Set on a 25-acre peninsula with five private coves on the ocean and a marina on the bay, Cambridge Beaches draws a mix of international travelers, many of whom return year after year. This is the type of place where guests gather for high tea in the afternoon, then dress for a formal dinner in the elegant main house. Evenings often end with dancing to live music on a terrace that overlooks the resort's private marina.

Sunlight dapples the indoor swimming pools at the Ocean Spa, a traditional Bermudian cottage with pink-stucco walls and a ridged roof. Guests here relax on a terrace where refreshments are served. The glass dome that covers the pools is open during warm months.

The spa offers treatments hard to find outside Europe. Cathiodermie facials by Guinot of Paris incorporate gentle stimulation of skin tissue with rollers that cause a tingling sensation. Using a clay mask, the therapist dissolves impurities and toxins, leaving the tissue feeling rejuvenated. Ionithermie treatments using electrical stimuli firm and tone skin and help rid the body of cellulite. These treatments can be combined with body wraps using seaweed, plant extracts, and other natural ingredients.

The Classic Spa Day package might start with a consultation with a therapist who conducts a computerized body-fat analysis, followed by exercise, sauna, and massage. A half-day program for men includes massage, facial, and hair treatment. Both full-day and half-day packages include lunch on a bayside terrace.

Accommodations are in cottage rooms and suites with traditional furnishings. Most have a whirlpool bath. Only a handful of the rooms have televisions, but there are others that can be rented.

Cambridge Beaches is in Somerset, a tiny parish of shady lanes and old homes. A short hike from Cambridge Beaches brings you to Scaur Hill Fort, built in the 1870s to protect the Royal Naval Dockyard. Now it's a 22-acre park with breathtaking views of the Great Sound and its armada of sailboats. You can charter a sailboat here or go snorkeling at an underwater trail for novice snorkelers.

INSIDER TIP Passionate about cricket, Bermudians gather for matches every Sunday during the summer. Try to catch one.

Equipment: Free weights, stair climbers, stationary bikes, treadmills, weight-training circuit. **Services:** Aromatherapy, massage, paraffin body wraps, reflexology, reiki, salt glow, seaweed wrap. **Swimming:** Indoor and outdoor pools, beaches. **Classes and Programs:** Computerized body-fat analysis, fitness consultation, nutrition consultation. **Recreation:** Bikes, boating, canoeing, croquet, kayaking, mopeds, snorkeling, tennis, windsurfing.

🛏 69 rooms, 19 suites.

✕ Meals included. Breakfast buffet. Lunch in the Mangrove Bay Terrace or the Café. Dinner in the Tamarisk Room. **Sample Meals:** Pesto pasta with shrimp and lemon, fish chowder, chicken–macadamia nut salad (lunch); seafood jambalaya, chicken breast with couscous, linguini with shrimp (dinner).

💳 Nightly rate $295–$420 per room. 5-night spa package $2,049 per person, includes meals and spa treatments. MC, V.

✉ *30 Kings Point Rd., Sandys MA 02, Bermuda,* ☎ *441/234–0331 or 800/468–7300,* ℻ *441/234–3352. www.privilege-spa.com*

SONESTA BEACH RESORT

LUXURY PAMPERING

You'll find the pinkest beaches you've ever seen at the Sonesta Resort, located right in the middle of Bermuda's South Shore, a privileged area close to island attractions yet secluded and peaceful.

Boasting an impressive array of treatments and exercise equipment in a compact space, the Bersalon Spa is a great place to drop by between business meetings or rounds of golf. The facility has 11 treatment rooms, an aerobics studio, a strength-training and cardiovascular room, and well-equipped lounges for men and women.

If you simply want to be pampered, there are four-day spa sampler packages that allow you to try treatments not available in the United States, such as the Oriental Wisdom, which combines Chinese- and Japanese-style massage with aromatherapy.

Set on a 25-acre peninsula, the resort has three beaches with gentle surf, tennis courts, and water sports. For swimmers, the freshwater swimming pool has an all-weather glass-dome enclosure.

The guest rooms and suites are in a six-story structure with ocean and bay views. Rooms have a balcony or patio. Spacious split-level units have a sitting area and dressing room, modern rattan furniture, and floor-to-ceiling windows.

INSIDER TIP Bring the kids to this big resort. While youngsters enjoy summer camp, you can be pampered at the spa.

Equipment: Free weights, stair climbers, stationary bikes, treadmills, weight-training circuit. **Services:** Aromatherapy, herbal wrap, loofah body scrub, paraffin body treatment, reflexology, salt-glow skin polish. **Swimming:** Indoor and outdoor pools, beaches. **Classes and Programs:** Personal training, snorkeling instruction, tennis lessons. **Recreation:** Badminton, croquet, scuba diving, shuffleboard, Ping-Pong, tennis, volleyball, windsurfing. **Children's Programs:** Activities for ages 5–12.

🛏 403 rooms.

✕ Meals à la carte. Lunch served at the SeaGrape and Boat Bay Club. **Sample Meals:** Vegetarian quesadillas, avocado sandwich with tomato and cheese (lunch); grilled swordfish, vegetarian lasagna, vegetable skewers with sea scallops (dinner).

✉ Nightly rate $115–$440 per room. 3-night spa sampler package $895–$2,085, single or double occupancy. AE, DC, MC, V.

✉ *Box HM 1070, Shore Rd., Southampton, Bermuda SN02,* ☎ *441/238–8122 or 800/766–3782,* ℻ *441/238–8463. www.senesta.com*

BONAIRE

HARBOUR VILLAGE BEACH RESORT

LUXURY PAMPERING

The spa at Harbour Village Beach Resort is a cool and calm retreat from the beach scene. After a day of swimming or snorkeling, you can retreat to the spa for a sports massage, body exfoliation, and the calming effects of breathing class. This is the best place to experience treatments with Bonaire sea salts, used for body polishing and baths.

Fitness programs begin with exercise on the beach. Mornings feature nature hikes or a 4-mi bike ride along the island's rugged but beautiful coastline to some cliffs called 1,000 Steps. Welcome to Bonaire's natural stair climber.

The two-story spa building has an aerobics studio and workout room with cardiovascular and weight-training equipment. Treatments are in nine air-conditioned and windowed rooms or outdoors in massage cabanas. Signature treatments include a seaweed masque, body wrap, and botanical soak. There's an outdoor pool for aerobics and toning classes as well as a tranquil lounging pool into which cascades refreshing desalinated water.

While the landscape is arid, underwater spectacle is the big draw. The nearby coral reef is home to more than 200 species of fish. A snorkeling program introduced by the island government in cooperation with *Skin Diver* magazine provides in-depth looks at prime sites. Established in 1979 to safeguard these treasures, Bonaire National Park is much like a museum, with guides and information to round out the experience as you float peacefully or explore with scuba equipment. There are also a 64-slip marina and a full-service dive shop.

Rooms and suites are in two-story, red-tile-roof villas clustered around courtyards and on a private beach. Ground-floor suites have verandas facing the beach. Furnished with rattan seating, all rooms have ceiling fans as well as air-conditioning.

INSIDER TIP Try the sea-accented Phytomer products from France, used in facials and aromatherapy massage.

Equipment: Rowing machines, stair climbers, stationary bikes, treadmills, weight-training circuit. **Services:** Aromatherapy, body polish, hydrotherapy bath, massage, reflexology, sea salt exfoliation, shiatsu. **Swimming:** Pool, ocean beach. **Classes and Programs:** Aerobics, aquaerobics, Pilates, yoga. **Recreation:** Deep-sea fishing, diving, sailing, snorkeling, tennis. **Children's Programs:** Supervised activities for ages 5–11.

⚊ 60 rooms, 18 suites.

✕ Meals à la carte. Four restaurants serve Caribbean, Spanish, and Tex-Mex cuisine, as well as spa items. **Sample Meals:** Smoked turkey sandwich, charbroiled catch of the day (lunch); cannelloni, poached wahoo fish, braised chicken (dinner).

🎫 Nightly rate $275–$405 per room. 7-night spa package program $1,395–$1,628 per person, double occupancy. Half-day spa package $132. AE, D, MC, V.

✉ *Box 312, Kralendijk, Bonaire, Netherlands Antilles,* ☎ *5997–7500,* FAX *5997–7507. Reservations:* ☎ *305/567–9509 or 800/424–0004,* FAX *305/567–9659. www.harbourvillage.com*

DOMINICAN REPUBLIC

RENAISSANCE JARAGUA HOTEL & CASINO

LUXURY PAMPERING

There is no beach at the Renaissance Jaragua Hotel & Casino, but you'll hardly notice. With an oversize swimming pool surrounded by tropical gardens, Scandinavian saunas, a Turkish steam bath, and a Roman whirlpool, the hotel's Wellness Place spa is an ideal spot to while away the hours.

From your room it's a pleasant walk through the garden and alongside the lagoon to the spa. There you can treat yourself to a body scrub, herbal wrap, facial, or massage. You can even just relax in your complimentary robe and slippers and enjoy the fresh fruit and juices available throughout the day. At the freestanding fitness facility, all marble and glass, you can work out on exercise equipment, join a step class in the aerobics studio, or an aquaerobics class in the Olympic-size pool.

Secluded on 14½ palm-fringed acres, the hotel has rooms with the same modern look as other Renaissance resorts. Dining options range from a New York deli to a pizzeria, with a formal dining room that features fresh seafood.

INSIDER TIP Stroll the hemisphere's oldest street, Santo Domingo's Calle las Damas, and visit the cathedral where explorer Christopher Columbus is said to have been buried.

Equipment: Free weights, rowing machines, stationary bikes, treadmills, weight-training circuit. **Services:** Herbal wrap, massage, reflexology, salt glow. **Swimming:** Pool. **Classes and Programs:** Aerobics, aquaerobics. **Recreation:** Tennis.

🛏 292 rooms, 6 suites.

✕ All meals à la carte. Choice of heart-healthy options at three international restaurants. **Sample Meals:** Rice and beans, fruit plate, spinach salad (lunch); charbroiled or grilled steak on a spit, stir-fry of Chinese vegetables, homemade pasta with shrimp (dinner).

💰 Nightly rate $115–$145. AE, DC, MC, V.

✉ *367 George Washington Ave., Santo Domingo, Dominican Republic,* ☎ *809/221–2222 or 800/468–3571,* FAX *809/686–0528. www.renaissancehotels.com*

GRENADA

LASOURCE

LUXURY PAMPERING

Don't expect a structured program at LaSource. Here you set your own schedule. That's a good thing because, like LeSport, its sister resort on St. Lucia, LaSource offers the all-inclusive Body Holiday, which includes accommodations, excellent cuisine, and a seemingly endless list of activities, from scuba diving in the crystal blue water to teeing off on a private 9-hole golf course.

Treatment rooms are centrally located in the Oasis, which is just steps from the beach and pool. After a brief examination by the resort's nurse, you choose from a list of treatments—massages, wraps, rub, and baths. Seaweed body wraps, aromatherapy massage with essential oils, and other treatments are given by well-trained local people and involve products imported from France. You're free to sign up for any number of treatments if they're available. Getting appointments for spa services here is sometimes difficult, as demand sometimes exceeds capacity, especially between December and April, so sure to sign up for treatments as soon as you arrive.

Aerobics classes (including step, stretch, and tone) and meditation, yoga, and tai chi instruction are offered daily in the resort's new relaxation pavilion. In the summer months guest experts in such specialties as funk and hip-hop workouts, kick boxing, and aquatic fitness conduct master classes. A group jog on the beach takes place early each morning at 7. Afterward, cool your heels in the sauna or simply relax in the outdoor whirlpool.

Secluded amid 40 acres of lush gardens on Grenada's southwestern coast, LaSource evokes a Victorian-era West Indian village. The elegant colonial buildings feature handcrafted wooden trellises and rooms with high ceilings, some of them beamed. Marble floors, handmade rugs, and custom-carved four-poster beds add to the charm of the accommodations. All rooms have terra-cotta tile balconies or terraces. Suites come with a bay window and pullout sofa bed. There are no televisions, however.

Make sure to leave time for exploring. St. George's, the picturesque capital city, can be toured on foot in several hours. Visiting bustling, noisy Market Square on Saturday morning is a definite entry for your "to do" list. Most shops are closed Saturday afternoon and all day Sunday, so head back to the beach or schedule another massage.

Equipment: Free weights, rowing machines, stair climbers, stationary bikes, weight-training circuit. **Services:** Aromatherapy, massage, seaweed body wrap, thalassotherapy. **Swimming:** Pools, beach. **Classes and Programs:** Couples massage, aerobics, meditation, stretch and tone, tai chi, yoga. **Recreation:** Archery, fencing, golf, Ping-Pong, scuba diving, snorkeling, tennis, volleyball, water sports.

🛏 91 rooms, 9 suites.

✗ Meals included. Breakfast buffet. Lunch every day and dinner twice a week are served at the Terrace Restaurant. The rest of the week international cuisine is served at the Great House. Special dietary requirements can be accommodated. **Sample Meals:** Local vegetables in a puree of callaloo (vegetable similar to spinach), cabbage roll of risotto (lunch); chilled beet root and ginger soup, pork fillet medallions with onion confit and oregano sauce, fusilli with mixed peppers and a basil and red pepper sauce, grilled crab cakes with a sweet pepper sauce (dinner).

📧 Nightly rate $200–$425 per person, double occupancy, includes all meals, activities, and spa treatments. AE, MC, V.

✉ *Box 852, St. George's, Grenada, West Indies,* ☎ *473/444–2556 or 800/544–2883,* FAX *473/444–2561.* *www.lasourcegrenada.com*

GUADELOUPE

CENTRE DE THALASSOTHÉRAPIE MANIOUKANI

MEDICAL WELLNESS ∘ MINERAL SPRINGS

Set on a hillside overlooking the ocean, Centre de Thalassothérapie Man-ioukani uses fresh seawater in its baths and in the exercise pool where fitness classes are held every morning. The heated seawater is said to improve circulation in your legs and to help provide relief to persons suffering from rheumatism.

Opened in 1995, this attractive facility is owned and operated by Pierre and Cordinne Saint-Luce. Consultation with a physiologist, chiro-practor, and dietitian can be included in a program tailored to your needs.

Aches and pains are soaked away in a huge pool filled daily with fresh seawater. Exercise sessions in the water are provided by a personal trainer. Stressed-out visitors can simply come for a massage, then relax in the solarium overlooking sailboats in the marina. Serious muscular prob-lems are treated in a hydromassage tub of seawater and with a body masque of Phytomer seaweed products imported from France.

Guadeloupe, which is really two islands that form a butterfly shape, moves to a Creole beat, part French and part African. Manioukani is in the south-western part of Basse-Terre, the butterfly's left wing, not far from La Soufrière, the island's still-puffing volcano. Spend mornings reclining on black-sand beaches or take an excursion to Bouillante (which literally means "boiling") and bathe in the aromatic thermal springs.

A new 25-bed lodging section has been added at Manioukani, but rooms are small. There are also excellent accommodations nearby. Free trans-portation is provided for guests staying in the nearby town of Saint-Claude at the Hotel Saint-Georges (☎ 590/80–10–10). Within walking distance of the Manioukani are the elegant cottages of Le Jardin Malanga (☎ 590/92–67–57).

INSIDER TIP If you're feeling adventurous, you'll find plenty of opportuni-ties for hiking on mountain trails or scuba diving at nearby Cousteau Un-derwater Park.

Services: Algae wrap, herbal bath, hydromassage, thalassotherapy, Vichy shower. **Swimming:** Pools. **Classes and Programs:** Aquaerobics, personal training.

⌂ 25 rooms.

✕ No meal plan.

Spa treatments are à la carte; each costs about $27. 2-day spa package $133 per person. 6-day dietetic program $487 per person. No credit cards.

✉ *Marina Rivière-Sens, 97113 Gourbeyre, Guadeloupe,* ☎ *590/99–02–02,* FAX *590/81–65–23.*

ESPACE SANTÉ DE RAVINE CHAUDE

MINERAL SPRINGS

La Soufrière was erupting when Spanish explorer Christopher Columbus stepped ashore here on November 4, 1493. Although the volcano is no longer active, the spring waters emanating from La Soufrière are still being tapped for therapeutic use.

The curative virtues of the spring waters emanating from La Soufrière were documented as far back as the 17th century. In 1658 a French historian wrote: "Guadeloupe has bubbling waters that experience has shown to cure all sorts of illnesses having origin in the cold." The spa complex at Espace Santé de Ravine Chaude, which opened in 1992, still attracts a large French clientele.

The spa is in the rugged, green countryside of northern Basse-Terre, just 10 minutes from the region's principal city of Pointe-à-Pitre. The spa offers a wide range of thermal-water therapies that are on a par with those available at resorts in Brittany and the French Riviera. The facilities at Ravine Chaude include baths and two swimming pools filled with the thermal waters. A doctor is on staff to consult with visitors on treatments.

Although a weekend package including lodging and meals is available, there are no accommodations on the premises. Visitors generally stay at the nearby Hotel Relais des Sources (☎ 590/25–31–04).

INSIDER TIP Don't miss a trip to bustling Pointe-à-Pitre, where vendor stalls are filled with herbs, home remedies, and medicines with exotic names: *matriquin, zhébe-gras, fleupapillon, bois-de-l'homme, bonnet-carré,* and the like.

Services: Lymphatic drainage, mud body masks, pressotherapy. **Swimming:** Pools. **Classes and Programs:** Antistress workshops, medical consultations. **Recreation:** Hiking.

⊞ None. Rooms available at nearby Hotel Relais des Sources.

✗ Meals à la carte. Two restaurants on the premises. Most area restaurants serve creole cuisine, based on fresh native fish and produce.

Cost of treatments ranges from $25 for a mud wrap to $47 for complete facial treatments. 1-night weekend package $233, includes meals, 4 treatments, and 1 night of lodging.

✉ *Centre Thermale René Toribio, Ravine Chaude, 97129 Le Lamentin, Guadeloupe,* ☎ *590/25–75—92,* FAX *590/25–76–28. www.ravine-chaude.gp*

JAMAICA

THE ENCHANTED GARDEN

LUXURY PAMPERING

The Enchanted Garden more than lives up to its name. Here you can stroll through a rain forest, float in a natural pool beneath a cascading waterfall, or retreat to one of the private garden nooks where a massage therapist awaits with aromatic oils.

The emphasis here is on all things natural, from facials with gel made from freshly cut aloes to aromatherapy with oils from jasmine picked straight from the garden. Many essential oils are available, allowing you to custom-mix a blend to suit your mood. The menu of services includes treatments with vegetable mud and micronized seaweed.

The spa's scheduled group classes range from dancercise to yoga. The limited selection of exercise equipment may be a disappointment for fitness buffs, though the facilities do include a Turkish steam bath and a Swiss shower with multiple heads.

A typical day may begin with a power walk through the exquisite botanical gardens and to the top of the falls. Lunch can be at the beach or by the pool. The all-inclusive plan allows you to dine at several specialty restaurants, selecting spa cuisine options that are low in fat, sodium, and calories.

Accommodations are in rooms and suites in buildings scaling the hillside gardens. There are also a number of town houses with sunken living rooms, private patios with plunge pools, and kitchens. A complimentary shuttle transports you to a beach club (approximately 10 minutes away) where you can enjoy water sports and the blue waters of the Caribbean. A daily shuttle takes you to town for crafts, souvenirs, and duty-free shopping.

More adventurous types will want to rent a car and drive along the coastal route to Dunn's River Falls (a slippery challenge to climbers) and visit Musgrave Market in the town of Port Antonio, where island produce such as *naseberries, cho-chos,* star apples, and tiny fig bananas are heaped on stands. Nearby, Boston Beach is lined with smoky shacks selling jerk pork and chicken barbecued over a pimiento wood fire.

INSIDER TIP The resort's soaring aviary provides close-up views of the island's birds.

Equipment: Cross-country ski machines, free weights, rowing machines, stationary bikes, treadmills. **Services:** Aromatherapy, body polish, body wraps, massage, reflexology, salt glow, shiatsu. **Swimming:**

Pools, beach. **Classes and Programs:** Aerobics, tai chi, yoga. **Recreation:** Tennis, water volleyball.

▣ 60 rooms, 53 suites.

✕ Meals included. Restaurants serve pasta, Middle Eastern, and Asian food. Spa cuisine available. **Sample Meals:** Warm curried crab and papaya salad, cold poached scallops with tomato vinaigrette (lunch); grilled marlin, mahimahi fillet with papaya relish, pepper-crusted beef with white beans (dinner).

▨ Nightly rate $140 per person, double occupancy. Full-day spa package $100–$210. AE, MC, V.

⊠ *Box 284, Ocho Rios, St. Ann, Jamaica, West Indies,* ☎ *876/974–1400 or 800/847–2535,* ⅂ₐ⅂ *876/974–5823.*

GRAND LIDO SANS SOUCI

LUXURY PAMPERING ○ MINERAL SPRINGS

Charlie's Spa at the Grand Lido Sans Souci resort takes a fresh approach to fitness. It's more hedonistic than health oriented, and the pampering treatments complement the vigorous workouts in the gym. This is a pleasant place to tone up or slim down.

With the sea on one side and a cascade of mineral water on the other, the hillside spa provides instant stress reduction. You can soak in a whirlpool or join an exercise class in the pool. You can also head down the hill to the exercise room for a workout or to the open-air pavilion, where group exercise sessions are scheduled twice a day during the week.

After a fast-pace walk through the terraced gardens and along the curve of beach, you may head to the tennis courts for a few games or to the marina for water sports. The sound of a violin or flute may draw you to the beach restaurant, where a band of roving musicians entertains. Buffet breakfast and lunch here is a sampler of island fare, along with Continental and Japanese favorites.

Be sure to make an appointment for spa treatments at the tiny office alongside a pool where Charlie, a huge sea turtle, thrives in the mineral water. Spa director Margaret Spencer has turned the spa terrace into a quiet place for alfresco reflexology treatments. A charming gazebo is just big enough for a private massage. Facials and other treatments are given inside tiny wooden cottages clinging to the rocks. Seaweed and mud wraps are given in rock-walled wet-treatment rooms.

A beach-level grotto conceals a dry sauna and treatment area for skin exfoliation with sea salt, followed by a rubdown with cleansing oil and a walk into the sea. The shallow water here is ideal for washing off oils and salts used for body scrubs (which, depending on your skin type, include aloe, peppermint, or coconut).

All suites overlook gardens and the sea. Most have private balconies and marble bathrooms, and many have whirlpool tubs. The all-inclusive program attracts a wide variety of people—honeymooners, families with children, and single spa goers. About half the guests in recent years have been couples, many taking marriage vows in a wedding gazebo.

INSIDER TIP For a special treat take a dip in a spring-fed pool hidden in a grotto on the beach.

Equipment: Free weights, rowing machine, stair climbers, stationary bikes, treadmill, weight-training circuit. **Services:** Aromatherapy, body scrub, fango, mud wrap, reflexology, seaweed wrap. **Swimming:** Pool, beach. **Classes and Programs:** Aerobics, aquaerobics. **Recreation:** Basketball, bicycles, croquet, kayaking, scuba diving, snorkeling, volleyball, water sports.

▦ 186 rooms, 24 suites.

✗ Meals included. Three restaurants serve Italian, Jamaican, and gourmet cuisine. **Sample Meals:** Grilled tuna sandwich, shrimp seviche, pasta primavera, spinach and ricotta cannelloni (lunch); seafood fettuccine, smoked marlin, broiled lobster, vegetarian lasagna (dinner).

✉ Nightly rate $285–$445 per person, double occupancy. AE, D, DC, MC, V.

✉ *Box 103, Ocho Rios, St. Ann, Jamaica,* ☎ *876/994–1353 or 800/ 859–7873,* FAX *876/994–1544.*

HALF MOON GOLF, TENNIS & BEACH CLUB

LUXURY PAMPERING ○ SPORTS CONDITIONING

Of all the terms you might apply to Half Moon Golf, Tennis & Beach Club, one of the most appropriate is "comprehensive." This sprawling resort on 400 manicured acres surrounding lovely Half Moon Bay has an 18-hole golf course designed by Robert Trent Jones, four squash courts, more than a dozen tennis courts, and 52 swimming pools, as well as a state-of-the art fitness center and—oh, yes—a spa.

Before you begin spa treatments, you don a fluffy robe and recline on a chaise lounge in the relaxation room. With soft music playing in the background, you can meditate while awaiting your treatment. Four massage rooms are used for muscle-soothing Swedish massage, detoxifying body wraps, invigorating body scrubs, and facials that employ natural Jamaican herbs. Those who believe water is the most therapeutic healer for revitalizing and lifting the spirit will take pleasure in the hydrotherapy facilities.

The weight room has Nautilus Next Generation equipment, where the fit (and those trying to be) can work out on a variety of machines. If that's not enough, you can work out on treadmills, bicycles, and step machines while watching cable television or listening to the radio. A personal trainer is available for guests who want to design their own fitness program.

Accommodations are elegant but informal, with decor that blends Queen Anne and Chippendale furniture made by local craftspeople from Jamaican mahogany. A 26-acre nature reserve is maintained on the property, and many of the fruits, vegetables and herbs used in the resort's restaurants are grown there.

....
INSIDER TIP Just 7 mi east of the airport in Montego Bay, Half Moon is much easier to get to than many other resorts in Jamaica. You'll get there so quickly, you might be able to squeeze in an extra spa treatment or two.
....

Equipment: Free weights, stair climbers, treadmills, weight-training circuit. **Services:** Aromatherapy, body scrub, body wrap, hydrotherapy, reflexology, Swiss shower, Vichy shower. **Swimming:** 52 swimming pools, beach. **Classes and Programs:** Diet program, fitness classes. **Recreation:**

Badminton, basketball, bicycling, boccie, croquet, fishing, golf, horseback riding, Ping-Pong, polo, sailing, scuba diving, snorkeling, squash, tennis, windsurfing, volleyball.

▥ 44 rooms, 176 suites, 32 villas.

✕ Meals à la carte. Seagrape Terrace, Sugar Mill and Il Giardino serve international cuisine; La Baguette serves informal fare. Special diets accommodated. **Sample Meals:** Jerk chicken, thin lobster medallion atop mixed greens with passion fruit dressing (lunch); osso bucco braised in wine and served on olenta, lamp wrapped with crispy phyllo dough with garlic eggplant and light cumin tomato sauce, mahimahi fillet in papillote with stir-fried vegetables and sweet pepper coulis (dinner).

▧ Nightly rates $120–$595 per person, double occupancy. Meal plans $75 for breakfast and dinner, $100 for all meals. Day spa packages $175 per person, includes meals and spa services. AE, D, MC, V.

✉ *Box 80, Montego Bay, Jamaica,* ☎ *876/953–2211 or 800/626–0592,* FAX *876/953–2731. www.halfmoon.com.jm*

SWEPT AWAY

SPORTS CONDITIONING

Those who find the pace on Negril's beaches to be a little too laid-back will love Swept Away. The secluded resort, set amid 20-acres of lush gardens, offers a gym full of exercise equipment and a studio for group exercise classes. There are 10 tennis courts lighted for night play, air-conditioned racquetball and squash courts, a professional-size basketball court, and a 25-meter pool.

From the resort's open-air reception area, paths lead to 26 two-story villas set rather close together in beachside gardens. The standard villa has four small suites arranged on two levels around a plant-filled atrium. Each unit has a private veranda, spare furnishings, and a large step-in shower. It is a quiet environment, but plenty of action vibrates at the pool, tennis complex, and around the beach bar. Most guests are young couples; some are honeymooners.

The sports center, across the island's main road from the villas, offers more than 12 exercise classes, from body sculpting to low- and high-impact aerobics. Joggers can check out a nine-station par course on the half-mile running track. Tennis buffs get workouts with pros at three daily clinics. Those into weight lifting will head to the open-air pavilion filled with high-tech German equipment. Diehards will be glad to know the gym stays open until 11 PM.

There are plenty of options outside, too. Golfers get unlimited play at the nearby Negril Hills Golf Club, an 18-hole, par 72 course set on 6,600 yards of rolling hills. There's unlimited use of water-sports equipment for windsurfing, kayaking, sailing, paddle-boating, and waterskiing. Snorkeling gear is also provided, as are outings in a glass-bottom boat. For certified divers trips to nearby reefs depart three times daily in the resort's own dive boat.

The staff can arrange outings such as a horseback ride through the tropical backcountry and a sunset catamaran cruise to caves near Rick's Cafe. Local outfitters take hikers to scenic waterfalls and a natural whirlpool, and for a walk through the bush.

After all that, you'll need a rubdown. Massages are given in thatch-roof pavilions at the center of the sports complex. Get into an island mood with hydrotherapy in a rock-wall tub filled with seawater to relax and soothe tired muscles. Facials and bodywork, such as wraps, scrubs, and waxing, are also available. Spa services are not part of the all-inclusive package, however.

INSIDER TIP One of the best ways to see the island is by mountain biking on trails along the beach. The activities desk can arrange an outing with a local guide.

Equipment: Cross-country ski machines, free weights, rowing machines, stair climbers, stationary bikes, weight-training circuit. **Services:** Body scrub, herbal and mineral bath, massage, reflexology, seaweed wrap. **Swimming:** Pools, beach. **Classes and Programs:** Tennis instruction, scuba lessons, personal training. **Recreation:** Basketball, diving, jogging, kayaking, racquetball, soccer, squash, tennis, volleyball, windsurfing.

▥ 134 suites.

✕ Meals included. An open-air pavilion serves buffet meals, a beach grill serves lighter fare, and a formal restaurant serves Continental cuisine. Spa menu available. **Sample Meals:** Steamed vegetables, grilled-chicken Caesar salad, plum tomatoes with goat cheese and olive oil (lunch); fettuccine with baby shrimp and okra in vermouth sauce, pan-fried snapper with red wine–caper sauce, goat chops in phyllo dough, curried-goat stew (dinner).

▤ 3-night package $910–$1,125 per person, double occupancy; 7-night package $1,925–$2,380 per person, double occupancy. AE, DC, MC, V.

✉ *Box 77, Norman Manley Blvd., Negril, Jamaica,* ☎ *876/957–4061 or 800/545–7937,* FAX *876/957–4060. www.sweptaway.com*

MARTINIQUE

CENTRE DE THALASSOTHÉRAPIE DU CARBET

MEDICAL WELLNESS

The indoor pools of the Centre de Thalassothérapie, north of Martinique's capital city of Fort-de-France, draw those who believe in the healing properties of seawater. The four-step rejuvenating treatment, called Remise en Forme, takes about 2½ hours and costs about $53.

You begin with a plunge into a seawater pool heated to 91°F, where you may participate in group exercises or simply relax. The pool has built-in underwater jets to massage sore muscles. Next comes a more intense underwater massage in a private tub with jets designed to effect lymphatic drainage. The third step is a *douche à affusion,* a full-body massage under a continuous shower of seawater. The final douche is in a shower stall lined with high-pressure jets aimed at cellulite points, the abdomen, and the vertebrae.

Other services available include electrotherapy designed to help muscles heal after injury, an algae body mask, and treatments to stave off aging and arthritis. The center also offers the inhalation of seawater mist for asthma sufferers.

The center, which is closed on Sunday, is on the island's northwestern coast, about a 40-mi drive from Fort-de-France. The beach here, Grand'Anse, is a favorite among locals. There are no public facilities, so change at the center. While you're here, visit the island's lush interior and the ruins of St-Pierre, the old capital that was destroyed in 1902 by an eruption of Mont Pelée.

INSIDER TIP On this most French island of the French Antilles, the town of Carbet has some of the best French restaurants you're likely to find this side of Paris.

Services: Electrotherapy, massage, pressotherapy, seaweed treatments, thalassotherapy.

🏨 Nearby hotels include: Hotel Marouba (☎ 596/78–00–21; FAX 596/78–05–65), which has 125 rooms, charges $100–$150 per person, double occupancy. Hotel Christophe Colomb (☎ 596/78–05–38; FAX 596/78–06–42), has 10 single or double rooms priced at $41–$50.

✕ No meals available. In Carbet a few very good creole restaurants offer fresh seafood.

✉ *Grand'Anse, 97221 Carbet, Martinique,* ☎ *596/78–08–78,* FAX *596/78–09–80.*

NEVIS

FOUR SEASONS RESORT NEVIS

LUXURY PAMPERING ○ SPORTS CONDITIONING

Pristine beaches, aquamarine seas, and tropical rain forests are what you'll find at the Four Seasons Resort on the tiny island of Nevis. Guests set their own pace here, choosing from among a number of outdoor activities ranging from golf to tennis. Spa services are limited to massage, and the fitness program does not include organized classes, but the exercise equipment is first rate.

Upon arrival in St. Kitts, Nevis's sister island, visitors are welcomed aboard a private launch for the 30-minute voyage to the resort. As an alternative, you can take a private plane to the minuscule Nevis airstrip.

A sports package, available year-round, is an excellent value, offering unlimited tennis and golf. The tennis complex has 10 courts supervised by pros who provide clinics and one-on-one training. At the 18-hole course designed by Robert Trent Jones II, you play on the slopes of cloud-capped Nevis Peak, which inspired explorer Christopher Columbus to call the island *Las Nieves,* or "the snows." Joggers and walkers can circle the links on a paved path leading through lush forest and up into the foothills.

Swimmers enjoy two free-form swimming pools. If that isn't enough to refresh you, pool attendants spritz you from time to time with Evian water. With a prime location on lovely Pinney's Beach, the entire complex is designed to provide easy access to the ocean and a variety of water-sports equipment, from sailboards to snorkeling gear.

The air-conditioned health club has a selection of cardio equipment that few island resorts can match, from high-tech rowing machines to the latest stair climbers. There's also an aerobics studio equipped with 10 units for step aerobics. Details make the difference here: iced facecloths and pitchers of fresh fruit juices are arranged in the exercise room, and in-room massages are available if you overdo it during your workout.

The 12 plantation-style guest cottages have screened porches and private patios. Each building has about a dozen rooms and suites outfitted with TVs, VCRs, and minibars. The decor, with traditional furniture, is rather austere. Each cottage has extralarge bathrooms and a complimentary self-service laundry facility.

The legacy of 300 years of British rule is still evident on the 36-square-mi island. In centuries past the British called Nevis, once home to 83 sugar plantations, the "queen of the Caribbees." British admiral Horatio Nelson came to Nevis for the restorative mineral baths and stayed on to marry his wife at her family's plantation. A visit to their home is a highlight of an island tour. History buffs can also join a walking tour of the island's tiny capital, Charlestown, to view thermal springs bubbling from a hillside next to the ruins of the once-exclusive Bath Hotel, built in 1778.

INSIDER TIP A perfect way to end the day is on Nevis Peak, where the sunset is spectacular and you might catch a glimpse of wild monkeys with 6-ft tails.

Equipment: Free weights, rowing machines, stair climbers, stationary bikes, treadmills, weight-training equipment. **Services:** Aromatherapy, massage. **Swimming:** Pools, beach. **Classes and Programs:** Aquaerobics, step, stretch-and-tone. **Recreation:** Billiards, croquet, darts, fishing, golf, kayaking, sailboarding, scuba diving, shuffleboard, snorkeling, tennis, volleyball, water sports. **Children's Programs:** Day-long activities for children ages 3–10.

▣ 179 rooms, 17 suites, 20 villas.

✕ Meals are à la carte. The Dining Room features seafood and international cuisine, as well as an alternative menu lower in fat and calories. **Sample Meals:** Herbed smoked chicken with mixed seasonal greens; salad with sweet peppers and marinated Spanish onions, Caesar salad (lunch); seafood gumbo, blackened red snapper with sautéed spaghetti squash, seared salmon with warm bean-sprout salad, local yellow tomato with Maui onion and roasted-pepper vinaigrette (dinner).

▧ Nightly rate $325–$850 per room. 7-night Romance in Paradise package $4,487–$8,219 for 2 persons, includes breakfast and dinner. AE, D, DC, MC, V.

✉ *Box 565, Charlestown, Nevis, West Indies,* ☎ *869/469–1111 or 800/332–3442 reservations in U.S., 800/268–6282 reservations in Canada,* 𝔽𝔸𝕏 *869/469–1112. www.fourseasons.com/nevis*

PUERTO RICO

GOLDEN DOOR

LUXURY PAMPERING

The Golden Door—perched on a 300-ft bluff where the Atlantic Ocean meets the Caribbean Sea—is a spa experience you won't easily forget. You'll always know you're in the Caribbean from the breathtaking views afforded from just about everywhere—the exercise room, the juice bar, and even some of the treatment rooms.

In the highly rated Las Casitas Village, the spa is part of the 500-acre Wyndham El Conquistador Resort & Country Club. You can opt to stay in one of Las Casitas' 90 Spanish colonial–style villas (complete with butler service) or in rooms near the marina, nestled into the side of a cliff, or in the main hotel. No matter where you stay, you an take advantage of the vast array of diversions—a casino, a marina, an 18-hole golf course, and an offshore island where you can sun, swim, and take part in water sports.

A sister facility of the Golden Door in Escondido, California, this 26,000-square-ft facility offers some of that legendary spa's famous treatments, such as the Golden Door Massage and the Golden Door Custom Facial. It also has added tropical touches, including its own Rainforest Facial—an 80-minute treatment that tantalizes you with the sweet smell of wild fruits and berries. You are transported to the rain forest with a recording of rustling leaves and chirping tree frogs.

The spa, housed in a plantation-style building surrounded by lush tropical plants and flowers, uses warm cream and yellow tones. Before treatments you can receive a relaxing massage from falling streams of water in the Japanese O-furo bath. There's also a tearoom that can be used before or after treatments (complete with small foot-massage machines) and a juice bar that also serves light food.

In addition to massage therapies, ayurvedic body treatments, wraps, scrubs, and polishes, the spa also offers a wide array of fitness programs, including aerobics, tai chi, and yoga. There's a weight-training room, and the staff is happy to conduct fitness assessments and put together custom workout programs.

An Edouard de Paris salon on premises offers all kinds of hair services in a room with huge windows overlooking the ocean. You can move to the balcony for some treatments, including manicures.

Special treatments for teenagers (14 and over) and men are available. The spa's daily membership fee is complimentary for guests at Las Casitas and is waived for guests staying in other parts of the resort if they purchase spa services.

INSIDER TIP The views are to die for here. Make the most of them by taking a daytime or evening yoga or tai chi class on the lawn overlooking the ocean.

Equipment: Free weights, stair climbers, stationary bikes, treadmills, weight-training equipment. **Services:** Aromatherapy, craniosacral therapy, fango, herbal wraps, hydrotherapy, reflexology, reiki, salt glow. **Swimming:** 6 outdoor pools, beach. **Classes and Programs:** Boxing, nutrition consultation, personal training, Pilates, spinning, tai chi, yoga. **Recreation:** Golf, diving, tennis, scuba, snorkeling, water sports. **Children's Programs:** Camp Coquí for ages 3–12.

▦ 809 rooms, 109 suites, 90 villas.

✕ Breakfast included. 11 restaurants throughout the resort serve varied cuisine; spa serves spa cuisine. Special menu programs can be arranged. **Sample Meals:** Salad with apple, corn, carrots, and beets in a corn ginger, and honey dressing (lunch); grilled swordfish with tropical salsa, turkey burger, lemon chicken with rice noodles and grilled vegetables (dinner).

▧ $545–$2,275; Las Casitas Village $1,195–$2,295. 4-night Golden Door Spa Vitality & Tranquility package $3,425–$8,385; 7-night package $5,640–$13,935. AE, MC, V.

✉ *1000 El Conquistador Ave., Las Croabas sector, Fajardo, Puerto Rico 00738,* ☎ *787/863–1000 or 800–WYNDHAM,* ℻ *787/863–6500. www.wyndham.com*

THE RITZ-CARLTON SAN JUAN HOTEL & CASINO

LUXURY PAMPERING

A surprisingly wide range of treatments—from aloe body wrap to a signature massage with *parcha* (passion fruit juice)—awaits guests at this luxurious oceanfront spa in the posh Ritz-Carlton San Juan Hotel & Casino. The Balinese massage and the Javanese lulur treatment are offered here, making the spa one of a handful outside Indonesia to offer these treatments.

A relaxing tropical ambience reigns inside this 12,000-square-ft spa, which gleams with marble floors, pale stone walls, and crystal chandeliers. Sunlight brightens the reception area on the ground floor where a boutique, beauty salon, and fitness center full of state-of-the-art equipment are located.

Upstairs, the à la carte menu of spa treatments features the latest techniques, including sea-salt glows, body polishes, shiatsu and reiki massages, collagen infusions, and cellulite treatments. The spa's signature San Juan Facial involves wavelike movements done to the sound of the ocean and includes an arm massage and heated hand masques. The ultimate treatment for many guests is the Windchimes Beachside Massage, done near the ocean while wind chimes play gently in the breeze. Pre- and post-tan care are available with special scrubs, conditioners, and body wraps.

Spa director Katherine Calzada brought in a special trainer to teach other therapists Balinese massage. In a treatment room draped with Balinese fabrics and lighted with candles, therapists use a special blend of massage oils and techniques such as skin rolling and thumb walking. The Javanese lulur treatment comes from a ritual for brides of royal families in central Java. You'll feel like royalty throughout the two-hour indulgence as the scent of exotic spices and sweet flowers fills the room. The treatment begins with a massage, followed by exfoliation with light rice powder and turmeric. A soothing yogurt moisturizer is smoothed on the skin and followed by a soak in a tub filled with flower petals. The ritual ends with a massage scented with jasmine and frangipani blossoms.

The spa has a private suite for a couple or family where different treatments can be performed simultaneously. It also offers kids' services, such as manicures, pedicures, facials, and massages (a parent or guardian must accompany children under 16). A spa menu is offered on an outdoor patio.

INSIDER TIP The many treatments here may make it hard to choose just one. Create your own package and get a 15% discount.

Equipment: Free weights, stair climbers, stationary bikes, treadmills, weight-training equipment. **Services:** Aromatherapy, body wrap, craniosacral therapy, mud masques. **Swimming:** Pool, beach. **Classes and Programs:** Aerobics, aquaerobics, Spinning, tennis lessons, yoga. **Recreation:** Tennis, water sports. **Children's Programs:** Ritz Kids program for ages 4–17.

▥ 403 rooms, 11 suites.

✕ Meals à la carte. 3 restaurants serving Continental cuisine; spa menu offered on terrace. **Sample Meals:** Steamed artichoke heart, Belgian endive salad with baby leeks, melon salad with buffalo mozzarella, basil and garlic pesto, fruit salad, pineapple and mango spring roll with orange carrot sorbet.

✉ Nightly rate $285–$319 per room. All spa packages are customized for the individual. AE, MC, V.

✉ 6961 *Avenue of the Governors, Isla Verde, Carolina, Puerto Rico 00979,* ☎ *787/253–1700 or 800/241–3333,* ℻ *787/253–0700. www.ritzcarlton.com*

LA CASA RESORT SPA

NUTRITION AND DIET ○ HOLISTIC HEALTH

In the foothills of the Caribbean National Forest, the rain forest commonly known as El Yunque, La Casa Resort Spa mixes ecotourism with holistic health and wellness programs. You'll feel at one with nature here, where health-oriented workshops and seminars are offered alongside treatments such as seaweed body wraps, sand immersion, and mud therapy.

Thirty minutes from San Juan, La Casa Resort Spa offers guests two types of accommodations. Some of the best views are found in the upper annex, where a renovated farmhouse with four guest rooms sits on a 10-acre farm. Rooms that are more modern, including six two-bedroom villas with hot tubs, are adjacent to the spa in an area known as the lower annex.

The spa, owned by New York–based psychoanalyst Jane G. Goldberg, hosts holistic health weeks, weekend workshops, and special seminars featuring healers from all over world. Workshops include "Falling in

Love with the Earth," through walking, hiking and swimming in mountain streams in El Yunque, and "Healthy Fun," with daily meditation and classes in natural living.

Treatments employ tropical plants and herbs grown on the grounds—eucalyptus, mango, papaya, banana, and *ylang-ylang*—formulated to be either calming, energizing, or detoxifying. To really enjoy the lush surroundings, you can request outdoor treatments. Aerobics, tai chi, and yoga classes are offered in open-air pavilions.

Excursions organized for La Casa guests include hikes to pre-Columbian petroglyphs in the rain forest or a canoe trip down the Río Grande. You can take it easy on Luquillo Beach, a crescent-shape strip of white sand that was once home to a thriving coconut plantation and now draws locals for picnics and family get-togethers.

INSIDER TIP Take advantage of the ecotourism trips offered at the facility, such as documenting endangered leatherback turtles spawning offshore on Culebra.

Services: Aromatherapy, acupuncture, colonic irrigation, herbal wrap, mud pack, polarity therapy, reiki, sea glow massage, seaweed wrap. **Swimming:** Pool, river. **Classes and Programs:** Aerobics, nutritional consultation, meditation and yoga instruction. **Recreation:** Boating, hiking, horseback riding.

▣ 13 rooms, 6 villas.

✗ Breakfast included. Mostly vegetarian diet emphasizes raw fruits and vegetables grown on the property. **Sample Meals:** Miso soup, organic salad, falafel (lunch); Chinese stir-fry, home-made chutney, freshly sprouted green salad (dinner).

▨ Nightly rate per person, double occupancy $120 in upper annex, $250 in lower annex. 5-day workshops $600 and up. MC, V

⊠ *Box 1916, Río Grande, Luquillo, Puerto Rico 00745,* ☎ *787/887–4359 or 888/3–lacasa,* FAX *787/887–4359. www.lacaspa.com*

ST. JOHN

OMEGA JOURNEYS

HOLISTIC HEALTH

A week at Maho Bay Camps, a world-famous ecotourism resort, should be more than enough to replenish mind, body, and soul. Workshops in health, music, movement, and personal growth are mixed with fun in the sun during five weeklong programs that the New York–based Omega Institute holds each January and February. The focus of Omega Journeys may be on getting back to basics, but here that includes peace, quiet, and spectacular views.

Early birds can start the day with sunrise meditation, tai chi, or yoga. Workshops run two hours each morning and afternoon, allowing participants to cover several subjects. During a typical week you will meet international experts in holistic health, stress management, and lifestyle change.

On 14 acres overlooking white-sand beaches, Maho Bay Camps is a sustainable tent-cottage community. Perched in thickly wooded hillsides, the canvas-walled tent-cottages are set on cantilevered plank decks. Each 16-by-16 unit has two beds and a living/dining area with a two-burner propane stove, a sofa, and lounge chairs. Linens and bedding are supplied, but there is no maid service. Boardwalks connect your unit to the toilets, showers, open-air dining pavilion, activities center, and commissary.

INSIDER TIP Take advantage of the lectures on St. John's wildlife and colorful history and culture conducted by the U.S. National Parks Service.

Swimming: Beach. **Classes and Programs:** Meditation, nutritional consultation, tai chi, yoga. **Recreation:** Hiking, kayaking, sailing, scuba diving, snorkeling, volleyball, windsurfing.

🏠 114 tent-cottages, with shared toilet/shower facilities.

✕ Meals included. 3 vegetarian buffets daily. Some fish and dairy products are available. **Sample Meals:** Green salad with sprouts and nuts, whole wheat bread, vegetable soup, lentil loaf (lunch); vegetarian lasagna, baked eggplant Parmesan, tofu casserole (dinner).

💲 1-week package $1,100 per person, double occupancy, includes programs and meals. D, MC, V.

✉ *Box 310, Maho Bay, St. John,* ☎ *340/776–6240. Reservations:* ✉ *Omega Institute, 260 Lake Dr., Rhinebeck, NY 12572,* ☎ *914/266–4444 or 800/805–3976,* FAX *914/266–4828. www.eomega.org*

ST. LUCIA

THE JALOUSIE HILTON RESORT & SPA

LUXURY PAMPERING ○ MINERAL SPRINGS

Arriving at the Jalousie Hilton Resort & Spa by helicopter is like being transported to an episode of *Fantasy Island*. Framed by two deep-green peaks called the Pitons, the resort sits by a crescent-shape beach in a 325-acre nature preserve.

At the top of a hill, overlooking both the Atlantic and Caribbean, sits a full-service spa and fitness center. Hiking there beats a stair-climber workout, though you can also take a van from the villas below. Several cottages have private treatment rooms and air-conditioned racquetball courts. An airy gym has an aerobics studio and cardio equipment. Here you can join exercise classes every morning, doing step and low-impact aerobics. Sheltered from the wind, four tennis courts are lighted for night play.

Treatments at the spa feature cosmetics made from organic and marine elements. FloraSpa facials include deep-cleaning the skin with a seaweed masque followed by an herbal balancing lotion. Hydrotherapy comes with algae-infused water bubbling from 47 underwater jets. There are body wraps, manicures, and pedicures. The ultimate luxury here is a massage combined with a soak in the whirlpool in a hilltop pavilion with a view of the sea.

About five minutes from the hotel are the free mud baths at Sulphur Springs. Take an old bathing suit and smear the smelly mud on whatever muscular aches or skin problems need attention. There are also thermal baths at Mt. Soufrière, a dormant volcano, that have been used since French forces occupied the island during the 17th century.

The area occupied by the resort was once a sugar plantation, and the 17th-century sugar mill now houses a gourmet restaurant and deluxe suites. Dotting the hillside above are individual villas with beamed ceilings, sitting areas, and private plunge pools on the verandas. Native fruit trees, flowering shrubs, palms, and tall coconut trees abound. A call to the transportation desk brings a van to take you to the beach club, where you can enjoy a sumptuous buffet lunch.

INSIDER TIP The poolside bar is the perfect place to sip a tropical drink while enjoying the sunset.

Equipment: Free weights, rowing machines, stationary bikes, treadmills, weight-training equipment. **Services:** Body polish, body scrub, hydrotherapy, sea-salt glow, seaweed wrap. **Swimming:** Pool, beach.

Classes and Programs: Step and low-impact aerobics. **Recreation:** Basketball, golf, horseback riding, racquetball, scuba diving, snorkeling, squash, tennis, water sports, windsurfing. **Children's Program:** Learning Center for ages 5–17.

⊡ 64 villas, 36 villa suites, 12 deluxe suites.

✕ Meals à la carte. The Plantation Restaurant serves Mediterranean and Asian fare. The Pier House serves seafood and creole specialties. Poolside restaurant serves lighter fare. **Sample Meals:** On-beach buffet of seafood, fresh salads, stew, and island vegetables (lunch); grilled grouper, lobster, chicken, and pasta (dinner).

▨ Nightly rate $475–$650 per room. Day spa packages available. AE, MC, V.

⊠ *Box 251, Soufrière, St. Lucia, West Indies,* ☎ *758/459–7666 or 888/ 744–5256,* FAX *758/459–7667. www.jalousie-hilton.com*

LESPORT

LUXURY PAMPERING ○ SPORTS CONDITIONING

The elegant Oasis Relaxation Centre, a hillside spa built to resemble Spain's Alhambra Palace, is where you'll find sophisticated European spa treatments, including a hydrotherapy tub and Swiss needle shower. Within the Moorish-style building on the grounds of LeSport you can indulge in a massage, bathe in algae, relax with a seaweed wrap, or enjoy Institut Clarins beauty treatments. You can simply enjoy the architecture by taking a dip in the swimming pool.

A checkup with the staff nurse precedes any treatment. After your blood pressure, heart rate, and weight are noted, the prescribed course of treatments may include the "hydrator," a bubbling bath with herbs and sea algae in which underwater jets smooth the fatty tissue found on the upper arms, thighs, and calves. Some guests, however, are intimidated by a seawater spray with a jet hose that is said to improve circulation.

Meditation, exercise sessions, and outings are scheduled daily at LeSport. In the air-conditioned aerobics studio you can join a yoga class or work with a personal trainer at no charge. All guests can join morning walks and hikes, archery sessions, guided bike trips, and water aerobics.

Accommodations are in plantation-style buildings with four levels of rooms. Some rooms have balconies or patios with views of the ocean or the garden. Cool, contemporary interiors are accented by marble floors, rattan furniture, and floral-print fabrics. Secluded on a private cove, the clublike facilities open to a large swimming pool where the social scene is nonstop. This may be part of the reason that LeSport is so popular among young people.

INSIDER TIP Most of St. Lucia's most spectacular scenery is on the southwest part of the island. A catamaran cruise along the coast is a perfect way to relax while taking in the island's natural beauty.

Equipment: Free weights, rowing machines, stair climbers, stationary bikes, treadmills, weight-training circuit. **Services:** Aromatherapy, body wrap, hydrotherapy, massage. **Swimming:** Pools, beach. **Classes and Programs:** Golf and tennis lessons, personal trainer, tai chi, yoga. **Recreation:** Archery, biking, croquet, fencing, golf, scuba diving, tennis, volleyball, waterskiing, windsurfing.

⌕ 145 rooms, 9 suites.

✕ Meals included. Breakfast and lunch buffets. International fare is available at Cariblue, and Tao serves East-West fusion cuisine. Special dietary requirements can be accommodated. **Sample Meals:** Stuffed chicken legs in leek-and-cream sauce with wild rice, julienne of carrots and zucchini (lunch); wok-steamed lobster with coriander and lemongrass sauce and Basmati rice, char-grilled chicken with Parmesan polenta and tomato-basil cream sauce, five-peppercorn filet mignon with straw mushrooms in a wine reduction (dinner).

▨ Nightly rate $195–$475 per person, double occupancy, includes meals and spa treatments. AE, D, MC, V.

✉ *Cap Estate, Box 437, Castries, St. Lucia,* ☎ *758/450–8551 or 800/ 544–2883,* ℻ *758/450–0368. www.lesport.com.lc*

ST. MARTIN/ ST. MAARTEN

PRIVILEGE RESORT & SPA

LUXURY PAMPERING ◦ SPORTS CONDITIONING

Panoramic views are part of the pampering at the Privilege Resort & Spa, perched on hills overlooking the beach and marina at Anse Marcel on the French side of the island. This unique hideaway provides European treatments to rejuvenate sun-damaged skin and aching muscles, as well as six-day courses for fighting stress, losing weight, or simply relaxing.

For a sampler of French balneotherapy, try an underwater massage in the high-tech Doyer tub, or try the Swiss shower temple, a multijet cabinet equipped with a control panel for cascades of varying intensity. The sea-oriented treatments make use of Phytomer algae and seaweed imported from Brittany.

Sports training can be combined with the spa program or arranged to fit your own schedule. Aerobics classes are held in the morning or late afternoon. Close by the pool is the sports complex with tennis, squash, and racquetball courts and a state-of-the-art fitness center. A trainer is available for bodybuilding tips or a few rounds of boxing-bag technique.

The Privilege Resort & Spa provides privacy and service not found in neighboring resorts. Most guest rooms are in Creole-style cottages with terra-cotta floors. Suites have marble bathrooms, large living rooms, and private balconies. Although all accommodations are air-conditioned, there is no screening to protect against mosquitoes if you prefer fresh air at night.

INSIDER TIP The resort organizes sailing excursions to neighboring islands. The trip, which includes lunch, is at no extra charge.

Equipment: Free weights, stationary bikes, weight-training equipment. **Services:** Hydrotherapy, massage, mud wrap, seaweed wrap, shiatsu, underwater massage. **Swimming:** Pools, beach. **Classes and Programs:** Aerobics, aquaerobics. **Recreation:** Racquetball, sailing, squash, tennis, water sports.

▥ 23 rooms, 8 suites, 1 7-bedroom villa.

✗ Breakfast included. No spa menu. **Sample Meals:** Caribbean fish soup, grilled tuna steak with steamed vegetables (lunch); salmon *escallope* in a creole sauce, carpaccio of fish Tahitian style, snails in pastry with white wine and mushrooms, scallop ravioli with leeks, duck breast with mango compote (dinner).

☎ Nightly rate $450–$760 per room, includes breakfast. 7-night program $3,750–$6,100 per person, double occupancy, includes breakfast, spa treatments, and car rental. AE, MC, V.

✉ *Anse Marcel, 97150 St. Martin, French West Indies,* ☎ *590/87–3838 for reservations* ☎ *800/874–8541,* FAX *590/87–4412. www.privilege-spa.com*

HEALTH & FITNESS

CRUISES

With the bracing sea air, the rush of breaking waves, and a seemingly endless expanse of blue skies, cruises offer an invigorating departure from your at-home fitness routine. In addition to enjoying the amenities of a luxury hotel and services of a full-service spa, you can travel anywhere you want. Although the Caribbean and the Bahamas account for the vast majority of cruise destinations, a steadily growing fleet on the Pacific coast makes Alaska, Hawai'i, and Mexico exciting alternatives. The Panama Canal, the Galapagos Islands, and Asia offer even more intriguing choices.

If you can withstand the temptations of lavish midnight buffets, a cruise can provide a truly healthy escape. Many ships have adopted the American Heart Association's Eating Away From Home program. Outstanding examples include Michel Roux's vegetarian menu for Celebrity Cruises' liners, the spa menu aboard Cunard's *Queen Elizabeth 2,* Holland America Line's Light and Healthy cuisine, Carnival Cruises Spa Nautica menu, and Crystal Cruises Innovative Spa menu.

You'll find the gyms filled with health enthusiasts easily working out for an hour or two a day. The top fleets all offer well-equipped gyms and interesting classes to help you maintain your fitness goals. For newcomers to working out, another advantage of a cruise is the opportunity to inaugurate a new personal fitness routine. Staff instructors offer one-on-one individualized training you'll be able to take back home to enhance your training.

Several lines provide free entrée to racquet clubs, golf courses, and fitness centers in the ports they visit, so ask your ship steward to direct you to the right place. Shore excursions on most cruises offer another great way to atone for the nightly array of mouthwatering desserts. Princess Cruises and the Disney Cruise Line schedule nature walks and bicycle tours. Crystal offers biking and kayaking excursions in Alaska. Special Expeditions offers hiking at various levels almost daily on its Sea of Cortez sailings.

If you are looking to travel for less, remember discounted rates are available at certain times of the year, depending on the destination. Some lines also offer discounts for early bookings, repeat passengers, kids under 18, and seniors. The best advice is to be proactive. Stay in touch with your booking agent, even after you've paid. You may even want to make a quick phone call to your agent every week to see whether the price has dropped. If it has, you'll usually be eligible for a price adjustment, which could be several hundred dollars. But if you don't ask, you won't receive.

In the pages that follow we have included cruise fares available at the time of publication. Prices may change by the time of your booking. You usually reserve a cruise either with passage only or as a package including round-trip airfare. Port taxes and ground transfers from the airport to the dock may not be included. For additional information ask for a referral to a knowledgeable travel agent by contacting the Cruise Lines International Association at 212/921–0066.

CARNIVAL CRUISE LINES

LUXURY PAMPERING

With the launch of its 2,758-passenger ship, the *Victory,* in August 2000, Carnival unveiled its largest health and fitness facility. It includes 15,000 square ft of exercise equipment, two whirlpools (of a total of seven onboard), and a ⅛-mi open-air jogging track encircling the Spa Deck.

The spa itself offers the usual steam rooms and saunas, as well as treatment rooms for European therapies offered by Steiner. Similar services are available on the other "Destiny Class" ships, the *Triumph* and the *Destiny*. In fact, all 15 of Carnival's ships offer fully equipped gyms, expansive workout facilities, soothing treatments, and full-service salons. But within the Destiny Class, the spa, gyms, and salons are expanded and take up two levels.

On the *Victory*, for example, equipment includes Keiser progressive resistance machines and a variety of stationary bikes, stair climbers, treadmills, rowing equipment, and free weights. Instructor-led classes throughout the day include step and senior aerobics, as well as specialized stretching, relaxation, and calisthenics sessions in the mirrored studio. Personal trainers, fitness evaluations, and wellness counseling are also available for a fee. Appointments can be made immediately after embarkation, and services are generally available on days when ships are in port.

On all ships the Carnival Line features its signature Nautica Spa Fare. These guilt-free dishes are lower in sodium, calories, cholesterol, and fat content. Meats, fish, and poultry are roasted or broiled, salads are paired with diet dressings, and desserts are made with sugar substitutes. Vegetarian entrées are also available at each meal, a salad bar in the grill area is open for lunch and dinner, and a pasta station serves up made-to-order selections.

INSIDER TIP Want a preview of your cruise? Order a "Fun Ship" video by calling 800/227–6482.

Exercise Equipment: Free weights, rowing machines, stationary bikes, stair climbers, treadmills, weight-training circuit. **Services:** Aromatherapy, eucalyptus steam inhalation, herbal pack, loofah scrub, massage, reflexology. **Children's Programs:** Complimentary kids program available year-round for ages 2–17.

🚢 3- to 16-day cruises to Alaska, the Bahamas, Canada, the Caribbean, Hawai'i, Mexico, and the Panama Canal. Fares without airfare range from $739–$2,189 for a 7-day cruise to the Caribbean, per person, double occupancy, including port charges.

✉ *Carnival Cruise Lines, 3655 N.W. 87th Ave., Miami, FL 33178-2428,* ☎ *305/599–2600 or 800/227–6482. www.carnival.com*

CELEBRITY CRUISES

LUXURY PAMPERING

Celebrity Cruises features one of the largest spa facilities afloat. Owned by Royal Caribbean, Celebrity has the youngest fleet of any major cruise line, with six ships and three slated to be launched by the end of 2002. Its new 1,950-passenger ship, the elegant *Millennium,* is the perfect example of what's to come.

Millennium features Celebrity's unique AquaSpa, a combination of treatments and eye-pleasing spa facilities. Spa packages, which can be booked prior to cruising, feature a choice of 20 treatments combined with classes, body-composition analysis, and personal-training sessions. In the massive solarium, you can schedule a dip in thalassotherapy seawater pools or hydrotherapy baths blended with seaweed, minerals, or aromatherapy oils; massage with an invigorating high-pressure water-jet massage; or an "aqua meditation," with three swirling warm-water shower heads simultaneously massaging your body. A beauty salon also offers hairstyling and manicure and pedicure services. All services are provided by Steiner spa professionals using their namesake products, as well as those by La Therapie Paris.

An international staff leads fitness classes ranging from step aerobics to relaxation. In addition to a plethora of cardio and weight machines, you can run the outdoor track or play shuffleboard or table tennis.

Dieters choose between the regular menu (which highlights items that are low in sodium and cholesterol) and a delicious vegetarian menu designed by chef Michel Roux. Many of his products (cookbooks and cookware) are sold in an onboard boutique. Delicious spa cuisine is also served at breakfast and lunch in the spa's soothing solarium, with its panoramic views of the sea. Don't miss the "portholes" built into the floor of the Ocean Café, where you can spot the waves below. The fine dining Olympic Restaurant and midnight buffets offer bountiful opportunities for indulgence. You can always spend an afternoon sipping a cappuccino to live harp music in the Cova Café Milano.

All *Millennium* staterooms have a telephone with voice mail and a multifunctional interactive television. The 32 Sky suites include a private whirlpool tub, a veranda, a flat-screen computer with Internet access, and a sitting area with sofa bed and lounge chairs. Finishes of wood, marble, etched glass, and polished granite distinguish the ship's decor. Suites are equipped with showers and doorways that accommodate wheelchairs and make it ideal for passengers who are older or have mobility problems.

INSIDER TIP Book a suite and enjoy a personal butler, who can also serve as a personal assistant, booking everything from dinner reservations to treatments at the AquaSpa.

Equipment: Cross-country ski machines, free weights, rowing machines, stationary bikes, treadmills, weight-training circuit. **Services:** Body brushing, body-fat analysis, cathiodermie facial, massage, personal fitness analysis, personal training, reflexology, seaweed treatments. **Children's Programs:** Supervised daily programs for ages 3–17 with a special staff of youth counselors. Private sitting for infants under 3 and a nightly slumber party are available for an additional fee.

🖾 Cruises to more than 100 ports and destinations in Alaska, Bermuda, Caribbean, Europe, Mexico, Panama Canal, Pacific Coast, and South America. Cruise-only fares start at $799 per person, double occupancy, for a 7-day voyage from New York to Bermuda, including port charges.

⊠ *Celebrity Cruises, 1050 Caribbean Way, Miami, FL 33132,* ☎ *305/ 539–6000 or 800/437–3111. www.celebrity-cruises.com*

COSTA CRUISE LINES

LUXURY PAMPERING

Costa Cruises is the outgrowth of an olive oil business in Genoa, Italy. When company founder Giacomo Costa passed away in 1916, his sons purchased a freighter to cut transport costs. Only after World War I did they begin passenger service, which has continued to grow.

Seven ships currently comprise the fleet, which sails a diverse itinerary, including the Canary Islands and Egypt and Israel. Certain ships are known for particular features. In the newest ship, the 2,112-passenger *CostaAtlantica*, a whopping 78% of cabins, including some 700 rooms with verandas, feature ocean views. A full service spa and fitness center compliment three pools, including one with a retractable dome for all-weather swimming.

The *CostaAtlantica* features several options for dining, including the two-level main restaurant, a buffet of international cuisine, and a pizzeria. As an alternative, passengers can also dine at the Ristorante Magnifico by Zeffirino, where chef Paolo Belloni has designed sumptuous menus already well known at his Genoa restaurant. And, reminiscent of St. Mark's Square in Venice, an onboard café resembles the 18th-century landmark Caffe Florian. At every meal a Health Spa selection is prepared with fewer calories and less fat, salt, and cholesterol.

But dining isn't the only pastime. On the *CostaAtlantica* and *CostaVictoria*'s eastern and western Caribbean itineraries, golf enthusiasts can enroll in Costa's Golf Academy at Sea. Private lessons and videotaped golf-swing analysis by a Professional Golfers' Association instructor augment onboard golf clinics. You'll be able to test your new skills at some of the Caribbean's best-known golf courses, including Mahogany Run, in St. Thomas; Teeth of the Dog, in Casa de Campo, and Runaway Bay, in Jamaica.

When you're ready for a luxurious spa experience, you can dive into the beautiful indoor pool at the *CostaVictoria*'s Pompei Spa & Fitness Center. Services include classic sauna, Turkish bath, thalassotherapy, and hydrotherapy. Spa treatments include deep-cleansing facials, reflexology, body scrubs, and seaweed or moor mud wraps.

Workouts come with great views of the sea in a window-walled fitness center, complete with weight-training equipment, stationary bicycles, treadmills, and stair climbers. An aerobics studio and a 500-meter jogging track offer more ways to workout. And for after-workout relaxation, all Costa ships feature massage rooms, steam rooms, saunas, whirlpools, and Roman baths.

INSIDER TIP Costa's onboard currency is the Italian lira, which says it all. Costa offers a distinct Italian flair, including a Roman-style spa, fabulous Italian cuisine, and even Italian lessons for little ones.

Equipment: Free weights, stationary bikes, weight-training circuit. **Services:** Aromatherapy, hydrotherapy, moor mud wraps, seaweed body wraps, reflexology, thalassotherapy. **Children's Programs:** Daily programs for ages 3–17. Two complimentary parents' night out allow kids to spend the evenings with peers while parents relax and dine alone. Baby-sitting is available for a fee.

⌨ Cruises of 7 days and more sail to the Caribbean, Mediterranean, northern Europe, and South America. Fares for a 7-day Caribbean cruise without airfare, reserved 120 days in advance, range from $699 to $4,399 per person, double occupancy, including port charges.

✉ *Costa Cruise Lines, 80 S.W. 8th St., Miami, FL 33130-3097,* ☎ *305/ 358–7325, or 800/462–6782. www.costacruises.com*

CRYSTAL CRUISES

LUXURY PAMPERING

Crystal Cruises' two ships, the *Crystal Harmony* and the *Crystal Symphony,* are among the highest-rated large luxury cruise ships afloat. It's not hard to understand why. Crystal is synonymous with a spectacular array of services and amenities. And the hotel and dining staff readily exhibit its schooling in the fine art of genteel service.

But that's only the beginning. When it comes to getting active, you can practice your swing using Callaway equipment, get tips from a PGA golf pro, and practice on the driving range and putting green. Onboard, you can also work out independently using state-of-the-art equipment with a spectacular ocean view. You can take aerobic, step, stretch, and yoga classes with the experienced staff, or work out with a personal trainer. The Steiner-operated spa offers French hand and foot treatments, seaweed or mud wraps, massages, exfoliation, and reflexology. And when you reach port, escorted excursions take you biking, kayaking, or on other adventures, including a floatplane ride over Alaska.

All this will likely leave you ravenous, and you'll be glad you worked up an appetite. Sumptuous gourmet meals are served at your choice of time in the formal dining room or in your stateroom. A poolside burger bar (fish, chicken, beef, veggie), an ice cream and cookie bar, a French bistro, and a midnight buffet are also available at no additional charge. But don't despair, lighter fare (low in calories, fat, cholesterol, and sodium) is always available. And if that doesn't satisfy you, you can sail during the Wine & Food Festival, in which celebrity chefs, such as Jacques Pepin, demonstrate their techniques.

You may choose to relax in your room watching CNN and ESPN or a video from the 600-plus videotape lending library. You can always take in a flick at the theater, or a soak in the whirlpool under the Alaskan sun, which seems never to set. Eventually, though, the wonderful meals and entertainment (musical theater and variety acts) compete for your attention. And you'll be wishing each day could stretch a bit longer.

INSIDER TIP Before you cruise, pick up the recommended reading list from www.crystalcruises.com. The classic literature, travel guides, and even cookbooks on the list complement every itinerary.

Equipment: Free weights, rowing machines, stair climbers, stationary bikes, treadmills, weight-training circuit. **Services:** Body scrub, herbal wrap, personal training. **Children's Programs:** Flexible program for ages 3–7, 8–12, and 13–17.

Cruises of 7 days and more to 300 ports, including Alaska, the Amazon, Asia, the Caribbean, Europe, and the Panama Canal. Fares for a 7-day cruise on the Mexican Riviera range from $2,355 to $9,950 per person, double occupancy, including port charges.

Crystal Cruises, 2049 Century Park E, Suite 1400, Los Angeles, CA 90067, 310/785–9300 or 800/446–6620. www.crystalcruises.com

CUNARD LINE

LUXURY PAMPERING

If you're looking for very cosmopolitan atmosphere, Cunard is a good choice. Almost 60% of Cunard's clientele hail from outside North America. The unparalleled *Queen Elizabeth 2* is still the most famous of all cruise ships currently in service. The company operates only one other ship, *Caronia,* the former *Vista Fjord,* which was extensively refurbished in 1999.

The Steiner spa aboard the *QE2* is a treat for body, mind, and spirit. The spa, in a separate enclave on the ship's lowest deck, has a hydrotherapy pool in which bubbling jets of seawater massage your muscles while you sink into a deeply relaxed state. If you like, London-trained therapists usher you into one of 10 private treatment rooms for a seaweed body mask, enveloping you in a mixture of algae and massaging you for a full hour to recorded sounds of the sea. Other treatments you might select include a hydrotub bath with freeze-dried seaweed, herbalized steam, and aromatherapy inhalations to clear your sinuses, or a water blitz massage in which concentrated jets play across your body. You can also head upstairs to the salon, where you can undergo anticellulite body-slimming treatments and cathiodermie facials.

On all voyages, including Caribbean and Bermuda cruises, passengers can participate in the fitness center's scheduled classes. One-on-one training is offered for a fee, as well as nutritional assessments and fitness evaluations. All dining rooms dish up spa cuisine, which can also be made to order in the grill rooms.

The 665-passenger *Caronia* keeps an international audience happy with its fine European hospitality and understated British elegance. The *Caronia* also has a spa, but it is much smaller than the *QE2*'s. The typical array of Steiner treatments as well personal training sessions are available.

When it comes to fitness, *Caronia* guests enjoy indoor and outdoor pools, hot tubs, aerobics and aquaerobics classes, and a variety of cardiovascular machines. Light cuisine is offered on every menu.

For golf lovers, cruises with PGA professionals are available on both ships. And, like all the best lines, Cunard takes its passengers to the world's most prestigious courses.

INSIDER TIP In the spirit of the classic transatlantic voyage, you can sail alone on the Cunard Line without paying a single supplement.

Equipment: Rowing machines, stair climbers, stationary bikes, treadmills, weight-training circuit. **Services:** Aromatherapy, cathiodermie facial, hydrotherapy, seaweed body mask, thalassotherapy body scrub, personal trainer. **Children's Programs:** A nursery for children under 5 is open daily on the *QE2*. On selected cruises, group activities for children are available. Baby-sitting is available.

QE2 has 15 to 20 6-day transatlantic crossings from New York to Southampton, England, each year. Fares on the *QE2* range from $2,270–$25,590, per person, double occupancy, including port charges and one-way airfare between London and 117 North American cities.

Caronia sails on itineraries of 12 days and more. Ports include the Amazon, the Caribbean, the Mediterranean, Europe, and the Norwegian Arctic. Fares for a 12-day northern Europe cruise range from $4,700–$18,230, including port charges.

✉ *Cunard Line, 6100 Blue Lagoon Dr., Suite 400, Miami, FL 33126,* ☎ *305/463–3000 or 800/223–0764. www.cunard.com*

DISNEY CRUISE LINE

LUXURY PAMPERING

With two of the largest and most elaborate spa and fitness centers at sea, Disney Cruise Line provides a dazzling range of opportunities for recreation and rejuvenation. On each of the fleet's two ships, the *Disney Magic* and the *Disney Wonder,* the 9,000-square-ft Vista Spa &

Salon offers sweeping ocean views and bird's-eye glimpses into the captain's bridge. You can work out with a personal trainer, take an aerobics class, try aquaerobics, dip into the three pools (one for adults, families, and kids), or take a ride down the super-fun waterslide.

After your satisfying workout in the state-of-the-art fitness center, treat yourself to an underwater massage or a Vichy shower with water jets that massage your entire body. Finish the day in Disney's unique Tropical Rain Forest, which features heated beds, soothing music, pore-opening aromatic showers, a scented steam room, and a refreshingly cool fog mist. The pampering continues on shore as well, where you can hike, bike, and snorkel in a protected lagoon, and catch an open-air massage overlooking the brilliant blue water.

If you're feeling low on energy, there's an onboard lecture series offering fascinating talks and interactive workshops on everything from animation to cooking. You could entertain yourself for hours sampling the artwork that makes these ships floating museums of Disney memorabilia. The whole family can take in a Disney movie or live performance every night, or the grown-ups can sneak away for a comedy show or spin around the dance floor in a variety of onboard nightclubs.

You can enjoy a different dining experience every night, from mouthwatering classic French and northern Italian cuisines to colorful Caribbean. Sample the sumptuous breakfast and lunch buffets and enjoy pizza, ice cream, and hot dogs on the pool deck or, if you'd rather relax indoors, order something from the 24-hour room service. But at least come out for the midnight buffet and dance away the calories under the stars.

INSIDER TIP Turn your knowledge of Disney trivia into plush toys and other prizes by playing shipboard tournaments such as "Who Wants to Be a Mousketeer?"

Equipment: Free weights, stair climbers, stationary bikes. **Services:** Hydrotherapy, massage, Vichy shower. **Children's Programs:** 15,000 square ft of supervised, age-specific activities for ages 3 and up. In-room baby-sitting on a first-come, first-served basis.

🚢 3- and 4-day cruises to the Bahamas and Disney's private island, Castaway Cay. Fares, without airfare, range from $434 to $3,049 per person, double occupancy, excluding port charges. 7-day resort and cruise packages range from $829 to $4,299 per person, double occupancy, and include unlimited admission to Disney theme parks.

✉ *Disney Cruise Line, Box 22804, Lake Buena Vista, FL, 32830,* ☎ *407/566–7000 or 800-WDW-CRUISE. www.disneycruise.com*

HOLLAND AMERICA LINE

With its Passport-to-Fitness program aboard each of its 11 ships, Holland America Line offers one of the best values in health and fitness cruises. Passengers pick up a passport aboard the ship to earn stamps for fitness classes, team sports, and beauty treatments. Even ordering lunch and dinner from the Light and Healthy menu earns a stamp (the menu includes such items as grilled sea bass with warm tomato salad, or chicken breast salad). T-shirts, gym bags, and other prizes are your rewards.

Immaculately maintained and decorated with an extensive collection of art and antiques, the flagship of the Holland America Line is the

1,316-passenger *Rotterdam VI*. But the fleet has been rapidly expanding, adding the *Volendam* in 1999 and the *Zaandam* and the *Amsterdam* in 2000.

These grand ocean liners offer all services and amenities of classic transatlantic travel. And like the other ships in the fleet—the 1,266-passenger *Maasdam Statendam, Veendam,* and *Ryndam*—they offer aerobics classes, strength-training equipment, stationary bicycles, treadmills, stair climbers, rowing machines, and free weights. Tennis and golf programs and a scuba certification course are offered on shore excursions on some cruises. The Steiner-operated spa features aromatherapy, body wraps, hand/foot therapy, and reflexology as well as hair and nail salon services.

INSIDER TIP Holland America has a no-tipping policy, so don't worry about calculating how much you would like to give to your room steward, waiter, and so on.

Equipment: Free weights, rowing machines, stair climbers, stationary bikes, treadmills. **Services:** Massage, mud treatments, reflexology. **Children's Programs:** Club Hal offers daily supervised activities for ages 5–8, 9–12, and 13–17.

✈ Cruises to Alaska, Canada, the Caribbean, Europe, Hawai'i, the Mediterranean, Mexico, the Panama Canal, South America. A 7-day Caribbean cruise, without airfare, ranges from $899 to $1,086 per person, double occupancy.

✉ *Holland America Line, 300 Elliott Ave. W, Seattle, WA 98119,* ☎ *206/281–3535 or 800/426–0327. www.hollandamerica.com*

LINDBLAD EXPEDITIONS

LUXURY PAMPERING

Unlike a typical cruise line, a voyage with Lindblad Expeditions focuses on expanding your mind as well helping you to relax. With its five expedition ships, two riverboats, and single day cruiser, Lindblad Expeditions takes its passengers to some of the most interesting places on the planet.

All expeditions are greatly enhanced by guided hikes and explorations with guides trained in the flora and fauna of every locale. Days are spent snorkeling, kayaking, or hiking, depending on the destination and the weather. A handpicked staff of naturalists and historians shares its expertise in geology, history, and archaeology. If you prefer hiking instead of kayaking, or birding instead of snorkeling, just inform the staff. Whatever you chose, evening recaps of the day's highlights allow you to hear how your fellow passengers fared.

Small ships, ranging in size from 30 to 110 passengers, visit everywhere from the Sea of Cortez to Botswana, from the Galapagos to Antarctica. Despite their size, most ships have some exercise equipment on the deck. Meals are hearty, palate-pleasing events and are geared to special diets—vegetarian, low cholesterol, and so forth—at no extra charge. There are buffet breakfasts and lunches and sit-down dinners, all with casual, impromptu seating. If you get hungry between meals, just tuck a complimentary soda and some trail mix into your backpack before you go ashore to explore.

Equipment: Free weights, stationary bicycles.

🖫 Cruises cover some 40 itineraries in 21 countries. Fares range from $2,980 to $5,140 for a 10-day Galapagos expedition and from $7,520 to $12,800 for a 14-day Antarctica adventure, per person, double occupancy, without airfare, port charges included.

✉ *Lindblad Expeditions, 720 5th Ave., New York, NY 10019,* ☎ *212/765–7740 or 800/397–3348. www.expeditions.com*

NORWEGIAN CRUISE LINE

LUXURY PAMPERING

If you love football, hockey, basketball, or baseball, your ship may have come in with the Norwegian Cruise Line. On its popular theme cruises you'll meet hall-of-famers and legendary athletes from each sport.

Two additional theme cruises offer even more opportunities to improve your form. On the Sports Illustrated Afloat cruise you can get pitching and batting instruction, analyze your golf swing, slam dunk on a full-size basketball court, or participate in a slap-shot tournament. Athletes such as Olympic gold medal–winning swimmer Matt Biondi and basketball star James Worthy give "chalk talks" about their sports. Sports enthusiasts and athletes will also love the Powerade Champions Fitness voyages featuring a wide array of fitness gurus sharing their expertise.

Among the Norwegian Cruise Line's fleet of six ships, the *Norway*'s spa is one of the best. There's a seawater aquaerobics pool and an exercise room with computerized cardiovascular equipment. This sybaritic enclave employs European-trained specialists in thalassotherapy, hydrotherapy, reflexology, and a wide range of beauty treatments. Services can be booked à la carte or in packages.

The *Norwegian Sky*'s spa best represents where the company is headed, and two more ships expected by 2002 will follow this ship's lead. Its full-service Steiner-operated spa and beauty salon are paired with a gym and aerobics area, offering state-of-the-art exercise equipment including stationary bikes and stair climbers. In addition to two pools, a shallow pool with a waterfall is designed especially for kids.

On all ships, active passengers enjoy an In Motion on the Ocean fitness program, which awards prizes for participating in the various physical activities scheduled daily.

There are five eateries in addition to two main dining rooms, with everything from gourmet pizza and pot stickers to chocolate fondue and flaming cherries jubilee. Midnight buffets are regular fixtures aboard the Norwegian ships, as is 24-hour room service. Low-calorie meals through the ships' *Cooking Light* program are also available. More than 160 recipes from *Cooking Light* magazine are rotated on breakfast, lunch, and dinner menus.

Equipment: Cross-country ski machine, free weights, rowing machine, stair climbers, stationary bikes, weight-training circuit. **Services:** Massage, personal training. **Children's Programs:** Activities are available for kids in four age groups: 3–5, 6–8, 9–12, and 13–17. Group baby-sitting for potty-trained children is available for a fee.

☎ Cruises to 200 ports including Alaska, Australia, the Caribbean, Europe, Hawai'i, the Mediterranean, Mexico, the Panama Canal, Southeast Asia, South America, and Scandinavia. Fares for 7-day eastern Caribbean cruises range from $499 to $3,500 per person, double occupancy.

✉ *Norwegian Cruise Line, 7665 Corporate Center Dr., Miami, FL 33126,* ☎ *305/436–4000 or 800/327–7030. www.ncl.com*

PRINCESS CRUISES

LUXURY PAMPERING

Of the 11 ships in the Princess fleet, the 2,600-passenger *Golden Princess* is the newest. It is a remarkable 19 stories high and three football fields long. Recalling the days of the great ocean liners, the teak decks and decorative accents in brass, warm woods, and marble enhance spacious staterooms. Eighty percent of all outside cabins have a private balcony.

With views overlooking the bow, the Steiner spa offers massages, facials, body wraps, and a hydrotherapy soak in seaweed or herbs. A spacious beauty salon has foot and hand treatments. Exercise options are equally diverse, with more than a dozen pieces of exercise equipment in the expansive fitness center, plus an outdoor ⅙-mi jogging track, swim-against-the-current pool, sauna, and a computerized golf center. Like its sister ship, the *Grand Princess*, the *Golden Princess* features five swimming pools (one just for laps), nine whirlpools, and dining rooms on three decks.

The fitness facilities are part of the Cruisercise® program, which awards prizes for participation in scheduled fitness activities. On all ships a daily schedule of classes includes walk-a-mile, stretch and tone, high- or low-impact aerobics, and aquacise.

The dining room menu offers heart-healthy items low in sodium and cholesterol, prepared according to American Heart Association guidelines. Dining options include a 24-hour food court in the Lido Café, pizzeria, patisserie, grill, ice cream bar, and Southwestern and Italian restaurants.

INSIDER TIP Princess offers wheelchair-accessible staterooms and gangways, smoke detectors and door knockers with flashing lights, text telephones, and other ways to accommodate passengers with disabilities.

Equipment: Free weights, rowing machines, stair climbers, stationary bikes, treadmills. **Services:** Body wrap, moor-mud facial mask. **Children's Programs:** Children as young as six months are welcome. For children up to 17, "Love Boat Kids" offers a daily supervised program. Individual baby-sitting is available for a fee.

☎ 150 itineraries to 230 ports including Africa, Alaska, the Panama Canal, the Caribbean, and Europe. Cruise-only fares for 7 days in the Caribbean range from $749–$4,049 per person, double occupancy.

✉ *Princess Cruises, 10100 Santa Monica Blvd., Los Angeles, CA 90067,* ☎ *310/553–1770 or 800/421–0522. www.princess.com*

RADISSON SEVEN SEAS CRUISES

LUXURY PAMPERING

With ships accommodating from 180 to 700 passengers, the Radisson fleet combines the luxury of smaller ships with the facilities of larger ones. Radisson operates the *Radisson Diamond,* the *Radisson Navigator,* the *Paul Gauguin,* the *Mariner,* the *Hanseatic,* and the *Song of Flower.* Radisson ships have swimming pools, excellent dining, and top-notch service, and all but the *Song of Flower* and the *Paul Gauguin* have a jogging track. Spa and exercise facilities vary among the uniquely crafted vessels.

The *Paul Gauguin,* which cruises Tahiti and French Polynesia, carries the first and only floating Carita of Paris Spa. Beyond the spa's marbled reception room, the pleasant French staff offers gentle massages, hydrotherapy, and facials. Try hydromassage/bubble bath, which uses hundreds of small jets to direct seawater toward specific muscle groups, quickly releasing tension, easing soreness, and providing a perfect prelude to a massage. The small fitness center is adequately equipped with treadmills, stair climbers, and stationary bicycles, but it can't compare to the outdoor fun beckoning in the clear blue Polynesian lagoons.

The ship's submersible, retractable water deck allows for kayaking, windsurfing, and waterskiing. A complete dive program helps beginners get certified and tantalizes experts with shark-feeding expeditions. With daytime temperatures ranging from 80° to 90°, the islands themselves are ideal for biking, hiking, jogging, and swimming.

Other Radisson ships offer equally alluring amenities. The entire top deck of the *Diamond* is devoted to a jogging track and a spa. The selection of Steiner services ranges from a cathiodermie facial to a thalassotherapy body scrub. The *Diamond* also offers extensive fitness opportunities. Scheduled twice each morning and afternoon, classes are held in the main lounge or on deck. You can join a stretch or walk class at 7:30 AM and follow up with a class on water aerobics or line dancing. The outdoor swimming pool and hot tub are tiny, but in port you can swim in a floating marina equipped for snorkeling, windsurfing, and jet skiing. And for days at sea the onboard fitness center offers a seven-unit weight-training circuit, stair climbers, stationary bikes, treadmills, and free weights.

Radisson's newest ships, the *Seven Seas Navigator* and the *Seven Seas Mariner* each carry Judith Jackson spas, complete with sauna, steam room, and massage therapy. Both vessels also offer personal trainers and a range of exercise equipment that includes stationary bikes, rowing machines, and treadmills. The *Mariner* makes its maiden voyage in March 2001.

Open-seating policies reign in Radisson's main dining rooms, which offer five-course European meals as well as healthy, lower-fat options on the Well-Being Menu and healthier versions of classic fare on the Simplicity Menu. Radisson chefs also accommodate special requests, such as low-cholesterol or low-sodium meals. Evening entertainment varies between boats but usually includes a show in addition to bars, casinos, and videotape libraries.

INSIDER TIP Aboard Radisson's ships, soft drinks, wine with lunch and dinner, 24-hour room service, and breakfast in bed are all included in the ticket price.

Equipment: Free weights, stair climbers, stationary bikes, treadmills, weight-training circuit (on some ships). **Services:** Massage, facials, hydrotherapy, manicures, pedicures, hair styling.

⌘ Cruises to the Caribbean, Mexico, Tahiti, the Panama Canal, Europe, Central America, India, New Zealand, Asia, Alaska, Antarctica, and Australia. 7-day Caribbean cruise-only fares $1,950–$9,695 per person, double occupancy. 7-day Tahitian cruises $2,895–$9,695 per person, double occupancy. Port charges are not included.

✉ *Radisson Seven Seas Cruises, 600 Corporate Dr., Suite 410, Fort Lauderdale, FL 33334,* ☎ *800/477–7500 or 800/285–1835. www.rssc.com*

ROYAL CARIBBEAN INTERNATIONAL

LUXURY PAMPERING

Amid Royal Caribbean's fleet of megaships, the 3,100-passenger *Voyager* is a playground at sea. You can scale a 200-ft rock-climbing wall, practice figure eights on an ice rink, or play a pick-up game of hoops. There are on-deck jogging and in-line skating tracks, a driving range, and a 9-hole miniature golf course. Kids can ride a water slide into the pool or watch colorful tropical fish swim in onboard aquariums. There's even a four-deck shopping mall.

In addition, 15,000 square ft of workout, aerobics, and spa facilities and a 10,000-square-ft solarium for relaxation comprise one of the largest health-and-fitness complexes afloat. The gym area features 20 ocean-view treadmills and 50 other training machines. There is a wide variety of classes, from stretching to body sculpting. For working out, you earn ShipShape Dollars, which you redeem for sports gifts.

There is also no shortage of dining options, including three main dining rooms. Guests may sample ShipShape healthy menus with less than 30% of calories from fat, vegetarian choices, and kosher meals. Other alternatives include a hamburger stand, a grill, café, ice cream bar, and a fine Italian restaurant.

INSIDER TIP It may be impossible to score tickets for the famed La Scala in Milan, but on *Voyager,* you can catch celebrities like Rita Rudner, Charo, and Ben Vereen at the 1,350-seat La Scala.

Equipment: Free weights, stationary bikes, treadmills, weight-training circuit. **Services:** Hydrotherapy, massage. **Children's Programs:** Free Adventure Ocean program of scheduled activities kids 3–17. Group or in-room baby-sitting is available.

⌘ *Voyager* cruises from Miami to Royal Caribbean's private island, Labadee (off Haiti), to Jamaica, and to Cozumel, Mexico. Fares start at $1,199 per person, double occupancy, for a 7-night Caribbean cruise, port charges included. Other Royal Caribbean ships sail to Alaska, Australia, the Bahamas, Bermuda, the Caribbean, Europe, Hawai'i, Mexico, the Middle East, the Panama Canal, New England, and New Zealand.

✉ *Royal Caribbean International, 1050 Caribbean Way, Miami, FL 33132-2096,* ☎ *305/539–6000 or 800/327–6700. www.royal-caribbean.com*

SEABOURN CRUISE LINE

LUXURY PAMPERING

One of the finest small fleets at sea, Seabourn is distinguished by an extensive spa aboard the 758-passenger *Seabourn Sun*. Seabourn's smaller all-suite ships all offer spa and gym facilities, although they are less extensive.

The Roman-theme Spa du Soleil, which was extensively refurbished in 1999, features an impressive array of treatments. Thalassotherapy rooms offer relief for sore muscles and there is a traditional Turkish steam room especially designed for couples. One room contains a dry float table that resembles a water bed, while another boasts a large, ornate Cleopatra bath with massaging minijets.

The elaborate window-wall gym boasts cardiovascular machines including treadmills, stair climbers, cross-trainers, rowing machines, and stationary bikes, as well as a weight-training circuit and free weights. Classes in aerobics, aquaerobics, and stretch, along with two pools (including one for laps), give you plenty of additional choices for working out.

For golf lovers, a PGA professional is available on every cruise to help with your game. There are also driving cages, a 13-hole putting course, and a golf simulator that allows you to virtually play 12 of the world's most challenging courses.

Besides the main dining room, you can choose the Venezia, which features Italian regional cuisines. Buffet breakfast and luncheons and bistro cuisine are served some nights at the Garden Café. All meals are modern classic cuisine, concentrating on fresh, seasonal, and regional ingredients. Every Seabourn menu offers a "Simplicity Suggestion" for a low-fat, low-calorie, and low-cholesterol meal.

INSIDER TIP Seabourn carries on the classic tradition of bon voyage parties. Obtain passes for your nonsailing guests four weeks prior to the voyage.

Equipment: Cross trainers, free weights, rowing machines, stationary bikes, weight-training circuit. **Services:** Thalassotherapy, massage, seaweed therapy, personal training sessions, water jet massage.

⌨ Cruises to 200 ports in 75 counties. Fares for a 14-day Mediterranean cruise range from $2,460 to $24,320 per person, double occupancy, without airfare, including port charges.

✉ *Seabourn Cruise Line, 6100 Blue Lagoon Dr., Suite 400, Miami, FL 33126,* ☎ *305/463–3000 or 800/929–9391. www.seabourn.com*

SILVERSEA CRUISES, LTD.

LUXURY PAMPERING

Silversea's four ships, the *Silver Cloud, Silver Wind, Silver Shadow,* and *Silver Mirage,* constitute another award-winning fleet of luxurious small ships. Some 75% of the all-suite accommodations feature private verandas. Guests also enjoy complimentary overnight accommodations in a deluxe hotel on most cruises.

Health-oriented passengers build their days around the spa and workouts in the fitness center. Special theme cruises focus on Cordon Bleu cooking, fly fishing in the Great Barrier Reef (or remote streams of New

Zealand), golf at some of the world's most challenging courses, and lectures by *National Geographic* photographers and journalists who share their expertise on your specific itinerary.

Light and Healthy menu selections highlight the chef's choices for low-fat, low-cholesterol, and low-sodium gourmet dining. Meat and fish may also always be ordered grilled or broiled or without sauces.

INSIDER TIP You can relax on a Silversea ship, as virtually everything is included in the stateroom cost, from gratuities and port charges to wines and spirits.

Equipment: Free weights, walking track, weight training circuit. **Services:** Aromatherapy, body wraps, hydrating baths.

Silversea sails to the Mediterranean, northern Europe, New England, the Caribbean, the Panama Canal, South America, Asia, and Africa. Fares range from $4,840 to $12,095 per person, double occupancy for a 7-day Barcelona-to-Rome sailing, including airfare, port charges, and all onboard gratuities.

✉ *Silversea Cruises, Ltd., 110 E. Broward Blvd., Fort Lauderdale, FL 33301,* ☎ *954/522–4477 or 800/722–9955. www.silversea.com*

WINDSTAR CRUISES

LUXURY PAMPERING

Windstar's four-ship fleet offers more than the romance of cruising under sail. Since the smaller ships stay away from the routes of the large cruise ships, there's a true sense of getting away from it all.

The newest ship, the 312-passenger *Wind Surf* boasts 10,000 square ft of spa and fitness services. Everything from a couples massage lesson to fango body masks is available. The $259 Simple Pleasures package includes a facial, aromatic body massage, manicure, pedicure, and hydrotherapy bath.

The crew organizes complimentary outings, such as waterskiing, windsurfing, kayaking, and snorkeling. Scuba diving is scheduled for both certified divers and novices. And shore excursions for hiking, horseback riding, and visits to golf and tennis resorts are also available.

INSIDER TIP Tend to eat too much on vacation? The Sail Light menu and vegetarian cuisine developed by renowned chefs Joachim Splichal and Jeanne Jones may help save your waistline.

Equipment: Free weights, rowing machines, stair climbers, stationary bikes, treadmills, weight training circuit. **Services:** Body masks, wraps, and polishes, personal training, stress management.

Cruises to 65 ports in Belize, the Caribbean, Central America, Costa Rica, Europe, the Mediterranean, the Panama Canal, and Mexico. Fares for a 14-day cruise from Lisbon to Barbados range from $3,160 to $4,658 per person, double occupancy, including port charges.

✉ *Windstar Cruises, 300 Elliott Ave. W, Seattle, WA 98119,* ☎ *206/ 281–3535 or 800/258–7245. www.windstarcruises.com*

GLOSSARY

A **abhyanga.** Herbalized-oil massage performed by two therapists, sometimes followed by hot towel treatment.

acupressure. Ancient Chinese massage technique intended to restore the flow of qi, or energy, by stimulating pressure points on the body.

acupuncture. Ancient Chinese medicine using the painless insertion of needles into key spots on the body in order to restore the flow of qi and allow the body to heal itself. Disposable needles are typically used for hygiene and safety.

Alexander Technique. A massage system created in the 1890s by the Australian actor F. M. Alexander designed to improve posture and correct physical habits that cause stress.

aquaerobics. Aerobic workouts in a pool that combine water resistance and body movements.

aromatherapy. Massage and other treatments involving essential oils from plants intended to relax the skin's connective tissues and stimulate the natural flow of lymph fluid.

asana. A posture used in yoga.

ayurveda. A 5,000-year-old Indian philosophy of well-being that uses oils, massage, herbs, and diet and lifestyle modification to restore a body to perfect balance.

B **Bach flower remedies.** Healing with floral essences and oils developed in London in the 1930s by Dr. Edward Bach.

balneology. Traditional water-based treatments using geothermal hot springs, mineral water, or seawater to improve circulation, strengthen immunity, and relieve pain and stress.

bindi. An ayurvedic treatment in which herb-infused oils are applied to the face and body.

body brushing. Exfoliating treatment involving the dry brushing of skin to remove dead cells and stimulate circulation.

body composition test. A computerized system that determines what percentage of a person's body is fat.

body polish. Use of large sea sponges to gently cleanse, exfoliate, and hydrate the body.

boxaerobics. High-energy aerobics incorporating boxing movements.

C **circuit training.** The combination of aerobics and use of weight-resistance equipment.

clay wrap. See *mud wrap*.

cold plunge. Deep pool used to stimulate circulation after sauna.

colonic irrigation. Enema to cleanse the entire colon to remove impurities.

contouring. Calisthenics for deep toning of muscle groups.

craniosacral therapy. Massage therapy focusing on the head and neck.

cure. Course of treatments. Also called *kur*.

D **Dead Sea mud.** Mineral-rich mud from the Dead Sea used to remove toxins, promote healthy skin, and relieve muscle and joint pain.

deep-tissue massage. Vigorous manipulation of bodily tissues to relieve knots, tension, inflexibility, pain, and discomfort.

dosha. The term for one of three body types in ayurvedic philosophy: pitta, vata, or kapha.

drinking cure. Medically prescribed regimen of mineral water consumption.

dulse scrub. Application of powdered dulse seaweed combined with oil or water to remove dead skin and enrich the skin with minerals and vitamins.

dry brushing. Brisk brushing of the skin to exfoliate and promote circulation. Often performed in advance of a body wrap or other treatment.

E **exfoliation.** The process of removing a thin layer of dry skin cells with a loofah or other lightly abrasive materials.

F **fango.** A mud pack or body coating intended to promote the release of toxins and relieve muscular and arthritic pain.

Feldenkrais Method. System developed by Israeli physicist Moshe Feldenkrais in the 1940s to reprogram the nervous system through movement augmented by physical pressure and manipulation.

flotation tank. An appliance filled with about 12 inches of highly salty, mineral-enriched water used to promote deep relaxation and serenity.

G **glycolic exfoliation.** A treatment that breaks down the bonds that hold dry skin on the face and softens lines and smoothes skin.

gommage. A cleansing and moisturizing treatment that makes use of creams applied with massage movements.

guided imagery. Visualization used to stimulate the body's immune system.

H **hatha yoga.** System of yoga that focuses on physical exercise used to achieve bodily control. See *asana*.

haysack wrap. Treatment with steamed hay intended to detoxify the body.

Hellerwork. A system of deep-tissue bodywork, stress reduction, and movement reeducation developed by educator Joseph Heller.

herbal wrap. A treatment in which the body is wrapped in hot linens and blankets imbued with herbal essences. It is intended to promote muscle relaxation and the elimination of toxins. Also called *aromabath, herbal bath*.

herbology. The therapeutic use of herbs in treatments and diet.

holistic medicine. A philosophical approach to health and healing that addresses the body and the mind.

homeopathy. Alternative medicine in which patients consume minute quantities of symptom-causing substances in order to stimulate self-healing.

hot stone massage. Massage using smooth stones heated in water and applied to the skin, either with pressure, with strokes, or by simply resting on the body.

hydrotherapy. Underwater massage, alternating hot and cold showers, and other water-oriented treatments.

hydrotub. Underwater massage in deep tubs equipped with high-pressure jets and hand-manipulated hoses.

I **interval training.** A combination of alternating high- and low-intensity aerobic activity.

Iyengar yoga. Exercise system developed in India by B. K. S. Iyengar.

J **Javanese lulur treatment.** A traditional prenuptial treatment in Indonesia that combines exfoliation, massage, and bathing.

K **kickboxing.** A form of self-defense that involves punching, kicking, and blocking.

Kneipp kur. Treatments combining hydrotherapy, herbology, and a diet of natural foods developed in Germany in the mid-1800s by Sebastian Kneipp.

kripalu yoga. A form of yoga that combines physical postures with meditation.

kur. See *cure*.

L **lap pool.** A pool with swimming lanes for working out.

loofah. A naturally occurring coarse sea sponge used to exfoliate the skin and stimulate circulation.

lomi lomi. Traditional Hawaiian massage.

lymphatic drainage. Massage technique designed to gently drain away toxins and excess water.

M **massage.** Manipulation of body tissue for therapeutic purposes. Types of massage include acupressure, reflexology, and shiatsu.

meditation. A technique that involves focusing on a particular thought, word, image, or sound for a length of time in order to promote wellness and reduce stress and anxiety.

microdermabrasion. An intense facial designed to help reduce the appearance of fine lines, pigmentation, and scarring. Involves the application of tiny aluminum crystals that are brushed against the skin.

moor mud. Natural peat or mud, rich in organic matter, applied to the skin to remove toxins and ease muscle and joint pain.

mud wrap. Body treatment using warm mud to cleanse pores and draw out impurities.

N **naturopathy.** Natural healing prescriptions that use plants and flowers.

NIA. Created by San Francisco dancers Carlos and Debby Rosas, the low-impact workout program called Neuromuscular Integrative Action blends techniques such as yoga, tai chi, and aikido with aerobics and modern dance.

O **ovo-lacto diet.** A diet regimen, usually vegetarian, that includes eggs and dairy products.

P **panchakarma.** A type of massage therapy that uses warm herbalized oils and aims to restore balance to the body.

parafango. Treatment using a combination of volcanic mud and paraffin. See *fango*.

paraffin wrap. Process of removing dead skin cells by brushing on paraffin wax.

parcourse. A trail, usually outdoors, equipped with exercise stations. Also called *parcours, vitacourse*.

phytotherapy. Plant-based treatments incorporating essential oils, seaweed, and herbs applied through massage, wraps, inhalation, and other methods.

Pilates. Strength-training movements developed in Germany by Dr. Joseph Pilates during the 1920s.

polarity therapy. Treatment developed by Dr. Randolph Stone that balances the body's energy through a combination of massage, meditation, exercise, and diet.

pressotherapy. Treatment using pressure cuffs on the feet to improve circulation.

pressure-point massage. Bodywork using pressure on designated body parts that connect to major nerves.

power yoga. Form of yoga that requires rapid movements.

Q **qigong.** Chinese exercise using breathing and body movements to recharge energy. Also spelled *chi kung*.

R **rebirthing.** A yoga breathing technique combined with guided meditation to relax and clear the mind.

reflexology. Massage of the pressure points on the feet, hands, and ears.

reiki. An ancient Japanese healing method that teaches universal life energy through the laying on of hands and mental and spiritual balancing. Intended to relieve acute emotional and physical conditions. Also called *radiance technique*.

Rolfing. A bodywork system developed by biochemist Ida Rolf that improves balance and flexibility through manipulation of muscles, bones, and joints.

Roman bath. A whirlpool bath.

Rubenfeld Synergy. A method of integrating body and mind through movement, verbal expression, and gentle touch, developed by Ilana Rubenfeld 35 years ago.

Russian bath. Steam bath used to flush toxins from the body.

S **salt glow.** Rubbing the body with coarse salt to remove dead skin. Also called *salt rub*.

sauna. A heated wooden room, usually with benches, useful for opening pores and eliminating toxins through sweat.

Scotch douche. A showerlike treatment with high-pressure hoses that alternate hot and cold water intended to improve circulation through rapid contraction and dilation of the capillaries.

seaweed wrap. A wrap using seawater and nutrient-packed seaweed.

shiatsu. Acupressure massage developed in Japan that uses pressure applied with fingers, hands, elbows, and feet.

shiroabhyanganasya. Head, face, and neck massage, followed by herbal steam treatment, heat packs, and herbal drops for nasal passages.

shirodhara. Ayurvedic massage in which warm herbalized oil is streamed onto the center of the forehead, then gently rubbed into the hair and scalp.

spa cuisine. Low-calorie, low-fat, and low-cholesterol food served by many spas that typically relies on fresh produce, whole grains, and fish.

Spinning. Trademarked name for exercise using special stationary bicycles that provides aerobic conditioning by pedaling quickly at varied resistance levels.

sports massage. A deep-tissue massage to relieve muscle tension, stress, and residual pain from workouts.

step aerobics. Low-impact aerobic exercise involving rhythmic stepping on and off a small platform.

stress management. A program of meditation and deep relaxation intended to reduce the ill effects of stress on the system.

sweat lodge. A Native American–inspired purifying ritual that takes place in a natural sauna made of rocks.

swedana. Herbalized steam treatment designed to reduce tension and release impurities through the skin.

Swedish massage. A treatment using stroking, kneading, and tapping to relax muscles gently. It was devised at the University of Stockholm early in the 19th century by Per Heinrik Ling.

Swiss shower. A multijet bath that alternates hot and cold water, often used after mud wraps and other body treatments.

T **tai chi.** An ancient Asian discipline for exercise and meditation combining slow, focused breathing and graceful dancelike movements and postures. Also called *tai chi chuan*.

thalassotherapy. Water-based treatments developed by the ancient Greeks that use seawater, seaweed, algae, and sea air.

Trager massage. A technique developed by Dr. Milton Trager that employs a gentle, rhythmic shaking of the body to release tension from the joints.

V **Vichy shower.** Treatment in which a person lies on a cushioned, waterproof mat and is showered by overhead water jets.

Vodder massage. Manual lymph drainage technique developed by Danish-born Emile Vodder in the 1950s.

Y **yoga.** Stretching and toning the body through a series of movements or postures, controlled deep breathing, and relaxation.

Z **Zen shiatsu.** A Japanese method of acupressure intended to relieve tension. Also called *shiatsu*.

DIRECTORY 1:

ALPHABETICAL LISTING OF RESORTS

A   Abbey Resort *214*
       The Aerie Resort *224–225*
       Alta Crystal Resort *203*
       The American Club *215–216*
       Antelope Retreat and Education Center *217*
       Aquae Sulis *117–118*
       Arizona Biltmore *14–15*
       The Ashram *43–44*
       Aspen Club *62–63*
       Auberge Du Parc Inn *242–243*
       Avandaro Golf & Spa Resort *262–263*

B   Bally's Park Place *145–146*
       Balnearios *263–265*
       Banff Springs Hotel *221–222*
       Bellevue Club *203–204*
       Berkeley Springs State Park *210–211*
       Bernardus Lodge *25–26*
       Birdwing Spa *128–129*
       Black Hills Health and Education Center *177–178*
       Boulder Hot Springs *133*
       The Boulders *15–16*
       Breitenbush Hot Springs Retreat *168*
       The Broadmoor *63–64*

C   Caba Real Resort *254–257*
       Cal-A-Vie Spa & Health Resort *44–45*
       Calistoga Spa Hot Springs *26–27*
       Cambridge Beaches *284–285*
       Canyon Ranch *16–17*
       Canyon Ranch in the Berkshires *122–123*
       Canyon Ranch Spaclub *138*
       Carnival Cruise Lines *313–314*
       Carson Hot Mineral Springs Resort *204–205*
       Casa Palmero *27*
       Casablanca Resort *138–139*
       Celebrity Cruises *314–315*
       Centre de Santé D'Eastman *243–244*
       Centre de Thalassothérapie Du Carbet *299*
       Centre de Thalassothérapie Manioukani *292–293*
       Château Élan *98–99*
       Château Whistler Resort *225–226*
       Chena Hot Springs Resort *13*
       Chico Hot Springs Resort *134*
       The Chopra Center for Well Being *45–47*
       Claremont Resort & Spa *27–28*
       The Cloister on Sea Island *99–100*
       Club Tremblant *244–245*
       The Colony Beach & Tennis Resort *78–79*
       Coolfont Resort *211–212*
       Cooper Aerobics Center *180–181*
       Copperhood Inn & Spa *153–154*
       Costa Cruise Lines *315–316*
       Crystal Cruises *316–317*
       Cunard Line *317–318*

D   David Walley's Hot Springs Resort *139–140*
       Deerfield Spa Resort *171*
       Desert Inn *140–141*
       Disney Cruise Line *318–319*

Disney's Grand Floridian Resort *79–80*
Dr. Wilkinson's Hot Springs Resort *29–30*
Don Cesar Beach Resort *80–81*
The Doral Golf Resort and Spa *81–82*
Double Eagle Resort & Spa *28–29*
Duke University Diet & Fitness Center *162–163*

E Echo Valley Ranch *226–227*
Ecomed Natural Health Spa *227–228*
Eden Rock Resort & Spa *82–83*
The Elms Resort and Spa *131–132*
The Enchanted Garden *294–295*
The Equinox *191–192*
Esalen Institute *30*
Espace Santé De Ravine Chaude *293*

F Fairmont Hot Springs Resort (British Columbia) *228–229*
Fairmont Hot Springs Resort (Montana) *134–135*
Fairmont Scottsdale Princess *17–18*
Feathered Pipe Ranch *135–136*
Fess Parker's Wine Country Inn & Spa *30–31*
Fisher Island Club *83–84*
Four Seasons Resort and Club *181–182*
Four Seasons Resort Aviara *31–32*
Four Seasons Resort Hualalai *101–102*
Four Seasons Resort Nevis *300–301*
Foxhollow *118–119*
French Lick Springs Resort *114–115*

G Glen Ivy Hot Springs Spa *47–48*
Glenwood Hot Springs Lodge & Pool *64–65*
Global Fitness Adventures *65*
Gold Lake Mountain Resort & Spa *66*
Golden Door (California) *48–49*
Golden Door (Puerto Rico) *302–303*
Golden Eagle Resort *192*
Grand Geneva Resort & Spa *216*
Grand Lido Sans Souci *293–294*
Grand Wailea Resort & Spa *106–107*
Gray Rocks *245–246*
Green Mountain at Fox Run *193–194*
Green Valley Spa & Tennis Resort *187–188*
The Greenbrier *212–213*
The Greenhouse *182–183*
Gurney's Inn *154*

H Half Moon Golf Tennis & Beach Club *296–297*
Harbour Village Beach Resort *287–288*
Hartland Wellness Center *197*
Health Spa Napa Valley *32–33*
The Heartland Spa *113*
Heartwood Institute *33–34*
The Hills Health Ranch *229–230*
The Hilton at Short Hills *146*
Hilton Head Health Institute *175*
Hilton Waikoloa Village *102–103*
The Himalayan Institute *172*
Hippocrates Health Institute *84–85*
Holland America Line *319–320*
Hollyhock *230–231*

The Homestead *198–199*
Hosteria Las Quintas *267–268*
Hot Springs National Park (Arkansas) *24*
Hot Springs State Park (Wyoming) *218*
Hotel Comanjilla *258*
Hotel Hacienda Cocoyoc *268–269*
Hotel Hana-Maui *107–108*
Houstonian Hotel Club & Spa *185–186*
Hyatt Regency Aruba *277–278*
Hyatt Regency Beaver Creek Resort & Spa *66–67*
Hyatt Regency Kaua'i Resort & Spa *105–106*
Hyatt Regency Pier Sixty-Six Resort *85–86*
Hyatt Regency Waikīkī *109*

I Indian Springs Resort (California) *34–35*
Indian Springs Resort (Colorado) *68*
The Inn at Manitou *235–236*
Ixtapan Resort & Spa *265–266*

J The Jalousie Hilton Resort & Spa *307–308*

K Kah-Nee-Ta Resort *169*
Kalani Oceanside Eco-Resort *103–104*
Kerr House *165–166*
Kingsmill Resort *199–200*
Kripalu Center for Yoga and Health *123–124*
The Kushi Institute of the Berkshires *124–125*

L La Casa Resort Spa *304–305*
La Costa Resort & Spa *49–50*
La Quinta Resort & Spa *50–51*
Lake Austin Spa Resort *183–184*
Lakeview Scanticon Resort *213*
Langdon Hall *236–237*
Lasource *290–291*
The Last Resort *188*
Le Château Bromont *246–247*
Lesport *308–309*
Lido Spa Hotel & Health Resort *86–87*
Lindblad Expeditions *320–321*
Lithia Springs Inn *169–170*
The Lodge & Spa at Cordillera *68–69*
The Lodge at Skylonda *35–36*
Loews Ventana Canyon Resort *18–19*

M Maharishi Ayur-Veda Medical Center *125–126*
Mandalay Bay *141*
Manoir Richelieu *247–248*
Mario's International Spa and Hotel *166–167*
Marriott Ihilani Resort & Spa *109–110*
Marriott's Desert Springs Resort *51–52*
Marriott's Spa at Camelback Inn *19–20*
The Marsh *129–130*
Meadowood Napa Valley *36–37*
Melia Cancun Resort & Spa *273–274*
Merv Griffin's Resort Hotel *52–53*
The MGM Grand Spa *141–142*
Millcroft Inn *237–238*
Miraval *21*
Mirror Lake Inn and Spa *155*

Misión Del Sol *269–270*
Mohonk Mountain House *155–156*
Mount View Spa *37–38*
Mountain Escape at Lake Louise Inn *222–223*
Mountain Trek Fitness Retreat & Health Spa *231–232*

N Nemacolin Woodlands *173–174*
New Age Health Spa *156–157*
New Life Hiking Spa *194*
New Moon Spa *23*
Northern Pines Health Resort *120–121*
Norwegian Cruise Line *321–322*
Norwich Inn and Spa *75–76*
Notaras Lodge *205–206*

O The Oaks at Ojai *53–54*
Ocean Place Resort *146–147*
Ocean Pointe Resort Hotel & Spa *232–233*
Ojai Valley Inn & Spa *54–55*
Ojo Caliente Mineral Springs *148–149*
Omega Institute *157–158*
Omega Journeys *306*
Optimum Health Institute of Austin *184–185*
The Option Institute *126–127*
The Orchid at Mauna Lani Resort *104–105*
Osmosis Enzyme Bath & Massage *38*

P The Palms *55–56*
Paradise Village Beach Resort *271–272*
The Peaks Resort & Spa *69–70*
PGA National Resort & Spa *87–88*
The Phoenician *22*
Pier House *88–89*
Pillar and Post Inn *238–239*
Plaza Resort *89–90*
Pointe Vedra Inn & Club *90*
Poland Springs Health Institute *121*
Post Ranch Inn *38–39*
Potosi Hot Springs Resort *136*
Preventive Medicine Research Institute *39–40*
Princess Cruises *322–323*
Pritikin Longevity Center (California) *56*
Pritikin Longevity Center (Florida) *91*
Privilege Resort & Spa *310–311*

Q Qualton Club & Spa Puerto Vallarta *259–260*

R Radisson Seven Seas Cruises *323–324*
The Raj *116–117*
Rancho La Puerta *252–253*
Red Mountain Spa & Fitness Resort *188–189*
Renaissance Jaragua Hotel & Casino *289*
Río Caliente *260–261*
The Ritz-Carlton San Juan Hotel & Casino *303–304*
Rosario Resort *206*
Royal Caribbean International *324*
Royal Hideaway Playacar *274*

S Saddlebrook Resort Tampa *91–93*
Safety Harbor Resort *93–94*
Sagamore Resort & Spa *158–159*

St. Helena Center for Health *40–41*
Ste. Anne's Country Inn & Spa *239–240*
Salish Lodge & Spa *206–207*
Sandals Royal Bahamian Resort and Spa *279–280*
Sanibel Harbour Resort & Spa *94–95*
Saybrook Point Inn and Spa *76*
Seabourn Cruise Line *325*
Silversea Cruises Ltd. *325–326*
Sivananda Ashram (Québec) *248–249*
Sivananda Ashram Yoga Farm (California) *41*
Sivananda Ashram Yoga Ranch (New York) *159–160*
Sivananda Ashram Yoga Resort (The Bahamas) *280–281*
Skamania Lodge *207–208*
Smith College Adult Sport/Fitness Camp *127*
Snowbird Resort *189–190*
Sol Duc Hot Springs Resort *208*
Sonesta Beach Resort *285–286*
Sonnenalp Resort *70–71*
Sonoma Mission Inn & Spa *41–43*
The Spa at Chaa Creek *282–283*
The Spa at Grand Lake *77*
Spa Hotel & Casino *57*
Spirit Rock Meditation Center *57–58*
Structure House *163–164*
Sun Mountain Lodge *209*
Sun Valley Resort *111–112*
Swept Away *297–298*
Sycamore Mineral Springs *58–59*

T Tan-Tar-A Marriott Resort *132*
Tassajara Zen Mountain Center *43*
Tazewell Club *200*
Ten Thousand Waves *149*
Tennessee Fitness Spa *179*
Topnotch at Stowe *195*
Truth or Consequences *150–151*
Turnberry Isle Resort & Club *95–96*
Two Bunch Palms *59–60*

V Vail Athletic Club *71–72*
Vail Cascade Resort *72–73*
Vatra Natural Weight Loss Spa *160–161*
Ventana Inn & Spa *60–61*
Vista Clara Ranch Resort & Spa *151–152*

W Waterville Valley Resort *143–144*
Westglow Spa *164*
The Westin Maui *108*
Westin Resort *176*
Wheels Country Spa at Wheels Inn *240–241*
The Wickaninnish Inn *233–234*
Wiesbaden Hot Springs Spa & Lodgings *73*
Windstar Cruises *326*
Women's Quest Fitness Retreats *73–74*
Woodstock Inn & Resort *196*
Wyndham Resort & Spa *96–97*

Y Yogaville *201–202*

DIRECTORY 2:

LISTING OF RESORTS
BY PROGRAM

Holistic Health

Antelope Retreat and Education Center 217
The Ashram 43–44
Black Hills Health and Education Center 177–178
The Boulders 15–16
Breitenbush Hot Springs Retreat 168
Canyon Ranch 16–17
Centre de Santé D'Eastman 243–244
The Chopra Center for Well Being 45–47
Coolfont Resort 211–212
Echo Valley Ranch 226–227
Ecomed Natural Health Spa 227–228
Eden Rock Resort & Spa 82–83
The Elms Resort and Spa 131–132
Esalen Institute 30
Feathered Pipe Ranch 135–136
Foxhollow 118–119
Global Fitness Adventures 65
Heartwood Institute 33–34
The Himalayan Institute 172
Hippocrates Health Institute 84–85
Hollyhock 230–231
Kalani Oceanside Eco-Resort 103–104
Kerr House 165–166
Kripalu Center for Yoga and Health 123–124
The Kushi Institute of the Berkshires 124–125
La Casa Resort Spa 304–305
The Last Resort 188
Maharishi Ayur-Veda Medical Center 125–126
The Marsh 129–130
Miraval 21
Misión Del Sol 269–270
Mountain Escape at Lake Louise Inn 222–223
Mountain Trek Fitness Retreat & Health Spa 231–232
New Age Health Spa 156–157
New Life Hiking Spa 194
New Moon Spa 23
Northern Pines Health Resort 120–121
Norwich Inn and Spa 75–76
Omega Institute 157–158
Omega Journeys 306
Optimum Health Institute of Austin 184–185
The Option Institute 126–127
The Phoenician 22
The Raj 116–117
Río Caliente 260–261
Sivananda Ashram (Québec) 248–249
Sivananda Ashram Yoga Farm (California) 41
Sivananda Ashram Yoga Ranch (New York) 159–160
Sivananda Ashram Yoga Resort (The Bahamas) 280–281
Spirit Rock Meditation Center 57–58
Tassajara Zen Mountain Center 43
Vista Clara Ranch Resort & Spa 151–152
Women's Quest Fitness Retreats 73–74
Yogaville 201–202

Luxury Pampering

Abbey Resort 214
The Acrie Resort 224–225
Alta Crystal Resort 203
The American Club 215–216

Aquae Sulis *117–118*
Arizona Biltmore *14–15*
Aspen Club *62–63*
Auberge Du Parc Inn *242–243*
Avandaro Golf & Spa Resort *262–263*
Bally's Park Place *145–146*
Banff Springs Hotel *221–222*
Bellevue Club *203–204*
Bernardus Lodge *25–26*
Birdwing Spa *128–129*
The Boulders *15–16*
The Broadmoor *63–64*
Caba Real Resort *254–257*
Cal-A-Vie Spa & Health Resort *44–45*
Cambridge Beaches *284–285*
Canyon Ranch *16–17*
Canyon Ranch in the Berkshires *122–123*
Canyon Ranch Spaclub *138*
Carnival Cruise Lines *313–314*
Casa Palmero *27*
Casablanca Resort *138–139*
Celebrity Cruises *314–315*
Château Élan *98–99*
Château Whistler Resort *225–226*
Claremont Resort & Spa *27–28*
The Cloister on Sea Island *99–100*
Club Tremblant *244–245*
The Colony Beach & Tennis Resort *78–79*
Copperhood Inn & Spa *153–154*
Costa Cruise Lines *315–316*
Crystal Cruises *316–317*
Cunard Line *317–318*
David Walley's Hot Springs Resort *139–140*
Desert Inn *140–141*
Disney Cruise Line *318–319*
Disney's Grand Floridian Resort *79–80*
Don Cesar Beach Resort *80–81*
The Doral Golf Resort and Spa *81–82*
Double Eagle Resort & Spa *28–29*
Echo Valley Ranch *226–227*
Eden Rock Resort & Spa *82–83*
The Elms Resort and Spa *131–132*
The Enchanted Garden *294–295*
The Equinox *191–192*
Fairmont Scottsdale Princess *17–18*
Fess Parker's Wine Country Inn & Spa *30–31*
Fisher Island Club *83–84*
Four Seasons Resort and Club *181–182*
Four Seasons Resort Aviara *31–32*
Four Seasons Resort Hualalai *101–102*
Four Seasons Resort Nevis *300–301*
Foxhollow *118–119*
French Lick Springs Resort *114–115*
Gold Lake Mountain Resort & Spa *66*
Golden Door (California) *48–49*
Golden Door (Puerto Rico) *302–303*
Grand Geneva Resort & Spa *216*
Grand Lido Sans Souci *293–294*
Grand Wailea Resort & Spa *106–107*
Green Valley Spa & Tennis Resort *187–188*
The Greenbrier *212–213*
The Greenhouse *182–183*

Gurney's Inn *154*
Half Moon Golf Tennis & Beach Club *296–297*
Harbour Village Beach Resort *287–288*
Health Spa Napa Valley *32–33*
The Hilton at Short Hills *146*
Hilton Waikoloa Village *102–103*
Holland America Line *319–320*
The Homestead *198–199*
Hosteria Las Quintas *267–268*
Hotel Hacienda Cocoyoc *268–269*
Hotel Hana-Maui *107–108*
Houstonian Hotel Club & Spa *185–186*
Hyatt Regency Aruba *277–278*
Hyatt Regency Beaver Creek Resort & Spa *66–67*
Hyatt Regency Kaua'i Resort & Spa *105–106*
Hyatt Regency Pier Sixty-Six Resort *85–86*
Hyatt Regency Waikīkī *109*
The Inn at Manitou *235–236*
The Jalousie Hilton Resort & Spa *307–308*
Kah-Nee-Ta Resort *169*
Kerr House *165–166*
Kingsmill Resort *199–200*
La Costa Resort & Spa *49–50*
La Quinta Resort & Spa *50–51*
Lake Austin Spa Resort *183–184*
Lakeview Scanticon Resort *213*
Langdon Hall *236–237*
Lasource *290–291*
Le Château Bromont *246–247*
Lesport *308–309*
Lindblad Expeditions *320–321*
The Lodge & Spa at Cordillera *68–69*
The Lodge at Skylonda *35–36*
Mandalay Bay *141*
Manoir Richelieu *247–248*
Mario's International Spa and Hotel *166–167*
Marriott Ihilani Resort & Spa *109–110*
Marriott's Desert Springs Resort *51–52*
Marriott's Spa at Camelback Inn *19–20*
Meadowood Napa Valley *36–37*
Melia Cancun Resort & Spa *273–274*
Merv Griffin's Resort Hotel *52–53*
The MGM Grand Spa *141–142*
Millcroft Inn *237–238*
Miraval *21*
Mirror Lake Inn and Spa *155*
Misión Del Sol *269–270*
Mohonk Mountain House *155–156*
Mount View Spa *37–38*
Mountain Escape at Lake Louise Inn *222–223*
Nemacolin Woodlands *173–174*
Norwegian Cruise Line *321–322*
Norwich Inn and Spa *75–76*
Ocean Place Resort *146–147*
Ocean Pointe Resort Hotel & Spa *232–233*
Ojai Valley Inn & Spa *54–55*
The Orchid at Mauna Lani Resort *104–105*
Osmosis Enzyme Bath & Massage *38*
Paradise Village Beach Resort *271–272*
The Peaks Resort & Spa *69–70*
PGA National Resort & Spa *87–88*
The Phoenician *22*

Pier House 88–89
Pillar and Post Inn 238–239
Plaza Resort 89–90
Pointe Vedra Inn & Club 90
Post Ranch Inn 38–39
Princess Cruises 322–323
Pritikin Longevity Center (California) 56
Privilege Resort & Spa 310–311
Qualton Club & Spa Puerto Vallarta 259–260
Radisson Seven Seas Cruises 323–324
Rancho La Puerta 252–253
Renaissance Jaragua Hotel & Casino 289
The Ritz-Carlton San Juan Hotel & Casino 303–304
Rosario Resort 206
Royal Caribbean International 324
Royal Hideaway Playacar 274
Saddlebrook Resort Tampa 91–93
Safety Harbor Resort 93–94
Sagamore Resort & Spa 158–159
Ste. Anne's Country Inn & Spa 239–240
Salish Lodge & Spa 206–207
Sandals Royal Bahamian Resort and Spa 279–280
Sanibel Harbour Resort & Spa 94–95
Saybrook Point Inn and Spa 76
Seabourn Cruise Line 325
Silversea Cruises Ltd. 325–326
Skamania Lodge 207–208
Snowbird Resort 189–190
Sonesta Beach Resort 285–286
Sonnenalp Resort 70–71
Sonoma Mission Inn & Spa 41–43
The Spa at Chaa Creek 282–283
Sun Mountain Lodge 209
Sycamore Mineral Springs 58–59
Tan-Tar-A Marriott Resort 132
Tazewell Club 200
Topnotch at Stowe 195
Turnberry Isle Resort & Club 95–96
Two Bunch Palms 59–60
Vail Athletic Club 71–72
Vail Cascade Resort 72–73
Ventana Inn & Spa 60–61
Vista Clara Ranch Resort & Spa 151–152
Westglow Spa 164
The Westin Maui 108
Wheels Country Spa at Wheels Inn 240–241
The Wickaninnish Inn 233–234
Windstar Cruises 326
Woodstock Inn & Resort 196
Wyndham Resort & Spa 96–97

Medical Wellness

Aspen Club 62–63
Canyon Ranch 16–17
Canyon Ranch in the Berkshires 122–123
Centre de Thalassothérapie Du Carbet 299
Centre de Thalassothérapie Manioukani 292–293
Cooper Aerobics Center 180–181
Ecomed Natural Health Spa 227–228
The Elms Resort and Spa 131–132
Green Mountain at Fox Run 193–194

The Greenbrier *212–213*
Hartland Wellness Center *197*
Heartwood Institute *33–34*
The Hills Health Ranch *229–230*
Hilton Head Health Institute *175*
Kripalu Center for Yoga and Health *123–124*
Maharishi Ayur-Veda Medical Center *125–126*
Mario's International Spa and Hotel *166–167*
Marriott's Spa at Camelback Inn *19–20*
The Marsh *129–130*
Northern Pines Health Resort *120–121*
Omega Institute *157–158*
Optimum Health Institute of Austin *184–185*
Poland Springs Health Institute *121*
Preventive Medicine Research Institute *39–40*
Pritikin Longevity Center (California) *56*
Pritikin Longevity Center (Florida) *91*
The Raj *116–117*
St. Helena Center for Health *40–41*
The Spa at Grand Lake *77*

Mineral Springs

Balnearios *263–265*
Banff Springs Hotel *221–222*
Berkeley Springs State Park *210–211*
Boulder Hot Springs *133*
Breitenbush Hot Springs Retreat *168*
Calistoga Spa Hot Springs *26–27*
Carson Hot Mineral Springs Resort *204–205*
Centre de Thalassothérapie Manioukani *292–293*
Chena Hot Springs Resort *13*
Chico Hot Springs Resort *134*
David Walley's Hot Springs Resort *139–140*
Dr. Wilkinson's Hot Springs Resort *29–30*
The Elms Resort and Spa *131–132*
Esalen Institute *30*
Espace Santé De Ravine Chaude *293*
Fairmont Hot Springs Resort (British Columbia) *228–229*
Fairmont Hot Springs Resort (Montana) *134–135*
French Lick Springs Resort *114–115*
Glen Ivy Hot Springs Spa *47–48*
Glenwood Hot Springs Lodge & Pool *64–65*
Grand Lido Sans Souci *293–294*
The Greenbrier *212–213*
The Homestead *198–199*
Hot Springs National Park (Arkansas) *24*
Hot Springs State Park (Wyoming) *218*
Hotel Comanjilla *258*
Indian Springs Resort (California) *34–35*
Indian Springs Resort (Colorado) *68*
Ixtapan Resort & Spa *265–266*
The Jalousie Hilton Resort & Spa *307–308*
Kah-Nee-Ta Resort *169*
Lithia Springs Inn *169–170*
Marriott Ihilani Resort & Spa *109–110*
Notaras Lodge *205–206*
Ojo Caliente Mineral Springs *148–149*
Poland Springs Health Institute *121*
Potosi Hot Springs Resort *136*
Río Caliente *260–261*
Safety Harbor Resort *93–94*
Sol Duc Hot Springs Resort *208*

Sonoma Mission Inn & Spa *41–43*
Spa Hotel & Casino *57*
Sycamore Mineral Springs *58–59*
Tassajara Zen Mountain Center *43*
Ten Thousand Waves *149*
Truth or Consequences *150–151*
Two Bunch Palms *59–60*
Wiesbaden Hot Springs Spa & Lodgings *73*

Nutrition and Diet

Aspen Club *62–63*
The Ashram *43–44*
Avandaro Golf & Spa Resort *262–263*
Birdwing Spa *128–129*
Cal-A-Vie Spa & Health Resort *44–45*
Canyon Ranch *16–17*
Canyon Ranch in the Berkshires *122–123*
Coolfont Resort *211–212*
Cooper Aerobics Center *180–181*
Deerfield Spa Resort *171*
Duke University Diet & Fitness Center *162–163*
Echo Valley Ranch *226–227*
The Elms Resort and Spa *131–132*
Global Fitness Adventures *65*
Golden Door (California) *48–49*
Green Mountain at Fox Run *193–194*
Green Valley Spa & Tennis Resort *187–188*
The Greenbrier *212–213*
The Greenhouse *182–183*
Gurney's Inn *134*
Hartland Wellness Center *197*
The Heartland Spa *113*
The Hills Health Ranch *229–230*
Hilton Head Health Institute *175*
Hippocrates Health Institute *84–85*
Kerr House *165–166*
The Kushi Institute of the Berkshires *124–125*
La Casa Resort Spa *304–305*
La Costa Resort & Spa *49–50*
Lake Austin Spa Resort *183–184*
The Last Resort *188*
Lido Spa Hotel & Health Resort *86–87*
Mountain Trek Fitness Retreat & Health Spa *231–232*
New Age Health Spa *156–157*
New Life Hiking Spa *194*
Northern Pines Health Resort *120–121*
The Oaks at Ojai *53–54*
Optimum Health Institute of Austin *184–185*
The Palms *55–56*
The Peaks Resort & Spa *69–70*
The Phoenician *22*
Preventive Medicine Research Institute *39–40*
Pritikin Longevity Center (California) *56*
Pritikin Longevity Center (Florida) *91*
Rancho La Puerta *252–253*
Red Mountain Spa & Fitness Resort *188–189*
Río Caliente *260–261*
Safety Harbor Resort *93–94*
St. Helena Center for Health *40–41*
The Spa at Grand Lake *77*
Structure House *163–164*
Tassajara Zen Mountain Center *43*

Tennessee Fitness Spa 179
Topnotch at Stowe 195
Vatra Natural Weight Loss Spa 160–161
Westglow Spa 164

Sports Conditioning

Aspen Club 62–63
Château Whistler Resort 225–226
Club Tremblant 244–245
The Colony Beach & Tennis Resort 78–79
Disney's Grand Floridian Resort 79–80
The Doral Golf Resort and Spa 81–82
Eden Rock Resort & Spa 82–83
The Equinox 191–192
Fairmont Scottsdale Princess 17–18
Four Seasons Resort and Club 181–182
Four Seasons Resort Nevis 300–301
Global Fitness Adventures 65
Gold Lake Mountain Resort & Spa 66
Golden Eagle Resort 192
Gray Rocks 245–246
Green Mountain at Fox Run 193–194
Half Moon Golf Tennis & Beach Club 296–297
The Hills Health Ranch 229–230
Houstonian Hotel Club & Spa 185–186
Hyatt Regency Beaver Creek Resort & Spa 66–67
The Inn at Manitou 235–236
Kalani Oceanside Eco-Resort 103–104
Kingsmill Resort 199–200
Lakeview Scanticon Resort 213
Lesport 308–309
The Lodge & Spa at Cordillera 68–69
Loews Ventana Canyon Resort 18–19
Manoir Richelieu 247–248
Miraval 21
Mirror Lake Inn and Spa 155
Mohonk Mountain House 155–156
Mountain Trek Fitness Retreat & Health Spa 231–232
Nemacolin Woodlands 173–174
The Peaks Resort & Spa 69–70
PGA National Resort & Spa 87–88
Pointe Vedra Inn & Club 90
Potosi Hot Springs Resort 136
Pritikin Longevity Center (California) 56
Privilege Resort & Spa 310–311
Saddlebrook Resort Tampa 91–93
Sanibel Harbour Resort & Spa 94–95
Smith College Adult Sport/Fitness Camp 127
Snowbird Resort 189–190
Sun Valley Resort 111–112
Swept Away 297–298
Tazewell Club 200
Topnotch at Stowe 195
Vail Athletic Club 71–72
Vail Cascade Resort 72–73
Waterville Valley Resort 143–144
Westin Resort 176
Women's Quest Fitness Retreats 73–74
Woodstock Inn & Resort 196
Wyndham Resort & Spa 96–97